# The
# Court-Martial
# of
# Mother Jones

# The
# Court-Martial
## of
# Mother Jones

Edward M. Steel, jr, Editor

The University Press of Kentucky

Copyright © 1995 by The University Press of Kentucky

Scholarly publisher for the Commonwealth,
serving Bellarmine College, Berea College, Centre
College of Kentucky, Eastern Kentucky University,
The Filson Club, Georgetown College, Kentucky
Historical Society, Kentucky State University,
Morehead State University, Murray State University,
Northern Kentucky University, Transylvania University,
University of Kentucky, University of Louisville,
and Western Kentucky University

*Editorial and Sales Offices:* The University Press of Kentucky
663 South Limestone Street, Lexington, Kentucky 40508-4008

**Library of Congress Cataloging-in-Publication Data**

The court-martial of Mother Jones / edited by Edward M. Steel, Jr.
    p.    cm.
    Includes bibliographical references and index.
    ISBN 0–8131–1941–3 (alk. paper).–ISBN 0–8131–0857–8 (pbk. :
alk. paper)
    1. Jones, Mother, 1843?–1930–Trials, litigation, etc.  2. Strikes
and lockouts–Miners–West Virginia.  3. Courts-martial and courts
of inquiry–West Virginia.  4. United Mine Workers of America–
History.  I. Steel, Edward M.
KF223.J66C68   1995
344.754′01892822–dc20
[347.54041892822]                      95-11135

# CONTENTS

Preface        vii
Introduction
        Arrest        3
        Habeas Corpus        13
        Court-Martial        25
        Writ of Prohibition        31
        The Court-Martial Resumed        39
        Sentences and Settlement        55
        Repercussions        61
        Conclusions        74
Notes        85
Transcript of the Court-Martial        97
Index        307

*Illustrations follow page 52*

# PREFACE

In the spring of 1913, forty-eight civilians were tried in Pratt, West Virginia, by a court-martial of the West Virginia National Guard. The state government preserved no record of the trial, but the official transcript survived, and I found it while seeking materials for editions of the letters, speeches, and writings of Mary Harris "Mother" Jones. Although it appeared to be a significant discovery, I had to defer any close exploration of it until the completion of the other volumes.

In the Introduction, I have placed the court-martial against the background of the Paint Creek and Cabin Creek strike, with the narrative centering on the figure of Mother Jones. She was not present at the beginning of the strike in April 1912, but she played a prominent role in the controversy from the end of June until the settlement of the strike a year later. She was one of the principal defendants in the court-martial, and she supplies the main threads connecting various aspects of the strike and the trial. Inevitably, to focus on her is to play down the role of her codefendants and the other strikers, but it gives coherence to many scattered events. Such a focus also shows her command of the techniques of protest—marches in the street that played to the newsreel cameras, mass petition movements alleging the invasion of civil rights, refusal to recognize the jurisdiction of a court, public protest rallies, and other appeals that impress the reader with their similarity to modern battles for public opinion. The trial took place seven years before the founding of the American Civil Liberties Union (ACLU) and may have been an example leading to the establishment of that organization, for Mother Jones was acquainted with Roger Baldwin, the founder and for many years director of the ACLU. She understood civil rights not only as an abstraction but from decades of practical experience as an agitator. In her career she faced injunctions, forcible deportations, threats of violence, and jail, though no civil court ever convicted her of anything more than a misdemeanor, such as making a public speech without a permit. She sometimes even provoked imprisonment so that she could play the martyr, and "raise hell in jail." Her comments in her autobiography and later speeches, as well as occasional interviews with reporters, throw light on the strike and trial.

For details on the legal proceedings and the strike generally I have relied heavily on the three volumes, *Conditions in the Paint Creek District, West Virginia* (Washington: GPO, 1913), transcripts of the hearings of a subcommittee of the Senate Committee on Education and Labor, in which many of the participants gave sworn testimony. As James Hamilton has pointed out in *The Power to Probe: A Study of Congressional Investigations* (New York: Random, 1976), the congressional investigation is primarily a twentieth-century phenomenon, and it was the furor over the imprisonment of Mother Jones in part that brought about the creation in 1913 of the first subcommittee to investigate a labor controversy. Once the ice was broken, Congress went on almost immediately to authorize two more such investigations, into conditions in the copper mining industry in Michigan and in mining in Colorado. Another simultaneous investigation, the "Money Trust" hearings, helped prepare the way for the Federal Reserve Act, the Clayton Antitrust Act, and the Federal Trade Commission. Besides aiding in the creation of regulatory commissions, congressional investigations have continued to play a significant role in American government and politics, especially in the era of television. When the Senate held hearings in Charleston, West Virginia, in 1913, the now familiar procedures had not yet been devised. Rather than relying on their own legal staff, the senators permitted lawyers for the coal miners and the operators to present witnesses and cross-examine them, almost paralleling an adversarial courtroom proceeding. Thus, the hearings often recapitulate the court-martial, but they also contain further evidence and self-justification by the participants.

The Paint Creek and Cabin Creek strike of 1912–13 fits the analysis of the industrialization of Appalachia in Ronald D. Eller's *Miners, Millhands, and Mountaineers: Industrialization of the Appalachian South, 1880-1930* (Knoxville: University of Tennessee Press, 1982), but Eller's regional approach does not permit much attention to individual states. Since the West Virginia government and officials played such prominent roles, the general reader will find more pertinent background material in histories of the state of West Virginia, especially John Alexander Williams's *West Virginia: A Bicentennial History* (New York: Norton, 1976) and *West Virginia and the Captains of Industry* (Morgantown:West Virginia University Library, 1976). The Paint Creek and

Cabin Creek strike has been frequently studied and written about. Winthrop D. Lane's *Civil War in West Virginia* (New York: Huebsch, 1921) set the pattern for much of the subsequent writing, emphasizing the violence and the disruption of society in a series of contests between the miners and coal operators that reached its climax in battles involving literally thousands of men in 1921. Nearly fifty years later Howard B. Lee's *Bloodletting in Appalachia* (Morgantown: West Virginia University, 1969) echoed the same themes. The widest-ranging scholarly investigation of recent years is David Corbin's *Life, Work, and Rebellion in the Coal Fields: The Southern West Virginia Coal Miners, 1880–1922* (Urbana: University of Illinois Press, 1981), an example of the new labor history that explores the development of a working-class culture among West Virginia miners.

Rather than retelling the whole story of the strike, I have concentrated on those elements that contribute to an understanding of the legal history. This view brings into prominence the role of George S. Wallace both as a key advisor to Governors William E. Glasscock and Henry D. Hatfield and as the prosecutor in nearly all the cases that arose during the periods of martial law. Fortunately, he gave to the West Virginia and Regional History Collection a substantial body of papers, some of which bear on the strike and the trial.

The transcript of the court-martial by the official court reporter is preserved in several forms. A bound version, consecutively paginated, is to be found in a collection entitled "West Virginia Mining Investigation Committee." It contains some editorial instructions for printing. Page 387 (of 445) is blank except for the notations, "Mother Jones' Speeches," and a separately paginated volume holds transcripts of five speeches. The George S. Wallace Papers contain a second copy, unbound but in stapled sections, some of which bear the notation "Wallace's copy." A third version, in the collection entitled "Coal Strikes. Records. 1912–1914," is the apparent source of the preceding two and consists of the transcribed notes of the court-martial, each session a separate unit, with typed copies of the written evidence submitted as additional units. Some of these sections bear handwritten directions for joining to other sections. A comparison of these three transcripts shows discrepancies mainly in pagination; for convenience, the bound copy was used.

Anyone who tries to reconstruct a trial from a transcript soon finds deficiencies in that source. He is totally at the mercy of the court reporter, who supplies whatever continuity and context the document has, such as "The court then adjourned until two o'clock." Desired information may or may not appear. In taking down the proceedings of this court-martial, the reporter excluded from the record some exchanges. When counsel made objections, the court "withdrew," heard arguments, emerged with a ruling, and continued with the presentation of evidence. Since no jury was hearing the case, suspending the stenography while attorneys approached the bar to argue points of law made no sense; the legal arguments were merely a continuation of the proceedings and should have been taken down by the reporter. With a multiple court such as the military commission such exchanges could have included remarks from the five members of the commission as well as the prosecutor and defense counsel. Was there dissent among the judges on their rulings, and, if so, did the president of the commission poll them? The record gives no hint of the procedures.

The court reporter does not explain the recess in the trial beginning on Tuesday and lasting into the afternoon of the next day. He breaks off at a point where the defense objected to Harrison Ellis's being put on the stand to testify against himself, with the lawyers approaching the bench to argue over the objection. From the transcript, a cursory reader might conclude that the twenty-four hour delay in the trial came because the court could not reach a quick decision on this point. Instead, from other sources it can be learned that Governor Henry D. Hatfield issued an order suspending the trial and that the attorneys went to Charleston to argue a related case.

The transcript, of course, gives no description of the physical setting of the trial, which took place in an upstairs room, the meeting place of a fraternal organization in the town of Pratt, West Virginia, a railroad junction on the C. & O. Railroad some twenty-five miles from Charleston. The hall was barely large enough to hold the court, the witnesses, the forty-eight defendants, and a few spectators, and the building was so rickety that the court limited the number of people admitted. Fortunately, newspaper reporters who were there supplied brief descriptions of the site of the trial.

Much can be inferred about the relations among the attorneys from the presentation of evidence and the arguments, but such things as demeanor and attitude are not the stuff of transcripts. The two junior officers who served as defense counsel both held appointive offices in state government. Were they overawed by their civilian or military superiors, the prosecutor and the commissioners? From the record, they clearly deferred to their senior nonmilitary colleague, M.F.

Matheny, an experienced trial attorney who was not dependent on the goodwill of the court. What was the impact on the final day when an ex-congressman who had not even been present during most of the trial joined the defending counsels? The transcript suggests some of the relationships among the lawyers, but the reader has only shaky inferences and imagination to give him the ambience of the court.

The transcript shows that informality prevailed in the courtroom, for the attorneys on either side interrupted one another and made offhand remarks taken down by the reporter, and members of the court frequently intervened in the questioning when evidence was being presented. One reporter commented on the fact that a witness was allowed to roam the courtroom freely and even talk to her during the trial. Other reporters noted that Mother Jones and some of her codefendants talked to one another while the proceedings were in progress. Formally, the court attempted to follow the general rules of procedure for contemporary West Virginia trials.

Newspapers and official legal reports of related civil cases, as well as works already mentioned, help to flesh out the bare bones of the transcript.

In the era immediately preceding World War I, judges, legislators, and executives at both the state and national level were adapting old laws and institutions or creating new ones—administrative and investigatory bodies as well as statutes and court decisions—to meet the needs of a changing society. Governor William E. Glasscock created a commission to provide factual information that might help settle the Paint Creek strike, and he even offered to serve as a personal mediator between the parties, an unusual role for a governor. For the first time in the state's history he proclaimed martial law in a district. His experiment with martial law and the court-martial as a social control raised constitutional questions that continue to be unresolved to the present. All told, over the course of seven months, more than two hundred civilians were tried by court-martial, a procedure that had few counterparts in American legal history except during and immediately after the Civil War.

The contestants in the Paint Creek and Cabin Creek strike of 1912–13 battled in the courts of law and in the wider court of public opinion, as well as with armed men in the coal camps and the hills. I hope that this record and account of legal maneuvering will add to the understanding of the roles of governments, organizations, and individuals in the history of American labor.

It is a pleasure to acknowledge the help of others. Franklin D. Cleckley, professor in the College of Law at West Virginia University, and Thomas A. Green, professor of law and professor of history at the University of Michigan, assisted me with their suggestions, and Nancy Grossman, J.D., has been a valued reader. None of them can be held responsible for the interpretation, or the errors, of the author. Members of the staff of the West Virginia and Regional History Collection at West Virginia University have been unfailingly helpful in providing the documents that they conserve.

# INTRODUCTION

# Arrest

On 13 February 1913, police officers arrested Mary Harris "Mother" Jones, the labor agitator, on a street in downtown Charleston, West Virginia, as she was leading a group of citizens to seek an interview with Governor William E. Glasscock at the Capitol. The delegation bore with them a petition protesting conditions in the Paint Creek and Cabin Creek districts of Kanawha County, where the governor had declared martial law because of repeated acts of violence during a long strike of coal miners. At meetings in Smithers and Long Acre, just outside the military zone, union miners had adopted the resolutions and named the men to present the petition, along with their spokeswoman.[1]

At the direction of T.C. Townsend, the county prosecutor, policemen took Mother Jones from Charleston to the area under martial law and turned her over to the military authorities. There she remained under guard until the week of 7 March when she and forty-seven other individuals faced charges of murder and conspiracy to murder in a military court. Immediately after the trial, some who had been held innocent gained their freedom, and some who were convicted received conditional pardons by the governor, but Mother Jones and eleven others remained in custody. The military authorities detained her at Pratt, West Virginia, until 7 May.

The court-martial of Mother Jones in West Virginia was to bring her unprecedented publicity, but her flair for dramatic actions had already spread her fame nationally.[2] In the 1890s she had participated in various political activities as a member of the Populist and Socialist Labor parties, and when "General" Jacob S. Coxey led an army of unemployed people on a march to Washington in 1894, she was one of his lieutenants. In Pennsylvania strikes, she had organized brigades of women with mops and brooms to add to the protest marches of striking miners. She gained greater prominence in labor affairs after she accepted in 1900 a position as an organizer for the United Mine Workers of America, the only woman so employed by the national UMWA. In

1902 her two years of organizing, largely in West Virginia, reached a climax when federal marshals arrested her for making a speech in violation of an injunction issued by Judge John J. Jackson.

In 1903 Mother Jones led an army of child textile workers who marched from Philadelphia to Oyster Bay to enlist the backing of Theodore Roosevelt for a national child labor law. The two following years saw her in Colorado, again organizing the miners there for the UMWA but also participating in the concurrent Cripple Creek strike of the Western Federation of Miners. Dissatisfied with the settlement of the Colorado coal strike arranged by John Mitchell and other leaders, she left the UMWA in 1905 and devoted herself to lecturing for the Socialist party in the southwest, becoming involved from time to time with the activities of the Western Federation of Miners in the area. She also became the champion of the Mexican revolutionaries in the United States who were trying to overthrow the government of Porfirio Diaz in Mexico. After Diaz fled Mexico, Mother Jones conferred with the leaders of the new revolutionary government of Mexico on labor policies.

In 1911, when she reckoned her age at eighty, Mother Jones resumed her position as organizer for the UMWA, now headed by John P. White, and she remained on the payroll of the union for the next twelve years. Although most closely associated with the coal miners, she left them from time to time to assist in strikes of textile workers, metalliferous miners, telegraphers, garment workers, and railroad men. Her first assignment after her return to the miners was among the strikers in the Greensburg district of Pennsylvania, but she soon went to Colorado, where the struggle to establish the union was continuing. In the copper mining center of Butte, Montana, in July 1912, she read of the failure of contract negotiations between miners and operators on Paint Creek, West Virginia, canceled her projected speaking dates in California, and hastened back to Paint Creek to throw herself into the fray.

The strike in West Virginia began in April 1912, when the UMWA sought an advance in wages and a renewal of their contract with the operators in the Kanawha Valley. After a brief work stoppage at some mines, most of the operators north of the Kanawha River settled with the union in May, but the Paint Creek Colliery, one of the largest operations south of the river, refused to renew its contract. The men struck, and a rising tide of violent incidents in July led Governor William E. Glasscock, at the request of the sheriff, to send in first one company and then the entire National Guard to preserve order in the Paint Creek area.[3]

Governor Glasscock was a mild Progressive—he was one of the seven Republican governors who requested Theodore Roosevelt to run for president in 1912—who had been chosen by the state Republican machine as the candidate for governor in 1908. A former court clerk and superintendent of schools in Monongalia County, he was also a practicing attorney and an ardent party worker. The Republican leaders of the state saw in his mild progressivism a chance to unify the two wings of the party for the contest in 1908. As governor he proposed many Progressive reforms, a few of which were enacted before he left office. On several occasions while he was governor his fragile health sent him to a hospital for treatment and rest; he was, however, tenacious in his attempts to deal with the problems that confronted him. He blamed the failure of his many efforts to settle the strike on the inaction of Kanawha County officials and on the unreasonable stance of the operators.[4]

On Paint Creek, Quinn Morton was the leading operator, with mines at Barnwell and Mahan, where union labor had been employed since 1904; he was also one of the principal negotiators in the conferences between the Kanawha Coal Operators Association and the UMWA in March and April. Although a stockholder in the Imperial Coal Company at Barnwell, he was essentially a manager for investors outside the state. When negotiations broke down, he brought in guards from the Baldwin-Felts detective agency, evicted strikers from the company-owned houses, and began importing nonunion workers. The strikers set up a tent colony at Holly Grove near the mouth of Paint Creek. Clashes between Morton's guards and the strikers mounted through the summer, particularly in July after the arrival of Mother Jones.[5]

Violent incidents increased in August, when Mother Jones managed to bring the workers on adjacent Cabin Creek out on strike. The dominant operator there was Charles Cabell, who was the very model of a paternalistic mine manager. He lived on the creek with his family and mingled with the men, many of whom he knew by their first names. He built a swimming pool for his miners; established a YMCA with a reading room and other recreation; provided churches open to any organized religious group; and paid an exorbitant price for the land on which a saloon was located, so he could close down the drinking place.[6] But he was adamantly antiunion and for years had employed

Baldwin-Felts guards to prevent union organizers from entering his area. The narrow, winding valley, accessible only by rail and a road that sometimes ran along the bed of the creek, made it easy for guards to spot strangers, and the special railroad police who rode the trains up from the main line cooperated with the Baldwin-Felts men. Any visitors who tried to travel the twenty-mile stretch of creek that Cabell controlled had to state their business to the guards, and if their answers were unsatisfactory, the company police barred their admittance. For nine years, known union organizers had not only been denied entry but had frequently received beatings by the guards. Except in the incorporated town of Eskdale, which had its own mayor and police, the operators and their guards reigned supreme.[7]

Mother Jones broke this tight seal on 4 August when she made a trip up Cabin Creek on a train carrying some of the militia assigned to the area. She spread leaflets announcing a rally and two days later held a meeting at Eskdale, inducted many of the miners on Cabin Creek into the UMWA, and brought them out to join their striking brothers on Paint Creek. Mayor Walter Williams not only permitted her to speak but also became an enthusiastic supporter of the strikers. A week later she led a march from Eskdale of some 150 strikers, some of them armed, for another speech and demonstration further up the creek at Red Warrior. [8]

Prodded by mine operators and Charleston businessmen who indicated to him that he was not vigorous enough in his handling of the strike, Governor Glasscock issued a Peace Proclamation for the disturbed area and called on the county officials to convene a special grand jury to deal with the violence there. The criminal court judge and the prosecuting attorneys refused, insisting that they could not rely on either grand or petit jurors to be fair in cases arising out of the strike.

This judgment rested in part on an experience early in the strike, when a group of Baldwin-Felts guards exchanged fire with several armed Italian strikers. One Italian died in the exchange of gunfire, and a black man was wounded. At the June grand jury, the Baldwin-Felts men sought to bring assault charges against the Italians, but the grand jurors indicted the guards instead. The prosecutors, for lack of a key witness, did not pursue the case at the June term of court. The judge granted a change of venue to the Greenbrier County court, and there the case was postponed. Samuel B. Avis, the prosecuting attorney who was running for Congress in the November elections, insisted that politics did not interfere with the performance of his duty, but he may very well have wished not to alienate some voters by appearing prominently before the public in controversial cases. In any event, he left the management of the grand juries for the June and October terms in the hands of his assistant, Frank Burdette, and it was Burdette, not Avis, who conferred with Judge Henry K. Black and the governor about a special grand jury. "I really was of the opinion that we could not accomplish much," Burdette testified later, "but I was willing to make the effort." The governor was also pessimistic, but, as he told the Senate investigating committee, "I did believe it was my duty to exhaust every known remedy before anything else was done." The judge, who alone could convene a grand jury, had the decisive voice, and he opposed the procedure. One commentator suggested that the decision in the last analysis was political: "The campaign was going on, and it might not have been a good thing."[9]

Neither the Peace Proclamation nor the presence of troops in the area prevented another clash between Baldwin-Felts guards and strikers, and after a trip on 30 August to inspect the site of the conflict at Dry Branch, Governor Glasscock reluctantly issued a declaration of martial law, the first in the state's history. Soldiers then confiscated all arms they could find in the Paint Creek and Cabin Creek districts, whether in the hands of guards or of miners. All Baldwin-Felts guards were excluded from the area. Shortly thereafter, Governor Glasscock set up a military commission to try offenders in the martial law zone, thrusting into prominence George Selden Wallace, the judge advocate general of the National Guard, who prosecuted nearly all the cases that came before the commission over the next seven months.[10]

George S. Wallace had practiced law in Huntington, West Virginia, for some fifteen years, interrupted by a tour of duty as a first lieutenant of the Second West Virginia Volunteers in the Spanish-American War. As a member of the National Guard, he had attained the rank of lieutenant colonel, and his service as prosecuting attorney of Cabell County (1904-8) made him a logical choice as judge advocate general of the West Virginia National Guard. With civil authority superseded by military, Wallace began a series of prosecutions of all persons, military or civilian, charged with offenses within the martial law zone. Since the West Virginia constitution, the first version of which was written during the Civil War, provides that civilians shall not be tried by a military court, attorneys for the UMWA challenged the legality of the proceedings.[11]

Under martial law, relative quiet came to the Paint Creek and Cabin Creek area. The mine operators insisted that, because the

Baldwin-Felts men had been expelled, they needed guards of some kind to protect their property. After several meetings of operators, the commander of the National Guard, and–indirectly–the UMWA, the conferees worked out a system by which the coal companies would hire watchmen chosen from the National Guard, which would release them from their military duties for the civilian employment. Under this system the companies would acquire willing guards from a list that the UMWA could winnow of any individuals they considered objectionable. As the new watchman system got under way, Governor Glasscock began withdrawing troops and on 15 October declared martial law at an end. Throughout the period, the governor made strenuous efforts to bring the mine operators and the miners together to work out their differences. He finally invited representatives of both sides to the Capitol and, since the operators refused to meet face to face with the union representatives, carried a set of proposals back and forth between different rooms, trying to bring the parties to some agreement. The miners were willing to negotiate or to accept arbitration, but the operators rejected all the proposals.[12]

Political campaigning exacerbated the economic tensions as the day for state and national elections approached. The Democrats, Republicans, and Bull Moosers did not align themselves openly with either side in the strike. For the most part they confined themselves to deploring violence and lawlessness and to expressing concern over the economic consequences of the strike. For the Socialists, on the other hand, the cause of the miners became the main issue in the campaign in West Virginia, and their principal orators, Harold W. Houston and John W. Brown, used it as the departure point for their indictment of the capitalistic system.[13]

The election results of 1912 did little to clarify political alignments in the state, except to show that changes were in the air. In the national contest Woodrow Wilson won the presidency and included the electoral votes of West Virginia in his column. On the state level, the old, dominant Republican machine of Stephen B. Elkins was disintegrating, and the Bull Moose defection from the regular party and presentation of rival tickets for local offices posed problems for the future. Still, the Republican candidate for governor, Henry Drury Hatfield, won in the face of the national trend toward Wilson. The Democrats could take heart at the emergence of a strong newcomer in Congressman Matthew Mansfield Neely, but they had narrowly lost one congressional seat and were still the minority party. The Democrats shared the new legislature almost equally with two factions of Republicans, promising a fierce battle over the selection of a United States senator when the legislators met in January. Leaders of both parties viewed with concern the rapid growth of the Socialist vote. Although it remained small, it could be a decisive factor in future elections, and the Socialist appeal to miners was particularly disturbing to insiders in both regular parties.

Mother Jones's relationship with the Socialists during the political campaign was ambiguous. A year earlier she had accused the secretary of the national Socialist Party of misconduct, but a special committee appointed to investigate her charges had exonerated him. The party then officially expelled her. She felt that the leaders of the party had treated her badly, but since the Socialists were strongly supporting the striking miners in West Virginia, she worked with them. She remained a socialist with a small "s" and went so far as to endorse Thomas Tincher, a miner, in his race on the Socialist ticket for sheriff of Kanawha County. At the rally she held in Montgomery on 4 August she shared the platform with John W. Brown, one of the leading Socialist orators, a candidate for the legislature, and he introduced her to the crowd at a meeting in Charleston. The *Huntington Socialist and Labor Star* and the *Charleston Labor Argus,* weekly newspapers that supported the Socialist party, featured her prominently in their columns, focusing on her role in the strike, not her political opinions. Though she was clearly working closely with the Socialists, the newspapers reported only one occasion when she publicly campaigned for the party ticket, whatever her private opinions may have been.

Mother Jones's relationship with the UMWA was almost equally ambiguous. Now, as it was at the time, it is impossible to say which of her actions during the strike bore the approval of the union. Tom Cairnes, president of District 17 of the UMWA, disclaimed all responsibility for the utterances or actions of Mother Jones. He stated publicly that District 17 did not employ her and that she did not represent his organization.[14] In a review of her career ten years later, Mother Jones maintained that the officers of the national union did not know that she was going to Paint Creek and that she acted on her own in organizing the Cabin Creek miners. Yet she added that during the strike she had made several secret trips to Indianapolis to consult with the international union leadership, and President John P. White "stood behind me in every move I made."[15]

While the leaders of the UMWA may not have directed or

approved of all the actions she took, it probably suited them to have a militant Mother Jones act "independently" so that their own image as reasonable negotiators would make them more acceptable to the operators and the public.[16]

From her headquarters in Charleston, Mother Jones traveled frequently to the strike area to hold rallies encouraging the strikers, and in a series of public meetings in Montgomery and Charleston from 4 August to 21 September she conducted a crusade for civil rights for all citizens in the strike area, as well as economic justice for the miners.

Speechmaking was only one of her activities. As she had done in previous confrontations, she organized the women in the coal camps to take a visible part in the protests of the strikers. Some gathered at the railroad depots and sidings to inspect cars that might be carrying scabs, or "transportation men" as they were usually called, subjecting them to jeers, insults, curses, and sometimes to stones and other missiles. A brigade of women paraded through the settlements along the creeks, showing support for their miner husbands and sons. Preparing the way for a demonstration in Charleston, the old agitator announced to newspapermen: "We are coming back to our capitol again and twice as strong. The men are going to bring their children along and their wives."[17] The parade before her next speech in Charleston included a company of children carrying placards.

After the declaration of martial law and the removal of all Baldwin-Felts guards, the strikers increased their opposition to the importation of scabs by those operators who tried to continue production. The managers of the coal companies advertised within and outside the state for workers, and made contracts with employment agencies whereby the coal company would pay by the head for all workers delivered to their premises. The Cabin Creek operators turned to the Industrial Corporation, which had offices in New York, Cleveland, and Chicago, where men signed contracts on the promise of good daily wages and transportation to the workplace. A hiring company agent would shepherd them aboard a train and supply them with food during the journey to southern West Virginia. At junctions on the main line they would transfer to trains going up the creeks, and when they reached their destination guards would escort them to company housing. There the new workers found themselves trapped, strangers without money, surrounded by hostile demonstrators, and dependent on the company for protection, food, and housing.[18]

The operators could bring in scabs to replace their striking workers, but the strikers could also use disgruntled scabs against the employers. The UMWA held a press conference at its headquarters in Charleston at which twenty-one men told of how the companies had lured them with false promises into scabbing. When their new employers mistreated them, they eluded the guards in the coal camp and took refuge in the tent colonies of the UMWA.

Mother Jones knew the value of publicizing such stories and concentrated her efforts on two of the men at the press conference. John Stehl, aged eighteen, and John Wister, aged seventeen, signed contracts with a New York employment agency that promised them good wages and did not inform them where they would be working or under what conditions. After five days on the job they decided to quit, but when they asked for their wages they found no pay was due to them because they had not yet worked out the cost of their transportation. Moneyless, they walked down to the mouth of the creek, where strikers fed and housed them and brought them to Charleston. Mother Jones, who was planning a speaking tour in the East, took these two young men along with her to Washington to lodge a complaint at the Department of Commerce and Labor against the mine operator and the employment agent for practicing peonage.[19]

She also intervened to help C.R. Shaw, a Parkersburg carpenter who took what he thought was a job paying three dollars a day, opening a new mine at Mucklow on Paint Creek. Once there, he found he had been deceived but felt compelled to stay. After a month on the job he and his wife decided to abandon their household goods and walked out of the valley with their six children. At Holly Grove, Mother Jones met them, bought them tickets to Charleston, and maintained them there until Shaw found work in a lumberyard. The newspaper reporter who wrote this story made it into a sentimental melodrama with Mother Jones as the rescuing angel who "hugged the tired and mud-stained little children and the brave wife and mother and gave personal assistance in taking care of them."[20]

More important than sentimental newspaper publicity was the work that Mother Jones did behind the scenes to stop the flow of scabs into the area. By law in Ohio, employment agencies had to inform men if they were replacing workers on strike, and the commissioner of labor kept a close eye on the Industrial Corporation in Cleveland to see that the employment agent obeyed the law. "He had to," said the manager of the company. "Mother Jones was on his trail all the time."[21]

All along the branch lines of the railroads, striking miners and their families mounted demonstrations against newcomers, and a scab caught by strikers away from whatever protection the company afforded him was a likely object of violence. These protests against the scabs brought the strikers into direct conflict with the railroad police, and Mother Jones and UMWA officials got in touch with the manager of the C. & O. Railroad to try to remove the special officers, and particularly their machine guns, which they regarded as provocative, from the trains running up the creeks. Briefly, the manager tried the experiment, but soon reverted to the earlier practice, feeling that the railroad company owed its passengers protection so long as they were on railroad property.[22]

In October 1912, Governor Glasscock began withdrawing units of the National Guard from the strike area even though the miners continued to display hostility against "transportation men." Mainly, the strikers confined themselves to epithets and stones hurled at the railroad cars that brought the men through their tent colonies. However, at times shots were fired into the trains, and these incidents, along with other violence around election time, led the governor to reimpose martial law on 15 November. With the reintroduction of the militia, a sullen peace descended over the district, while all parties awaited the report of a fact-finding commission that the governor had appointed.[23]

The Donahue Commission, presided over by the Catholic bishop of Wheeling, began taking testimony in the Paint Creek and Cabin Creek area, and to a lesser degree elsewhere in the state, shortly after Governor Glasscock appointed them on 28 August 1912. On 27 November they submitted their report, which pleased neither miners nor operators. In support of the miners, they declared that the Baldwin-Felts guard system was un-American, that company stores often overcharged, that excessive docking of miners for slate in loads of coal existed, and that some operators had used blacklists. On the other hand, they found that wages and living conditions in the strike district were as good as or better than comparable mining camps in the state. Most important of all, the commission supported the view that the basic cause of the strike was the attempt by the UMWA to organize the mines and that UMWA organizers and outside agitators, in concert with coal operators in other states, had brought on the troubles on Paint Creek and Cabin Creek.[24]

The Donahue Commission report therefore failed to break the existing stalemate. The miners insisted on negotiation or arbitration to settle their differences; the operators south of the Kanawha River refused to deal with the UMWA in any way. With nonunion labor, operators were able to maintain partial production at some mines, but many other mines had to close their tipples. After Mother Jones spoke at Eskdale in August, said J.E. Staton, "We never turned another wheel."[25] The strikers who had been evicted from company houses settled in the tent towns that the UMWA had set up at Holly Grove and elsewhere, or drifted on to other jobs. Neither tent colonies nor working coal camps were safe havens, for company guards and strikers occasionally fired into them from the surrounding hills, but most of the incidents seemed to be for the purpose of intimidation rather than of inflicting casualties.

The governor rescinded his second martial law proclamation on 12 December, but he kept his decision secret for fear that knowledge of the repeal might lead to more conflict. He kept a skeleton force of the National Guard in place in the strike zone. The relative quiet may also have been owing to the absence of Mother Jones during much of the period. About 15 November, she made a trip to Washington, D.C. In the first three weeks of December, she spoke in Cleveland, Cincinnati, New York, and Washington, trying to generate support for the strikers. Just before Christmas she returned briefly to the "free town" of Eskdale and to the strikers' camp at Holly Grove. Early in January she was again on the road, speaking at the Victoria Theater in Wheeling on the fifth, and at the Armory in Washington, D.C., on the tenth. The potential for violence in the strike zone remained high, but at the beginning of the new year, Charles Cabell, the "czar of Cabin Creek," felt safe in taking a Florida vacation.[26]

≈    ≈    ≈    ≈    ≈

# Habeas Corpus

Anxious to lay down the reins of office and return to his law practice in Morgantown, Governor William E. Glasscock nevertheless hoped to see the legislature complete at least part of his Progressive agenda at its meeting in January. If the hair-thin Republican majority held together and if some Democrats voted for reforms, he could achieve many of his goals. As he wrote a friend in his hometown, "if I can only succeed in having this incoming legislature pass some needed legislation I shall leave Charleston very happy indeed."[27] Thanking Henry

D. Hatfield, who would succeed him in March, for his promise of support, he predicted that it would be a historic session, surpassing any in the state's history. In his address to the legislature and in other public statements, he outlined a long list of reforms for enactment: a new primary election law; a corrupt practices act; the abolition of the fee system for paying local officers; initiative, referendum and recall measures; a child labor act; old age pensions; a minimum wage law; a state constabulary; improvement of the workmen's compensation law; a state utilities commission; a law giving the governor the power to remove sheriffs, prosecuting attorneys, and justices of the peace who did not carry out their duties; and improvement of the company guard system.

Factional quarrels among the Republicans dashed Glasscock's hopes. For weeks, the legislators who met in January could not even complete their formal organization, and when they did, they proceeded to the election of a United States senator that produced a series of deadlocks. In the face of these disruptions, little legislation moved to completion. Of Glasscock's proposals, only three made it through the legislative process: establishment of a public service commission; the Bloch bill, which amended the workmen's compensation act; and the Wertz bill, which forbade the appointment of company guards as deputy sheriffs. This latter act had begun as a complete ban on the employment of company guards, but amendments watered it down merely to deny them official status as law enforcement officers. Clarence F. Jolliffe, later to be president of the court-martial, introduced a bill to establish a state constabulary, but it failed of passage.[28]

Quiet had prevailed in the strike area while the legislature was quarreling over its organization, but renewed violence burst out with random shooting attacks on towns along Paint Creek early in the first week of February. Then, on 7 February 1913, Ben Burks, a nonunion miner, suffered a serious injury to his leg in a mining accident. Dr. J.C. Anderson, Jr., a company physician, treated Burks at the mine, but decided that he should take him to the hospital outside the strike zone to attempt surgical repairs to the damaged leg. Anderson arranged for a wagon and driver to convey his patient from Mucklow to the hospital for surgery. As the doctor, the patient, and his driver passed through Holly Grove, striking miners subjected them to gunfire. The driver whipped up the mules, and Dr. Anderson, who was walking alongside the ambulance wagon, made his escape into the woods. The injured man was bleeding to death in the wagon in front of the hospital when

Dr. Anderson caught up with it. Anderson telephoned back to headquarters, and a group of armed guards set out from Mucklow to Holly Grove to retaliate against the strikers, only to be met by a superior force of miners who drove them back with rifle fire. Strikers took up positions in the hills above Mucklow and poured a hail of bullets into the headquarters of the watchmen.[29]

In Charleston, Quinn Morton received a phone call from Mucklow informing him that the town was under fire from snipers in the hills. Immediately, he got in touch with Sheriff Bonner Hill to ask for protection. He also went to Lowenstein's Hardware and bought thirty rifles and ammunition to take to his beleaguered town. Tom Little, the deputy in the strike area, had already reported to Sheriff Hill on the new violence, and the sheriff began organizing a posse of ten men to accompany him to Paint Creek. By the time Morton and Hill had assembled their men and arms, they had missed the last regular train at 4:30, but Morton called the superintendent of the C. & O. Railroad and, with a confirming call from Sheriff Hill, got permission to use an armored train that the railroad kept constantly prepared for trips into the strike zone. Quinn, the sheriff, and his posse went aboard the Bull Moose Special, which mounted two machine guns and had protective steel plates installed on the engine and one car. Joining them were five or six special deputies on the railroad company payroll who added to the firepower of the force that arrived at Paint Creek Junction at 10:30 in the evening.

The train started up the winding tracks from the junction toward Mucklow, running without lights. The accounts of what happened next differ widely. Residents of the tent colony at Holly Grove asserted that, without provocation, men on the darkened train shot into the camp with both rifles and machine guns. Those on the train insisted that they merely returned fire that riflemen in the tent colony directed at them. In any event, the fusillade from the train killed a miner named Estep and wounded a woman. The train proceeded to Mucklow, where Morton delivered the guns and ammunition he had bought and made plans for the defense of the town. The next morning Morton and Hill returned to Charleston to confer with the governor.[30]

While the resentment of the strikers was rising over this latest incident, Mother Jones had returned from her speech-making tour in eastern cities to her room at the Fleetwood Hotel in Charleston on Sunday, the ninth. Almost immediately, she went to Paint Creek, where she spoke at the funeral of Sesco Estep, and no one who knew her would have expected her to be temperate in her remarks. Accounts of what she said are brief and suspect, but the *Charleston Daily Mail* quoted her as urging the men "to get their guns and shoot them (watchmen) to hell."[31]

During the weekend, someone cut the telephone wires running up Paint Creek so that no outsider could acquire accurate information from the area. In Charleston, the garbled reports of renewed violence in the strike zone came in the midst of intense political conflict that had absorbed the legislature since the beginning of its session. The newspapers announced that police had arrested five members of the legislature on charges of selling their votes in the senatorial election, with more possibly to be indicted. This sensation was still agitating the public mind when the news arrived of the renewed violence on Paint Creek. Governor Glasscock summoned legislative leaders of all factions, who with other advisers unanimously urged him to declare martial law in the zone once again. He issued his third martial law proclamation on Monday, 10 February 1913. The troops who had gone home during the previous two months received new calls to active duty and began their return journey by train to the martial law district.[32]

Back on the creeks, tempers were running high. Although some miners abandoned their vulnerable tents at Holly Grove, others stayed, and the prevailing hostile mood throughout the strike region found a focus in the watchmen who had their headquarters at Mucklow. Exactly who coordinated the assault on Mucklow is the subject of the court-martial, but the general plan of operations is clear from the trial evidence. Armed strikers numbering perhaps fifty were to gather early in the morning of Monday, 10 February, on the mountain above Beech Grove, follow a trail along the crest of the ridge, and from the high ground be able to command the town of Mucklow, where the watchmen had their headquarters.

The guards did not sit idly awaiting the attack. A force numbering twenty-five, composed of watchmen, company office workers, and volunteer nonunion workers, armed with the rifles brought by Quinn Morton, prepared to man defensive positions on the eastern slope of the mountain above Mucklow.

The result was predictable. On the heavily wooded ridge, a group of strikers surprised a detachment of nonunion men at a machine gun. The defenders challenged the interlopers, and firing broke out. In the ensuing exchange of fire, the defending force lost one man killed and another wounded. A general engagement began that was to go on intermittently throughout the day as reinforcements joined both sides. Some participants fled immediately, others became lost, and some found themselves cut off from their fellows for hours, not knowing what was going on. By evening, men from both sides made their way toward home, just as the first soldiers of the National Guard began to arrive at Paint Creek Junction. The defenders of Mucklow had prevented an attack on the town and captured some opponents but had suffered casualties and lost a machine gun. The strikers had also suffered casualties and may have looked forward to regrouping and continuing the action the next day, when the National Guard intervened and began arresting all suspicious characters. All told, the military authorities rounded up some fifty-one strikers and held them for trial; none of the nonstrikers in Mucklow was arrested.[33]

The frustrations and anger of the miners after the battle of Mucklow and the later arrests culminated on Wednesday the twelfth in a mass meeting outside the strike zone at Smithers, north of the river. The union leaders urged the men there, who had gone out on strike in sympathy with the miners south of the river, to return to work. Mother Jones also spoke at the meeting, advising against further violence. Instead, she advocated another protest to the governor against the unwarranted arrests of the strikers. In the morning she once more talked to a meeting of miners at Long Acre before she left aboard the K. & M. train to Charleston with a delegation bearing a petition to the governor. [34]

Thursday provided much excitement for the citizens of Charleston. The Gazette printed a story indicating that Mother Jones was planning a march at the head of a body of five hundred armed miners to assassinate the governor. Authorities rang the bell at city hall as a riot warning, and many citizens poured into the streets to try to find out what was happening. All city and county police units were called to duty, and members of the National Guard who were in the city assembled to defend the grounds of the Capitol.[35]

Mother Jones and her delegation never reached the governor. Special Officer Dan Cunningham arrested her shortly after she arrived at the Charleston depot on a warrant issued by a justice of the peace that charged her with complicity in the murder of the slain defender at Mucklow. Later in the day he took her to Pratt and handed her over to the military authorities. There the military prosecutor charged her, along with forty-seven of the men they had arrested in the military zone immediately after the battle at Mucklow, with conspiracy to murder. An early court-martial of the prisoners was expected.[36]

While they awaited trial, she and the other prisoners had to face harsh conditions. Temporarily, the militiamen used railroad boxcars to confine the suspicious characters whom they had rounded up. Then the National Guard took over the C. & O. freight station and converted it into a holding pen. Most of the men slept in one big room, badly heated, ill-lit, and poorly ventilated. One end, formerly a partially walled office, served as a preliminary holding area and as a place where prisoners could see visitors under the eyes of guards. At mealtimes the prisoners lined up and marched in groups of twenty to another building, used as a mess hall. The march also served as their exercise period. Sentries kept close guard on all sides of the building, but the jailers allowed the prisoners to see visitors, who could bring them food and clean clothes. The authorities singled out from the others a few men whom they considered ringleaders in the battle of Mucklow and kept them in a private house.[37]

For Mother Jones, and briefly for some other women who soon gained their freedom, the Guard commandeered a boardinghouse, a two-story frame building with a porch, set behind a picket fence. Mother Jones occupied the first-floor parlor and other women prisoners the second story. The number and names of these women do not appear in the unofficial records; they were apparently arrested, held for some time, and released, never being brought before the court-martial. The authorities contracted with the landlady, Isabel Carney, to house and feed them. For lack of records, no direct connection can be made between the other occupants of the boardinghouse and Mother Jones. One of her standard techniques in a strike was to work with the women to play a public part in the fight. These female prisoners at Pratt could have been among those whom she had organized to march in demonstrations or harass scabs, or they could have been simply part of the general roundup after the Battle of Mucklow of armed men and their accomplices.

The principal prisoner had contact only with Isabel Carney, her captors, and on occasion with visiting journalists, who interviewed her under close supervision by a Guard officer. Her jailers permitted her to use the porch, and one of the officers began to take her regularly on brief walks about the neighborhood when her inactivity seemed to be affecting her health adversely. Two sentries also patrolled this house. The provost marshal permitted her to receive letters, packages, and newspapers but was authorized to open her mail. She protested the interference with her mail and charged that her captors withheld some items.[38]

Their security measures may not in fact have been as tight as the military authorities thought. In an interview years later, Dallas Stotts told how when he was sergeant of the guard he let Mother Jones persuade him to accompany her to the nearby village of Hansford to get some beer. They left Carney's house about dusk, and walked the two miles to Hansford. Mother Jones had her beer and bought some more to take back with her, and they returned to her prison quarters in something under two hours.[39]

In one of her letters at this time, Mother Jones expressed surprise that her old friend William B. Wilson, newly appointed secretary of labor, was not exerting himself in her behalf. On the contrary, he was working manfully to secure her freedom, impelled not only by his own inclinations but also by the political pressure that the issue was generating nationally. Letters and petitions for the federal government to intervene in her behalf were flooding in to President Wilson and members of Congress, and the recipients routinely directed them to the new secretary of labor for information, advice, and action. No less than seven files of letters and petitions are preserved in the National Archives.[40] Old friends in the labor movement were urging action on William B. Wilson, some even suggesting the possibility of violence: "I have carried a gun three times in industrial wars in this country," wrote T.J. Lewellyn from Indiana, "and by the eternal, if any harm comes to the old mother, I'm not too old, nor by the same token, too cowardly to carry it again. But we don't want that in this country and age."[41]

Secretary Wilson, trying to organize a new cabinet department with a minuscule staff and no appropriation, had to turn to other branches of the government for action. One answer was a congressional investigation, and he had already set that process in motion. While still a member of Congress, he had proposed a resolution to investigate the conditions of coal mining in West Virginia. Senator John Worth Kern, the majority leader, introduced it as a Senate resolution and kept it high on the party agenda. Next, Secretary Wilson turned to the Post Office Department and sent a registered letter with enclosures to Mother Jones in her prison in Pratt, requesting a notice of delivery. When he received no return receipt, he sent first an informal and then a formal request to the postmaster general for an immediate investigation. The postal department initiated inquiries by telephone and by letter and later sent postal inspectors in person to explore Wilson's charges.[42]

Not knowing of Wilson's efforts and convinced that the coal

operators were intercepting her mail, Mother Jones had devised some alternative lines of communication. She persuaded her landlady, Isabel Carney, to serve as a secret courier when she went to visit her mother, carrying mail to another post office not subject to control by operators or soldiers. She also arranged with sympathizers among the soldiers who guarded her to pick up communications, which she lowered through loosened floorboards into the basement or crawl space of Carney's boardinghouse. It was through this latter secret line of communication that she dispatched a telegram to Senator John Worth Kern that he read during the debate in the U.S. Senate over the question of setting up a committee to investigate conditions in the coalfields of West Virginia.[43]

On 16 February, A.J. Hollis, an enterprising reporter for the Pittsburgh *Leader,* made his way through the basement and loose floorboards of Carney's house and conducted a long unsupervised interview with Mother Jones. The day after their talk, the provost marshal arrested Hollis and held him for several hours in the bull pen before Lieutenant Colonel George S. Wallace and other officers questioned him. He finally produced a letter from his editor to Governor William E. Glasscock, and after the Guard officers had checked his bona fides in the capital they released him. Hollis returned to Pittsburgh and began to file a series of byline articles that appeared in his newspaper over the next two weeks, the first of them dealing with his own incarceration.[44]

Between her arrest and the end of her court-martial, Mother Jones left her prison quarters in Pratt on only one occasion, to attend a habeas corpus proceeding before the Supreme Court in Charleston. On the same day that the police in Charleston had placed her under arrest, they had also taken into custody Charles H. Boswell, editor of the Socialist *Labor Argus,* and two international organizers of the UMWA, Charles Batley and Paul J. Paulsen. Three days after their detention, Albert M. Belcher and Harold W. Houston, attorneys for the UMWA, began habeas corpus proceedings for the four prisoners. The next day an official served the writ on the military authorities in Pratt, who were ordered to produce the prisoners before the Supreme Court the following week.

*In re Mary Jones et al.* was the third habeas corpus proceeding that tested the power of Governor Glasscock to impose martial law, military trials, and punishment. In the first, *In re Shanklin,* the lawyers for the applicant for a writ argued that his arrest, trial, and imprisonment in the state penitentiary were illegal. The court addressed itself only to the question of arrest, which they held to be constitutionally authorized, and the justices did not consider their decision important enough to be printed. The typed opinion is noteworthy mainly for the fifty-page recital of events in the strike area up to the arrest of J.R. Shanklin.[45]

In the second habeas corpus case, two men, S.F. Nance and L.A. Mays, sought release from the state penitentiary. The military court that had tried them had found them guilty of offenses that under the civil code would have been misdemeanors but had sentenced them to five years imprisonment in the penitentiary. The incident that led to Nance's imprisonment involved Mother Jones. On 7 November, in the interval between the first and second declarations of martial law, S.F. Nance and his wife were at a railroad station awaiting a train that would take them to visit relatives in Kentucky when they saw a crowd chasing and beating a black man who they thought was a scab worker. The man took refuge in the women's waiting room but was ejected, and the mob, estimated at seventy-five men, continued to chase and beat him until he appealed to Mother Jones. She had been watching the activities from a distance but now told the strikers that they had gone far enough and gave the beaten man her protection. An officer and two soldiers, though somewhat intimidated by its size, ordered the crowd, including the Nances, to the other side of the railroad. While Mrs. Nance was crossing the tracks, she slipped and fell, and Nance cursed the officer and shook his fist in his face. He and his wife continued on their trip to Kentucky, but when he came back the military authorities arrested him and charged him with obstructing an officer in the performance of his duty. At his court-martial he received a sentence of five years in the state penitentiary.[46]

Lawyers for Nance and Mays in the habeas corpus hearing maintained that their arrest was illegal, as were their subsequent trials and imprisonment. Their lawyers argued their case before the Supreme Court in the third week in December. The justices held that the arrest and detention of Nance and Mays were constitutional and remanded them to the custody of the warden of the state penitentiary. George S. Wallace, who had presented the case for the state, responded to the congratulations of Bishop P.J. Donahue with the triumphant report that a lawyer friend had told him "it looked like I had written the opinion."[47] The defense counselors, Albert M. Belcher and Harold W. Houston, announced their intention to appeal the decision to the federal courts as soon as it was published. The official opinion was delayed for three weeks, but a preliminary version appeared in the newspapers. On Christmas Eve Governor Glasscock prevented any appeal to the federal courts by issuing pardons to Nance, Mays, and several other men whom the military court had turned over to the warden of the penitentiary for imprisonment.[48]

Shortly after the arrest of Mother Jones and two organizers in February, the UMWA through its attorney Albert M. Belcher began habeas corpus proceedings to gain her release. Here was another chance to force the Supreme Court to pronounce on the legality of the military trials. The justices set 18 February 1913 as the day for argument on the third habeas corpus case, *In re Mary Jones et al.*, but later delayed the hearing until the twenty-fifth. On that day, however, the prisoners did not appear in court, and despite the arguments of George S. Wallace that their presence was unnecessary, the justices postponed the case until the next day and directed the military authorities to comply with the order of the court to produce the prisoners in court in person.[49]

For Mother Jones, Albert M. Belcher and Harold W. Houston contended that the civil courts were open and that she was outside the martial law zone at the time of her arrest. Her transfer to the control of the military authorities who were preparing to try her before a court-martial was contrary to various provisions of the constitution, specifically the ban on any trial of civilians by a military court. In addition, the military authorities were denying her other fundamental civil rights, such as presentment by a grand jury and trial by a jury of her peers.[50]

The basic argument of Wallace and his associate counsel followed the same line taken in the Nance and Mays case. As a sovereign state, West Virginia had the inherent power to preserve itself when threatened by invasion, insurrection, or riots.

In the face of such threats the state constitution gave the governor the power to declare martial law in cities, towns, districts, or counties. Once he had issued his proclamation, the only law in the area designated as a martial law zone was the will of the commander in chief, the governor. The military authority completely superseded civil authority. By statute the governor had the authority at such times to detain anyone contributing to the riot or insurrection that had brought about the declaration of martial law.

The court held that the original warrant charging Mother Jones with complicity in the murder of Bobbitt was properly sworn out. The county prosecutor and the magistrate had acted on their own in transferring her to the military zone, and not at the instigation of other governmental officers. The military authorities rearrested her when she came into their jurisdiction and charged her with the same offenses under the constitutional and statutory powers already confirmed. Thus, due process had been observed; the method by which she came into the martial law zone was irrelevant.[51] In holding that the authorities had followed due process, the court cited its previous decisions in *In re Shanklin* and in *Nance and Mays v. Brown*. In the *Mother Jones et al.* cases, a majority of the court refused to go beyond the legality of martial law and the power of the governor to detain people who threatened the preservation of law and order. By conferring on him the power to declare martial law, the constitution "vests tremendous power in the governor, and its exercise may produce frightful consequences, but . . . it is the necessary means of prevention of still worse results." The declaration of martial law "made the inhabitants of the district technically enemies of the state." Section 6 of Chapter 14 of the code gave the governor power to apprehend and imprison all persons contributing to the disturbance of the peace of the area. Nothing in the terms of the statute limited the exercise of this executive power, and he or his agents could make such arrests either inside or outside the military district. With these constitutional and statutory powers lodged in the governor, the arrest of people giving aid and comfort to the enemy "amounts to due process of law, within the meaning of the Fourteenth Amendment."[52]

Again, as in the previous Nance and Mays case, Justice Ira E. Robinson filed a long and vigorous dissent from the majority of the court. He dismissed the plea of necessity, pointing out that the constitution itself declared its provisions to be "operative alike in a period of war as in time of peace and any departure . . . under the plea of necessity, or any other plea, is subversive of good government and tends to anarchy and despotism." Though admitting the power of the governor to declare martial law and even to arrest and detain people within the zone, he denied the right to try or punish them. The majority opinion, he averred, "deals with a part of Kanawha county as enemy country. In this it can not be sustained by reason or authority. Cabin Creek District has not seceded!" The constitution declared the military to be subordinate to the civil power, and the proper role of the National Guard was to assist the civil authorities; they could not supersede them. "The militia is not an imperial army," he asserted. The National Guard in a martial law zone should confine itself to seeing that law and order prevailed and should turn over to the civil government any people arrested for supposed violations of law. Nothing whatever, he continued, "prevented the taking of offenders, arrested by the militia in the quelling of disorder, before our civil courts and there subjecting them to trial in constitutional form. . . . If the militia could . . . secure witnesses for its own assumed court, it could do so as readily for the legally organized courts." When civil authorities arrested Mother Jones and her associates and turned them over to the military, "the law is reversed, and the civil authorities are used to aid the military power." In their reliance on *Moyer v. Peabody* (212 U.S. 78), cited frequently in the majority opinion, the other justices disregard Governor James H. Peabody's disclaimer of any intention to supplant Colorado's civil courts by military ones and his direct answer "that he was only acting in aid of the civil authorities." Robinson ended his opinion with a lament: "Unfortunate indeed is the generation that forgetteth the memories of its fathers."[53]

In the three habeas corpus cases, the Supreme Court of West Virginia gave their sanction to the actions of the governor and the military authorities. In the first, *In re Shanklin,* they confirmed the power of the governor to declare martial law and the right of the military authorities to arrest and detain individuals within the zone. In the second, *Nance and Mays v. Brown,* they supported the power to arrest even though martial law had temporarily been lifted. In the third, *In re Jones,* they approved the arrest, even outside the martial law zone, of persons charged with contributing to lawlessness within the zone. The second decision was the broadest one, for it recognized not only the right to arrest but also the right of the authorities to set up a military court to try offenders and commit them to the state penitentiary.

After the hearing, Belcher and Houston informed reporters that they would refuse to appear before the military commission, whose jurisdiction they did not recognize. They would advise their clients also to deny its right to try them and to stand mute before the court. They stated their intention to appeal immediately to the Supreme Court of the United States, and if they won there to file civil suits against all the parties implicated in railroading their clients to the penitentiary. Lieutenant Colonel George S. Wallace was anticipating an appeal, which he expected to take place in April.[54]

The Supreme Court remanded Mother Jones, Batley, Boswell, and Paulsen to the custody of the military authorities, and they returned under military guard to their places of imprisonment in Pratt to await the court-martial.

≈    ≈    ≈    ≈    ≈

# Court-Martial

Henry D. Hatfield, who took the oath of office as governor of West Virginia on 4 March 1913, was a physician by profession. Elected to the legislature, he had risen quickly to a position of leadership among the Republican members. As governor, he showed himself to be decisive and energetic in approaching the problems that faced him. Somehow, he had to break the deadlock that had existed for eleven months. The wounds of Holly Grove and the battle of Mucklow were still festering, and he had to make at least some gestures to conciliate the miners. At the same time, he needed to emphasize his support for law and order. Peace in the coalfields was imperative for the economic health of the state. Only the existence of a surplus in the previous year's budget had prevented the expenses of the National Guard from playing havoc with the state's finances. A final settlement that was acceptable to both sides would end those costs as well as restore production in the state's leading industry. In his inaugural address and earliest actions, he projected himself as a strong supporter of law and order but a fair man, committed to neither side in the strike. In the just concluded habeas corpus cases the Supreme Court had confirmed the broad power that he could exercise as commander in chief, without having to rely on the help of a divided legislature or the civil courts. He determined that the military trial of Mother Jones and her associates, scheduled just three days after his inauguration, should go forward.[55]

The trial began on 7 March and lasted for a week, with Sunday off and a twenty-four hour delay from Tuesday to Wednesday afternoon. It is a curious amalgam of military and civil court procedures. The law establishing the National Guard in West Virginia incorporated the court-martial procedures of the United States Army, which the West Virginia authorities followed during the strike. In general orders to the guard, Governor Glasscock directed them to enforce the laws of the state, and the military commission adopted for its trials both the pleading and rules of evidence then in use in West Virginia courts. Defendants before the military commissions could employ civilian attorneys, but the court appointed military officers who were attorneys to represent those defendants who did not hire their own lawyers. The military commission acted as both judge and jury, and its recommendations were subject to review only by the commander in chief, the governor, who could affirm or alter them at his will.

At Pratt, the prosecutor charged Mother Jones and her associates with conspiracies as defined in the Red Men's Act, a broadly worded statute enacted in 1882. The court-martial completed its deliberations and delivered its verdicts under seal to Governor Hatfield, probably on the afternoon of the fourteenth.[56]

Several newspaper reporters, along with members of the prisoners' families, crowded into the Odd Fellows Hall, the largest public room available in Pratt, which the National Guard had commandeered for their headquarters. With the members of the court-martial, guards, the defense counsels, the stenographers, witnesses, and nearly fifty prisoners, there was very little room for the spectators, and latecomers could only gather at the bottom of the outside stairs leading up to the courtroom and wait for those inside to relay news to them.[57]

The trial opened with necessary formalities. Stripped of their military jargon of charges and specifications, the accusations were that the defendants conspired together to steal a machine gun, and that in pursuit of that aim two men were murdered and three other men were feloniously wounded. In addition, the defendants all conspired as accessories after the fact to aid those involved in the murder of Fred Bobbitt to escape. One defendant, Ernest Creigo, was accused of carrying a concealed weapon, a revolver. After the reading of the charges, five of the defendants—Mother Jones, John W. Brown, Charles H. Boswell, Charles Batley, and George F. Parsons—made brief statements denying the jurisdiction of the court. They stood mute before the court and pleas of not guilty were entered for them.[58] The other defendants by their attorneys pleaded not guilty. The prosecution then called its first witnesses.

The initial testimony concerned some sixteen telephone calls that originated in a store in Hansford from the seventh to the tenth of February. A clerk from the telephone company brought records of longdistance calls and explained them. The prosecutor was attempting to identify John W. Brown, George F. Parsons, and Charles H. Boswell as the leaders of the armed strikers who took part in the battle above Mucklow. To that end, he questioned F.W. Howery, who had kept his store in Hansford open so the strikers could use his telephone. Unfortunately for the prosecutor, it was difficult to show many facts from one end of an overheard telephone conversation, particularly when the witness was hostile. If modern wire-tapping devices and techniques had been available to the prosecution, they might have been able to construct stronger proof of conspiracy between Brown and Parsons, the leaders of the Socialist party, and Charles H. Boswell, editor of the Socialist newspaper, the *Labor Argus*, to have organized the miners into armed units and to have supplied them with ammunition. As the testimony stood, Brown and Parsons clearly had been present on the scene in Hansford before the battle, perhaps in a leadership capacity, and they had been in touch with the office of the *Labor Argus* in Charleston, but the prosecutor could not show the meaning of their conversations conclusively.

Wallace put on the stand two black defendants who testified about their part in the events of the ninth and tenth of February. Charles Wright and John Jones told how they had attended a meeting at Beech Grove near Hansford on the evening of the ninth, at which the assembled miners agreed that armed men would meet at six the next morning on the mountain and move south, but the purposes were vague: to protect the Holly Grove inhabitants generally, to intimidate scabs at Barnwell, or to capture a machine gun that the guards had located on the mountain. Wright and Jones admitted that they had been on the mountain with rifles and named some of their companions, but cross-examination revealed that they saw no one fire a gun; they merely heard shooting up ahead, threw down their own weapons, and ran away. Cross-examination also brought out the fact that one of these witnesses had been promised his release if he testified for the prosecution. There are hints in the transcript that Wright and Jones, surely adepts at evasion in a Jim Crow society, had failed on the stand to be as "good" witnesses as they had been when Wallace interviewed them before the trial.[59]

Testimony from three mine guards showed the circumstances of the battle at Mucklow: how observers had seen men on the heights, how James Pierce, the mine superintendent, led a group of about twenty armed guards up the hill, and how he challenged the armed strikers they met. A shot rang out and a battle followed. However, only one of the defendants was identified as being present when shooting took place. One witness admitted that he had made some earlier identifications on the basis of the clothes that people wore, not sight of their faces.

The testimony of James Pierce, superintendent of the Wacomah Coal Company, took up most of the next morning (Saturday). He told of having a picket on the mountain report to him by phone that he had seen thirty-nine men moving along the mountaintop. Pierce had then assembled a group of about twenty volunteers, had led them up the mountain, had challenged some men they met, and had fought a battle with them. By his estimate, two groups of opponents besides the ones he originally challenged, totalling perhaps 150, also participated in this round of shooting. Two of his men were killed and another wounded. Two other men who were on the mountain with Pierce confirmed his account. However, neither Pierce nor his men were able positively to identify any of the defendants as having been present on the mountain or of having fired any guns.

The prosecutor recalled F.P. Howery, his recalcitrant witness of the previous day, and extracted from him the admission that he understood that John W. Brown and George F. Parsons were in charge of affairs at Hansford on 8, 9, and 10 February and that he had heard Brown call for red-blooded men and specific kinds of ammunition.

In the afternoon session, the prosecutor shifted to the events of the afternoon of 10 February, detailing through many witnesses the adventure of a three-man patrol headed by Lieutenant Taylor, formerly of the National Guard but now the employee of a coal company. Taylor and his two companions went up the mountain from Dry Branch and met a group of men who fired at them. Though wounded, Taylor managed to make it back to Dry Branch and send help for the more seriously wounded Crockett. Heffner, the third member of the patrol, sustained no injuries. Again, under cross-examination none of the witnesses was able to identify any of the defendants as having been among the men who fired on them.

The prosecutor turned then to the afternoon of 10 February and brought to light accounts of the arrest of some of the defendants. At Dry Branch, company guards arrested Ernest Creigo and Harry Craise as they were trying to make their way to the river. Four other defendants were arrested at Sharon as they went down Cabin Creek in the direction of the river–Carl Morgan, John and Ernest O'Dell, and Joe Prince. Shortly afterward company guards stopped four more miners heading toward the river–Grady Everett, William Bainbridge, Bert Nutter, and Charles Lanham. The guards handed all these men over to the custody of Sheriff Bonner Hill, who in turn delivered them to the military authorities.

The sensation of the trial, and a complete surprise to the defense counsel, was the testimony in the afternoon of Frank Smith, a detective from the J.W. Burns agency. For some five months, Smith had posed as a miner in the area. He had a card from the local union at Mossy, West

Virginia; whether it was genuine and how he acquired it did not emerge in the questioning, but it served him well as a passport among the strikers. Smith told how on 10 February he had gone from Charleston to Holly Grove. There in the afternoon he had seen many of the defendants armed and following the instructions of John W. Brown and George F. Parsons. He had seen men moving dynamite from Howery's establishment to a storage shed and had heard that the armed men were setting an ambush for the Bull Moose Special train. When suspicious strikers surrounded and questioned him, John W. Brown intervened, advised him to get out of the area, and accompanied him some way down the tracks to Hansford, telling him that he had saved his life. Taken aback by this unexpected testimony, the counsel for the defendants deferred their cross-examination until Monday.

At the end of the second day, then, the prosecution had begun rounding out its case with well-substantiated accounts of what happened when two different men, James H. Pierce and R.L. Taylor, led armed guards up on the mountain to challenge men whom lookouts had seen moving along the trail near the top of the ridge. Direct testimony about the arrest of ten of the defendants placed them armed and near the scene of the battle above Mucklow in the afternoon of 10 February. Yet none of the witnesses was able to say certainly that any of the defendants actually fired a gun at other men on the mountain. Detective Frank Smith had identified many of the defendants as armed, and under the leadership of Brown and Parsons, but only in the evening, hours after the battle. His statement that they were planning to plant dynamite on the tracks of the Bull Moose Special contributed to the idea of a general conspiracy but was far from constituting proof of the complicity of the defendants in the Mucklow battle.

When the trial resumed on Monday, the Burns detective was the first witness, but M.F. Matheny did not get very far with his cross-examination. The attorney tried to discover who had hired Smith, but the court sustained the prosecutor's objection to the question. Matheny then waived further questions, and Smith left the witness stand.

Lieutenant Colonel Wallace then proceeded to question more witnesses who had accompanied Superintendent Pierce in the attempt to intercept the men who had been spotted on the mountain, and whose confrontation had set off the battle. However, these witnesses added only a few details to the already established facts, and, like the previous ones, they were unable positively to identify any of the defendants as having been on the mountain.

The prosecutor then brought forward several officers and noncommissioned officers of the West Virginia National Guard who gave an account of their arrival on the scene on the evening after the battle of Mucklow. They had orders to pick up all suspicious characters, and they had arrested a number of the defendants, including John W. Brown and George F. Parsons. Despite the driving rain and the darkness, the defendants did not challenge them, try to evade them, or resist arrest. Parsons even invited Captain H.C. McMillen and his men into his home out of the rain. These National Guardsmen were able to establish ownership of various weapons by some of the defendants they had arrested.

In an attempt to speed up the trial, both the prosecutor and the defense counsel stipulated a number of background facts about the course of the strike. The court also gave the judge advocate an hour's delay while he chose excerpts from the *Labor Argus* over the previous twelve months to submit as evidence of editor Charles H. Boswell's complicity in the conspiracy. Matheny, who had left the case in the hands of his associate counsel in the afternoon, had earlier agreed to the introduction of such testimony. When Captain Charles R. Morgan, one of the appointed defense lawyers, saw the extent of the excerpts from the newspaper (fifty typed pages), he raised an objection, but the court overruled it. The members of the court repeated this scene when the prosecutor introduced a hundred pages of transcribed stenographic notes of speeches delivered by Mother Jones in August and September 1912. After these submissions of written evidence, the court adjourned until the next day.

When the trial resumed on Tuesday, two witnesses reported on what Mother Jones had said in speeches that were not included in the hundred pages already in evidence. The defense counsel objected because the events had taken place beyond the limits of military control, but the court overruled the objection.

Lieutenant Colonel Wallace then put on the stand Harrison Ellis, a black man and one of the defendants. When he began questioning him, defense counsel objected that Ellis was being forced to testify against his will and that the prosecutor was contravening his basic right not to testify against himself. The court interrupted the regular proceedings in midmorning for the lawyers to argue the question. No conclusion was reached before the luncheon break, nor in the afternoon session, which again was adjourned. The break in the trial continued through the morning of Wednesday, and at two o'clock the court finally sustained the defense objection and ruled that Ellis could not be forced to testify against himself.

~     ~     ~     ~     ~

# Writ of Prohibition

The suspension of the court-martial on Tuesday afternoon came about on a direct order from the commander-in-chief, Governor Hatfield, in response to a legal action commenced on the eve of the trial by Albert M. Belcher and Harold W. Houston. On 6 March they applied to the circuit court judge, Samuel D. Littlepage, for a writ to prohibit the military trial the next day, and the judge responded with an order directed at the members of the commission and other military authorities to desist from holding the court-martial. The next morning Sheriff Bonner Hill went to Pratt to serve the writ, arriving just as the court-martial was about to begin. Soldiers met him at the train and escorted him to the provost marshal, who informed him that he would not be allowed to make service on the commission. The sheriff returned to Charleston and informed Judge Littlepage of his failure. When Belcher and Houston learned Friday evening that the provost marshal had not allowed the sheriff to serve the writ of prohibition, they issued a statement to the *Kanawha Citizen* in which they deplored the refusal of the military to recognize the supremacy of the civil authority, contrary to the constitution. "This action upon the part of the military officers," Belcher and Houston asserted, "is only a counterpart of the action of Colonel Bell in the Colorado labor struggles when he said, 'To hell with the constitution.' " [60] Judge Littlepage also issued a brief statement: "I believe the military commission to be unlawful and unconstitutional, and I did all in my power to see that the defendant should have trial elsewhere."[61]

    Friday evening the judge advocate conferred in Charleston with the governor,[62] and on Saturday morning, at the invitation of the governor, Judge Littlepage joined for two or more hours in a conference with Governor Hatfield, Attorney General A.A. Lilly, Belcher, and Houston. Governor Hatfield told the conferees that the situation was grave and that he could cope with it only by using the militia. He wanted a free hand to deal with the situation and no divided responsibility. In effect, he presented Judge Littlepage with an ultimatum: Either withdraw your prohibition, or I will withdraw the troops. "If Judge Lit-tlepage would be responsible for law and order," he was quoted as saying, "he would turn the situation over to him, and Judge Littlepage replied that he could only try cases as they came before him."[63] On Monday the UMWA attorneys amended their petition to include Governor Hatfield in the writ of prohibition, but their basic contentions remained the same. Constitutionally, the petitioners could not be deprived of life, liberty, or property without due process of law. They were being denied a trial by jury. As civilians, they were not subject to the jurisdiction of the military court, and the civil courts were open to try them in a normal manner. Finally, the state constitution specifically forbade the trial of civilians by a military court. On these grounds, the court should prohibit the trial.

George S. Wallace had not been present at the Saturday con-ference in Charleston, since he was busy conducting the court-martial in Pratt, but he kept himself informed and over the weekend helped to prepare the response to the amended application for a writ of prohibi-tion. On Tuesday Attorney General A.A. Lilly appeared for Governor Hatfield before Judge Littlepage, filing a plea in abatement. Immedi-ately following the hearing, Governor Hatfield issued his order sus-pending the court-martial, and that afternoon Wallace and other lawyers from the court-martial went to Charleston to argue the case before Judge Littlepage. About noon on Wednesday, the judge an-nounced his decision. Although he continued to believe that the court-martial was unconstitutional, the Supreme Court pronounce-ments in *Nance and Mays v. Brown* compelled him to hold that his court had no jurisdiction within the military zone. At the conference on Saturday Judge Littlepage had been no match for the forceful governor, but in obiter dicta in his ruling the judge had a last word, offering to adjourn his court and serve as a mediator in the dispute between the miners and the operators, and concluding with a comment: "There is no doubt, though, in my mind that true friendship, peace and good will will never be restored to Paint and Cabin Creeks with blood and iron."[64]

Describing the proceedings, George S. Wallace gave a some-what different view of the case when he wrote to his friend Lieutenant Colonel W.A. Bethel, who taught military law at West Point:

> We then filed a return denying jurisdiction of the Court to
> award a prohibition against the Military Commission, but as
> a stinger thereto we put a concluding paragraph setting out

the condition in the strike district, the efforts made to restore law and order and without waiving our legal rights to detain and try prisoners if the Judge would take the responsibility of protecting life and property in the district we offered to deliver prisoners to him and withdraw the proclamation. This last position was more political than legal. The Judge, in the language of the street, went straight up. He refused the writ and announced from the bench that the whole military proceedings were illegal, but in as much as the Supreme Court had decided the question he would be liable to impeachment if he went in the face of its decision, but as a man, if the matter would be submitted to him he could manage it in great style.[65]

The eleventh-hour effort to prevent the court-martial had failed. The UMWA attorneys could still seek relief in the federal courts, but by the time they received a cease and desist order the court-martial might well be over. If the militia continued to hold the prisoners of the habeas corpus proceedings in custody, they could appeal to the United States Supreme Court, a course they had already announced they would pursue.

Publicity, not the law, was Mother Jones's principal weapon during her imprisonment and trial. She continued to bombard influential friends on the outside with letters, even though she felt sure the authorities were censoring her mail. As newspaper reporters came to Pratt to cover the court-martial, she seized every chance to make statements, however restricted her contacts.

Two reporters managed to get brief interviews with Mother Jones. General Charles D. Elliott of the National Guard invited William Bruce Reid, a reporter for the *Charleston Kanawha Citizen,* to cover the military trial, but with the understanding that he would photograph neither the courtroom, the bull pen, nor any other place where prisoners were kept. The ban on photographs did not forbid him to look, however, and when he saw Mother Jones standing on the veranda of Carney's house he accosted her. "I said, 'How do you, Mother Jones? How are you feeling?' She said, 'Not very well; so so.' I said, 'Have you any statement to make or you would like to make?' She said, 'Yes.' So she made a short statement, and I took it down and put it in my pocket, and I was chatting with her and up came a little corporal and a lot of soldiers came running up and I paid no attention to them, and the corporal touched me on the shoulder and said, 'You are under arrest.' "[66] After keeping Reid in the bull pen for about ten minutes, the military authorities released him with a warning not to talk to any of the prisoners.

Next day, the *Citizen* carried Mother Jones's defiant assertion: "The only statement I have to make to the American people is that it is not the first time that I have had to measure steel with the minions of the ruling class. I have never yet raised the white flag, and I shall fight so that the red flag of industrial freedom shall not perish on the bosom of young Columbia."[67]

Cora Older, a San Francisco writer, marketed two articles based on her experiences in the strike zone to magazines with large national circulations. A well-known journalist in her own right, she was also the wife of Fremont Older, the crusading editor of the *San Francisco Bulletin*. Puzzled by the lack of news of the strike that came to them in California, she traveled to Pratt, where she found that the Associated Press correspondent was an officer of the militia and, in fact, the provost marshal of the strike zone. She interviewed miners and housewives and was talking to Isabel Carney when an officer interrupted them and took her before the provost marshal. After she explained her presence, he permitted her to continue her general interviewing but banned contact with any of the defendants. Later, General Charles D. Elliott overruled the provost marshal and gave her permission to talk to the prisoners. At Carney's house, Mother Jones, curling tongs in hand, met her at the door. " 'Mother Jones, they say you must choose between leaving the State and going to jail.' She laid down the curling tongs. 'I choose jail now. I can raise just as much hell in jail as anywhere, but it is to be peace.' "[68]

In her magazine articles, Cora Older expressed her outrage over the military control and especially her discovery that the Associated Press correspondent, rather than reporting news from the strike zone, used his position as provost marshal to keep outsiders from knowing what was going on there. Although in Pratt for only two days, Older managed to interview many of the principals in the drama and to write telling sketches of them and others, showing her admiration for Mother Jones and her sympathy for the strikers.

During the twenty-four hour delay in the court-martial, Mother Jones also gave a statement to the reporter for the Socialist daily, the *New York Call.*

> It is a rule of law in Anglo-Saxon civilization, gained through centuries of political struggle and warfare, that a prisoner

cannot be placed on the stand by the prosecution to testify in the matter in which he is a defendant, unless he voluntarily waives that right.

The Constitution of the United States and of all the States guarantee that right.

But look what happened yesterday. Judge Advocate Wallace, prosecutor of the military court, called to the witness stand Harrison Ellis, one of the miners arrested, and demanded that he testify. Can you imagine anything worse than this?

We are not afraid to testify, but we demand that our rights as citizens of this republic be recognized and whatever the military court may say, I maintain that no body of men in West Virginia has the power to suspend the Constitution of the United States.[69]

Somehow Mother Jones also issued a statement addressed to the miners, which her old friend Marlin E. Pew, editor of the *Philadelphia News-Post*, quoted in an article late in March.

You know why they have locked me up charging me with inciting to murder. It is merely because they cannot bear to permit me to talk to you. I am an old woman and I have not long to live. I am ready for the eternal sleep. If they take me to the gibbet it will be all right and I will die gladly, because it will cause thousands of millions to think of the misery of all you poor workers, your miserable wives and children, who are denied the comforts and blessings that you should have in this great country. String me up to your tree, you soldiers and detectives and judges, if you will. That is the only way that you can still my voice.[70]

Mother Jones was more interested in affecting public opinion than in winning lawsuits, and imprisonment by the military authorities enabled her to play the martyr who suffered because she was trying to publicize the grievances of the miners. Her writ of habeas corpus, the writ of prohibition, and the court-martial were all merely incidents in the larger battle she was fighting.

At this late date, no one can speak authoritatively about public opinion during the strike, and it must have varied with the changing events. At the time of the Jones habeas corpus hearing, both the *New York Call* and the *United Mine Workers Journal* assessed public opinion to be on the side of the striking miners.[71] The attitudes of some representative individuals and groups can be identified with certainty. Broadly speaking, the local daily press was pro-operator and antistriker, with the *Charleston Gazette* and *Charleston Daily Mail* leading the way. The third local daily, the *Kanawha Citizen,* was more sympathetic to the miners, though by no means unreservedly prolabor. The weekly *Labor Argus,* on the other hand, had nothing good to say about the coal operators and only praise for the miners. In most stories in all papers, state officials are represented as hostile to the strikers. The operators, said the socialist editor of a Wheeling paper, "are aided by a willing governor, house of delegates, senate, state and county courts, sheriff, and justices of the peace."[72]

Outside of Charleston, editors in West Virginia often expressed approval for the miners or condemned the operators. "Let us repeal the iniquitous private guard law, and make every miner a free citizen, instead of a slave," urged the *Keyser Mountain Echo* (13 September 1912). Commenting on a recent report of strikers firing guns at a train, the *Wayne News* said, "Heretofore they have had the sympathy and respect of the populace of the state in their warfare against capital" (21 November 1912). "But . . . back of all the violence, and indications of violence, were the greed and rapacity of the operators," asserted the *Weston Independent* (19 September 1912). Several journals criticized the refusal of the operators to submit to arbitration or even to talk with the union leaders, and two editors called for the enactment of laws for compulsory arbitration. Miners had every right to belong to a national union, according to the editor of the *Morgantown Post-Chronicle.* "The sooner our operators recognize this fact the better it will be for all concerned" (18 September 1912). The *Parkersburg News-Dispatch* deplored the fact that anyone who crossed the river into the military zone lost his civil rights. "Possibly the czar of Russia or maybe the president of Nicaragua may have more authority than the Adjutant General" (7 September 1912).

On the whole, a majority of the people living in the strike area who were not miners seem to have sided with the strikers. The best proof of this is the decision by the judge and the prosecuting attorney not to call a grand jury, for fear that it would not be "fair." The mayor of the town of Montgomery participated in a rally organized by Mother Jones in August 1912. The town, just outside the strike zone, was named for Senator Samuel B. Montgomery's family, which had lived in the area for a hundred and fifty years. Montgomery also spoke at the rally, and throughout the strike he supported the UMWA, although he deplored the violence, which he thought the operators, not the miners, instigated. In a letter to the president of the military commission protesting the court-martial, he asked how, when a battle had taken place with casualties on both sides, the military court could claim to be fair when they were trying only miners and their leaders for murder; not one single mine guard or operator had been arrested, much less tried.

Montgomery's charges stung the court, and George S. Wallace immediately haled him before them and took a twenty-five page statement under oath, insisting in his questioning that the court was seeking the truth and that if they could find strikers willing to testify they would receive equal treatment from the court. When Montgomery asked him if he had even talked to the president of the district UMWA, Tom Cairnes, he replied that he had not.

> [Wallace:] Invite him up here Monday and I will question him. Any of your men can come here with impunity and we will treat them nicely and send them home.
> [Montgomery:] Some of them have heard that they might be incarcerated if they came here as the leaders of the miners.
> [Wallace:] . . . we will not humiliate or mortify anybody at all and they will be given the same courtesies as anyone else.[73]

Despite his resentment of charges of bias, there was no doubt where the sympathies of the judge advocate lay. George S. Wallace saw the strike from the coal mine operators' viewpoint and actively sought their advice and assistance. While preparing for the Nance and Mays habeas corpus case, he submitted his brief to the Charleston law firm that represented the operators on Paint and Cabin Creeks and received from a senior partner suggestions on how to improve it. In the court-martial he turned again to Brown, Jackson and Knight for aid in preparing his case, and they supplied his most effective witness in the trial, the Burns detective whom they had hired as an undercover agent among the strikers. Wallace had in his possession one of detective Frank Smith's sworn reports to his employers, and to it was appended a note, "We will endeavor to furnish the names of some of the witnesses who heard 'Mother' Jones' speech at Boomer, February 12." The same firm also supplied him with the hundred-page transcript of the speeches of

Mother Jones, which they had instructed their stenographer to take down in shorthand. Wallace's closeness to the lawyers of the coal mine operators helped him immeasurably in preparing his cases.[74]

In striking contrast, the commander of the National Guard, General Charles D. Elliott, publicly declared his sympathy for the miners. It was he who countermanded the order of the provost marshal and allowed Cora Older to interview the prisoners, and he specifically invited a Charleston reporter to come to Pratt to cover the court-martial. After ten months of commanding the troops in the field, he released a long statement about the end of an era of cheap labor in industrial America: "Here in the mountains of West Virginia, the coal operators demanded the cheapest sort of labor, and they got it. The worm has turned . . . [Some operators] refuse to give their miners square deals in the mines and . . . maintain dirty, filthy, insanitary camps for their employes. . . . There is a great truth behind the strike of the coal miners in this state, and that truth is that employers must treat their workers more like men than like machines."[75] He blamed the owners for conditions at one dirty and dilapidated coal camp, which he declared he intended to burn to improve the sanitary conditions on the water-shed.

The National Guard drew its officers mainly from the business and professional communities in the state, and some of these officers, following an old American tradition, used their associations and titles in the militia to political advantage. If the principal actors in the court-martial are taken to be representative, nearly all had connections with the economic and political power structure of the state. Walker, Carskadon, and Morgan were lawyers, and also members of the state bureaucracy. Walker's brother was a member of the railroad police, who cooperated closely with the mine guards. Clarence F. Jolliffe, the president of the court, was a country squire who presided over an agricultural community in Wetzel County. Although a member of the bar, he confined his practice to making wills and conveyances for his neighbors and devoted his time instead to politics, cattle raising, farming, and his general store that served the needs of the community. In addition to commanding the regiment from the northern section of the state, he was a member of the West Virginia Guard team that won the national shooting championship in 1913.[76]

The rank and file of the National Guard was more heterogeneous than the officer corps, made up largely of workingmen, including some union members. One commentator said that "most of them have hard hands."[77] Town dwellers, such as shopkeepers and clerks, and a sprinkling of farm boys filled out the ranks of the Guard. Mother Jones had no trouble finding sympathizers among the soldiers to set up her alternative lines of communication. When the militia first came into the strike area, the strikers welcomed them as protectors against the brutalities of the company guards, but after troops were used to evict strikers and protect scabs, union members began to regard the Guard with less favor. Strikers sometimes jeered the soldiers along with the scabs they were protecting, but there was no general resistance to the National Guard by the strikers.[78]

~      ~      ~      ~      ~

# The Court-Martial Resumed

On Wednesday afternoon, when the court-martial reconvened, a different attitude prevailed in the courtroom. The presentation of additional evidence was almost perfunctory, compared with the detailed testimony earlier in the trial. The prosecutor gave up any attempt to identify people who were present at the battle above Mucklow or the responsibility of particular individuals for specific charges. In fact, many of the defendants in the court-martial were never mentioned by name. One can speculate that when the court ruled that Harrison Ellis could not be forced to testify against himself, Wallace had to abandon plans to convict the defendants out of their own mouths. It must have been frustrating for the prosecutor, whose notes of interviews with defendants show that they had in some cases admitted that they were on the mountain with guns. However, very few of them could or would name their companions, and their stated intentions were either innocuous—visiting relatives or looking for a cow—or vague, such as protecting the residents of the tent colony at Holly Grove. If he had been able to elicit testimony from them as witnesses, his case would have been greatly strengthened.[79]

The new attitude of the prosecution shows up particularly in the failure to make a better case against Mother Jones. The principal evidence against her was the transcript of the speeches she had delivered the previous August and September. In this final afternoon of the trial the judge advocate, George S. Wallace, once again brought forward witnesses to testify to the nature and effect of speeches they had heard

Mother Jones deliver, but he had difficulty in getting his witnesses to characterize them as inflammatory. Superintendent T.H. Huddy reported that after Mother Jones spoke at Boomer on 29 September, his mine had work stoppages that he attributed to her words. J.C. Bell, a clerk for Boomer Coal and Coke Company, testified about the same speech but to little advantage for the prosecutor. The most damaging statement that another coal company clerk who listened to the same speech could provide was that Mother Jones had advised the miners to hold on to their rifles and not participate in a proposal that all gun owners in the area turn in their weapons to local authorities. At first glance it is inexplicable that the prosecutor focused on these speeches when he had a much more direct line that he could have pursued.

According to newspaper reports, Mother Jones arrived back from a trip to Washington on Sunday, 9 February, just in time to speak at the funeral of Sesco Estep, the miner slain in the shooting at Holly Grove. The *Charleston Mail* quoted her as urging the men "to get their guns and shoot them (watchmen) to hell."[80] The meeting at Beech Grove occurred that night, and early next morning the force of strikers gathered on the ridge to march to the heights above Mucklow. A logical inference far stronger than some of his other proof would have connected Mother Jones with the battle of Mucklow. On the other hand, he may have despaired of getting reliable witnesses on the stand. Dan Cunningham, the officer who arrested Mother Jones, was trying hard to find for him people who would testify to Mother Jones's speeches. When he interviewed Sally Holly, she told him how disgusting she had found Mother Jones's cursing and incitement to violence at a meeting in November, but she believed her husband would perjure himself before he would tell what Mother Jones said and had threatened to kill her if she told Cunningham.[81] Another unknown volunteer helper in the search for witnesses had found one in "an exceptionally smart colored man," C.C. Wood, who "says he does not desire to talk for publication but will tell all he knows if legally summoned by the commission."[82]

On the other side of the argument, it seems strange that the defense attorneys never recalled Frank Smith, the Burns detective, to subject him to stiff cross-examination. They had given up questioning him when they failed to establish who employed him. It may be that they feared that further queries would merely introduce more damaging statements. Instead, they attempted by evidence and argument to impugn his character and brand him as a hireling of the coal operators.

Late in the afternoon, Adam B. Littlepage, former congressman from the district, was added to the list of defense counsel. Shortly thereafter, the prosecution rested its case. The defending attorneys immediately asked that the evidence be stricken and that the accused be acquitted. When the commissioners denied that motion, they then entered in evidence the proclamations of martial law by Governor Glasscock, the report of Governor Glasscock's Donahue Commission, and a stipulation with the prosecution that prior to the beginning of the strike the citizens in the martial law zone had been peaceable and law-abiding.

The witnesses for the defense were few in number. Two officers of the National Guard testified that the defendants had been quiet and orderly while in their custody. W.R. Gray, a prisoner but not a defendant, then testified that Frank Smith had tried to suborn evidence from him against the defendants. One final witness gave evidence that Cal Newman, one of the defendants supposed to have been among the armed men on the mountain, instead spent most of the day in Crown Hill trying to arrange for a boar to be put to a sow that he owned. The court then adjourned until seven o'clock, when the lawyers would make their closing arguments.

During the course of the trial, both sides had submitted extensive written evidence, some of which, such as stipulations about the general course of the strike, need no comment. Of the remainder, three are long and detailed. After three months the Donahue Commission, already alluded to, had submitted a report that antagonized both the miners and the operators. It did supply a factual basis for generalizations about conditions in the West Virginia coalfields that might be useful for one side or the other in argument. The prosecutor also entered as evidence two other long written pieces that he intended to use primarily against the defendants Charles H. Boswell and Mother Jones.

Prosecutor George S. Wallace had charged Charles H. Boswell with being one of the principal leaders in organizing the miners who participated in the battle at Mucklow, and very specifically with bringing three suitcases, presumably filled with ammunition, from Charleston to a train station across the river from Paint Creek. The witnesses who supplied his evidence for this had been present at Howery's store and had overheard phone calls. Other witnesses had seen Boswell at railroad stations. Properly connected, this chain of evidence would directly link Boswell to the violence on Paint Creek.

The written evidence against Boswell consisted of editorials and news stories from the weekly *Labor Argus*, which he edited. By them the prosecutor hoped to prove that Boswell participated in the more general conspiracy that promoted riots and violence as a part of the plan to organize the miners in the West Virginia coalfields. The excerpts reach back to the early months of the strike and continue up until the day after Boswell's arrest, when a special edition defiantly avowed that the paper would continue publication even though the editor had been arrested.

The following pieces extracted from the fifty pages of *Argus* articles and editorials illustrate the nature of the evidence. Whether or not the words that the prosecutor chose from the *Labor Argus* buttress his case against Boswell as a conspirator, they leave no doubt that the editor was addicted to using vituperative language. He customarily referred to Baldwin-Felts guards as thugs and occasionally as human hyenas—"these off-scourings gathered from the lowest depths of capitalistic society and commissioned as 'police' and 'deputies' by the prostituted puppets of an 'Invisible Government.' "[83] Governor William E. Glasscock was "Little Willie" or "Weary Willie," a weak-kneed tyrant, a criminal, a pawn of the Elkins political machine, and a tool of the coal operators. Two days after Glasscock handed over the reins of government to Henry D. Hatfield, the *Argus* outdid itself in a farewell editorial:

GOOD-BYE GLASSCOCK. For four years West Virginia has been afflicted with you and now we fear neither hell nor hereafter. Forced upon us, the bastard child of a political rape, you have lived up to the natural reputation of your political parentage and we have paid for your degeneration with blood and tears. You are hated by the masses whose deadly and stealthy enemy you have been, and the gluttonous powers which have used you as their pliant tool have only a wreath of contempt to lay upon your political grave. . . . To mention the word "justice" in the same column with the name Glasscock is a crime, and the mere suggestion of a man appointing a court to try citizens of West Virginia without a jury or any other of their constitutional guarantees is a damnable, outrageous insult that our hardy forefathers would have wiped out with the blood of its author. George III was the last tyrant who tried to force upon Americans the brutal rule of the soldier and his red-coated Hessians were driven into the Atlantic. Let the coal barons' yellow-coats listen to the still re-echoing thunders from Bunker Hill and Yorktown—and take warning. [6 March 1913]

Moving from intemperate language to actual incitement to violence, the editorials and articles contained violent statements couched as warnings that under some conditions violence might occur:

> The West Virginia miners are determined to drive the Baldwin thugs from the state or die in the attempt. . . . If Governor Glasscock does not want a repetition of the Kanawha County bloodshed and violence he had better keep Mr. Baldwin and his thugs moving until they are beyond the state borders. If the executive of the state fails to do his duty and use his official power to move the Baldwin thugs out the state the miners will move them by force. [5 September 1912]

A month later, the *Argus* asserted that the miners were determined to win the strike at any cost or "die in the attempt." The newspaper continued: "If the militia officials pursue their plans to eject the miners with the soldiers a condition will arise that even the state militia will not be able to handle" (10 October 1912).

"The people should rise in a body and protest against such an outrage on humanity," said the *Argus* in a story about eviction of miners from their homes, "and teach the spineless officials that they are the servants and not the masters of the people" (5 December 1912).

Toward the end of January the *Argus* became more militant in its statements, though it generally presented them in conditional sentences:

> If there is a law to deprive the workingman of his liberty and railroad him to the penitentiary on the smallest pretext and no law to protect the lives of the workers or to punish those who maim and murder them, then we may say to hell with the law and will advise the working class to take the law in their own hands and redress their own wrongs. (23 January 1913)

∾   ∾   ∾

> If they uphold the vicious decision of the state court, then the miners in the name of justice and humanity will lay their case before the court of last resort and let the people be the judge. And to the tools of plutocracy who are wielding the power

of this government, we say beware how you persecute a long-suffering people, lest patience ceases to be a virtue and they rise in their just and righteous indignation and demand a day of reckoning. [23 January 1913]

~  ~  ~

If a stop is not put to their [company guards'] tactics the miners will be forced to defend themselves as best they can. . . . If some steps are not taken to stop the depredations of the guards and gunmen, the miners will have to follow the example set by the state's executive and take the law in their own hands. [23 January 1913]

~  ~  ~

The deputized thugs and hired gunmen only drive the miners to desperation, and when they see their elected officials prostitute the law in the interest of the greedy coal barons they will lose faith in the law and depend on their own manhood for protection. [30 January 1913]

~  ~  ~

We will warn the powers that be that unless a stop is put to the brutalities of the hired thugs there will be more civil war in West Virginia. . . . if a stop is not put to them, history will repeat itself this summer. . . . Self-preservation, that first law of nature, is their [the miners'] only thought and they will fight with a desperation that knows no defeat. [30 January 1913]

The next week, just before the renewal of widespread violence, the *Argus* asserted that Governor William E. Glasscock "overrode the constitution of the state and nation and established a military despotism, outraged justice and assassinated liberty" and added:

This is a class war; for every wrong suffered by the workers the master class should be made to pay. "An eye for an eye, a tooth for a tooth and a life for a life." When the miners learn to exert their manhood and retaliate on the masters and their hirelings every wrong they suffer at their hands they will put a stop to these outrages. [6 February 1913]

Not until the machine-gunning of the tent colony at Holly

Grove and the fight at Mucklow is there endorsement of the use of arms for self-defense.

> At last, driven to desperation by the sight of the mangled corpse of their comrades, the suffering of their wounded women, and the frantic fear of their wives and children, the miners at last took up arms to protect themselves, and the man who would not fight under these circumstances is indeed a craven coward, not deserving the name man.
>
> It is a deplorable state of affairs when the sovereign citizens are forced to resort to arms to protect their lives and the lives of their families in a state that claims to be civilized. [13 February 1913]

~ ~ ~

> They [the miners] are only asking for their constitutional and legal rights and they are going to have those or die fighting for them. Justice is all the miners are asking for and this fighting and bloodshed will never stop until they get it. [13 February 1913]

~ ~ ~

> The governor's military despotism under the guise of martial law amounts to no more than political persecution, and the prisoners railroaded to the penitentiary by that illegal and tyrannical court, the military commission, are nothing more than political prisoners in exile from their homes for no other cause than their activities in the interest of the working class. [13 February 1913]

~ ~ ~

> The southern slave barons hung John Brown and brought about the Civil War. It would be wise for the coal barons of West Virginia to profit by their experience or they might start a revolution that will be equally as disastrous to their interest. [13 February 1913]

After the Supreme Court had denied the writ of habeas corpus for Mother Jones and her companions, including the editor of the *Argus,* the newspaper mentioned the word *revolution.*

When the highest court of law in West Virginia on last Friday said, in effect, that the writ of habeas corpus was a useless instrument, that the provisions of the Constitution of the United States were never intended for the toilers of the land, that the written laws of the state could be swept ruthlessly aside by the "invisible" hand that guides their prostituted actions, and the tyranny of a military despotism would be built upon the ruins of Freedom's chapel–it sounded the doom of Justice and Liberty, or it lighted the signal fires of an oncoming revolution. The decision which sent a gray-haired woman of four-score years back to the hell of a despot's prison stinks to high heaven, for it was supplied from an incision in the bowels of the putrid coal interests and the odor will cling to the bench for eons to come. [6 March 1913]

Bobbitt, with whose murder the defendants in the court-martial were charged, "met his well deserved end at the hands of men exercising the natural law of self-preservation," maintained the *Argus*. "The miners have guns, which is their right, and they know how to use them in self-defense–which accounts for their survival among the pack of murderous curs that have been turned loose on them" (6 March 1913).

Here, then, are the most violent expressions to be found in the *Labor Argus*. It seems that the prosecutor was relying on the aggressive and defiant tone of the editorials and news stories, rather than actual calls for violent acts. Whether such a tone, together with name-calling and exaggerated description of "outrages," could be regarded as inciting to riot was one more of the uncertain facts which the members of the military commission were called on to decide.

Another hundred pages of written evidence contain speeches delivered by Mother Jones at Montgomery and Charleston in the preceding August and September. From these, the coal company lawyers selected passages to be printed in the report of the Senate investigating committee. Although it must be presumed that they looked on these excerpts as indicating her guilt as a conspirator during the strike, it is difficult to find in these selected quotations any direct calls for violence, although she did make threatening statements, such as her claim that forty thousand men "are ready for battle"; and "we are breaking the chains that bind you; we are putting the fear of God into the robbers"; and "If the governor proclaims martial law, bury your guns" (*Hearings,* 2261). In another speech after the declaration of martial law she exhorted a crowd of miners in Charleston, "If you were men with a bit of revolutionary blood in you, you wouldn't stand for the Baldwin guards, would you?", adding later "we will carry on this fight, we will make war in the State until the Baldwins are removed" (2281).

The speech that Mother Jones delivered from the steps of the Capitol on 15 August is quoted in its entirety, and once again she did not call directly for violence but rather issued conditional threats:

> We will give the governor until tomorrow night to take them guards out of Cabin Creek.

> ∼  ∼  ∼

> Here on the steps of the Capitol . . . I say that if the governor won't make them go then we will make them go.

> ∼  ∼  ∼

> I have been in jail more than once, and I expect to go again. If you are too cowardly to fight, I will fight.

> ∼  ∼  ∼

> It is freedom or death, and your children will be free. [These quotations and those in the following paragraphs are all drawn from the speech at the Capitol on 15 August, pp. 2262-75.]

But in the same speech an equal number of passages can be found in which she urges the miners to obey the law, to remain quiet and sober, to cooperate with the militia, and to protect private property.

It was the tone of her speeches rather than specific incitement to violence that made them unacceptable to some people. Religious leaders should be in the forefront of reform, she said, but the preachers "are owned body and soul by the ruling class" and would not preach against the guard system or the unjust prices at the company stores. "O you preachers! You are going over to China and sending money over there for Jesus. For God's sake, keep it at home; we need it." Instead of the church, she felt, it was the union that stood for humanity: "No church in the country could get up a crowd like this, because we are doing God's holy work. . . . Did the church make the operators run and go into the cellar?" "The operators dock you for slate in the coal and then they give to Jesus on Sunday." "They give your missionary women a couple of hundred dollars and rob you under pretense of giving to Jesus. Jesus never sees a penny of it, and never heard of it. They use it for the women to get a jag on and hollow for Jesus."

She also showed disrespect for the governor and for the dominant officeholders. "You have voted for the whole gang of commercial pirates every time you get a chance to free yourselves," she told the crowd. "Elect judges and governors from your own ranks," she urged. "I want to say to you that the governor will not, can not, do anything for this reason: The governor was placed in this building by Scott and Elkins [senators and bosses of the state Republican party] and he don't dare oppose them."

"The prosecuting attorney," she added, "is of the same type—another fellow belonging to the ruling class. She publicly ridiculed the sheriff and a mine operator, who when faced by a crowd of angry miners took refuge in a store and hid under a pile of dirty clothes in the cellar. Ex-presidents were not exempt from her scorn: "The politicians are cutting each other's throats, eating each other up; they are for the offices. Teddy, the monkey chaser, had a meeting in Chicago. He was blowing his skull off his carcass about race suicide. God Almighty, bring him down the C. & O. and he will never say another word about race suicide. The whole population seems to be made up out of kids. Every woman has three babies in her arms and nine on the floor."

Here was a disturber of the peace in a broad sense, someone who foretold a complete overturn of society: "This [meeting on the steps of the Capitol] is an uprising of the oppressed against the master class." "I will tell you why we are not going to destroy your property, Mr. Governor: Because one of these days we are going to take over the mines."

In focusing on the rhetoric and the tone of the speeches, the lawyers who cited them failed to recognize that Mother Jones had taken a dispute over the renewal of a contract and had converted it into a struggle for civil rights. The mass meeting of miners and sympathizers in Montgomery on 4 August could not have been held in the mining camps controlled by the Baldwin-Felts guards, and its purpose was to gain endorsement of a petition to the governor to insure the rights of citizens to be secure in their persons, to assemble peacefully to discuss their grievances, and to ask the authorities for redress.

> It is respectfully represented to your excellency that the owners of the various coal mines doing business along the valley of Cabin Creek, Kanawha County, W. Va., are maintaining and have at present in their employ a large force of armed guards, armed with Winchesters, a dangerous and deadly weapon; also having in their possession three Gatling guns, which they have stationed at commanding positions overlooking Cabin Creek Valley, which said weapons said guards use for the purpose of browbeating, intimidating, and menacing the lives of all the the citizens who live in said valley, who are not in accord with the management of the coal companies, which guards are cruel, and their conduct toward the citizens is such that it would be impossible to give a detailed account of.
>
> Therefore suffice it to say, however, that they beat, abuse, maim, and hold up citizens without process of law; deny freedom of speech, a provision guaranteed by the Constitution; deny the citizens the right to assemble in a peaceable manner for the purpose of discussing questions in which they are concerned. Said guards also hold up a vast body of laboring men who live at the mines, and so conduct themselves that a great number of men, women, and children live in a state of constant fear, unrest, and dread.
>
> We hold that the stationing of said guards along the public highways and public places is a menace to the general welfare of the State. That such action on the part of the companies in maintaining such guards is detrimental to the best interests of society and an outrage against the honor and dignity of the State of West Virginia.
>
> As citizens interested in the public weal and general welfare, and believing that law and order and peace should ever abide, that the spirit of brotherly love and justice and freedom should everywhere exist, we must tender our petition to you that you would bring to bear all the powers of your office as chief executive of this State for the purpose of disarming said guards and restoring to the citizens of said valley all the rights guaranteed by the Constitution of the United States and said State.[84]

Having gained the endorsement of the assembly to this petition, she then scheduled a mass meeting in Charleston for August 15. The UMWA helped to insure a crowd when it supplied the miners from Paint and Cabin Creek with money to pay the railroad fare to Charleston and back. On the steps of the Capitol, she and others spoke to the miners and the citizens of Charleston who had joined them. She and a committee delivered the petition to an official in the Capitol and then led a parade with banners proclaiming, "Mountaineers are always free" (the state motto), "Out of the State with the Baldwin murderers," "No Russia for us. To hell with the guard system," and "Nero fiddled while Rome burned. That is what the governor of West Virginia is doing." She was very much aware of the presence of newsreel cameramen and urged the crowd: "I want you to go in regular parade, three or four together. The moving-picture man wants to get your picture to send over the country."[85]

Subsequent speeches in Charleston continued to hammer on the same themes but were naturally tailored to the changing situation in the strike zone, where martial law had been imposed. The speech of 6 September attacked Governor William E. Glasscock because he had appointed no representatives of the miners to the commission to investigate conditions in the state coalfields. Mother Jones's brief speech on 21 September was preceded by a march through the streets of Charleston of miners' children carrying banners proclaiming, "We are the Babes that Sleep in the Woods," and "We Want to go to School and not to the Mines." The march was designed to put pressure on the delegates to a conference of state leaders called by the governor to discuss a compulsory arbitration statute and other economic legislation to be presented at the next meeting of the legislature. But Governor Glasscock's attempt to mobilize public opinion failed, for the conferees fell to bickering among themselves and adjourned without accomplishing anything.[86] The speeches, though militant in expression, were clearly part of a well-planned campaign to work within the system by petitions and demonstrations to influence the governor and others in authority in policy decisions and to gain public approval for the position of the miners.

At the court-martial, with the evidence, oral and written, all in and each side resting its case, the arguments were scheduled to begin in the evening, but before the final summaries of the contending parties the prosecutor reopened the presentation of evidence. He called Lieutenant Augustus S. Guthrie of the National Guard to the stand to refute the testimony of W.R. Gray that the Burns detective, Frank Smith, had tried to induce him to testify against the defendants. Guthrie said that he had been in the room on the occasion when the incident was supposed to have occurred and that no such conversation had taken place.

At the conclusion of this evidence M.F. Matheny for the defense objected strenuously to the presence in the courtroom of Frank Smith, and to the fact that he had been allowed the liberty of the courtroom throughout the trial, even when other people were excluded. Matheny's objections were overruled.[87]

In their final argument, the defense counsels divided their time unequally. The court-appointed attorneys, Captain Charles R. Morgan and Captain Edward B. Carskadon, together took up less than a third of the time used by the defense. Morgan directed most of his argument to the inadequacy of the evidence in proving conspiracy and the failure of the prosecutor to connect elements of his evidence in a chain of proof. Carskadon touched the same bases with greater specificity, pointing out that the prosecution had brought forward no witnesses against a majority of the defendants, and that the strongest statement ascribed to the editor of the *Labor Argus*, Boswell, was "It is time to fight," a phrase he had heard both the prosecutor and his colleague Matheny use on the hustings. As for Mother Jones, to Morgan she was an admirable old fighter for the rights of the laboring man who might have said some extreme things but who was no part of any conspiracy. Carskadon inquired sarcastically how the written evidence, speeches delivered months before the events that were the subject of the trial, bore any relevance whatsoever to the charges against her.

Adam B. Littlepage's speech was more rhetorical flourishing than argument, although he did enlarge the area of discussion when he raised the question of the proper relations of capital and labor in contemporary society. The property and rights of capitalists deserved protection, but equally deserving of protection were the rights and property of laborers, whose toil was as necessary for economic development as the money of the investor. He assailed strongly the character and testimony of the Burns detective, Frank Smith. His only references to Mother Jones alluded to her advanced age and, somewhat incoherently, to her unbridled speech.

M.F. Matheny, who bore the chief burden of argument, combined the legalism of his juniors and the broader view of Littlepage with some high-flying rhetoric of his own. He began by appealing to the progressive spirit of the age, alluding to comments of all the candidates in the recent presidential campaign on the division between wealthy and laboring classes and the need to create a more just society. Then he pointed out the laws that gave an employer in West Virginia a right to evict tenants from company houses by proceedings in magistrates' courts. Not content even with such summary process, the companies had used the guards they employed to evict tenants illegally in brutal fashion. Generally, hired guards carried out what should be the functions of public officers, and their arrogance had enraged the people. When appeals for redress went unheard it is not surprising that they countered violence with violence. Dragging these particular prisoners off to jail would not solve the problems of an unjust system.

Matheny insisted that the prosecution had not proved the existence of a conspiracy. They had cited speeches and the newspaper editorials that were no stronger in their condemnation of exploiters than the campaign speeches of Teddy Roosevelt, Woodrow Wilson, and William Jennings Bryan. Why single out the defendants, who had not been linked with any proven conspiracy, when thousands of armed miners and sympathizers live in this zone? The prosecution had presented no evidence at all concerning some of these defendants.

As for Mother Jones, Matheny likened her "inflammatory" speeches to similar pronouncements by presidential contenders in the recent election. Later, in comparing her to the treacherous Frank Smith, he launched into a soaring flight of rhetoric:

> They can condemn this gray-headed woman, whom the boys call "Mother;" it makes but little difference to her, because she has gone down the slope to that point where the sun, fast receding, strikes its golden rays high in the hilltops. But a few more days, at least, and it will be said of her "Well done;" but, gentlemen of the commission, where the white hair is this evening, there will be a halo of glory, all of gold, and her picture will adorn the walls of the children begotten in the tents and her face will shine from the frame of humble homes long after the man who has betrayed his trust has been consigned to oblivion, unwept, unhonored, and unsung.

Like Littlepage, Matheny attacked the credibility and character of the guards who gave evidence, and especially the Burns detective, Frank Smith, "a betrayer for money and for a price." Like Littlepage, too, he saw the case as a part of modern industrial warfare. "The state

Mother Jones. West Virginia and Regional History Collections, West Virginia University Libraries.

Mother Jones. Archives of Labor History and Urban Affairs, Wayne State University.

William Ellsworth Glasscock,
governor of West Virginia. West
Virginia and Regional History
Collections, West Virginia
University Libraries.

Lt. Col. George S. Wallace,
West Virginia National
Guard, 1913. West Virginia
and Regional History
Collections, West Virginia
University Libraries.

Henry Drury Hatfield,
governor of West Virginia.
West Virginia andRegional
History Collections, West
Virginia University Libraries.

William Bauchop Wilson,
U.S. secretary of labor,
1913-1921. U.S.
Department of Labor.

*Above:* Mother Jones leading a demonstration. West Virginia and Regional History Collections, West Virginia University Libraries. *Below:* With John R. Lawson (*left*) and Horace N. Hawkins, 1914.

They Asked Bread And Were Given Bullets

*New York Call*, 27 May 1913

*United Mine Workers of America Journal*, 3 July 1913

# THE MOTHER OF FIGHTING MEN

From the battlefield of West Virginia, Mother Jones will, tonight, report to the meeting at Carnegie Hall.

*Above:* Addressing strikers in Star City, West Virginia, 1920s. *Below:* With Sid Hatfield and others, 1921. West Virginia and Regional History Collections, West Virginia University Libraries.

*Above:* Isabel Carney's boarding house, where Mother Jones was imprisoned February through May 1913, shown today. Photo by Richard Fauss. *Below:* With Calvin Coolidge at the White House. National Archives.

Mother Jones. West Virginia and Regional History Collections, West Virginia University Libraries.

of West Virginia," he said, "cannot afford in this conflict to take one side of these contending armies and cast them in prison and in jail and deny them their rights, and disarm them and leave the other people in complete operation and complete control." Matheny ended his argument with a sentimental appeal to the feelings of the court, pointing out that nearly all of the defendants were young miners who were the sole support of wives and children and, in some cases, aged parents. It is the same kind of plea that he might have presented in a civil court to a jury composed of local residents, not a court consisting of military officers.

The judge advocate, Lieutenant Colonel George S. Wallace, began his closing argument with a defense of the procedure they were involved in. The military court, he maintained, had afforded the defendants every benefit that they would have had in a civil court. "Every time that counsel for the defendants have invoked the aid of the strict common law rule in the conduct of the case, this court has sustained them."

Wallace dealt first with the defense arguments, pointing out that references to industrial warfare generally were irrelevant, since the trial was about the facts in this particular armed conflict. As for the testimony of Smith, had not other witnesses corroborated it? The attempt by the defense to impute to him subornation of perjury was refuted by the testimony of Lieutenant Guthrie.

Quoting from the Red Men's Act, which specifically said that circumstantial evidence, rather than direct, was sufficient to prove conspiracy, Wallace pointed to the inflammatory writings by Boswell, phone conversations between Boswell and Parsons with the latter requesting ammunition, the trip of Boswell with suitcases to be met by Brown, the instructions issued to various groups by Brown and Parsons, the meeting at Beech Grove, and the arranged rendezvous at dawn on top of the mountain to march toward Mucklow. Then came the clash with the group of guards led by Superintendent Pierce, with Bobbitt and Vance dead as a result, and Crockett and Nesbitt wounded in subsequent firing. These defendants were apprehended in the area. They planned an attack on Saturday and Sunday, executed it on Monday, and were apprehended and jailed Monday evening. Witnesses had identified some of them as actually being on the mountain, while others had been clearly associated with them. There was no evidence, the prosecutor admitted, connecting the organizers for the UMWA, Batley and Paulsen, with the conspiracy; in effect, he called for their acquittal.

In presenting his case against Mother Jones, the prosecutor tried to show that her speeches had encouraged violence and conspiracy among the striking miners. In addition to the hundred pages of transcriptions of her speeches that he had read into the record, nine witnesses testified about other speeches that they had heard her make. Two army officers reported that they had heard her deliver speeches the preceding August at Hansford and Kayford, but neither officer considered her speech inflammatory. Three witnesses testified about a speech she delivered in Boomer in September, when she advised the miners not to turn in their guns to a group in Montgomery that had advocated disarming people in the area. Three other witnesses reported briefly on speeches in December and January, in which she accused the miners of having a yellow streak down their backs if they did not resist the arrogance of the guards and the importation of scabs. The most recent speech was one listed as having been delivered at Boomer in February. From newspaper reports this could only have been the speech that she gave on the day before her arrest, when she was organizing the delegation that carried the petition to Governor Glasscock asking for protection of the miners from arbitrary arrests. She advised the audience to keep their guns and that she would call on them if she needed them; that if any miner were sent to the penitentiary, "we would tear up the state."

Strangely, no defense lawyer pointed out that the crimes alleged in the charges all occurred before this speech, so that it could not have contributed to the conspiracy that led to the crimes. In fact, much of the evidence brought forward by the prosecution, including that of the private detective Frank Smith, pertained to actions that took place in the afternoon and evening after the events detailed in the major charges. Only a very loose interpretation of what constituted proof of conspiracy to abet the escape of known felons could justify the presentation of this ex post facto evidence.

The prosecutor stated that Mother Jones might have thought she was doing right but that by her speeches she had "largely contributed to this trouble." Even so, he admitted, "I do not think the evidence is very strong against her," adding that he would leave it to the commission to decide if she was guilty.

The judge advocate went out of his way to indict the civil authorities for failure to act. "If the criminal courts and juries of this county had done their duty, you and the balance of us would not be here performing this disagreeable and unpleasant duty."

Wallace's peroration included his assertion that he had as much sympathy for the defendants as did the defense lawyers but that he had a duty to fulfill, and he called upon the members of the court-martial to perform their duty and convict the defendants.

~ ~ ~ ~ ~

# Sentences and Settlement

Following the final argument by the prosecutor, the transcript of the trial contains several pages of forms that list the names of the defendants, with blank spaces for "guilty" or "not guilty" verdicts and other blanks for recommended sentences. Presumably, in the report sent under seal to Governor Henry D. Hatfield these forms were filled out. No such document appears in the Hatfield Papers or in the archives of the Hatfield administration, so that no official record exists to tell the fate of the defendants. However, a survey of the newspapers of the time permits the searcher to arrive at some conclusions about the verdicts.

On 20 March Governor Hatfield ordered the release of ten men—Tip Belcher, Clyde E. Bowe, Ed Gray, Cal J. Newman, W.H. Patrick, Will Perdue, Lawrence Perry, Oscar Petry, Jim Pike, and John Siketo—who, according to the *Charleston Daily Mail,* had been found not guilty. The next day, another fifteen men were released, including Charles Gillispie, Charles Batley, and Paul J. Paulsen, the latter two of whom were the UMWA organizers whom police arrested in Charleston the same day as Mother Jones. They too were held to be not guilty.[88]

On 22 March another nineteen prisoners received their freedom, but they apparently had been convicted on some charge, since their release was conditional on good behavior. "The executive admonished the men that should they violate the provisions of their freedom they would be returned to the military guard house and dealt with severely."[89]

Eleven more men were also held to be guilty of some offense and were transferred to civilian jails to await further disposition, which might entail being sent to the state penitentiary at Moundsville. Included in this group were Charles H. Boswell, John W. Brown, Ernest Creigo, Charles Kenney, A.D. Lavender, G.W. Lavender, Tom Miskel, George F. Parsons, John Seachrist, Cleve Vickers, and E.B. Vickers.

Mother Jones also remained imprisoned, inferring that she too had received a guilty verdict.[90] A search of the newspapers failed to reveal the names of four defendants, but reports in June said that all the prisoners had been released. By 21 June even John W. Brown, identified in the court-martial as the military commander who organized the miners for the battle at Mucklow, was free and in Charleston seeking a chance to testify before the Senate investigating committee.[91]

Three pages of notes among the prosecutor's papers tend to confirm these findings. The notes divide the names of the defendants into several groups and list a term of months or years for each group. Beside the name of Mother Jones is the phrase, "3 years." Beside the names of John W. Brown, Charles H. Boswell, and George F. Parsons are notations for ten years. Men who were found at Hansford with guns have "8 months" written beside them. For "men on the mountain" and "men at Sharon or Cabbin Creek Side," the listing is for five years. Twelve names bear the notation "No evidence" or "Not Guilty." Nine of these last names appear among the prisoners first released on 20 March and reported as not guilty by the newspapers. Similarly, all in the group listed for eight months were released on parole 22 March, according to the newspapers. It seems very likely that the prosecutor made these notes to help him prepare the sealed verdicts that he sent to the governor, but the papers have no official status.[92]

Governor Hatfield's only known public reference to the sentences came twenty years later when he was a senator from West Virginia: "One of the first acts I was called upon to perform as Governor was to attach my signature to the findings of a military court which, had I done so, would have sent to the penitentiary many mine workers of the State and their supporters for periods from five to twenty years. Among these commitments was one which would have sent Mother Jones to the State Penitentiary for a period of years. . . . I did not confirm the findings of the military court, in the case of Mother Jones nor any of the other cases."[93]

After the verdicts of the court-martial, Governor Hatfield showed clemency by releasing the lesser offenders on good behavior, but he had incarcerated nearly all the leading "trouble-makers" in the strike. So long as he did not officially confirm the sentences of the court-martial he held the ringleaders as hostages in any deals that he might contemplate with the national leaders of the UMWA. He had another UMWA hostage in the person of Lawrence Dwyer, who had emerged as the leader of the newly organized miners on Cabin Creek;

the sheriff of Raleigh County was detaining him in his jail on charges unrelated to the court-martial.[94]

Even before the trial was over, Governor Hatfield embarked on a plan to settle the strike that was as carefully timed and orchestrated as Mother Jones's campaign of the preceding August and September. As an incoming governor he had the advantage of control of the institutions of the state and the close attention of the newspapers. He began with a strenuous round of consultations with mine operators, leaders of the UMWA, and prominent citizens, all as the trial was coming to a close. A new offer by the UMWA representatives gave a faint hope of a break in the impasse, but it was offset by the threat of a statewide strike by all miners if the operators would not make concessions. The International Executive Board of the union had considered the possibility of such a strike but had left a final decision to the discretion of a three-man committee headed by John P. White. President White was due in Charleston the following week to consult with District 17 leaders. On Friday, operators from all over the state converged on Charleston to meet with the governor and discuss this new threat.[95]

On the following Tuesday Hatfield made his first visit to the martial law zone, where, in contrast to former Governor Glasscock, he spent his time talking with miners and prisoners rather than with the officers and men of the guard. Mother Jones was probably one of the prisoners he talked to, but his later recollection of the meeting is totally at odds with the contemporary sources. Recounting the events twenty years later, he said that he saw her on 6 March, found her suffering from pneumonia and running a temperature of 103°, transferred her to a hospital in Charleston, and released her after she recovered from her illness. However, she appeared before the military tribunal the morning after he said he saw her and continued to do so throughout the week. One news story mentioned that she was feeble and clung to the arm of John W. Brown as she climbed the stairs to the courtroom, but other reporters who talked to her during the same week characterized her as lively, cheerful, and defiant. Contemporary accounts agree that Governor Hatfield did not visit the strike zone until the week following the court-martial. Mother Jones wrote several letters from Pratt during the period in question.[96] Governor Hatfield could have treated her as a patient, but if he did no one else has reported it.

His role as a physician did enable him to create a positive image, for he returned the next two days for extensive tours up the creeks and took along his doctor's bag to conduct informal medical clinics for the striking miners and their families. He assured them that he intended to see that everyone received justice. At the end of his last day in the field, he freed ten of the defendants in the court-martial. Over the next two weeks, he released all the prisoners in boxcars or bull pen except eleven whom he had transferred to county jails to await further disposition. Significantly, all eleven of the men so held were identified as Socialists by a Socialist newspaper. Three had been active in the recent political contests: John W. Brown and George F. Parsons had been Socialist candidates for the legislature in the November election, and Charles H. Boswell edited the Socialist weekly, the *Labor Argus*.[97] The only other defendant, Mother Jones, remained imprisoned at Isabel Carney's house in Pratt. The court-martial scheduled no more civilian trials, although the governor kept the military commission intact. In the newspaper reports, the governor was characterized as an energetic, fair-minded, and compassionate man. "To my mind," said Hatfield, "it is infinitely more important that peace be restored and law and order permanently established than that past offenders be punished." [98]

While Hatfield was soothing the miners in the field, help toward a settlement of the strike came to Charleston in the person of President John P. White of the UMWA, who kept a low profile and refused to talk to reporters. Although he bore the responsibility for deciding whether a statewide strike should be called, he also had good news for the governor. Since early February he and other UMWA officials had been holding conferences in Scranton, Pennsylvania, with the president and other officers of the parent company of the Paint Creek collieries. On 21 March, White, international executive board member Thomas Haggerty, and Thomas Cairnes, president of District 17, announced from Philadelphia that they had reached an agreement that included the right to organize, bimonthly pay, short ton weight (some mines still used the long ton), a checkweighman on each tipple, and a grievance procedure that involved representatives of both management and miners. Additional understandings provided for the adoption of the Kanawha wage scale (which already prevailed north of the river) and an end to the importation of strikebreakers.[99]

When President White returned to Charleston on 25 March he outlined for Governor Hatfield his ideas for a general settlement, and an ad hoc citizens organization publicized them in the Charleston newspapers. Some momentum was created when the New River operators announced that they were in agreement with the nine-hour day, bimonthly pay, and checkweighmen. Even a flood that affected the whole Ohio River basin failed to stop progress, although it undoubtedly delayed it. Units of the National Guard had to be transferred to disaster relief duty in river towns, and Governor Hatfield toured devastated areas, while John P. White hastened back to Indianapolis to see to the safety of his family.[100]

Although both sides continued to air their differences in long letters and advertisements in the newspapers, the movement toward a general settlement gained headway. On 15 April, Governor Hatfield issued a set of proposals broadly paralleling the earlier agreement arrived at by the UMWA and the Paint Creek Colliery Company. All the Charleston newspapers wrote editorials in support of it, the business community swung behind it with a formal endorsement by the Chamber of Commerce, and T.L. Lewis, former president of the UMWA who was now a spokesman for coal mine operators, approved the plan. A hastily called convention of District 17 gave the governor an ovation when he addressed them and accepted his proposals conditionally. On 28 April, Governor Hatfield went to the strike zone with UMWA officials to urge the men to go back to work. Both sides declared themselves pleased that the yearlong strike was over.[101]

Governor Hatfield might work with the UMWA, but he had no intention of dealing leniently with their Socialist allies of the past year. The Socialists were labeling the Hatfield settlement a sellout, and on 29 April military authorities seized the *Labor Argus* and arrested its editors, later detaining one of the reporters. Similarly, by order of the governor, state officials seized the *Huntington Socialist and Labor Star*, confiscated its printing plant, and arrested five people associated with it. None of the major newspapers in the state raised their voices in protest against the suppression of the Socialist newspapers.[102]

For Mother Jones, the basic conditions of imprisonment remained the same after the court-martial, but her captors eased some restrictions on her contacts with outsiders. They permitted members of the International Executive Board of the UMWA to visit her, and Isabel Carney years later said that a secretary from District 17 headquarters in Charleston came to Pratt once a week to help Mother Jones with her correspondence. It may be that the beer-drinking adventure with Dallas Stotts took place during this time of eased tensions.

On the night of 7 May 1913, Captain R.E. Sherwood accompanied to Charleston the last prisoner in Pratt, Mother Jones. She took up temporary residence at the Fleetwood Hotel and had at least one interview with Governor Hatfield. Neither revealed what passed between them, although Mother Jones did say that they talked of economic conditions. She was unconcerned about her fate. "It doesn't matter to me what they do with me," she told a reporter. After a brief stay at the hotel, she departed for Washington, D.C.[103]

Mother Jones's release may have been a part of unwritten agreements between President White and Governor Hatfield, but even without them, if they existed, it would probably have taken place. The pressure from Washington had become severe. Senator John Worth Kern, the majority leader, was pushing to a vote his resolution for an investigation into conditions in the coalfields of West Virginia, and the debate about the use of the military and the imprisonment of an elderly woman were giving the state an unwanted image. When Senator Nathan Goff of West Virginia characterized her as the grandmother of all agitators and denied that she was imprisoned, saying she was merely "confined in a pleasant boarding house," Kern replied by reading the telegram that Mother Jones had smuggled out of her quarters at Pratt: "From out of the military prison walls, where I been forced to pass my eighty-first milestone of life, I plead with you for the honor of this Nation. I send you the groans and tears of men, women, and children as I have heard them in this State, and beg you to force that investigation. Children yet unborn will rise and bless you."[104] This telegram, the culmination of the publicity campaign that she had been waging, brought quick results. Three days after its dispatch the military authorities took her to Charleston and freed her.

After her release, Mother Jones was able to witness from the gallery of the Senate in Washington the last stages of the debate and the passage of the resolution for an investigation of the conditions in the coalfields of West Virginia. She addressed public meetings in New York and Pittsburgh before returning to Charleston in early June to attend the hearings of the Senate investigating committee. Most of the West Virginia miners had gone back to work in May, but militant unionists in a number of mines remained dissatisfied with the substance and wording of individual agreements and called for work stoppages if their demands were not met. A flare-up on Cabin Creek, where the miners charged that Charles Cabell was not living up to the Hatfield settlement, led Mother Jones to schedule a speech at Eskdale, but the controversy died after adjustments were made.[105]

In July 1913, a year after Mother Jones entered the fray, the miners of West Virginia were back at work, but at high cost to them, their opponents, and the general public. Perhaps fifty deaths, untold suffering, lost wages and profits, and the indirect costs of a general disruption of the economy and a military occupation had to be weighed against the grudging admission of the right to organize and some improvements in wages and the conditions of work. It would require determination to maintain their gains, and the use of company guards and deputy sheriffs paid by the coal operators had not been permanently banned. Wounds from the strike were healing, but the consequences of the conflict continued to echo through the succeeding months and years.

~   ~   ~   ~   ~

# Repercussions

Three months after the court-martial and one month after Mother Jones's release, the Senate subcommittee on Education and Labor began its investigation of conditions in the Paint Creek mining district of West Virginia. The nearly 2,300 closely printed pages of the Senate hearings contain a wealth of material about the strike and the court-martial. Private lawyers, rather than a senate staff, called and questioned witnesses, in some cases repeating or enlarging earlier testimony before the Donahue Commission or in one trial or another. However, the senators were often impatient with the lawyers and frequently intervened with their own questions. The Senate subcommittee spent more than a week taking testimony in Charleston, West Virginia. In September, after Congress took its summer recess, they resumed the hearings in Washington, D.C. Although some of the testimony was repetitious, much new information appeared when many of the principals in the strike and the trial gave testimony justifying their actions. In one dramatic moment, Senator James E. Martine verbally attacked Quinn Morton for his participation in the Holly Grove shoot-up and asked him "whether you deem it a civilized method to use a machine gun on helpless women and children." Morton replied: "I am tired of being browbeaten." In another exchange with Martine, Morton asserted: "I believe my conscience is as clear today as yours is, sir, and because you are a Senator you have no right to condemn me." In the sweltering heat, tempers flared. "Only the interference of the sergeant-at-arms prevented the two men coming to blows," reported the *Raleigh Register,* "when Morton intimated that Senator Martine was under the influence of liquor and added that he was 'an excitable old man.' "[106]

Governor William E. Glasscock explained his intentions and actions at length before the senators, and Governor Henry D. Hatfield, though not a witness, sent a long explanatory letter to the chairman. Lieutenant Colonel George S. Wallace testified, as did some of the witnesses in the court-martial and lawyers in that and other cases. Notable among those who did *not* testify was Mother Jones. It seems odd that she did not take the stand, since her role in the strike figured so largely in the debate that led to the hearings. President John P. White may have been responsible, following gentlemanly understandings with Governor Henry D. Hatfield, for it is probable that in their talks he and the governor mentioned her powerful presence. White was not so rash as to promise to muzzle her, but he could give instructions to the UMWA lawyers who were lining up the witnesses for the Senate hearings. The governor did not order her release until after the miners had gone back to work, but he did allow two old friends high in the councils of the UMWA, Frank Feehan and William Fairley, to visit her in prison at Pratt. They may have been able to convince her that negotiation and factual testimony, not dramatic militancy, would now gain the most for the miners in West Virginia. Although it is pure speculation, it seems likely that Governor Hatfield stated to President White his intention to release the last of the prisoners when a settlement had been worked out, while President White agreed to use his influence to keep Mother Jones quiet. In any event, the hearings in Charleston ended without Mother Jones's having testified, nor did she appear before the committee when it reconvened in Washington in September.[107]

In its hearings in the fall, the subcommittee spent most of its time exploring the corporate organization of the coal industry in West Virginia, markets, profitability, and other broad economic questions that might be pertinent to national legislation, but no bills can be identified as emerging from this committee. Yet the West Virginia mining investigation, with two later ones in Michigan and Colorado, when added to the report of the contemporaneous Commission on Industrial Relations, showed how the Congress was acquiring massive amounts of information that might be useful in writing new laws and establishing new institutions. During this administration, the federal government began to inject itself more directly into the economic life of the nation through regulatory commissions. The new Department of Labor organized its mediation service in time to play a role in the Colorado strike of 1913–14. The temporary management of the economy by the War Industries Board and the War Labor Board during World War I took shape partly on the basis of the information acquired during these investigations.

By the time the Senate committee resumed its hearings on conditions in West Virginia in September 1913, Mother Jones was in Trinidad, Colorado, calling on the coal miners of that state to strike. Over the course of the next year, there was an almost eerie replaying in Colorado of the same scenario as in West Virginia in 1912–13. Once again the UMWA led the miners in a strike, miners and company guards shot at one another in violent confrontations, the state militia took over control of a large mining area, and Congress approved another call for an investigation. Many of the company guards in Colorado were Baldwin-Felts men who had just served a tour of duty in West Virginia and were equipped with the same machine guns they used on Paint Creek. As at Holly Grove in West Virginia, an attack was made on a tent settlement of strikers in Ludlow, Colorado, and this one brought about the death of miners, women, and children, who perished in the burning tents. As in West Virginia, the Colorado militia imprisoned Mother Jones, but they released her the day before the state Supreme Court scheduled a habeas corpus hearing. Almost immediately they rearrested and reimprisoned her at another location for three more weeks.

Although there were many parallels between the Colorado strike of 1913–14 and the West Virginia strike of 1912–13, there were also major differences, the chief one being the rapid nationalization of conflicts between capital and organized labor. Overriding a chorus of state rights protests, congressional committees from the Senate and House in 1913 were authorized to investigate mining conditions in West Virginia, Michigan, and Colorado. In Colorado the executive branch also acted by sending mediators from the newly established Labor Department and by stationing federal troops to replace the Colorado National Guard, which had proved unable to preserve order. Eventually, President Woodrow Wilson proposed a settlement to the contending parties in Colorado, but the operators paid little attention to the president's attempt to act as an arbitrator.[108]

When Albert M. Belcher and Harold W. Houston had applied to Judge Samuel D. Littlepage for a writ ordering the military officers to stop the court-martial of Mother Jones, soldiers at Pratt prevented

Sheriff Bonner Hill from serving writs on them, and the trial began as scheduled. Belcher and Houston then issued a statement to the *Kanawha Citizen* in which they deplored the refusal of the military to recognize the supremacy of the civil authority, contrary to the constitution. "The lawyers of the state ought to immediately assemble," they said, "and take some action ... for the preservation of constitutional government."[109]

Although no spontaneous congress of attorneys sprang up to protest the decision in *In re Jones et al.*, lawyers in West Virginia continued over the next weeks and months to debate the legal points of the decision, together with the earlier pronouncements in *In re Shanklin* and *Nance and Mays v. Brown*. Articles in the monthly journal of the state bar association spoke approvingly of Judge Ira E. Robinson's dissenting opinions. The interpretation put on the constitution by the majority of the court, wrote the editor, "staggered those of us who had not given the subject special study and who were accustomed to read its plain provisions as meaning what they say in plain English."[110]

The decisions were the principal subjects at the meeting of the West Virginia Bar Association in July. In his presidential address, W.G. Mathews strongly attacked the use of courts-martial to prosecute civilian residents of West Virginia. He deplored the Supreme Court decisions that had upheld the extraordinary powers of the governor and the military authorities. He found it almost unbelievable that the court had endorsed the governor's right and power to enact laws, prescribe punishment, summon and try without presentment or indictment, without grand or petit jury, to award punishment and to enforce that mandate, to make laws retroactive, and to transform a misdemeanor into a felony. In the words of Montesquieu, he said, such a mixture of legislative, judicial, and executive powers was "the essence of tyranny."

Toward the end of his speech, Mathews declared: "I most respectfully, but with all the earnestness of which I am capable, desire to record an emphatic protest, a protest which I believe will be concurred in by the great majority of those acquainted with the ... constitutional history of our State."

After reviewing the facts of the strike, the violence, and the governmental responses of the past year, he proceeded to an analysis of the various errors he saw in the decisions of the Supreme Court, basing his argument almost exclusively on the West Virginia constitution. He went into detail on the wartime experiences of the makers of the constitutions of 1863 and 1872, and particularly the strengthening of the clauses that safeguarded civil rights and specifically provided that a citizen of West Virginia could not be tried by a court-martial. The language of the constitution, he asserted, "could no more plainly inhibit such trial and punishment had it named the petitioners in the habeas corpus cases and provided that they should not be so tried and punished." Mathews's speech was a virtual invitation to the members of the bar association to join him in a public protest.[111]

In a special session in the afternoon for discussion of the president's address, numerous leaders of the bar put forward their views, some with great vigor. A supporter of Mathews, Judge P.T. Jacobs, asserted: "I do not believe there is any authority existing under the constitution or elsewhere authorizing the military court to try a private citizen for any kind of crime." However, the former governor, George W. Atkinson, upheld the actions of the governors and the majority opinion of the Supreme Court. As discussion developed, it became apparent that the members of the bar could reach no consensus for an immediate endorsement of President Mathews's views. However, several members suggested referring the address to a committee that would prepare a statement or statements for further consideration by the membership. Proponents of various views wrangled about whether the referral should be to a special or a standing committee and with what instructions. Nearly all agreed that further deliberations were necessary, and even Albert M. Belcher, the UMWA attorney who had earlier called for a lawyers' protest, supported Howard N. Ogden's amended proposal to refer the matter to a committee. Belcher thought it important for the association to take a stand on the question "whether or not the will of one man can be substituted for the constitution of a great state." The delegates finally instructed the standing Committee on Judicial Administration and Legal Reform to bring in a report at the next meeting of the bar association.[112]

While the lawyers were debating in West Virginia, the bureaucratic machinery was grinding slowly in Washington. At the beginning of May Secretary of Labor William B. Wilson asked the postmaster general to investigate possible interference with Mother Jones's mail in Pratt, West Virginia. On 21 June the Post Office Department sent Wilson a return receipt for the registered letter that he had mailed to her, but as it bore neither postmark nor date, Wilson asked that they make further inquiries. By that time, the Senate had begun its own inquiry into conditions in the West Virginia coalfields, and the postal investigation had lost its high priority for Wilson. It continued at a leisurely pace, and the Post Office Department issued a final report in June 1914 summarizing the case and pointing to various conflicts in testimony that indicated that someone might have tampered with Mother Jones's mail. William B. Wilson considered carrying the matter to the federal courts, but the departmental solicitor advised against it, doubting that responsibility for a lost letter could ever be fixed.[113]

Even after the National Guard troops had gone back to their homes, Lieutenant Colonel George S. Wallace remained on call whenever some legal matter connected with the strike arose, and he defended both Governor Glasscock and Governor Hatfield in civil cases that grew out of their actions in the strike, as well as giving advice on legal strategies.

One case concerned Dan Chain, who was also known as "Few Clothes" Johnson, a colorful and aggressive black union leader who had been convicted by an early court-martial, had served time in the penitentiary, had been released by Governor Glasscock, and had been reimprisoned for breaking his parole. He had sought a habeas corpus hearing from the Supreme Court of the United States, but the justices denied his request because he had not yet exhausted the remedies available at the state level. He had applied for a writ of habeas corpus hearing before the West Virginia Supreme Court and might possibly go on appeal from there to the United States Supreme Court. Toward the end of April, Wallace reported to Governor Hatfield that the West Virginia court had continued the case. He recommended that Hatfield grant Chain a pardon, for the case was not worth the trouble and expense, "as probabilities are you will pardon him anyway."[114] The governor followed Wallace's advice and gave Chain an immediate pardon.

Another striker who had been confined in the penitentiary and released by Glasscock, S.F. Nance, brought a civil action against Glasscock for damages for the fifty-one days he had spent in jail. The case was scheduled for trial in November 1914 but must have been either dropped or settled out of court, as no record of it can be found in the circuit court where the hearing was set.

The Socialist Printing Company of Huntington, West Virginia, brought an action of trespass against Governor Hatfield and four National Guard officers for conspiring to destroy a printing office and to suppress the paper that they printed, the *Socialist and Labor Star,* to the amount of ten thousand dollars in damages. The guard officers appeared in open court 2 February 1914 and filed a special plea: They were agents of Governor Hatfield, who was their commander-in-chief; they were merely loyal officers carrying out the orders of their superior.

As they explained it, the situation was this: A settlement was pending in the coal strike in 1913, but the *Socialist and Labor Star* denounced it as a sellout. On 5 May, Governor Hatfield issued his warrant for seizing the paper. On the night of 8 May, the officers took possession of the newspaper office and pied the type.

The petitioners asked the Supreme Court to grant a writ of prohibition whereby Judge Jonathan T. Graham (of the 6th Judicial District) be stopped from trying the suit for trespass. The Supreme Court awarded the writ of prohibition, citing *Nance and Mays* (71 W. Va. 519) and *Moyer v. Peabody* (212 U.S. 78). The judges ruled that

1. The governor's actions and warrants are not subject to review by the courts.
2. The governor cannot be held liable for damages to private property when carrying out his duty.
3. The governor has power to arrest and detain disturbers of the peace, and power to suppress temporarily any newspaper.
4. Subordinate officers cannot be held liable for actions performed in the normal course of their duties.

In this case, Judge Ira E. Robinson dissented, citing his previous dissent in the Mother Jones habeas corpus case. "The unsound principle established by that decision permits a Governor to deal with private rights and private property as he pleases." It is "wholly un-American" and "inconsistent with constitutional government." "Reason and authority condemn it, and the administration of even-handed justice cries out against it."[115]

No other cases are known to have arisen out of the strike and the court-martial, but in 1915, Adjutant General John C. Bond was still trying to clear up expenses arising from legal proceedings connected with the Paint Creek strike.[116]

Lawyers from outside the state as well as within followed the legal maneuvers of the strike and continue to debate about *Nance and Mays v. Brown* and *In re Jones et al.* H.C. Carbaugh, in the first scholarly article to note the West Virginia Supreme Court decisions (1913), argued strongly for the inherent right of government to preserve itself and the power of the governor to declare martial law but asserted that the military when called in to support the civil authorities had no power to bring offenders to trial. In the summer a passionately worded article appeared by Henry Winthrop Ballantine, then dean of the University of Montana law school, calling the reasoning of the majority decision in *Nance and Mays v. Brown* "preposterous" and praising Robinson's "able opinion" in dissent. Ballantine expressed disapproval of the "dangerous misconceptions" of the majority in *In re Jones et al.,* and he characterized the Paint Creek military trials as "an abdication of the supremacy of law."[117]

Two years later in the *Yale Law Journal,* Ballantine returned to the subject of the use of troops, finding a tendency by the military to assume unwarranted power when called out to maintain order in industrial disputes and citing the West Virginia cases as instances of usurpations of the Bill of Rights. He felt that the whole question of emergency powers of the executive needed legal clarification. "The law is in a dangerous and disgraceful condition, misleading to the military, and fraught with peril to the community and to the citizen."[118]

George S. Wallace, whose experience and study had made him an expert on martial law and courts-martial, joined the scholarly fray. Even after all cases had been dismissed or settled, he continued to write to adjutant generals in various states, inquiring into their use of martial law and any litigation that had grown out of it. In September 1916, he presented before the American Institute of Criminal Law and Criminology in Chicago a paper entitled, "The Need, the Propriety and Basis of Martial Law, with a Review of the Authorities." In it he surveyed the use of martial law in six states in the previous three years, with many allusions to earlier cases. The use of martial law in West Virginia, though only one of six instances, naturally occupied a prominent place in his address.[119]

Ballantine was only the first of many scholars who pointed out the need for clarification of the term "martial law." In a long and thoughtful article in the *Illinois Law Review* in 1929, Charles Fairman, professor of constitutional law at the Harvard Law School, looked at some questions in the light of a recent case in Denver in which a federal court on a writ of habeas corpus released prisoners being held by the militia. In various decisions in the last twenty years, Fairman pointed out, state and federal courts had ruled sometimes against and sometimes for the wielding of extraordinary power by governors, including trials by court-martial. "The Supreme Court of West Virginia may claim the dubious honor of having pioneered this line of reasoning," said Fairman, citing *Nance and Mays v. Brown* and *In re Jones*.[120] Fairman concluded his article by calling for a study of the problems and the development of a legal system that carefully balanced conflicting social values. "How the military power of the state may be exerted to preserve ordered liberty without becoming arbitrary or biased is a problem which, to be settled rightly, will require legal statesmanship of a high order."[121]

The next year Fairman answered his own call for a study by publishing his book, *The Law of Martial Rule,* a broad investigation of the whole range of constitutional questions raised in the Paint Creek trial. In reviewing martial rule from its English origins, he pointed out that federal or state troops had been used to preserve order since the beginning of the republic but that the proclamation of martial law was a rarer occurrence. In addition to examining the general principles involved, he devoted two pages to legal questions arising from the Paint Creek strike. In his view, the term "martial law" should be restricted to the laws applying to the armed forces. However, troops may be used as police to support existing civilian authority. Finally, there had existed at various times and places what he termed "punitive martial rule," used largely in disorders arising out of labor disputes, which had been upheld by state and federal courts in some instances and denied in other decisions. The leading Supreme Court case was *Moyer v. Peabody* (212 U.S. 78), which broadly upheld the power of the governor of Colorado in restoring order during a strike, but to the contrary was the case of *Ex parte Milligan* (4 Wall. 2), where the U.S. Supreme Court disallowed the conviction of a Confederate sympathizer by a military court, because the civil courts of the state of Indiana were open and functioning at the time. Most of the later decisions by lower courts looked back to the principles stated in one or the other of these cases.[122]

In themselves, neither the Moyer nor the Milligan cases dealt with the question of the basic constitutional powers of governors. Since the U.S. Constitution prohibits states from declaring war, can a governor declare a state of war to exist, as Governor William E. Glasscock did in 1912? Can a governor justifiably call a labor disturbance a war? A number of state constitutions give governors the power to declare martial law without defining it, but can a governor suspend civil rights, even temporarily, to preserve order? If a governor exerts extraordinary powers during a crisis, are his actions reviewable by the courts at the time, or after martial law has been revoked, or at all? Is a governor liable for damages created by his actions during a crisis, or are his delegated agents, such as members of the militia, responsible for such damages? The decisions of state and federal courts on these points were contradictory. Did recent decisions of the Supreme Court "incorporating" the Bill of Rights into state law actually negate the Moyer decision?

A strong blow to the supporters of broad powers for governors came in 1932 when Chief Justice Charles Evans Hughes announced the court's opinion in *Sterling v. Constantin* (287 U.S. 378). The court restated the facts in *Moyer v. Peabody* and warned that the general language of the Moyer opinion must be taken in connection with the restatement, in which they found the soldiers acted "with reason." Thus the court now endorsed the idea of reasonableness, adopted in some other decisions, and projected it backward on Moyer. Despite this reversal, many constitutional questions remained unanswered.

Robert S. Rankin, in *When Civil Law Fails,* reviewed again the questions posed by Fairman and devoted twenty-eight pages to the West Virginia cases, examining especially the legal and constitutional bases for the declaration of martial law and comparing four conflicting views. Morris Shepp Isseks in an article in the *Oregon Law Review* was more critical of the West Virginia Supreme Court decisions upholding Governors Glasscock and Hatfield. Rankin, a professor of political science at Duke, though characterizing the *Nance and Mays v. Brown* decision as "certainly one of the most radical ever given by an American court concerning martial law," nevertheless tended to support the exercise of extraordinary power by governors; he merely hoped that their consciences, or fear of impeachment, would make them act with restraint. Both Rankin and Isseks recognized that the militia had been used primarily in industrial disputes and that the overall outcome was usually the protection of property rights at the expense of civil rights. Their general conclusions remained the same as Fairman's: that the term "martial law" needed definition and that there were irreconcilable contradictions in the decisions of both state and federal courts about the the powers of a governor who declared martial law to exist.[123]

The coming of World War II raised some of the same questions in new guises, such as the presidential military commission appointed to try German saboteurs who landed from submarines; the arrest and incarceration of Japanese, both citizens and aliens, in California; the declaration of martial law in the entire Territory of Hawaii; and martial law in Detroit in 1943 where regular army troops replaced the original Michigan National Guard. Fairman's *The Law of Martial Rule* appeared in a new edition (1943), as did Glenn and Schiller, *The Army and the Law*

(New York: Columbia Univ. Press, 1943), a standard treatment that in 1918 included a chapter on "Martial Law at Home."

In the decade following World War II, scholars continued to examine some of the same questions, usually in the context of whether the Bill of Rights applied to military tribunals and what power of review belonged to the courts.[124]

In the 1960s the conflicts between civil rights and the preservation of order by militia came more frequently in cases arising out of urban riots and student demonstrations and reached their climax in the shooting of students at Kent State by members of the Ohio National Guard. Just a year after that event, David Engdahl in the *Iowa Law Review* once again presented an updated review of the use of troops in civil disorders and emphasized the need to find a solution to the conflict between preserving civil rights and preserving order. In 1968 and 1970 respectively, the National Commission on Civil Disorders and the President's Commission on Campus Unrest made their reports that recognized the inherent constitutional problems of using troops to quell civil disorder. In 1972, Engdahl and two student assistants at the Law Revision Center of the University of Colorado, which Engdahl directed, proposed model legislation that would clarify the power of governors, generally restricting arbitrary actions and subjecting them unmistakably to review by the courts. That same year, James E. Roark reviewed once again the 1913 decisions of the West Virginia Supreme Court and recommended the adoption by the West Virginia legislature of Engdahl's model law, but no movement for such revision has developed to push the legislators toward action. In the light of eighty years of scholarly discussion, some legal questions connected with the court-martial of Mother Jones and her associates remain unsolved.[125]

Echoing through the strike, the court-martial, and on into the following years are the themes of race and ethnicity, but their importance is hard to measure. Black miners had been a part of the labor force in West Virginia from the earliest days, and more had been imported, sometimes as strikebreakers, as in 1903–4. In general, black and white miners seem to have gotten along well both below and above ground, and some blacks held office in the predominantly white union. However, there is reason to believe that some operators exploited racial differences to keep their employees divided.[126]

In addition, massive immigration to the United States over a generation was beginning to change the makeup of the West Virginia mining force, as the operators added the new arrivals to the old

American stock, black and white, that had supplied their labor in earlier days. Language differences sometimes made communication difficult and required special efforts to overcome. Public notices in the Boomer area in 1913 were bilingual to accommodate the large number of Italians in the mines there, and the UMWA catered to its diverse membership by publishing its journal in three languages: English, Italian, and Slavic. Many of the immigrants were Catholic, and Governor William E. Glasscock may have been recognizing the new ethnic elements when he appointed Bishop P.J. Donahue to head his investigating committee, symbolically admitting a Catholic prelate to the heretofore largely Protestant establishment in West Virginia.[127]

The racial and ethnic concepts that were characteristic of the time occasionally surfaced in words and customs during the strike and trial. The prosecutor addressed black witnesses by their first names but gave whites the title of "Mister." He began the evidence about the battle of Mucklow with the testimony of two black defendants, but their memories proved to be vague on crucial points. Although these two willing witnesses gave testimony for the prosecution, another black defendant, Harrison Ellis, later became the key witness who, the court ruled, could not be forced to testify against himself. In attempting to use these black men to make his case, was the prosecutor, consciously or unconsciously, trying to drive a wedge between the black and white strikers? Were black men easier to induce to testify or to intimidate? The action of Harrison Ellis indicates the contrary.

Ethnic labels and slurs formed part of the vocabulary of the day. Newspaper reporters and others concerned with the strike casually used such terms as "wop," and "hunky." Lieutenant Colonel Wallace assured the Senate investigating committee that he treated dagos the same as he did American citizens. One newspaper distinguished between the "American" and "Italian" miners at Boomer, characterizing the latter as more prone to violence. General Charles D. Elliott, the commander of the National Guard, took some coal operators to task for the disdain they showed for their immigrant labor: "There are coal companies which consider coal miners inferior beings. The 'Hunky' mother and the 'Wop' mother do not lose the mother instinct simply because they happen to be Italian, Slav, Hungarian, or Lithuanian. The 'Hunky' mother has a heart which aches when she can't find food enough for her children. The 'Wop' mother despairs when she has to leave her children so she can go into a mill and earn $6 a week with which to help pay excessive tenement rent."[128]

A survey of the manuscript census returns of Kanawha County for 1910 shows that along Paint Creek and Cabin Creek most of the inhabitants had been born in West Virginia, but the census marshals encountered substantial groups of immigrants there. Most of them were single men who lived in boardinghouses, were not naturalized, and had entered the United States since 1900. The largest number listed Russia as their country of origin, but the names appear to be mostly Polish or Lithuanian. Next most numerous were Italians, some of whom were married and took in fellow Italian boarders; they were also more likely to be citizens. After them in numbers came Slavs from the Austrian empire, Hungarians, and a few Germans, Scots, English, and Swiss. These were the elements that supplemented the native manpower for the new mines that had opened in recent years.

The names of twenty-two of the defendants were found in the census reports, and if the known outsiders—Batley, Boswell, Brown, Mother Jones, and Paulsen—are excluded, they constitute one half of those tried by the court-martial. A profile constructed from the census data shows that the typical defendant was twenty-seven years of age, a native West Virginian, whose parents were either West Virginians or Virginians. Most of them indicated that they had been employed all during the past year. Only 14 percent of them lived in houses that they or their families owned, yet in the three years that had passed since the census enumeration they still lived in the same area. Thus, a solid core of the defendants were drawn from the native population and were a relatively stable labor group. The names of those defendants who were not found in the census suggest that the Slavic and Italian elements were also represented among the forty-eight, but subordinate to the natives.[129]

The defense counsel compiled a list of the ages of the defendants that agrees generally with the profile constructed from the census data. Again excluding the known outsiders, thirty was the average age of the defendants, five of whom were teenagers and seven of whom were forty or above. Eighteen supported wives and children, averaging 3.4 per family; seven more maintained widowed mothers or other relatives. More than half, then, were family breadwinners, not roving, single laborers.[130]

In conducting the trial, the prosecution focused its attack on John W. Brown, Charles H. Boswell, and Mother Jones, the outside agitators whom they accused of leading the conspiracy and misleading the miners into acts of violence. It was the outsiders, with some socialist miners, who received the most severe sentences from the court-martial. All the others were either acquitted by the court or paroled by Governor Henry D. Hatfield shortly after the end of the proceedings. The ringleaders, on the other hand, were incarcerated for several more weeks. Even though they, too, were eventually released, their ideologies and their powers of communication were the obvious reasons for the governor to keep them in jail until he had concluded a settlement.

≈   ≈   ≈   ≈   ≈

# Conclusions

The court-martial of Mother Jones fitted precisely Sir Frederick Maitland's description of martial law as an improvised justice executed by soldiers. During the previous year, when those charged with the administration of justice failed to act, Governor William E. Glasscock reluctantly proclaimed martial law. He created a military court for which he set the jurisdiction, prescribed the laws, and reviewed and carried out the sentences, prompting more than one of his critics to compare the proceedings to the Court of Star Chamber. Yet the Supreme Court of Appeals of West Virginia endorsed the replacement of civil courts with military ones that tried both military and civilian offenders. After the renewal of violence on Paint Creek in February 1913, Governor Glasscock imprisoned those regarded as the worst troublemakers. It was an exercise in power, by which the authorities silenced and immobilized the leaders of the strike. The Supreme Court of Appeals again upheld the actions of the governor, and a date was set for the court-martial of Mother Jones and her associates.

Governor Henry D. Hatfield took over the reins of office in March, just before the trial was scheduled to begin. He used, but then dismantled, the system he had inherited. For him, the defendants in the court-martial became bargaining chips for a settlement of the strike. Hatfield gained public approval for his leniency in releasing some of the people convicted by the military court, but he held those regarded as the leaders as hostages until he worked out a strike settlement that balanced various interests. He then released the last of the military court prisoners and returned the administration of justice to civil officers. Unsatisfactory as Hatfield's actions might have been to some participants, the Socialists on the left or the diehard antiunionists on the right, he brought about a restoration of coal production to the profit of operators and miners, and he eliminated the heavy expense of maintaining the militia in the field. By freeing all the prisoners, he also put an end to litigation and avoided a test in the federal courts of the power of the state to use courts-martial to try civilians. If the newspapers are to be believed, his settlement enjoyed broad public support as well as the endorsement of major economic groups.

The political and economic leaders of West Virginia had demonstrated how far some members of an entrenched elite were willing to go to stop the activities of those they regarded as troublemakers, but their tactics aroused so much criticism nationally, particularly in the case of Mother Jones, that they brought unwanted notoriety to the state. Governor Hatfield, by acting promptly and decisively to end the strike and restore normal conditions in the mining area, softened the adverse criticism. The settlement he arranged between miners and operators prevailed for several years but rested more on tacit understandings than on laws that addressed the problems.

As a unique event the court-martial deserves recording, but in the history of American labor law it was an aberration. Whatever temporary utility it may have had in the eyes of West Virginia leaders was outweighed by the spectacle of military autocracy that it presented to the rest of the country. Nor did courts-martial for civilians become acceptable legal maneuvers elsewhere. It is noteworthy that in strikingly similar situations the following year in Colorado, the militia held no military trial of its prisoners, including Mother Jones.

The mainstream of American labor litigation is represented not by the court-martial, but by a case from northern West Virginia being decided contemporaneously. In December 1912, Judge Alston G. Dayton of the Northern District of West Virginia announced his decision in *Hitchman Coal and Coke Company v. Mitchell*. It too had arisen, five years earlier, out of an organizing drive of the UMWA. Although the company had agreements with individual miners that they would not join the union—"yellow dog" contracts—the UMWA was nevertheless able to organize the men and call a strike. The company sued the union and its officers (John Mitchell was then president), alleging restraint of trade as defined in the Sherman Anti-Trust Act. Dayton's decision in favor of the coal company was later upheld by the Supreme Court.[131]

The lawyers for the coal companies assisted the prosecution in the court-martial, but they could only have seen the procedure as an anachronism. As early as the 1880s they had begun to abandon the use of charges under state conspiracy laws to meet the threat of union opposition; instead, they sought injunctions, especially in federal courts. In 1902, for instance, seven different coal companies filed injunctions in the federal court for the Southern District of West Virginia against Mother Jones and other UMWA officials to prevent their activities in strikes in the area. In the same year, coal companies also named her in an injunction in the Northern District of West Virginia, and she was jailed briefly for violating it.[132] While they continued to make use of the injunction, lawyers for corporations in the first decade of the new century were developing the technique of prosecuting unions and their leaders under the Sherman Act, pioneered in the Danbury Hatters case and continued in the Hitchman case.

The attorneys for the coal mine operators in Kanawha County in 1913 had to watch while the military lawyers tried to make their case on a state conspiracy statute, a tactic that they had abandoned nearly a generation earlier. No sooner was the court-martial completed than the coal operators' lawyers began to speak of possible indictment of John P. White and other UMWA leaders under the Sherman Act. On the other side, the UMWA matched the operators lawyer for lawyer, tested the martial law powers and procedures in the state courts, and declared themselves ready to resort to the federal courts to overturn the convictions in the military trial. The settlement of the strike and the release of prisoners put an end to these suggested continuations of the legal battles.[133]

The legal and political aspects of the court-martial are inextricably entwined. The state and national elections took place almost midway between the beginning and end of the strike. The list of lawyers involved in one way or another reads like a Who's Who of the state's political leaders. Albert M. Belcher and Adam B. Littlepage, counsel for the defendants, were prominent figures in the state Democratic party; but, then, so too was George S. Wallace, the prosecutor. Samuel B. Montgomery, another UMWA attorney, was a Democratic state senator. Colonel Clarence F. Jolliffe, the president of the military court, had begun and then abandoned a run for the Democratic nomination for governor in 1908. Harold W. Houston, an early candidate for governor on the Socialist ticket in 1912, was concerned with the imprisonment and trial not only of Mother Jones but also of his fellow Socialists, Boswell, Brown, Parsons, and others. Samuel B. Avis, the prosecuting attorney of Kanawha County during the early months of the strike, won a seat in Congress in the election in November. Ira E.

Robinson, the dissenting justice on the Supreme Court, ran as the Republican candidate for governor in the next election. On the whole, Democrats seem to have preponderated among the lawyers who worked for the miners, but some of the most telling criticisms of the mine operators came from Adjutant General Charles D. Elliott, a Republican. Rather than emphasizing party affiliations, the court-martial and related legal proceedings show the leaders of the state, particularly the bench and bar, joining to make use of the legal system to solve an economic, social, and political crisis.

Here is a provincial elite, accustomed to wielding power in their state, who addressed the problems of the Paint Creek strike in narrow, legalistic, and personal terms. Many lawyers found in the court-martial opportunities for lucrative employment or self-advancement. George S. Wallace received a fee of five thousand dollars—very large for those times—for his services in presenting before the state Supreme Court the state's argument for the legality of the military trials. Adam B. Littlepage, when he volunteered as defense counsel, was undoubtedly looking to the next election, in which he won back the seat in Congress that he lost in 1912 to Avis. The Supreme Court showed itself a part of or subservient to the ruling elite by upholding the powers of the military authorities despite the clear and specific wording of the state constitution. The lawyers for the coal operators were jackals to the lions, feeding off the legal business of an expanding industry. Governor William E. Glasscock, himself a lawyer, took a legalistic approach to his many problems. Thwarted by the restrictions of the state constitution and code, he reluctantly resorted to martial law, which only temporarily quieted the violence when the soldiers occupied the territory. It is no accident that the final breakthrough that led to a settlement was worked out not by lawyers in positions of power in the state but by John P. White, an "outsider" with a national view, by absentee industrialists, and by Governor Henry D. Hatfield, a physician.

Personalities aside, the leaders of the state had to work within or around structural defects in the system of the administration of justice. The institutions that had so long served a rural America proved totally inadequate for the conditions that prevailed in the coal communities of West Virginia. Along thirty miles of a narrow valley there might be, as on Paint Creek, a population of fifteen thousand concentrated every mile or two in "coal camp" villages. A similar situation might exist over the mountain along the next creek; two coal camps, one union and one nonunion, might be five miles apart as the crow flies and forty miles away by rail. The services of two rural elected constables were certainly inadequate to provide even minimum police protection for the population of the whole district, and it is no wonder that the coal mine operators hired four men, supplied by the Baldwin-Felts Agency, to serve as resident police. The sheriff of Kanawha County appointed them as deputies, and they enforced the law on Paint Creek, apparently to the satisfaction of their employers. Some acceptance of their legitimacy even by the miners might be inferred from the fact that three of these resident guards married daughters of miners working on the creek. Within these families, the challenges of loyalty can only be imagined as the conditions in the area changed during the strike.

Just as the constables were inadequate for the policing of the area, so too were the justices of the peace for the trial of minor offenses and the formulation of more serious charges to be brought before the courts of record. In the society in which the system developed, justices of the peace were substantial landowners whose knowledge of their rural bailiwicks qualified them to hand down appropriate punishment for local offenders and refer more serious cases to higher authorities. In the West Virginia coal areas, the miners regarded the justices of the peace as servants of the coal operators. During the strike these magistrates proved inadequate as dispensers of justice locally. Over the many months when violent incidents occurred within their jurisdictions, they supplied to the county prosecuting attorney no information for the indictment of offenders in serious crimes. Nor did use of the ballot alter the situation. In the election of 1912, the Socialists swept the local ticket in the Cabin Creek District, outpolling the Democrats and Republicans combined, and elected "their own" constables and the magistrate. But the new justice of the peace found that the military authorities would not permit him to exercise his office, and, in fact, briefly imprisoned him when he tried to fulfill his function.

Neither sheriff who held office during the strike was able to command the respect of the mining population. When violence became widespread the governor had at his command no state constabulary that he might send in to assist or replace local police. Instead, he had to wait until the sheriff called on him for help. Such a request finally allowed Governor William E. Glasscock to call out the National Guard, but only by continual occupation could it quell the disturbances. When the governor asked for a special grand jury to be called, the prosecuting attorney of the county and the judge of the intermediate (criminal) court who had the power to do so advised against it. Since the law prescribed geographic restrictions in the choosing of grand jurors, the appointment of a "blue ribbon" panel was not possible. The attorney general had no power to intervene in the business of the circuit courts, except that at the direction of the governor he could lend his aid to the prosecution after indictment. The prosecuting attorney of the county had no investigatory power or budget; he was wholly dependent on the reports of magistrates, which he would then present to a grand jury. During the summer of 1912 no such reports from magistrates reached prosecutor Samuel B. Avis or his assistant, Frank C. Burdette, even though it was public knowledge that several people had died by violence in the mining areas. It is not surprising that in his testimony before the senate investigating committee Governor William E. Glasscock stated that lack of cooperation by local officials impaired his efforts to settle the strike, or that in desperation he turned to martial law and military trials. Contrary to the belief of some people at the time, he did not send in the National Guard at the behest of the operators. In fact, many of them opposed his declaration of martial law, while union leaders at first welcomed the militiamen as protectors against the arrogance of Baldwin-Felts guards.

Despite the revelation of many deficiencies in the machinery of government, when conditions returned to normal the leaders of the state generally failed to alter their institutions to meet future crises. The legislature enacted few items on Governor William E. Glasscock's Progressive agenda, and one looks in vain in the immediately following years for thoroughgoing improvements in the system. Most notably, the understanding at the time of the settlement that the guard system would be radically reformed was left unfulfilled. The constitution of the state underwent only minor modifications, and politics continued to be highly personal, with much power remaining in the hands of local officials, the "courthouse rings." The reforms of the political structure that characterized the Progressive movement in some states touched West Virginia hardly at all. The Hatfield strike settlement prevailed for a few years, but within a decade the operators and the miners' union returned to violent confrontation.

Nor did many of the industrial leaders of the state change their methods or attitudes. The nonunion mine operators in West Virginia saw themselves as heroic battlers against "foreign" enemies. If the "outside agitators" of the UMWA were successful in organizing their miners, then the national officers of the UMWA in conspiracy with operators in other states would set wage rates and make other demands that would ruin the West Virginia coal industry. Also parties to this alleged conspiracy were the railroads, which directly set freight rates that discriminated against West Virginia coal while indirectly hampering production by allocating insufficient numbers of coal cars or by delaying their assignment to West Virginia mines. Railroad companies such as the Norfolk and Western threatened the existing market for steam coal by their ownership of huge tracts of coal lands where they could develop captive mines. Governor Glasscock's investigating commission headed by Bishop Donahue endorsed elements of this conspiracy theory in its 1912 report, and Judge Alston G. Dayton's elaboration of it in his opinion in the Hitchman case was referred to in the Senate hearings, as well as being widely publicized in newspaper reports and editorials.

For the UMWA, the settlement in West Virginia that formally recognized certain already established rights and a small advance in wages could be called a victory only in relative terms and in the context of its struggles elsewhere. Although it was the largest American union, and was regarded as one of the strongest, the UMWA could barely keep pace with the expansion in its dynamic and highly competitive industry and had been wracked by internal power struggles during the presidency of T.L. Lewis, who preceded John P. White. In 1912–13, the UMWA was emerging from an abject defeat in the long and bloody Irwin strike in western Pennsylvania that had exhausted the treasury and was looking forward to a bitter fight in the Colorado fields, where trouble had been smouldering for years. The Hatfield settlement in West Virginia allowed the miners to escape with peace and minimal gains while their national organization began recruiting its forces for the struggle in Colorado. With the cooperation of the new Democratic administration in Washington, the miners' union brought on a senatorial investigation to help redress the balance of power between labor and capital in West Virginia, just as the next year they invoked presidential intervention in Colorado.[134]

In March 1913, William E. Glasscock, governor during most of the strike, retired thankfully to the obscurity from which he had come. A mild man of good will, he had done his duty as he saw it, but in the crisis of the Paint Creek strike he could find no legal way out of the dilemma except the imposition of martial law, which he thought of originally as a weapon against hotheads. It was never his intention, he told the senate investigators, that the sentences of the military court should run their full terms, and he issued conditional pardons in all cases, though not until some of those convicted had served time in the penitentiary. He felt he was forced into the use of the courts-martial by the inadequacies of local officials. One of the reforms he proposed to his last legislature would have given the governor the right to remove magistrates, prosecutors, and sheriffs who did not carry out their duties properly. He also maintained that if an earlier legislature had created the state constabulary he had recommended, he could have policed the area and have prevented a crisis from developing.

Facing the same circumstances, Governor Henry D. Hatfield acted more boldly. Mother Jones noted the differences between the characters of the two governors: Glasscock was "a good, weak man," while Hatfield was "dictatorial and with the instincts of a brute."[135] Unbound by legalisms, he played the game both ways, going ahead with the court-martial but releasing prisoners almost immediately as part of a wide-ranging settlement. He issued pardons conditioned on good behavior to some of those convicted in the military trial and blandly denied to the Senate investigating committee that the trial verdicts were official proceedings that deserved to be recorded. By threats and cajolery, and aided by the negotiations of the UMWA with Pennsylvania capitalists, he was able to bring contending interests into line. The settlement of the Paint Creek strike in its simplest terms was the work of two men, Hatfield and John P. White of the UMWA, neither of whom was certain that he could pull his constituencies behind him. They found their solution not in legal proceedings but in a broadly stated agreement, tacit understandings, and ambiguities. Time, too, was on their side, for the continued sufferings by all parties made the way easier for them to gain approval for their proposals. By settling the strike, Henry D. Hatfield placed himself at center stage in West Virginia politics, where he remained for years, capping his career by serving six years as senator from West Virginia. Under Governor Hatfield and his successors, both Democratic and Republican, West Virginia remained a stronghold of antiunion operators, who in 1921 succeeded in breaking the power of the miners' union for more than a decade.

On the national political scene, in contrast, a new status for labor was beginning to take shape at the time of the Paint Creek strike. Progressive Republicans joined with the incoming Democratic majority to create a Department of Labor, and Woodrow Wilson appointed William B. Wilson, the former secretary of the UMWA, to head the new department. Never before had a president had an experienced labor leader in his official family. As the Democrats took over the offices of government, William B. Wilson organized the new Department of Labor and set up a national system of mediation in industrial disputes, although too late for any use in the strike in West Virginia. In the opening months of the Democratic administration, Senator John Worth Kern pursued vigorously his resolution to investigate conditions in the Paint Creek strike, bringing the federal government into the West Virginia labor dispute as a fact finder. Later in the year other committees investigated the conditions of mining labor in Michigan and Colorado, and the president sent in federal troops to replace the Colorado militia. The administration of Woodrow Wilson went on to pass the Clayton Act and other legislation desired by labor leaders. During World War I, the creation of the War Labor Board recognized the importance of labor in setting and carrying out national policies. The fact that some of these trends faltered or were reversed after the war should not obscure the fundamental changes in attitudes and laws, or the models they furnished for the labor policies of the New Deal.

For Mother Jones, the Paint Creek strike was only one more in the long series of battles she had fought for working people. Once again she had proved her skill at organizing and getting publicity for the petitions, speeches, and protest rallies that presented the miners' cause. She had come in to Paint Creek uninvited but determined to preserve the union presence south of the river. Singlehanded, she had brought out the miners on nonunion Cabin Creek to join their striking neighbors on Paint Creek. Most of all, she had converted a wage dispute into a crusade for the civil rights of the inhabitants of the coal camps. Her oratory and personality made her a major force in the strike. Locally she had roused and enheartened the miners, and elsewhere in the state and out she had presented their case to the public. Her imprisonment had made her a martyr for the cause and aroused national attention, promoting the passage of the senate resolution to investigate conditions in West Virginia. She had held to her principles and had stood mute before the court-martial, and in the end her captors had been forced to free her to continue her work as she saw fit. Her fellow socialists might denounce the Hatfield settlement as a sellout, but she had a different view. As she told the miners of Colorado in 1915: "[The miners of West Virginia] came to me and asked my advice and I said: 'Take what you can get out of the pirates.' The newspapermen asked: 'What do you think of the settlement?' and I told them it was alright, it wasn't what we wanted, but what we could get."[136]

In the Paint Creek and Cabin Creek strike, she proved to be

more a trade unionist than a socialist. In fact, her experiences in the strike in West Virginia confirmed her break with the Socialist party. Her expulsion from the party in 1911 probably cost her publicity in Socialist organs that had once followed her activities closely. The New York *Call,* one of the few Socialist dailies in the nation, managed to run many stories on the strike in West Virginia without mentioning her name but eventually began to recognize her prominent role in the struggle. One editorial comment implied that she had been a victim of party infighting, but without referring to her expulsion from the organization. *The Appeal to Reason,* the most widely read Socialist weekly, took the lead in organizing petitions for federal intervention to obtain her release from imprisonment at Pratt. It might be concluded that by the spring of 1913 she had recovered her Socialist respectability, if not her party credentials, for Socialist groups sponsored the speeches she gave in New York following her release from jail, and the *Call* treated her as a heroine of the movement. She was not so forgiving of some party leaders and privately complained that they had not come to her rescue when she was in prison. It was the Morris Hillquit-Victor Berger-Algie Simon faction that she blamed for not taking action while she was jailed. Then and later she remained on friendly terms with Eugene V. Debs and other well-known Socialists.[137]

After the settlement of the West Virginia strike and the Senate hearings, Mother Jones went to Michigan to lend her aid briefly to the copper miners who were on strike there. Then it was on to Colorado, where her passionate speeches and other activities on behalf of the coal miners once again led to imprisonment by the state militia. Whether in the field leading a strike or in Washington lobbying for their cause, she continued to fight for laboring people all over the country. As M.F. Matheny predicted in his speech in her defense at the court-martial, she became a mythic heroine for the descendants of the miners in West Virginia, and no one remembers Frank Smith's name.

Memories of the Paint Creek and Cabin Creek strike still linger in the minds of West Virginians. Even those not very knowledgeable continue to associate Paint Creek with a violent strike long ago. The legal maneuverings of the time have occasionally caught the attention of scholars, but the court-martial, officially unrecorded, has nearly passed into oblivion. It was unique to its time and place, and it seems unlikely that after eighty years of legal and social change the people or the courts of West Virginia would now accept a court-martial as a means of settling a labor dispute.

The issues raised by the court-martial remain: What protections of civil rights do constitutions provide for those caught up in the throes of industrial disputes? What, precisely, *is* martial law? When a governor proclaims it, what powers do he and his subordinates have to impose law and order? What is the role of the National Guard or of the regular army in maintaining the peace, whether in industrial disputes or urban riots? How do governors and presidents differ in their powers to use military organizations as police? To what extent are such executive actions reviewable by the courts? In the years since the court-martial of Mother Jones, legal scholars and presidential commissions have recognized the need to clarify these questions, but neither legislators nor judges have solved the problems. Perhaps, as in 1913, only confrontations can raise the issues to the level of resolution.

# Notes

*Note: The letters WVU following a citation indicate manuscript collections in the West Virginia and Regional History Collection at West Virginia University.*

1. U.S. Senate, *Conditions in the Paint Creek District, West Virginia* (Washington: G.P.O., 1913), hereinafter referred to as *Hearings*: affidavit of T.C. Townsend (408-9) and testimony of W.B. Reid (20-40); *Charleston Gazette,* 14 Feb. 1913; *Charleston Mail,* 17 Feb. 1913; *UMWA Journal,* 13 Feb. 1913.

2. Mary Harris Jones, *The Autobiography of Mother Jones* (Chicago: Charles H. Kerr, 1925), 162-63, hereinafter referred to as *Autobiography,* is essential to understand Mother Jones's life but is inaccurate; Dale Fetherling, *Mother Jones, the Miners' Angel: A Portrait* (Carbondale: Univ. of Illinois Press, 1974), is the best biography but omits important aspects of her life, such as her Socialist connections; Priscilla Long, *Mother Jones, Woman Organizer, And Her Relations with Miners' Wives, Working Women, and the Suffrage Movement* (Cambridge: Red Sun Press, 1976), explores the significance of gender in Mother Jones's career, as does Mari Boor Tonn, "The Rhetorical Personae of Mary Harris 'Mother' Jones: Industrial Labor's Maternal Prophet," Ph.D. diss., Univ. of Kansas, 1987; see also the introductions and notes in Edward M. Steel, ed., *The Correspondence of Mother Jones* (Pittsburgh: Univ. of Pittsburgh Press, 1985), hereinafter referred to as *Correspondence,* and idem, *The Speeches and Writings of Mother Jones* (Pittsburgh: Univ. of Pittsburgh Press, 1988), hereinafter referred to as *Speeches and Writings.*

3. *Hearings*: testimony of William E. Glasscock (361-407), testimony of Quinn Morton (928-79), testimony of M.T. Davis (1258-63).

4. W.E. Glasscock to George C. Baker, 25 Sept. 1912, William E. Glasscock Papers, WVU; Hearings: testimony of William E. Glasscock (361-407); for Glasscock's career generally, see Gary Jackson Tucker, "William E. Glasscock, Thirteenth Governor of West Virginia" (Ph.D. diss., West Virginia Univ., 1978).

5. *Hearings*: testimony of Quinn Morton (928-79); Fred Mooney, *Struggle in the Coal Fields: The Autobiography of Fred Mooney* (Morgantown: West Virginia Univ. Library, 1967), 25; James Morton Callahan, *History*

*of West Virginia Old and New* (Chicago: American Historical Society, 1923), 3:497.

6. *Hearings*: testimony of Charles A. Cabell (1443-63); in the marshal's returns of the 1910 Census, the Cabell household consisted of C.A. Cabell, age thirty-nine, his wife, his three daughters, aged five to eleven, the daughters' governess, and two black servants, Friday and India Williams; Callahan, *History of West Virginia Old and New* 3: 589-90.

7. *Hearings*: testimony of Charles A. Cabell (1443-63); *Autobiography*, 148-49, 152-56; Mooney, *Struggle in the Coal Fields,* 15, 27-28; *Cincinnati Post,* 9 April 1912; *UMWA Journal,* 10 Aug., 5, 12, and 26 Sept. 1912.

8. *Hearings*: testimony of Charles A. Cabell (1443-63), testimony of J.E. Staton (1565-76); *Autobiography,* 152-60.

9. *Hearings*: testimony of Samuel B. Avis (318-52), testimony of Frank C. Burdette (409-17), testimony of William E. Glasscock (361-407), testimony of George S. Wallace (238-68). Burdette's difficulties with a recalcitrant grand jury continued, for the Oct. panel refused to indict a striking miner, Ray Morse, who witnesses said had assaulted a man named Bobbitt.

10. *Hearings*: testimony of William E. Glasscock (361-407); testimony of Samuel B. Avis (328-52); testimony of Frank C. Burdette (409-18). For the role of the National Guard in the strike, see Kenneth R. Bailey, *Mountaineers Are Free: A History of the West Virginia National Guard* (St. Albans, W.V.: Harless Printing, 1978), 103-16; for the National Guard generally, see John K. Mahon, *History of the Militia and the National Guard* (New York: Macmillan, 1983).

11. *Nance and Mays v. Brown,* 71 W. Va. 519.

12. *Hearings:* testimony of William E. Glasscock (361-407); testimony of Quinn Morton (928-79); testimony of M.T. Davis (1258-63).

13. Otis K. Rice and Stephen W. Brown, *West Virginia: A History.* (Lexington: Univ. Press of Kentucky, 1993), 214-15, 224-47; John Alexander Williams, *West Virginia and the Captains of Industry* (Morgantown: West Virginia Univ. Library, 1976) 246-47; Frederick Allan Barkey, "The Socialist Party in West Virginia from 1898 to 1920: A Study in Working Class Radicalism," Ph.D. diss., Univ. of Pittsburgh, 1971, has the most complete account and analysis of the campaign (117-26).

14. *Fayette Tribune,* 14 Sept. 1912; see also *Baltimore Evening Sun,* 8 Sept. 1912. Strictly speaking, Cairnes was correct; she was on the payroll of the international union, not that of District 17.

15. *Speeches and Writings,* 246.

16. See *Autobiography,* 152-53; *Hearings*: testimony of Paul J. Paulsen (896-97). As late as June 1913, Paulsen, a member of the International Executive Board of the UMWA, denied knowing whether Mother Jones was an organizer for the union.

17. *Parkersburg News-Dispatch,* 11 Sept. 1912; *Wheeling Register,* 2 Nov. 1912; *Huntington Advertiser,* 4 and 5 Nov. 1912.

18. *Hearings:* testimony of George Williams (1825-40).

19. *Kanawha Citizen,* 15 Nov. 1912; *Wheeling Register,* 15 and 16 Nov. 1912; *Bluefield Telegraph,* 16 Nov. 1912.

20. *Pittsburgh Leader,* 25 Feb. 1913; *Hearings:* testimony of C.R. Shaw (802-3).

21. *Hearings:* testimony of George Williams (1825-40).

22. *Hearings:* testimony of L. L. Scherer (1745-59).

23. *Hearings:* testimony of D.W. Shipley (1776-1804); testimony of G.C. Cowherd (898-905).

24. P.J. Donahue, *Report of West Virginia Mining Investigation Commission* (Charleston, W.V.; n.p., 1912).

25. *Hearings:* testimony of J.E. Staton (1565-76). Staton was assistant manager of the Halley-Stephenson Coal Company at Eskdale.

26. *Charleston Gazette,* 17, 26 Nov., 1912; *Hearings:* testimony of William E. Glasscock (361-407); testimony of Charles Cabell (1443-63).

27. William E. Glasscock to M.H. Brown, 14 Nov. 1912; see also Glasscock to Henry D. Hatfield, 29 Nov. 1912, William E. Glasscock Papers, WVU.

28. *West Virginia Journal and Bills of the Senate, 1913, passim.* It took the Senate three weeks and 111 ballots to choose a president; they then spent another three weeks in joint session with the House before electing Nathan B. Goff, a conservative Republican, United States Senator.

29. Statement of J.C. Anderson, Coal Strikes. Records, 1912-14, WVU.

30. *Hearings:* testimony of Quinn Morton (928-79); *Charleston Gazette,* 8, 9 Feb. 1913; *Charleston Daily Mail,* 8, 10 Feb. 1913.

31. *Charleston Daily Mail,* 11 Feb. 1913.

32. *Charleston Gazette,* 8, 9 Feb. 1913; *Charleston Daily Mail,* 8, 10, 11 Feb. 1913; *Hearings:* testimony of William E. Glasscock (361-407). On the following Friday the legislature passed a concurrent resolution pledging its support for "the use of all necessary means to restore order and to command respect for the law in those districts." In this, as in hardly any other matters, the legislators thought as one.

33. *Charleston Gazette,* 12 Feb. 1913. The *Gazette* reported sixteen killed and an unknown number wounded, but these figures proved to be exaggerated.

34. *Hearings:* testimony of James Claggett (1176-79); testimony of C.C. Woods (1179-81); *Pittsburgh Leader,* 2 Mar., 1913. Both the *Charleston Gazette* , 13 Feb. 1913, and the *Daily Mail,* 13 Feb. 1913, represented her remarks at the Smithers meeting as inflammatory.

35. *UMWA Journal,* 20 Feb. 1913; *Kanawha Citizen,* 14 Feb. 1913; *Charleston Gazette,* 13, 14 Feb. 1913.

36. *Pittsburgh Leader,* 2 Mar. 1913; *Charleston Gazette,* 13, 14 Feb. 1913; *Charleston Mail,* 11, 12, 13, 17 Feb. 1913; *Kanawha Citizen,* 10, 11, 12, 15 Feb. 1913;

*New York Call,* 15 Feb. 1913. Mother Jones denied statements attributed to her by the *Citizen,* and officials of District 17 insisted that contrary to the *Gazette* headline: "Governor's Life is Threatened," the meeting at Smithers had been an attempt to get the men, who had come out in sympathy with their comrades across the river, to go back to work.

37. *UMWA Journal,* 20 Mar. 1913; *Pittsburgh Leader,* 18, 19 Feb. 1913; *New York Call,* 13 Mar. 1913. To alleviate the crowded conditions, more than sixty men were later transferred to two vacant houses in Mucklow.

38. Mother Jones to Terence V. Powderly, 3 Mar. 1913, *Correspondence;* Fetherling, *Mother Jones, the Miners' Angel,* 38-39, 41-42, 120, 147-48. Charles Connor, "Roving the Valley," *Charleston Daily Mail,* 1 Feb. 1953; Dallas Stotts, Oral History Reel No. 149, WVU; Post Office Department investigation reports, RG 174 16/228, National Archives; *Pittsburgh Leader,* 18, 19 Feb. 1913; *Kanawha Citizen,* 9 Mar. 1913; Cora Older, "Answering a Question," *Collier's,* 19 Apr. 1913; *UMWA Journal,* 20, 27 Feb., 20 Mar. 1913. Captain R.E. Sherwood of the Guard said that he had never opened her mail, although authorized to do so, and Mother Jones accepted his word; she thought that the postmistress diverted her mail into the hands of the coal operators before delivering it to the Guard officers.

39. Dallas Stotts, Oral History Reel No. 149, WVU.

40. RG 174 16/013, National Archives. Typical would be Congressman William Kent to W.B. Wilson, 28 Apr. 1913, enclosing a letter of protest by Florence Kelly, Secretary of the National Consumers League, and Wilson's reply to Kent, 1 May 1913.

41. T.J. Lewellyn to William B. Wilson, ibid.

42. William B. Wilson to the postmaster general, 9 May 1913, RG 174 16/228, National Archives. The entire file 16/228 is devoted to the investigation.

43. *Autobiography,* 164; Mother Jones to Caroline Lloyd, 17 Mar. 1913, *Correspondence,* 109; *Charleston Daily Mail,* 1 Feb. 1953.

44. *Speeches and Writings,* 135-36; *Pittsburgh Leader,* 18, 19 Feb. 1913.

45. A typed copy of the decision is on file at the Supreme Court Library, Charleston, West Virginia.

46. Court-martial of S.F. Nance, George S. Wallace Papers, WVU. Two eyewitnesses who testified before the Senate subcomittee confirmed the general account of the incident related in Nance's court-martial, and one told of a very similar incident, only in this case Mother Jones did not intervene until the strikers had threatened the man's life. He was kneeling on the railroad tracks with a pistol at his head when she told the men they had gone far enough. Her phraseology and her presence on two occasions when scabs were beaten suggest that she approved of the violent tactics, if she did not actually instigate them.

*Hearings*: testimony of D.W. Shipley (1776-1804); testimony of G.C. Cowherd (898-905).

47. George S. Wallace to P.J. Donahue, 23 Dec. 1912, George S. Wallace Papers.

48. *Kanawha Citizen,* 20, 21, 22, 24 December 1912; see also *Nance and Mays v. Brown,* 71 W. Va. 519. The prisoners gained their freedom before the final written decision appeared.

49. *New York Call,* 8 Mar. 1913.

50. See brief of Albert M. Belcher and Harold W. Houston, *Supreme Court Record and Briefs,* vol. 71-F (1912–13). These volumes in the West Virginia Law Library contain the printed briefs, bound together, of attorneys appearing before the Supreme Court.

51. Ibid. Wallace was assisted by J.O. Henson, an assistant attorney general. Two law firms representing coal mine operators filed briefs as amici curiae supporting the position of the state.

52. 71 W. Va. 567. See also *Charleston Gazette,* 8 Mar. 1913; *Kanawha Citizen,* 7, 8 Mar. 1913.

53. 71 W. Va. 567. Although he based his dissent primarily on the state constitution, Robinson quoted at length from *Ex parte Milligan* (4 Wall. 120) and rejected the majority interpretation of that case, as well as the relevance of many of the other cases cited.

54. George S. Wallace to George N. Biggs, 20 Mar. 1913; Wallace to E.W. Van C. Lucas, 20 Mar. 1913; Wallace to W.A. Bethel, 21 Mar. 1913, George S. Wallace Papers, WVU; see also, *Wheeling Majority,* 6, 13 Mar. 1913.

55. *Kanawha Citizen,* 8 Mar. 1913.

56. *Charleston Daily Mail,* 20 Mar. 1913; *Charleston Gazette,* 21 Mar. 1913; *New York Call,* 20 Mar. 1913.

57. *Charleston Gazette,* 23 Mar. 1913.

58. John W. Brown to Eva Brown, 9 Mar. 1913, RG 174 16/013, National Archives, explained to his wife that, by denying the jurisdiction of the court, they could put up no defense, but this was a tactical maneuver they thought time would justify.

59. Typed summary of interviews with witnesses, George S. Wallace Papers, WVU.

60. *Kanawha Citizen,* 8 Mar. 1913; *Hearings*: testimony of George S. Wallace (1443-63).

61. *Charleston Daily Mail,* 12 Mar. 1913.

62. *Kanawha Citizen,* 8 Mar. 1913.

63. *Hearings*: testimony of A.A. Lilly (261-63). Belcher and Houston were present at the senate hearings and joined with Lilly to reconstruct the confrontation. The *Kanawha Citizen,* 6-13 Mar. 1913, supplied many details in its close coverage of the case.

64. *Charleston Gazette,* 13 Mar. 1913.

65. George S. Wallace to W.A. Bethel, 21 Mar. 1913, George S. Wallace Papers, WVU.

66. *Hearings*: testimony of William B. Reid (20-40).

67. *Kanawha Citizen*, 9 Mar. 1913.

68. Cora Older, "Answering a Question," *Collier's*, 19 Apr. 1913, and idem, "The Last Day of the Paint Creek Court Martial," *Independent*, 15 May 1913, 1085-88.

69. *New York Call*, 13 Mar. 1913. The newspaper story has no byline, and it is not clear whether the *Call* dispatched a reporter to the scene or depended on a local correspondent. Earlier, the *Call* asserted (18 Feb. 1913) that the news had been rigidly censored and that details "are not allowed to reach the outside world."

70. As quoted in the *New York Call*, 25 Mar. 1913. Marlin Pew, later for many years editor of *Editor and Publisher*, had first met Mother Jones when he was reporting on the anthracite strike of 1900, and they had kept in touch thereafter.

71. *New York Call*, 20 Feb. 1913; *UMWA Journal*, 27 Feb. 1913.

72. *Wheeling Majority*, 20 Feb. 1913; the Gazette called Mother Jones "the Bloody Mary of the UMWA," 11 Feb. 1913.

73. Statement of Samuel B. Montgomery, George S. Wallace Papers, WVU.

74. Coal Strikes. Records. 1912-14, WVU; see also, Edward W. Knight to George S. Wallace, 7 Dec. 1912, George S. Wallace Papers, WVU.

75. *Kanawha Citizen*, 24 Apr. 1913. General Elliott had political ambitions, but in 1916 he failed in his bid for a congressional seat.

76. Interview of Martha and Joe Jolliffe by E.M. Steel, 10 Apr. 1988; West Virginia *Blue Book*, 1916, 1917, 1918; *Hearings*: testimony of Quinn Morton (928-79). Antebellum politicians electioneered for both military and civil offices at the scheduled musters of the militia, and the tradition continued in West Virginia after the Civil War when the National Guard was created. See Clement Eaton, *A History of the Old South* (New York: Macmillan, 1966), 58.

77. Statement of Judge William R. Bennett, 4 Aug. 1912, West Virginia Mining Investigation Committee Papers, 1912-13, WVU.

78. Dallas Stotts, Oral History Reel No. 149, WVU; Interview of George Baker by E.M. Steel, 26 Dec. 1969; *Autobiography*, 152.

79. Coal Strikes. Records, 1912-14, WVU, case notes passim.

80. *Charleston Daily Mail*, 11 Feb. 1913.

81. Daniel W. Cunningham to Thomas and Davis, 18 Feb. 1913, Coal Strikes. Records, 1912–14, WVU.

82. Note added to affidavit of C.C. Wood, 15 Feb. 1913, Coal Strikes. Records, 1912-14, WVU.

83. *Labor Argus*, 27 Feb. 1913. Since no continuous file of the *Argus* is known to exist, the transcript is the only source for most of these newspaper

items, and the items are quoted liberally. The dates in parentheses
are those ascribed in the transcript.

84. *Speeches and Writings,* 89-90.

85. *Speeches and Writings,* 88-105; *Charleston Gazette,* 16 Aug. 1912; *UMWA
Journal,* 22 Aug. 1912.

86. *Speeches and Writings,* 106-18; *UMWA Journal,* 26 Sept. 1912.

87. Cora Older reported that Frank Smith's behavior in the courtroom was
brash and officious.

88. *Charleston Daily Mail,* 20 Mar., 2 Apr. 1913; *Charleston Gazette,* 21, 22 Mar.
1913; *Wheeling Majority,* 22 May 1913.

89. *Charleston Gazette,* 23 Mar. 1913; *Kanawha Citizen,* 13, 14 Mar. 1913;
*New York Call,* 14 Mar. 1913.

90. *Charleston Gazette,* 22 Mar. 1913; *Charleston Daily Mail,* 18, 19, 20 Mar., 2,
7 Apr. 1913; *Kanawha Citizen,* 20, 22, 23 Mar. 1913; *New York Call,*
20 Mar. 1913.

91. John W. Brown to Eugene V. Debs, 21 June 1913, Papers of Eugene V. Debs,
Indiana State Univ.

92. Coal Strikes. Records, 1912-14, WVU; *Kanawha Citizen,* 22, 23, 24, 25
Mar. 1913; *New York Call,* 24 Mar. 1913.

93. Press release of remarks by Senator Henry D. Hatfield on an NBC radio
network program, 1 May 1932, Henry D. Hatfield Papers, WVU.

94. *Kanawha Citizen,* 22 Apr. 1913. Dwyer was released from the Raleigh
County jail on 21 Apr. without having been tried.

95. *Kanawha Citizen,* 13, 14 Mar. 1913; *Charleston Daily Mail,* 28, 29 Mar., 1913;
*Charleston Gazette,* 1 Apr. 1913.

96. Press release of remarks by Henry D. Hatfield on NBC radio network, 1 May
1932; see also Henry D. Hatfield to William Binkley, 23 June 1952,
Henry D. Hatfield Papers, WVU; *New York Call,* 13 Mar. 1913.

97. Lucy Boswell Montague to William B. Wilson, 28 Apr. 1913, RG 174 16/013,
including excerpts from a letter from her brother, Charles H.
Boswell, who said that Hatfield had been making deals with some
of the prisoners. "Brown, Parsons and I are never taken into these
conferences or approached by the Governors messengers."

98. *Charleston Daily Mail,* 18, 19, 20 Mar., 2, 7 Apr. 1913; *Kanawha Citizen,* 20,
22, 23, Mar. 1913.

99. *Kanawha Citizen,* 22, 23, 24, 25 Mar. 1913.

100. *Charleston Daily Mail,* 28, 29 Mar., 2 Apr. 1913; *Charleston Gazette,* 1 Apr.
1913.

101. *Charleston Daily Mail,* 15, 16, 17, 21, 22, 28, 29 Apr. 1913; *Charleston Gazette,*
15, 17, 20, 23, 26, 27, 28 Apr. 1913. Omitted in the governor's
proposals were any references either to the right to organize or to the
use of company guards. The District 17 convention accepted them
with the understanding that the right to organize was implicitly

recognized, and after the men had gone back to work the governor issued a statement condemning the previous practices of company guards and promising to work with the legislature to reform the system.

102. *Charleston Gazette*, 1, 10 May 1913. For a more extended view of these incidents, see David Corbin, *Socialist and Labor Star*, (Huntington, W.V., 1971), passim; Frederick Allan Barkey, "The Socialist Party in West Virginia from 1898 to 1920: A Study in Working Class Radicalism," Ph.D. diss., Univ. of Pittsburgh, 1971, 139-43; and Leslie H. Marcy, "Hatfield's Challenge to the Socialist Party," *International Socialist Review* 13, no. 12 (June 1913): 881-87.

103. *Charleston Gazette*, 8, 9 May 1913; *Charleston Daily Mail*, 8 May 1913.

104. *Congressional Record*, 63rd Cong., 1st sess., 1913, 50, pt. 2:1403; see also *Kanawha Citizen*, 13 Apr. 1913. In a speech to the UMWA, Kern recounted some of the legislative history of the resolution and details about the congressional debate. John W. Kern, *Address of United States Senator John W. Kern to the Twenty-fourth Consecutive and First Biennial Convention of the United Mine Workers of America*, (Indianapolis: n.p., 1914).

105. *New York Times*, 19, 28 May, 1, 12 June, 1913; *New York Call*, 26, 27, 28 May 1913; *Hearings*: testimony of Charles Cabell (1443-63); David Alan Corbin, *Life, Work, and Rebellion in the Coal Fields: The Southern West Virginia Miners, 1880-1922* (Urbana: Univ. of Illinois Press, 1981), 99; Maier Bryan Fox, *United We Stand: The United Mine Workers of America, 1890–1990.* (Washington: United Mine Workers of America, 1990), 147-52.

106. *Raleigh Register*, 5 June 1913; *Hearings*: testimony of Quinn Morton (928-79).

107. *Kanawha Citizen*, 13 Apr. 1913. Letters to and from Eugene V. Debs during June support the conclusion that White and Hatfield had a number of understandings that White did not share with the Socialists, but the letters throw more light on internal dissension in the Socialist party than they do on the settlement of the strike. See the microfilm edition by J. Robert Constantine, *The Papers of Eugene V. Debs,* June 1913, passim.

108. Priscilla Long, *Where the Sun Never Shines: A History of America's Bloody Coal Industry* (New York: Paragon, 1989), emphasizes the crucial nature of the union's struggle in Colorado in 1913–14 and has the most complete account of Mother Jones's role there. See also George Stanley McGovern and Leonard F. Guttridge, *The Great Coalfield War* (Boston: Houghton, Mifflin, 1972).

109. *Kanawha Citizen*, 8 Mar. 1913.

110. "Has West Virginia a Republican Form of Government?" *The Bar* (June-

July 1913): 18-21; see also "A Nice Constitutional Question," *The Bar* (March 1913): 7-8.

111. West Virginia Bar Association, *Proceedings,* 1913, 16-40. The quoted words can be found on pp. 37 and 38. The Democratic senator from West Virginia, W.E. Chilton, gave Mathews's remarks wider circulation by having them printed as a Senate document. *Senate Documents* 63rd Cong., 1st sess., 22, no. 230.

112. West Virginia Bar Association, *Proceedings,* 1913, 58-85. Jacobs's words are on page 60; Belcher's, page 83. At the 1914 meeting the committee recommended no action. *Proceedings,* 1914, p. 110.

113. RG 174 16/228, National Archives.

114. George S. Wallace to Henry D. Hatfield, 26 Apr. 1913; see also, Wallace to W.A. Bethel, 21 Mar. 1913; Wallace to A.A. Lilly, 9 Apr. 1913; Lilly to Wallace, 2 Apr. 1913, George S. Wallace Papers, WVU; *Journal of the Supreme Court of the U.S.,* Oct. 1912, p. 121, (entry for 3 Feb. 1913), copy courtesy the Library of the Supreme Court.

115. 73 W. Va. 759.

116. A.A. Lilly to George S. Wallace, 27 Oct. 1913; George S. Wallace to J.O. Henson, 27 Oct. 1913; William E. Glasscock to George S. Wallace, 6 Nov. 1914; John C. Bond to George S. Wallace, 5 Jan. 1915, George S. Wallace Papers, WVU.

117. H.C. Carbaugh, "Martial Law," *Illinois Law Review* 7 (March 1913): 479-95; Henry Winthrop Ballantine, "Military Dictatorship in California and West Virginia," *California Law Review* 1 (July 1913): 413-26.

118. Henry Winthrop Ballantine, "Unconstitutional Claims of Military Authority," *Yale Law Journal* 24 (Jan. 1915): 188-216.

119. George S. Wallace, "The Need, the Propriety and Basis of Martial Law, with a Review of the Authorities," *Journal of the American Institute of Criminal Law and Criminology* 8, no. 2 (1917): 167-89, and no. 3 (1917): 406-19.

120. Charles Fairman, "Martial Rule and the Suppression of Insurrection," *Illinois Law Review* 23 (Apr. 1929): 766-88.

121. Ibid.

122. Charles Fairman, *The Law of Martial Rule* (Chicago: Callaghan, 1930), 67-68, 75-76, 103-5.

123. Robert S. Rankin, *When Civil Law Fails: Martial Law and Its Legal Basis in the United States.* (Durham: Duke Univ. Press, 1939); Morris Shepp Isseks, "The Executive and His Use of the Militia," *Oregon Law Review* 16 (June 1937): 301-39; see also an unattributed commentary, "Use of Military Force in Domestic Disturbances," *Yale Law Journal* 45 (Mar. 1936): 879-95.

124. Harold L. Kaplan, "Constitutional Limitations on Trials by Military Commission," *University of Pennsylvania Law Review,* 92 (Dec. 1943):

119-49, 272-94; Gordon D. Henderson, "Courts-Martial and the Constitution: The Original Understanding," *Harvard Law Review* 71 (Nov. 1957): 293-324; Frederick Bernays Wiener, "Courts-Martial and the Bill of Rights: The Original Practice," *Harvard Law Review* 72 (Nov. 1958): 1-49; 72(Dec. 1958): 266-304. Henderson and Wiener differed fundamentally on whether the founding fathers intended the Bill of Rights to apply to military trials.

125. David E. Engdahl, "Soldiers, Riots and Revolution: the Law and History of Military Troops in Civil Disorders," *Iowa Law Review* 57, pt. 1 (1971): 1-73; David E. Engdahl, Anthony F. Renzo, and Luize Z. Laitos, "A Comprehensive Study of the Use of Military Troops in Civil Disorders with Proposals for Legislative Reform," *University of Colorado Law Review* 43 (*June 1972*): 399-447; James E. Roark, "Constitutional Law–Martial Law–Preserving Order in the State: A Traditional Reappraisal," *West Virginia Law Review* 75 (Dec. 1972): 143-65; see also Ruthanne Gartland and Richard Chilcota, "When Will the Troops Come Marching In. . . .," *Journal of Urban Law* 45 (Spring-Summer 1968): 881-901, and Frederick Bernays Wiener, "Martial Law Today," *American Bar Association Journal* 55 (Aug. 1969): 723-30.

126. For the role of black miners in the strike, see Ronald L. Lewis, "The Black Presence in the Paint-Cabin Creek Strike," *West Virginia History* 46 (1985–86): 59-71. Black miners have been widely studied since the pioneering work of James T. Laing, "The Negro Miner in West Virginia," (Ph.D. diss., Ohio State Univ., 1933), and recently in southern West Virginia by Joe William Trotter, Jr., in *Coal, Class, and Color: Blacks in Southern West Virginia, 1915–1932* (Urbana: Univ. of Illinois Press, 1990); although Trotter's work focuses on a later period, the analysis of racial and ethnic divisions in West Virginia in his first chapter is useful. Generally, see Ronald L. Lewis, *Black Coal Miners in America: Race, Class, and Community Conflict, 1780–1980* (Lexington: Univ. Press of Kentucky, 1987), 121-64; see also Paul Nyden, *Black Coal Miners in the United States* (New York: American Institute for Marxist Studies, 1974.)

127. Frederick A. Barkey, "Immigration and Ethnicity in West Virginia: A Review of the Literature," in *West Virginia History: Critical Essays on the Literature,* ed. Ronald L. Lewis and John C. Hennen, Jr. (Dubuque, Iowa: Kendall/Hunt, 1993), lists the small but growing body of work on ethnic subjects.

128. *Kanawha Citizen,* 24 Apr. 1913.

129. U.S. Bureau of the Census, Marshal's Returns for Kanawha County, 1910, microfilm. Names are not reliable guides to nationality, of course; Joe Prince, one of the defendants, was identified in the trial as Italian.

130. List of defendants, with their residences, ages, and dependents, George

S. Wallace Papers, WVU. Insofar as the limited biographical data allow them to be classified, all the members of the court-martial and the civilian lawyers seem to have been, in popular jargon, male WASPS.

131. 245 U.S. 283; for Judge Dayton's original opinion, see 202 Fed 512, especially pp. 533-52. Justice Louis D. Brandeis, in a dissenting opinion in which he was joined by Justices Holmes and Clarke, took Judge Dayton to task for admitting the testimony of conspiracy against West Virginia coal interests, which was not germane to the points at issue. For the continuing influence of the case, see William E. Forbath, *Law and the Shaping of the American Labor Movement* (Cambridge: Harvard Univ. Press, 1991), 115-17, 123, 162.

132. Index, Federal Courthouse, Charleston, West Virginia. The case papers are in the judicial records stored at the Philadelphia branch of the National Archives; see also, Edward M. Steel, "Mother Jones in the Fairmont Field, 1902," *Journal of American History* 57, no. 2 (Sept. 1970): 290-307.

133. George S. Wallace to George N. Biggs, 20 Mar. 1913; George S. Wallace to E.W. Van C. Lucas, 10 Mar. 1913, George S. Wallace Papers, WVU. The judge advocate expected the Mother Jones habeas corpus case to be appealed to the United States Supreme Court in April, according to these two letters. The general trends in labor litigation have been observed by numerous scholars and discussed at length recently by Christopher L. Tomlins, *Labor Relations, Law, and the Organized Labor Movement in America, 1880–1960* (Cambridge: Cambridge Univ. Press, 1985), as well as Forbath, op. cit. For a view of judicial attitudes as revealed in a contemporaneous case, see Barry F. Helfand, "Labor and the Courts: The Common-Law Doctrine of Criminal Conspiracy and Its Application in the Buck's Stove Case," *Labor History* 18, no. 1 (Winter 1977): 91-114.

134. Long, *Where the Sun Never Shines;* McGovern and Guttridge, *Great Coalfield War,* see also, Manfred Franz Boemeke, "The Wilson Administration, Organized Labor, and the Colorado Coal Strike, 1913–1914," Ph.D. diss., Princeton Univ., 1983, especially chapters 3 and 4.

135. *Autobiography,* 170; *New York Call,* 27 May 1913.

136. *Speeches and Writings,* 153.

137. See *New York Call,* coverage of the strike, passim; Mother Jones to Caroline Lloyd, 4, 27 Apr. 1913; Mother Jones to Maude Walker, 27 Apr. 1913, *Correspondence, 109-113.*

# TRANSCRIPT
# OF THE
# COURT-MARTIAL

In the following pages, the comments of the court, the questions of the attorneys, and the replies of witnesses appear verbatim as recorded by the court reporter. He occasionally failed to name the lawyer who questioned a witness and no attempt has been made to supply speculative identifications. The editor has pruned many superfluous words and phrases from the continuity supplied by the reporter.

The printed evidence that was submitted is too voluminous for inclusion with the transcript, but much of it is available from other sources. The Donahue Commission report circulated widely as a printed state governmental document and the speeches of Mother Jones that the prosecutor placed in evidence have appeared in several collections, most recently in *Speeches and Writings,* 56-118. Since no full file of the *Labor Argus* exists, a substantial number of the articles chosen from it by the prosecution for evidence remain in the transcript, supplemented by quotations in the introduction from another fifty pages that were read into the record.

## PROCEEDINGS OF A MILITARY COMMISSION, CONVENED AT PRATT, WEST VIRGINIA, ON FRIDAY, MARCH 7th, 1913, at ten o'clock a.m.

The Commission proceeded to the trial of W.H. Adkins, alias Bunk Adkins, G.F. Parsons, John W. Brown, A.D. Lavender, Charles Wright, Charles Gillispie, Ernest Creigo, John Jones, E.B. Vickers, Bert Nutter, Grady Everett, William Brandridge, Carl Morgan, Charles Batley, C.H. Boswell, Charles Lanham, Paul Paulsen, Mary Jones, Robert Parrish, Sanford Kirk, Jim Pike, W.H. Patrick, Clyde E. Bowe, John Seachrist, W. Lawrence Perry, Ernest O'Dell, John O'Dell, Joe Prince, Harrison Ellis, John Siketo, Steve Yager, Charles Kenney, Frazier Jarrett, J.D. Zeller, alias Dutch Zeller, George W. McCoy, Leonard Clark, G.W. Lavender, Tip Belcher, Tom Miskel, Emory J. Sowards, William Price, Boyd Holley, alias Boyd Adkins, H.V. Craise, Cleve Vickers, Ed. Gray, W.H.H. Huffman, Oscar Petry, Cal J. Newman, and Will Perdue, who having been brought before the Commission, the Judge Advocate asked the defendants if they desired counsel.

Thereupon the defendants Mary Jones, C.H. Boswell, Charles Batley, John W. Brown, and G.F. Parsons, replied as follows:

John W. Brown: I notice you have taken the position, General Wallace, that the accused are to plead not guilty, do I understand that?

The Judge Advocate: That is the plea that will be entered.

John W. Brown: Now before making a plea in this matter, I would like to understand my status in the case. I am not represented here by any attorney. I understand that the Governor's declaration of martial law suspends the State and National constitutions. Am I correct?

The Judge Advocate: Go ahead with your statement.

John W. Brown: If I as a citizen of this Republic and of this State have no rights under the organic law of the State and the Union, if these are taken from me, I am reduced to the state of a subject and not a citizen, and I as one of the accused refuse to plead one way or the other.

The Judge Advocate: We will enter a plea of not guilty for you at the proper time.

C.H. Boswell: I wish to state that I have no defence to make. I am not going to enter a plea at all in this court.

The Judge Advocate: We understand that and we will enter a plea of not guilty for you at the proper time.

Mary Jones: Will you permit me to make a statement, General Wallace?

The Judge Advocate: Proceed, Mother.

Mary Jones: I have no defence to make. Whatever I have done in West Virginia, I have done it all over the United States, and when I get out, I will do it again.

The Judge Advocate: We will enter a plea of not guilty for you.

Charles Batley: I wish to make the statement that while I have got all the respect in the world for this Court that I can have, yet I have no defence to make.

The Judge Advocate: We will enter a plea of not guilty for you, Mr. Batley.

G.F. Parsons: General Wallace, I wish to make a statement in this regard. I make this statement for the whole bunch.

The Judge Advocate: You are then speaking on behalf of all the other defendants?

G.F. Parsons: Yes, I wish to make the statement that we refuse to make any defence whatever; this is for the whole bunch.

The Judge Advocate: For everybody?

G.F. Parsons: Yes, sir.

The Judge Advocate: We will enter a plea of not guilty for you.

Thereupon the other defendants [named] stated that they desired counsel and introduced M.F. Matheney, Esq., and Captain Carskadon and Captain Morgan, as counsel.

Austin M. Sikes and R.S. Douthat were duly and severally sworn as reporters.

The order convening the Commission and the order modifying the detail, was read to the accused, and they were asked if they objected to being tried by any member present named therein; to which they replied in the negative.

The members of the Commission and the Judge Advocate were then duly sworn.

The accused were then arraigned upon the following charges and specifications:

Charge 1: Conspiracy under the "Red Men's Act." Violation of Section 9, of Chapter 148 of the Code:

Specification 1: In this, that the said [named defendants], together with two or more persons whose names are unknown, did feloniously and unlawfully combine and conspire together for the purpose of inflicting punishment and bodily injury upon one, Fred Bobbitt, Thomas Nesbitt, and W.R. Vance, and that the said [named defendants], in pursuance of said combination and conspiracy did inflict bodily injury upon one, Thomas

Nesbitt, by then and there feloniously and unlawfully shooting the said Thomas Nesbitt, with intent to maim, disfigure, disable and kill.

This at or near Mucklow, Kanawha County, West Virginia, within the military district covered by the Governor's proclamation of February 10th, 1913, on or about the 10th day of February, 1913.

Charge 2: Murder.

Specification 1: In this, that the said [named defendants], feloniously, wilfully, maliciously, deliberately and unlawfully did slay, kill and murder one, Fred Bobbitt and W.R. Vance.

This at or near Mucklow, Kanawha County, West Virginia, within the military district covered by the Governor's proclamation of martial law of February 10th, 1913, on or about the 10th day of February, 1913.

Charge 3: Conspiracy under the "Red Men's Act." Violation of Section 9, of Chapter 148 of the Code.

Specification 1: In this, that the said [named defendants], together with two or more persons, whose names are unknown, did feloniously and unlawfully combine and conspire together, for the purpose of destroying, injuring and taking away personal property, not their own, in this to take away a certain machine gun, belonging to the Paint Creek Collieries Company, and in pursuance of said combination and conspiracy did inflict bodily injury upon one, Thomas Nesbitt, by then and there feloniously and unlawfully shooting the said Thomas Nesbitt, with intent to maim, disfigure, disable and kill.

This at or near Mucklow, Kanawha County, West Virginia, within the military district covered by the Governor's proclamation of February 10th, 1913, on or about the 10th day of February, 1913.

Charge 4: Conspiracy, under the "Red Men's Act." Violation of Section 9, of Chapter 148 of the Code.

Specification 1: In this that the said [named defendants] did feloniously and unlawfully combine and conspire together for the purpose of inflicting bodily injury upon one R.L. Taylor and John Crockett, and in pursuance of said conspiracy did then and there feloniously and unlawfully shoot the said R.L. Taylor and John Crockett, with intent to maim, disfigure, disable and kill.

This at or near Ronda, Kanawha County, West Virginia, within the military district covered by the Governor's proclamation of February 10, 1913, on or about the 10th day of February, 1913.

Charge 5: Accessories after the fact.

Specification 1: In this, that the [named defendants], then and there well knowing that a felony had been committed, at or near Mucklow, West Virginia, in this, that a number of persons, had then and there feloniously, wilfully, maliciously, deliberately and unlawfully killed and murdered one Fred Bobbitt at or near Mucklow, Kanawha County, West

Virginia, within the military district covered by the Governor's proclamation of February 10th, 1913, did then and there feloniously and unlawfully aid, abet, and assist the principal felons to escape.

This at or near Mucklow, West Virginia, within the military district covered by the Governor's proclamation of February 10th, 1913, on or about the 10th day of February, 1913.

Charge 6: Carrying weapons, in violation of Section 7, of Chapter 148 of the Code:

Specification 1: In this, that the said Ernest Creigo, did unlawfully, without then and there having a state license therefor, carry about his person a revolver.

This at or near Ronda, Kanawha County, West Virginia, within the military district covered by the Governor's proclamation of February 10th, 1913, on or about the 10th day of February, 1913.

To which all of the defendants, except Mary Jones, C.H. Boswell, John W. Brown, G.F. Parsons, and Charles Batley pleaded ["Not guilty" to all charges and specifications].

Thereupon the Judge Advocate entered a plea of "Not Guilty" for the defendants, C.H. Boswell, John W. Brown, Mary Jones, G.F. Parsons, and Charles Batley.

Thereupon, M.F. Matheny, counsel for the accused, stated as follows:

Gentlemen of the Commission, before proceeding to the taking of evidence in this case, we want to make a preliminary motion, which we presume will be overruled, but at the same time we want to save the point as a matter of record. We want to protest against the right of this Commission to try and determine the charges set forth in the specifications against the defendants, who have pleaded not guilty, making no appearance whatever for those who have not plead to the specifications. We will ask for a ruling on that motion.

Thereupon the accused, his counsel, the reporter and the Judge Advocate withdrew and the Commission was closed, and on being opened, the President of the Commission announced in their presence that the objection was overruled. To which ruling and opinion of the Commission, the defendants, by counsel, excepted.

Attorney Matheny: We next want to appear to the charges as filed and move that they be quashed as to each of the prisoners and this motion goes to the charges as a whole and each specification there.

Thereupon the accused, their counsel, the reporter and the Judge Advocate withdrew and the Commission was closed, and on being opened the President of the Commission announced in their presence that the motion to quash was overruled. To which ruling of the Commission the defendants, by counsel, excepted.

Captain Walker (Member of the Commission): I desire to make this statement:

I was taken off of the Military Commission appointed by General Orders No. 5, because Governor Glasscock was under the impression that I had signed the return in the writ of Habeas corpus proceedings of Mary Jones, and others, against the State. I want to say that I did not sign the return, nor did I read it or know what it contained, and if there is any statement in there as to the guilt or innocence of the persons now about to be tried, why I am not advised of it and had no part in making the return, and feel that I can sit in the trial of these cases and render a verdict according to the law and evidence.

Thereupon, F.W. Howery, a witness for the prosecution, was duly sworn, and testified as follows in direct examination by the Judge Advocate:

Q. Mr. Howery, how many of the prisoners do you know? Just identify them, those that you know.

A. Harrison Ellis, Emory Sowards, E.B. Vickers. That is all I see in this crowd that I know, and Mother Jones, I know her by sight but I don't know her personally. I am not acquainted with her, but I know her when I see her.

Q. Do you know Mr. Brown?

A. Yes, sir.

Q. Do you know Mr. Parsons?

A. I didn't see him.

Q. Stand up, Mr. Parsons. (The defendant G.F. Parsons stands to his feet.)

A. Yes, I know him.

Q. Do you know the gentleman (C.H. Boswell) sitting there at the left of Mother Jones?

A. No, I don't know him. I think that is all I know.

Q. Where do you live, Mr. Howery?

A. I live at Hansford.

Q. How long have you lived there, at Hansford?

A. About 20 years.

Q. What do you do there?

A. Sell some goods.

Q. Have a store?

A. Yes, sir.

Q. Were you there on the 7th, 8th, 9th and 10th of February, 1913?

A. Yes, sir; I was there all the time.

Q. All the time?

A. Yes, sir.

Q. What arrangement, if any, did you have with the defendants J.W. Brown and Mr. Parsons—G.F. Parsons—to leave your store open there, so they could have telephone communication during that period?

A. Well, one night they asked me to keep it open.

Q. Who asked you to keep it open?

A. Mr. Brown, I think.

Q. You know who did ask you; did he?

A. Yes, sir, Mr. Brown, I believe was the man.

Q. What night was that with reference to the time that they had the trouble at Mucklow? You heard of the Mucklow trouble, on the 10th?

A. Let me see. I kind of get mixed up on dates. I will have to study a little.

Q. Mucklow trouble was on Monday and the Holly Grove trouble was on the Friday before?

A. That must have been Monday night, the best of my recollection.

Q. Did you have that store open before that?

A. Before that?

Q. Before the Monday night, didn't you have it opened on Saturday and Sunday night preceding that?

A. Yes, but I was not asked to keep it open.

Q. But you did keep it open, as a matter of fact for them, Mr. Howery?

A. It was kept opened a while each night.

Q. What do you mean by a "while each night?"

A. I don't know just what time I did close up on that night. I closed up about 12 o'clock.

Q. What time was that on Monday night?

A. That I agreed to keep it open?

Q. Yes, all night?

A. I closed it before the soldiers come in. I don't know that they come in until the next morning.

Q. Didn't you on Saturday before the soldiers came in, the soldiers came in on Monday night, hear Mr. Brown and Mr. Parsons telephone to Charleston and ask them "to bring up the stuff" or "send up the stuff."

A. There was some kind of stuff. I don't just know exactly what, but they was to bring up some kind of stuff.

Q. You heard them having a conversation of that sort?

A. Yes, sir, something, I don't know what it was.

Q. On Sunday did you hear the defendant J.W.Brown put in a call; did he put in a call for Carbondale?

A. I don't think he did on Sunday, for I don't think I was open on Sunday. That is the best of my recollection now.

Q. You told me that in a conversation which I took down in shorthand?

A. Yes.

Q. You stated that you heard Brown call Carbondale and ask for Ernest Creigo, did you not?

A. No, sir.

Q. How?

A. No, sir. If you have got that, you have got it kind of wrong at Carbondale.

Q. What did you tell me then?

A. That he phoned up there and somebody, Dr. Wilson, I think, answered.

Q. Go ahead, what did he ask Dr. Wilson?

A. He asked him if those men had come there. I couldn't hear what Dr. Wilson said. He said, "I guess they will come over; I sent two up."

Q. Who was it that he had the conversation with?

A. It seemed like it was Wilson, that is the way I understood it.

Q. That is, Mr. Brown had the telephone—J.W.Brown was doing that telephoning?

A. Yes, Mr. Brown. He said "Get the men or boys together" or something, and "I will, up some time tomorrow morning."

Q. Was that on Sunday afternoon?

A. Well, I can't just say or I can not tell you exactly what date it was.

Q. Mr. Parsons was with him, was he not, at that time?

A. I don't remember of him being with him at that time. They was in there together a great deal, but I can't tell you each time they was together.

Q. On that particular Sunday were there quite a number of men, going in and out of Hansford, a great many of them armed with rifles and guns of various sorts?

A. I seems like I saw one squad, coming in from the river, coming up from the river is all I ever saw.

Q. Didn't you upon that occasion see Mr. Parsons and Mr. Brown with those men?

A. I don't remember seeing them with them at all, but Mr. Parsons was out on the streets, and I saw Mr. Brown occasionally. I was in the house most of the time.

Q. Now, you know you have told me two or three times what you saw Brown and Parsons doing on that particular day. Just tell these gentlemen what you told me.

A. I can't say that I saw Mr. Brown or Parsons talking to any squad of men, although I saw the men occasionally.

Q. Didn't you tell me in these two conversations with me at different times, when these men came in, you saw both Mr. Brown and Mr. Parsons go out and have a conference with them and you believe they were instructing the men?

A. I didn't aim to tell you that way, because I don't hardly think to my knowledge they met a crowd and told them to do anything. It was a time that every two men who met, would have a talk. When two men would meet, they would have something to say about this trouble, speak to one another. When a man would meet another, he would stop and talk together. Whenever there was anyone, no matter who it was, wherever two or three men were together, the crowd would come there. There was a great deal of trouble going on.

Q. Didn't you in your conversation with me, make the statement that Mr. Brown and Mr. Parsons were active leaders of the men upon that occasion?

A. I said they seemed to be the leaders; that is, I didn't hear anybody call them leaders, but they understood there that they would be the leaders, it seemed, if they were attacked there by the "Bull Moose," that is all they talked about, was the "Bull Moose" coming in to attack them, and they were going to defend themselves.

Q. And your men Brown and Parsons were leading your side of it?

A. I said they seemed to be.

Q. They seemed to be?

A. Yes, sir.

Q. Did you see the man or men who brought in the dress suit case of ammunition on Sunday morning?

A. No, sir.

Q. Your understanding was that it did come in, was it not?

A. No, sir. I never heard anybody say they brought the ammunition in.

Q. You knew that it had been telephoned for, the day before?

A. I was not out that morning at the post office. I didn't see anybody come up on that train. I didn't see anybody get off of No. 14 when she came in. They had to go right by the post office, if they had brought anything in.

Q. Didn't you understand that the ammunition had come up on Sunday morning?

A. No, sir.

Q. Didn't you hear that talked around generally?

A. No, sir.

Q. You didn't know that?

A. No, sir.

Q. I want for the purpose of refreshing your memory, I want to know if you did not have your store open all night Saturday night, and was it not Saturday night they kept that store open for telephoning, and not Sunday? I won't want you to be misunderstood about that.

A. No, sir. The store—my store was not kept open all night Saturday.

Q. Didn't you arrange so they could go in and out all Saturday night, for the purpose of using the telephone?

A. No, sir. I didn't give anybody my key.

Q. You say you didn't give anybody your key?

A. No, sir.

Q. How did you expect them to get in Monday night?

A. I stayed in with them all Monday night.

Q. You stayed with them Monday night?

A. Yes, sir. I stayed there to collect tolls.

Q. Do you know who they telephoned to?

A. No, sir, I don't know. They were calling numbers in Charleston mostly.

Q. Calling numbers in Charleston mostly?

A. Yes, sir.

The witness is turned over to the accused for cross examination.

Counsel for the defendants announce that they do not care to cross-examine Mr. Howery.

C.M. Boren, a witness introduced on behalf of the prosecution, being first duly sworn, testified as follows in direct examination by the Judge Advocate:

Q. Mr. Boren, I take it that you do not know any of these defendants?

A. No, sir; I do not.

Q. What position, if any, do you hold with the Chesapeake and Potomac Telephone Company?

A. District Manager.

Q. You were served, I believe, with a subpoena duces tecum to appear here and bring some records?

A. Yes, sir.

Q. Have you the toll records from Hansford for February 7, 8, 9, 10 and 11, showing who called and what places?

A. I believe the 10th was the last day, Colonel.

Q. Have you the toll record for the 7th, 8th, 9th and 10th of February, 1913, showing who did the telephoning, and where he telephoned to, during these days?

A. Yes, sir.

Captain Morgan: Who made the toll record?

A. The operator at East Bank.

Q. In the course of the usual business who makes up these toll records?

A. The operator.

Q. In the usual course of business the operator makes up these toll records, what is done with them?

A. They are sent into the accounting department, for the purpose of billing, and returned to our officer for permanent record.

Q. You are the custodian of the permanent records, are you?

A. Yes, sir.

Q. And these slips are a part of your permanent records?

A. Yes, sir.

Q. Of which you are the custodian?

A. Yes, sir.

Captain Morgan: You didn't make up these yourself?

A. No, sir.

Q. You do not know yourself whether they are correct or not, do you?

A. No, sir.

Q. You are not informed as to their correctness?

A. No, sir.

Counsel for the defendants object to any further testimony relative to these toll records. Objection overruled, to which ruling of the commission, the defendants, by counsel, excepted.

Q. On February 7 we find one call from Kauf, at Hansford. I will ask you to state to what place he telephoned?

A. To C.N. That is Charleston. That is an abbreviation for Charleston, the "C.N." is.

Q. What number was called?

A. That was No. 69, Fisher and Freit.

Q. Who are Fisher and Freit?

A. They are meat men there.

Q. Now on February 8 I hand you all your tickets for that day and ask you to read them; just read them into the record, who made the calls and to whom the calls were made.

A. Blont at Hansford called No. 2401, that is the *Labor Argus*, at Charleston. Scott called 114, Charleston.

Q. What place is that?

A. United Mine Workers.

Q. Go ahead, Mr. Boren.

A. Brown called 2401, that is the *Labor Argus*. Howery called 2401, that is the *Labor Argus*. Brown called 2401, that is the *Labor Argus*, Parsons called 2401, that is the *Labor Argus*. J.W. Blont called Dr. Wilson, at Carbondale, West Va., on the 8th.

Q. The next day I hand you is February 9. I will ask you to take these slips and say to whom the calls were made and by whom made.

A. Parsons called 2401, *Labor Argus*, at Charleston. Brown called the same place. Scott called the same. Parsons called the same. Parsons again called the *Labor Argus*. Parsons again called the same number. Parsons called the same number. Howery called "A.B." that is an abbreviation and stands for "Anybody" that answers the telephone at Carbondale.

Q. Is that all of your tickets?

A. Yes, sir.

The Judge Advocate thereupon offered in evidence to the commission, 16 toll records, dated February 7, 8, 9, and 10, 1913.

Counsel for the defendants objected to the introduction of said toll records. Objection overruled, to which ruling of the court, the defendants, by counsel, excepted.

Cross-examination by Captain Carskadon:

Q. You say you did not keep these records personally?

A. No, sir; no, sir.

Q. You do not know whether they are correct or incorrect?

A. No, sir.

Captain Morgan: You do not know anything about the conversations?

A. I do not; nothing whatever.

Dr. S.M. Wilson, a witness for the prosecution, was duly sworn, and testified as follows in direct examination by the Judge Advocate:

Q. Dr. Wilson, give the commission your name.

A. S.M. Wilson.

Q. What is your profession and where do you live?

A. Physician, Carbondale, West Va., Fayette County.

Q. Carbondale, West Va.?

A. Yes, sir.

Q. I will ask you to turn to the defendants there and pick out all the defendants that you know.

A. All that I know personally?

Q. Yes, sir, take your time and identify all that you know by name; commence at the back row.

A. Mr. Parsons and Mr. Nutter. I think it is Bert.

Q. Do you know that is his name?

A. Yes, sir. Do you want the names of any person, so that I know them?

Q. Yes, so you know them.

A. Joe Prince. There is a gentleman whose face I know.

Q. Will the gentleman stand up; what is your name?

The defendant: Harry Vrasic.

A. Yes, sir, I know Harry Craise. Mr. John Brown. Mother Jones, Mr. Boswell, Mr. Batley, that is all.

Q. I will ask you to tell where the defendants that you have identified live, if you know; or to simplify it, how many of them live on the opposite side of the river from here?

A. Just a moment. I see Grady Everett and I know him, also Ernest Creigo. Those that live on the other side of the river from here are Mr. Ernest Creigo, Mr. Grady Everett, Mr. Joe Prince and Mr. Harry Craise. They are all.

Q. Where does Bert Nutter live?

A. Mr. Bert Nutter lives at Carbondale.

Q. How do you come from Carbondale to Pratt, in the usual way of travelling, and about how far is it?

A. You could via Smithers Creek, to Montgomery, over the bridge to Montgomery, and from Montgomery direct to Pratt.

Q. About how many miles is it, as you travel it?

A. About six miles, I should say.

Q. Take your seat, Doctor. Where were you, Doctor, on Saturday and Sunday, February 8th and 9th, 1913?

A. Where was I on Saturday?

Q. Saturday and Sunday.

A. At Carbondale.

Q. Did you on either of these days have a telephone conversation with the defendant J.W. Brown?

A. Yes, sir.

Q. Which one of the days did you have the phone talk with him?

A. Not at all.

Q. Which days did he call you, and did you have the phone conversation with him?

A. Not that I know of at all.

Q. I asked if you had a phone call from him and you stated that you did; now I am asking you which day it was.

A. Saturday night.

Q. Saturday night?

A. Yes, sir.

Q. About what hour?

A. I think it was about six or seven o'clock.

Q. What request, if any, did he make of you at that time?

A. Now as I remember the conversation that took place over the phone, someone, I can't swear that it was Mr. J.W. Brown, but someone said that his name was John Brown called me up and said he was at Pratt, and the text of his conversation was as follows: He says, "He didn't know how I felt about this matter, but that something ought to be done." Now he said "the guards had shot up Holly Grove, and had killed a miner" as near as I understood it. That is just about what I understood of the conversation. Right there I stopped him. I told him to hold the phone a second, and I went over and got Mr. Creigo. Previous to this by way of explanation, Saturday evening, Mr. Creigo got off the train there at Carbondale station, I was going up the railroad, and he hollered to me and asked me if I would take a phone message that night, that he would not be up there, in the store, and would I take the message. I told him yes, I would, and that is all that passed between us. Then I stopped this man at the other end of the line, whoever he was and told him to hold the phone a second, and I went over and told Mr. Creigo to come over there and see to that phone message.

Q. Did you hear the Creigo end of the phone conversation, that took place after you called him?

A. No, sir, I was in my office.

Q. What connection, if any, has Mr. Creigo with the miners; is he employed by them in any way?

A. Yes, sir, he is the lobbyist at the State legislature.

Q. Did you see Mr. Creigo on the day following this telephone conversation?

A. Yes, sir, he was in my office.

Q. About what time in the day?

A. He was in my office about six o'clock, I think.

Q. Afternoon or morning?

A. Afternoon.

Q. What statement, if any, did he make to you, meaning Mr. Ernest Creigo, about coming over on this side of the river, to take part in the trouble going on?

A. He made this statement to me, standing at the foot of my bed. He says, "Doc," he says, "I have decided that it is my duty to go over there tonight." He says, "I never have been over there, but" he says, "I understand there is not to be any trouble but just a demonstration." He says, "I feel it is my duty to go over there." He says, "I think the crowd is going over from here," and he said, "heretofore I never have been over there, but I think it is my duty to go tonight." That is the very substance of what passed between us.

Q. Do you know whether or not he went over that night? What is your information about it?

A. I can't swear about that.

Q. What is your information as to whether or not he left there?

Counsel for the defendants object to this question. Objection sustained as to the form of the question.

Q. Doctor, do you know whether or not Creigo or any of the men whom you have identified, who live at Carbondale, left Carbondale on Sunday night or Monday night?

A. No, sir.

Q. Did you see the defendant, Boswell, on Sunday, February 9, 1913?

A. Yes, sir.

Q. Where did you see him?

A. He came to my boarding house.

Q. What was he doing when you saw him?

A. He came into my room. Mr. Boswell came into my room, just behind him came several men, one of them Mr. Nutter, he came with him.

Q. When you say "Mr. Nutter" you mean Bert Nutter?

A. Yes, sir.

Q. Go ahead with your statement, Doctor.

A. He came—the gentleman I have just forgotten his name—he came in and got some medicine for his wife, and Mr. Nutter came with him. They stayed for a few minutes and they left.

Q. Did you hear any conversation between those persons at the time you were in the room, Boswell and Nutter?

A. No, sir.

Q. What statement, if any, did Boswell, make to you as to the purpose—as to his purpose for being at Carbondale, that afternoon?

A. The only thing that I heard him say relative to this, was just after dinner, and we were going out from the dining room. I heard some one remark to Mr. Boswell if he was going over to the meeting, and he said, "No, he was not." "That he had just come over there to deliver a message." What that message was or its text or anything, I don't know. But prior to that time, that morning, when in my room, he was talking to me, after these parties left, and he asked me or said he wanted some information. I told him all right, and he asked me or he wanted to know if there was such a thing as maternal impression; what effect this fight would have on a child that was born of a woman in childbirth at the time of the fight. I expect we discussed that for one hour or so. We differed radically in regard to it and the discussion was a good long one. That is what he wanted to know, and from that he diverted on to some other texts, and I remember of him saying that he did not think there was going to be any trouble; that he understood the guards had left the creek, and the "scabs" were going out and he thought if the miners would make a demonstration, the strike would end. That is his opinion, and all he said about it.

Q. You made a statement to me in one of my interviews, that he made a statement, in substance, that if you could get 1,000 men to make a demonstration, which would end the strike. Now for the purpose of refreshing your memory, what did he say about it?

A. To get 1,000 men?

Q. Yes; that is the statement you made to me the other day, Doctor.

A. I don't remember that, Colonel. I don't remember of ever having said that.

Q. You recall all the conversation you had with me?

A. No, sir; you have my conversation mixed up with somebody else. I am satisfied I never made that assertion.

Q. What time did Parsons go over to Carbondale that morning?

A. Mr. Boswell?

Q. Boswell, yes?

A. About ten or eleven o'clock, I think.

Captain Morgan: What morning was this?

A. Sunday.

Q. Do you know where he came from that morning?

A. No, sir.

Q. Did he make any statement about where he had come from?

A. No, sir.

The witness is turned over to the accused for cross-examination by Attorney M.F. Matheny:

Q. Doctor, in regard to this young man, Creigo, I believe you stated that he told you he never had been over on this side, in any of this trouble, and that he understood there was going to be a demonstration, and he felt he ought to come over and join in the demonstration?

A. Yes, sir.

Captain Carskadon: You do not know whether he did come or not, do you, Doctor?

A. No, sir.

B.F. Backus, a witness introduced for the prosecution, being first duly sworn, testified as follows in direct examination by the Judge Advocate:

Q. What is your name?

A. B.F. Backus.

Q. Where do you live, Mr. Backus?

A. Carbondale.

Q. What is your business?

A. I am manager of the Sunday Creek Commissary.

Q. I will ask you to look over these defendants and pick out all of them that you know. Just start in and identify them and give their residence, as you identify them.

A. Mr. Creigo.

Q. Ernest Creigo?

A. Yes, sir, Ernest Creigo. Grady Everett.

Q. Where does he live?

A. He lives at Oakland, I believe. He works at our place. And Harry Craise.

Q. Harry Craise?

A. Yes, sir. Bert Nutter. This gentleman up here, I don't know his initials, Brown.

Q. The big man, J.W. Brown?

A. Yes, sir, I have seen him. I never have met him.

Q. Any more of them?

A. And Mother Jones. I have seen her but I never met her, that I know of.

Q. Were you at Carbondale, on Saturday night and Sunday, February 8th and 9th, 1913?

A. Yes, sir.

Q. Did you hear Ernest Creigo talk on the telephone with anybody on Saturday night?

A. He was at the telephone; yes.

Q. Did you hear what he said into the phone?

A. No, sir, I did not.

Q. Did you see Mr. Boswell, the gentleman sitting right there next to Mother Jones, on her left?

A. No, sir, I did not.

Q. Was he there; did you see him on Sunday?

A. No, sir, I didn't see him.

Q. What, if anything, do you know about any of these men that you have identified, leaving Carbondale on Sunday night for any purpose?

A. I don't know that they left. I don't know a thing in the world about it.

Q. You don't know anything about it?

A. No, sir.

Q. Did you hear Mother Jones make any speech at Carbondale, prior to this declaration of martial law?

A. I heard her speak about six or eight minutes, maybe six, at a school house, at a distance. I was at a distance and heard nothing that she said.

Q. You haven't heard anything since then?

A. No, sir.

Q. You know nothing about it?

A. No, sir.

The witness is turned over to the accused for cross-examination. Counsel for the accused announced they did not care to cross-examine the witness.

C.C. Woods, a witness for the prosecution, being first duly sworn, testified as follows in direct examination by the Judge Advocate:

Q. What do you do, Mr. Woods?

A. Miner, machine man, however.

Q. Where do you live?

A. Boomer.

Q. I will ask you to look at these defendants and see how many of them you know. Just stand up and identify them, one at a time.

A. I don't know any of them, except Mother Jones. I think that is the only one I know.

Q. How long have you known Mother Jones?

A. Why, not very long, possibly two or three years, something like that. I don't remember.

Q. Have you had occasion to be present when Mother Jones was making any speeches, immediately before the trouble that they had at the battle of Mucklow?

A. Once, I believe, is all.

Q. When was that?

A. When was it?

Q. About when was it, the best of your recollection?

A. I don't remember the date, but some time just after the trouble at Mucklow, I think.

Q. I will ask you to tell the commission what statement, if any, she made then, with reference to the trouble?

A. I didn't hear all of her speech. I heard part of it, when I went into the hall. There was so much noise I didn't understand distinctly what she said. I didn't hear very much of her speech. She was referring to the speech that she had made before, when I came in. At the time Governor Glasscock had ordered the Citizens Investigation of martial law or something, and she was telling the audience about how she had advised them before, not to give their arms up and repeated her speech that she had made before, some time before that.

Q. What statement, if any, did she make in regard to advising violence?

A. I don't remember any. She said nothing about any violence. She said something about, "I told you not to give your guns up before, and I think you were right" or something like that. Along that line.

Q. Have you any further statement that you wish to make regarding her speech?

A. Well, I don't know. I don't remember anything. I don't know what would be important.

Q. Did you hear her enticing any violence, or advising or encouraging any violence, on this side of the river?

Q. No, sir, I did not. I don't know that she referred to the trouble on this side of the river. I don't know that I would consider it that way.

The witness is turned over for cross-examination by M. F. Matheney:

Q. Where was this speech, you say, Mr. Woods?

A. At Boomer.

Q. When was that?

A. I don't remember the date. I think it was on Wednesday evening. I don't remember the date.

Q. What month?

A. I would judge it was last month possibly, or the latter part of the month before.

Harry King, a Witness for the prosecution, being first duly sworn, testified as follows in direct examination by the Judge Advocate.

Q. Mr. King, where do you live?

A. Holly Grove.

Q. I believe you are a striking miner?

A. Yes, sir.

Q. I will ask you to look at these defendants and identify those that you know. That is, start in with Mr. Brown, and tell how many of them you know.

A. How many of these men?

Q. Yes.

A. Do you want me to go through and count them?

Q. No, give their names.

A. I know Mr. Patrick, and Mr. Perdue. I know Willie Perdue. Frazier Jarrett, and Robert Parrish.

Q. For the purpose of expediting the matter. You know Mr. Brown and Mr. Parsons?

A. I know them when I see them but I am not personally acquainted with them.

Q. You know them when you see them?

A. Yes, sir.

Q. You were at Hansford on the Sunday preceding the battle at Mucklow, or fight at Mucklow, that is, on February 9, 1913?

A. Yes, sir.

Q. Did you see Mr. Parsons and Mr. Brown there upon that occasion?

A. What occasion?

Q. On Sunday, February 9, 1913, at Hansford?

A. Yes, sir, I believe I saw them there on Sunday.

Q. You believe you saw them there on Sunday?

A. Yes, sir.

Q. A good many persons in Hansford there on that Sunday were carrying guns, were there not?

A. No, I didn't see hardly anyone with guns.

Q. You made a statement here to me a few days ago, under oath, which I took down, you recall that, don't you?

A. Yes, sir.

Q. Didn't you state to me that you saw a good many men with guns?

Counsel for the defendants objected to this question. Thereupon the accused, his counsel, the reporter and the Judge Advocate withdrew and the commission was closed, and on being opened the president announced in their presence that the objection was overruled, which ruling of the commission the defendants, by counsel, excepted.

A. No response.

Q. Didn't you make the statement to me here some time ago under oath, that Sunday at Hansford, you saw strangers with guns?

A. Yes, sir, I told you I saw a few men there with guns on Sunday.

Q. Did you see Mr. Brown or Mr. Parsons at that time?

A. I don't remember whether I saw them right at that time or not, but I saw them on Sunday; yes, I saw them.

Q. What were they doing with reference to these people who had guns and were in the crowd there?

A. I don't know that they were with them. I don't think those men with them had guns.

Q. What was going on at Hansford on that Sunday, that you are talking about, Sunday, the 9th?

A. There was a good crowd gathered around there, that is all I know. I don't know whether there was anything particular or not.

Q. Who was the leaders, so far as you could tell, of the men that were collected at Hansford on Sunday, February 9th?

A. I don't know. I couldn't say because I didn't enquire.

Q. Didn't you make the statement to me upon the occasion I refer to, when you were up here and your statement taken down, that Brown was the leader of these men and that Parsons was assisting him?

A. No, sir, you asked me if I saw Mr. Brown there.

Q. And what did you tell me?

A. I told you he was standing there talking to the crowd of men.

Q. Didn't you make the statement that you understood who the leaders were, and didn't I ask you the questions, "Who did you understand were leaders?" and didn't you reply, "It looked like Brown was. He talked to the men he counted out." Now didn't you make that statement?

A. I told you he was talking to the crowd of men. I don't recollect of saying he counted them out.

Q. And didn't I ask you, "What do you mean by counting them out?" And didn't you reply, "First, one side and then another, and then talking to them. He would come out and talk to them and then go and talk to this side." Didn't you make that statement?

A. Yes, I believe I did.

Q. What did you mean now by that?

A. What do you mean?

Q. Yes, making this statement, that he took them out and talked to them, and then go and talk to the other side?

A. I don't know that I meant anything about it. I don't know what he was talking about.

Q. Didn't I ask you the further question, "Talking with the men with guns" and didn't you reply, "Yes, sir?"

A. No, sir, I don't think I did.

Q. I want to say this to you in all fairness, I want you to understand that what you are saying is being taken down in shorthand.

A. Yes, sir.

Q. You understand you are being sworn now?

A. Yes, sir.

Q. Didn't I propound to you another question, "Do you know what he said to them?" and didn't you answer, "No, sir, I was not up close enough to understand. I thought he was fixing up for business right. He was just walking from one bunch to another." Didn't you make that statement?

A. I said he was walking from one bunch to another; yes, sir.

Q. Didn't you say you thought he was fixing up for business right?

A. No, sir, I told you I didn't know what he was doing.

Q. What did you mean when you said you thought he was fixing up for business right, referring to Brown?

A. Well, I don't know. I don't know what he meant, because I was not close enough to them to hear what he said or nothing what he was fixing to do.

Q. Did you see Parsons upon that occasion?

A. I saw Mr. Parsons in Hansford on Sunday.

Q. Was he with Brown?

A. Not when I saw him he was not.

Q. Didn't I ask you the question, "Did you see Parsons?" and didn't you reply, "Yes, sir?"

A. Yes, sir, I saw him.

Q. Didn't I ask you "They were together?" and you replied, "Yes, sir?" "They were together," meaning Brown and Parsons, and didn't you reply, "Yes, sir?"

A. No, sir, I saw Mr. Parsons there in Hansford on the street.

Q. Didn't I ask you the further question, "You saw Parsons and Brown walking around, talking to men with guns; taking them off and talking to them?" and didn't you reply to it, "Yes, sir?"

A. Walking around and talking to guns?

Q. Talking to men with guns.

A. No, sir, I didn't make any statement like that.

Q. And then didn't I ask you, "Were they talking loud?" and didn't you reply, "No, sir, talked low?" Didn't you make that statement?

A. I told you I was not close enough to hear what they talked about. I heard them talking.

Q. And didn't I ask you the further question? I asked you about Scott, and you said, "Did not see Scott around. I went into his place and got a check. He was giving checks. Farley asked me if I was going to a meeting up in the grove; told me there was going to be a meeting up in the grove, and asked me if I was going to it and I told him no." Did you not make that statement?

A. What Scott is that?

Q. You can hear me, can't you?

A. Yes, sir.

Q. I asked you if you didn't tell me in reply to my question, if Scott was around, and didn't you say, "Did not see Scott around. I went into his place and got a check. He was giving checks. Farley asked me if I was going to a meeting up in the grove; told me there was going to be a meeting up in the grove, and asked me if I was going to it and I told him no." Did you make that statement?

A. I didn't see Scott.

Q. I am not asking you about Scott. I am asking you about that statement, didn't you tell me that?

A. I told you there was men asked me down there if I was going to a meeting in Beech Grove and I told you no; I told them no and I told you no too.

Q. What was that meeting for?

A. I don't know what it was for. I never went to it.

Q. When you came up to Hansford and went from Hansford to Holly Grove on the morning following, tell this commission whether or not you found that the men had gone?

A. (No response.)

Q. Don't you know Sunday night that men were held for that purpose, and the men were going up on the mountain Monday for some purpose?

A. No, sir, I was not in any of the meetings and I didn't hear anybody say they was going up there.

Q. And didn't you tell me when you came down the following Monday morning that you found the men had gone?

A. No, sir, I didn't tell you that the men had gone.

Q. Didn't I ask you this question, "Did you see Brown and Parsons down about the place when you came down at nine o'clock and heard that the men were gone?" And didn't you reply, "No, sir, they were gone." Didn't you make that statement?

A. On Monday?

Q. Yes.

A. No, sir. I told you I saw Brown and Parsons in Hansford.

Q. You didn't make that statement?

A. No, sir.

Q. Didn't I also ask you upon that occasion, "What do you know about some ammunition being brought up from Charleston?" What did I ask you about that?

A. (No response.)

Q. Didn't I ask you about that?

A. Yes, sir.

Q. What did you tell me?

A. I told you I heard some men was coming up with some, but I didn't know who the men was.

Q. Is that exactly what you said to me?

A. (No response.)

Q. Didn't you tell me that three suitcases had been brought up?

A. Yes, sir, but I didn't know who had.

Q. And didn't I ask who brought it up?

A. Yes.

Q. What did you tell me then?

A. I told you I didn't know.

Q. And didn't you say, "They didn't say. I heard them say they brought three suitcases up from Charleston. I heard it Sunday. Don't remember who said it; just heard it. They said they had plenty of ammunition. I know they were looking for three suitcases on the train or some would bring it." Did you make that statement?

A. Yes, sir.

Q. And didn't I ask you the further question, "And while that was being talked, Brown and Parsons were getting together these people who had guns?" And didn't you reply, "Yes, sir." Isn't that true?

A. No, sir.

Q. Then I asked you the further question, "You understood that the ammunition was being brought up from Charleston, something was going to be pulled off, and Brown and Parsons were making arrangements. Didn't I ask you that question?

A. You asked me if there was going to be anything pulled off, that I knowed of.

Q. I asked you this question, didn't I ask you, "You understood that the ammunition was being brought up from Charleston, something was going to be pulled off, and Brown and Parsons were making arrangements?" And then didn't you answer "Yes, sir." Now isn't that true?

A. No, sir, I didn't.

Q. You didn't?

A. No, sir. I told you that the suitcases had been brought up. I didn't tell you that Brown and Parsons were making any arrangements.

Q. Didn't I ask you upon that occasion, to use this as an illustration, didn't I ask if you would come into the room and was deaf and dumb and couldn't hear what was going on, if you couldn't pick out the men were conducting the affairs, and didn't you say, yes that you could see me, and didn't you upon that occasion, when I asked you if Brown and Parsons were not directing it, didn't you say, "Yes, sir?"

A. No, sir.

Q. You didn't say that?

A. No, sir.

Q. You understand now that you are on oath and what you have sworn to is going down into this record?

A. Yes, sir.

Q. You understand that you have before made a statement which was taken down in shorthand and has since been extended?

A. Yes, sir.

Q. You understand that?

A. Yes, sir.

The witness is turned over to the accused for cross-examination. Counsel for the defendants announce that they do not care to cross-examine the witness.

Charley Wright, a witness for the prosecution, being first duly sworn, testified as follows in direct examination by the Judge Advocate:

Q. Your name is Charley Wright?

A. Yes, sir.

Q. You are one of the defendants in these charges and specifications?

A. Yes, sir.

Q. I will ask you to get up and identify all the people that you know among these defendants, just get up and point them out.

A. I know Tip Belcher, Charley Kenney. I know this gentleman right there. Mr. George W. Lavender. I believe that is all I know.

Q. Do you know that big man with a white hat on?

A. No, I have seen him but I don't know him.

Q. This is Mr. Brown, where did you ever see him before?

A. I saw him down at Crown Hill one day.

Q. Anybody else in there that you know?

A. No, sir, I don't know all of these fellows; they are strangers to me.

Q. Where were you on the 10th day of February, 1913, at the time there was some shooting on the mountain at Mucklow?

A. I was up there.

Q. I want you to begin at the beginning and tell this commission how you happened to be up there, and all about it; just tell the story.

A. Well, how I happened to be up there, they said the news come there that there was a gatling gun on the hill, in the woods, somewhere, and they decided to go up there and get this gatling gun.

Q. Where were you when that decision was made, if you know, Charley?

A. Now it was just talked among some of the fellows there, right in front of where I lived. I don't know who the fellows were; they was strangers to me. I had not attended any of the meetings. I know nothing about any of the meetings at all, but I went up there with them. There was a crowd of fellows along; of course, I don't know all of the fellows that was along. I called the names of those that were along.

Q. These men that you identified were with you?

A. Yes, sir.

Q. Go ahead and tell what happened.

A. So we goes on around and there was a shot fired after we got over there at the spring, but who fired the shot or where it come from I am not able to tell. There were several shots fired, who fired them, whether it was men in our crowd shooting against these people on the mountain, I can't tell you. We run. I know I run, and I think most of the others in the crowd run.

Q. Were you armed?

A. Yes, sir, I had a gun.

Q. Did you have any cartridges?

A. Yes, sir.

Q. How many?

A. I had 16.

Q. Where did you get them; where did you get your gun and cartridges from?

A. I got my gun and cartridges from Mr. Darby.

Q. Who?

A. Old man Darby.

Q. Who is old man Darby?

A. William Darby.

Q. Were you at a meeting down here in the grove at Hansford, Sunday night?

A. No, sir, I was not.

Q. You knew there was such a meeting?

A. No, sir, I didn't know that there was such a meeting.

Q. When did you hear about them going around up on the mountain to capture the gatling gun?

A. I heard them talking about it Sunday night.

Q. Who was talking about it?

A. I can't tell you the men because I don't know their names. There was some men in there at the school house. There was some few fellows staying at the school house, but I don't know who they were. I don't know where they come from. I never asked them.

The witness is turned over to the accused for cross-examination by Captain Morgan.

Q. Where were you with reference to this spring, when the shots were fired?

A. This spring?

Q. Yes.

A. The first battle they had up there, you mean?

Q. In this battle that you are talking about, with reference to this spring, on the ground that you talk about.

A. Yes, sir, I was there. I was at Crown Hill.

Q. When this fight was up in the mountains, where were you?

A. When this fight was going on up in the mountain, I was up there, but I was working at Crown Hill.

Q. Were you at the spring?

A. No, sir, I was not at the spring. I was not at the spring, I was around the hill further.

Q. You were around the hill further?

A. Yes, sir, but I run and all I seen run. There was shooting but who shot it I can't tell, because I did not see either side shooting. I heard them shooting and I know I run; everybody I seen was running. I tried to get out and away.

Attorney Matheny: How badly were you scared, Wright, about the time the first shot was fired?

A. I was scared bad enough to run and get out from all of it.

Q. Where did you go?

A. I went back towards Cabin Creek, back down that hollow.

Q. You went fast, didn't you?

A. Yes, sir, I did.

Q. You don't know who was doing the shooting?

A. No, sir, I couldn't tell who was doing the shooting. I didn't see the guards or I didn't see any of the men shooting. I heard the first shot fired and I turned around and they commenced shooting and I lit out and all the rest of them lit out. I can't tell you. I didn't see nary a man with a gun up to his face but I heard them.

Q. Did you bring your gun out with you?

A. No, sir, I didn't. I left it in there.

Q. You left your gun in the mountains?

A. Yes, sir.

Q. So you don't know much about it, do you, Wright?

A. No, sir. I know I was there but I run when the shooting commenced, and everybody I seen was trying to get out of the way. I know I run.

Q. You don't even recognize the people that were there, getting out of the way?

A. No, sir, they were getting out of the way and getting out of the way fast.

Q. You don't know but what the guards were doing all of this shooting?

A. I can't say whether the guards was doing all the shooting, or the miners was doing all the shooting. I didn't see any man with a gun up to his face, who fired the shots I can't tell. There was one shot fired and then there were several shots fired; I can't tell how many. I can't tell, the men were running.

Captain Carskadon: How long have you lived at Hansford?

A. I don't live at Hansford; I live at Crown Hill.

Q. How long have you lived there?

A. I can't tell you exactly how long it was. I come there some time last year, directly after Christmas, last year some time.

Redirect examination by the Judge Advocate:

Q. You say you were pretty badly scared, were you, Charley?

A. Yes, sir.

Q. You were not so badly scared that you did not recognize the men that you identify; you know they were there?

A. Yes, sir, they were up there, because they went up there that morning, as I went up there.

Q. Give the names of those people that you saw up there. How many men did you go up on the hill with that day?

A. I didn't go up on the hill with anyone, I went right up behind them.

Q. You went up on the hill right behind them?

A. Yes, sir.

Q. How many men were up ahead of you, up on the hill.

A. I can't tell you. I don't know who was in ahead of me, because I didn't know them.

Q. I am asking you how many you saw, that you know of.

A. That I know of?

Q. Yes.

A. Oh, those that went up ahead of him, I didn't know none of them, because they were all strangers to me.

Q. What I am trying to get at, you told me when you were in here before, you told me the names of the persons that went up on the hill with you.

A. No, not with me. The persons I named I saw them on the hill.

Q. Did you see them up on the hill?

A. Yes, sir.

Q. That is what I am trying to get at.

A. Yes, sir.

Q. The names that you gave the other day, were Charley Kenney; you have identified him as being along or on top of the hill?

A. Yes, sir.

Q. Tip Belcher was there on that day?

A. Yes, sir.

Q. John Jones?

A. Yes, sir.

Q. This [illegible]

A. Yes, sir.

Q. Walter Deal, he is not here?

A. No, sir, he is not here.

Q. And A.D. Lavender?

A. George Lavender was the one that was along.

Q. Tell this commission whether or not you saw these men there on the hill the day of that shooting?

A. Yes, sir, they were up there.

Q. Were they armed?

A. Yes, sir, they were all armed.

Q. Were they with the party that was with you; were they all together in the same bunch?

A. Yes, sir, they all got scattered around. They were going along there like hogs, following each other.

Q. After you got up on the hill did you stop and have any conference of any sort?

A. No, sir, they just marched right on around the hill.

Q. You didn't do any talking up there?

A. No, sir, we didn't have any talk.

Q. Who was it that told you they were going up there to get the gatling gun?

A. The news come there to the place where I was boarding. I boarded at Mrs. Pollard's, and Miss Darby, Miss Edith, said that old man Koontz, her grandfather, said he was over on Cabin Creek and he met 12 guards. He said they had a gatling gun up on top of the mountain and they were going up to tie up the thing.

Q. That is what you understood and that is the purpose of going up there that morning?

A. Yes, sir.

Captain Walker: You stated a while ago, that you recognized Mr. Brown or had seen him at Crown Hill. You do not mean to say that he was up on the hill that day?

A. No, sir, in Crown Hill, in the bottom at the store.

Q. Then the other names that you mentioned were on the hill, except Brown and he was not on the hill?

A. No, sir, I never have seen Mr. Brown on the hill. I seen Mr. Brown down in the bottom at Crown Hill.

The witness is again turned over to the accused for cross-examination by Captain Carskadon.

Q. Didn't any of these men, so far as you know, whose names you mentioned, fire any of the shots up there?

A. I can't tell which side fired the shots because I was running. I heard the shots fired but I don't know who fired them.

John Jones, a witness for the prosecution, being first duly sworn, testified as follows in direct examination by the Judge Advocate:

Q. John, you are one of the defendants to these proceedings; you have been arrested?

A. Yes, sir.

Q. What were doing in February, on February 7th, 8th, 9th and 10th, 1913?

A. February 7th, I think it was that was on Friday, wasn't it?

Q. Yes.

A. I was working that day.

Q. You were working on the 7th?

A. Yes, sir.

Q. Where were you working?

A. Crown Hill.

Q. Working at Crown Hill, on the 7th?

A. Yes, sir.

Q. I do not want to go into the Holly Grove trouble at present. Were you at any meeting on Saturday, February 8, 1913?

A. No, sir, I was not. I started up to Hansford on Saturday, but I got up a piece, I didn't go. I believe I did go a little piece of the trip and turned around and went back.

Q. Were you at any meeting on February 9th, Sunday the 9th?

A. No, sir.

Q. Were you with the party that went up on the hill, toward Mucklow, when there was a conflict between the guards and the people and they had a fight?

A. Yes, sir, I was with them—with the crowd.

Q. You were with that crowd.

A. Yes, sir.

Q. I would like for you to tell the commission, first, how you happened to go up on the hill and what you went for, John?

A. So far as the purpose for which we went, Captain, I can't explain. We started, I didn't learn the course in which they were aiming to pursue, until I got up the hill, and they they said they were going to Burnwell.

Q. Who said that, now?

A. Walter Deal.

Q. That was one of the fellows in the crowd with you?

A. Yes, sir, Walter Deal said it.

Q. How many were in the party that went along with you; I will ask you to identify them that went along with you?

A. A.D. Lavender.

Q. That is A.D. Lavender here?

A. Yes, sir, and then George Lavender. The gentleman sitting right over there. No, the next one to him, Vickers. Cleve Vickers; both of them.

Q. Cleve Vickers?

A. Yes, sir.

Q. Was the old man Vickers there?

A. Yes, sir.

Q. E.B. Vickers?

A. Yes, sir. There was one statement that I made to you before, I would like to rectify in regard to a man I said was there, that is Cal Newman. I wouldn't be willing to say on my oath that Cal was up there.

Q. You don't know whether the defendant Cal Newman was up there or not?

A. No, sir.

Q. You have old man Vickers; who was the next one?

A. Tom Miskel.

Q. Who was the other one?

A. Charles Gillispie, from Elk Ridge, the only man there was I think from over on Elk Ridge, and other places.

Q. How about Tip Belcher?

A. Tip Belcher; yes, sir. As I told you before, I don't know whether Charley Kenney was right there when the shooting occurred. I think he turned way back down below there.

Q. Did he start from below and go on the hill?

A. Yes, sir, he was up on the hill, after I got up there.

Q. Where was the last place you saw him that day?

A. The last place I saw Charley Kenney–I can't say. I am not familiar with the mountains.

Q. What I am trying to get at, was it above the coal works, up on the hill, above the coal works at Crown Hill?

A. Yes, sir.

Q. Had you gotten to the top of the mountain?

A. Yes, sir, he was above there.

Q. Was the party with you that day armed?

A. Yes, sir, they all had arms.

Q. Now tell the commission whether or not you had any conference, after you got up on the hill?

A. Yes, sir. They stopped generally as we went along, they stopped to eat and some of us there got pretty far back behind and myself and George Lavender, and I think it was George, and I am pretty sure a couple of Italians were getting pretty far behind, and myself and these Italians had decided to turn back and one of them, his buddy, was going on just ahead of him. He called him. I don't know whether these people in front heard it or not but it seemed that they did and it attracted their attention and they stopped and called us to come up and stopped there and somebody suggested if we wanted to go back, I think it was Deal, now is the time to go back but we will take your ammunition from you, we won't let you have ammunition. Then somebody said something there was a resolution passed we were all to go, and they voted on that proposition and if I mistake not, make no mistake, that is, I don't know but I think some fellow then said, to make them all go and there wasn't anything said to the contrary by anybody not going.

Q. Where were you when the shooting began, John?

A. George Lavender, myself and Tom Miskel and several of the boys got pretty far behind and I heard the first shot, it seemed as though it came from below the mountain and the path was directly on top of the ridge and I was walking on this side because I knew where the Montgomery mine side was, because I worked there, and I thought if the guards come up and shot, I wanted to be clear on this side, when the shooting began I left and it seemed to me as though most of them all was running. There was men I thought was very brave but they outrun me, because I was getting away and clumsy. I never saw nary a guard. I couldn't see the front of the crowd that was along with me, the path was crooked, the path crooked around in a way so you could not see very far in front of you.

The witness is turned over to the accused for cross-examination by M.F. Matheny.

Q. You didn't wait to see who fired the shots?

A. I didn't see nary a shot fired.

Q. You didn't see a shot fired?

A. No, sir.

Q. You heard the report of some guns as you went off the mountain?

A. Yes, sir, I heard the shooting. I heard the first shot. It seemed to me to come from the lower side of the mountain and there were some fellows behind and they said run and one fellow remarked that these guards was getting in behind us. It looked like they had cut us off.

Q. It was your impression that the guards had dropped in behind you and had opened their fire on you?

A. Yes, sir.

Q. You never heard any of your men shooting?

A. There was a lot of shots fired but I don't know who fired them.

Q. You really do not know where you were going or where they were going?

A. Which do you mean?

A. The boys that were with you?

Q. I didn't know where they was starting to. I knew after they started, they said they had started to Burnwell. They said they were aiming to go to Burnwell.

Q. You say Deal said that?

A. Yes, sir.

Q. You never heard anybody else say that, did you?

A. No, sir, I don't know that I did.

Q. What inducements have been made to you; what induced you to make this statement?

A. To make this statement?

Q. Yes.

A. Well, I will tell you. I got lost, stayed out in the mountains that night. I stayed out in the mountains all night. I got lost from the rest of the boys and I wandered around there until it became night and I made a fire and camped out in the mountains that night and the next morning I was still lost. I didn't know where I was and I started to come out of there. I didn't know where I was. I thought I was going in the direction of Cabin Creek; my aim was to try to make it into Eskdale, on Cabin Creek, but the hollow in which I struck, I knew that hollow led to an outlet, somewhere, but where I didn't know—

Q. I did not ask you that; I asked you what induced you to make this statement?

A. I am trying to tell you now. I have no inducement. There was no inducement, only General Elliott said to speak the truth, and he said he had some information—

Q. Were you promised to be released if you did that?

A. Yes, sir.

Q. You are making the statement on the boys that you have been striking with, on the belief that you will be released?

A. I told the General then I was willing to take my punishment along with the rest, but then that is what they told me; yes, sir.

Q. But you believe you will be released?

A. Yes, sir, that is what they told me.

Q. Still you had a gun up there in the mountains and did as much as anybody else did?

A. Yes, sir, and I run and I saw the crowd run.

Q. That is what the rest of the boys did?

A. All that I saw.

Captain Walker: Did you make this same statement to anyone else other than General Elliott?

A. I think to Captain Bond and Major Davis, out on the train.

Q. In coming down this hollow that you started to tell about, where did that bring you out?

A. Standard on Paint Creek.

Q. Did you make any statement to anybody, to any other person?

A. To the guards. The guards caught me up there at Standard.

Q. Did you tell them where you had been, and did you make the same statement to them, that you have here?

A. Yes, sir, I was trying to make it out from Standard and they caught me.

Q. What we are trying to make out, whether you made this statement, that you were offered inducement, to any other person?

A. No, only just what I have told these gentlemen.

Captain Carskadon: Did you have your gun when they caught you?

A. No, sir. I left my gun in the mountains.

Redirect examination by the Judge Advocate:

Q. John, didn't you give Captain Bond a statement of what you have made here, on the train coming down, but nothing was said to you about it?

A. Yes, sir.

Q. And then after you made the same statement to him, afterwards I took it down?

A. Yes, sir.

Charles Gillispie, a witness for the prosecution, was duly sworn and testified as follows in direct examination by the Judge Advocate:

Q. Your name is Charley Gillispie?

A. Yes, sir.

Q. You are one of the defendants on trial; you are being tried on these charges and specifications? Is that right?

A. Yes, sir.

Q. Where do you work, Charley?

A. Elk Ridge.

Q. You were in the trouble that took place on the mountains near Mucklow, on the 10th day of February, 1913, when there was some shooting, and some men were said to have been killed and others wounded, I believe?

A. Yes, sir.

Q. I will ask you to tell this commission, first, how you came to be up on the hill and what you went up there for?

A. I don't know exactly what I was going for. There was some talk of transportation. I heard something about transportation being at Burn-well. I don't know for certain what they were going for.

Q. Did anybody go to Elk Ridge for you?

A. Yes, sir.

Q. Who was that?

A. Charley McCamic.

Q. What did he tell you?

A. He come and said he was looking for volunteers to go to Holly Grove, the guards was shooting up the women and children like dogs.

Q. Then what did you do?

A. I volunteered and come with him. I didn't come with him. I come out with some more fellows. He didn't come out of the creek.

Q. Where did you go to?

A. I come to Montgomery and they said that the soldiers would be in here before we could get here and the boys turned back and I come on down here Sunday.

Q. You came down here Sunday?

A. Yes, sir.

Q. Where did you stay Sunday night?

A. I stayed down at the works below Hansford. I don't know the name of the parties I stayed with. I don't know the name of the people.

Q. Were you at the meeting at the beech grove, Sunday night?

A. Yes, sir.

Q. Tell this commission what took place at that meeting.

A. Well, I don't know nothing that took place, only they agreed to meet the next morning at six o'clock there.

Q. I will ask you to look at these defendants and see how many of them you recognize as being at that meeting, in which they agreed to meet at six o'clock.

A. There is nary one in the crowd that I recognize. They was most all strangers to me down there.

Q. Did you meet with the crowd the next morning at six o'clock?

A. The crowd was on the hill when I come up from where I stayed that night. The crowd had done left there and there was some fellow went up the hill and we went up and met them at the top of the hill.

Q. Were you armed?

A. Yes, sir.

Q. I will ask you to tell this commission the men who went up on the hill with you on Monday, the 10th, when that shooting took place.

A. When we went up the hill there was John Jones there.

Q. John Jones was in the crowd with you?

A. Yes, sir.

Q. Did you see anybody else on top of the hill with you, that are not among the defendants?

A. Yes, sir.

Q. Who was it?

A. There was Tom Marie.

Q. Anybody else?

A. Everett Hendricks.

Q. Anybody else?

A. John Jackson.

Q. Anybody else?

A. That is all I believe I know in the crowd.

Q. Where were you when the firing began?

A. I was at the spring that is on top of the hill.

Q. Did you see the beginning of the shooting?

A. Sir?

Q. Did you see the beginning of the shooting?

A. No, sir, I never seen that shot fired at all.

Q. What did you or what do you know about the shooting?

A. I heard an awful lot of shooting is all I know about it.

Q. Then what did you do?

A. I broke and run.

Q. You broke and ran?

A. Yes, sir.

The witness is turned over to the accused for cross-examination by M.F. Matheny.

Q. You simply started down here in company with some other fellows, to defend some women and children at Holly Grove, that you heard were being mistreated?

A. Yes, sir, that is the communication we got there.

Q. Did any of those boys start with any intention of shooting at any of the guards, or into the town?

A. No, sir, I didn't hear them.

Q. You didn't see anybody shoot into any property?

A. No, sir, I didn't see any shots fired.

Q. Or tried to damage any property?

A. No, sir.

Q. And the whole country had been aroused over some alleged bad treatment to women and children down at Holly Grove; isn't that true?

A. Yes, sir.

Q. It was simply a move on the part of yourself and some other citizens to give these people protection?

A. Yes, sir.

Redirect examination by the Judge Advocate:

Q. You were not going over to protect women and children, when you were up on the hill, when you were going to Burnwell, you were not over there to protect women and children?

A. No, sir, as I told you before it was mentioned in the crowd something about transportation. I heard it mentioned in the crowd about transportation.

Q. All the men with you who went up into the hill, and were going to Burnwell to get transportation out, were armed?

A. Yes, sir, I believe they all had arms.

Q. Those that were not armed, what did they have?

A. I believe they were all armed.

Q. Some were carrying ammunition?

A. No, sir.

Q. Where did you get this gun for this expedition?

A. I had my own.

Q. Did you see anybody else furnish men with rifles?

A. No, sir, I did not.

The witness is again turned over to the accused for further cross-examination by Captain Morgan.

Q. You say you were going up there to get out some transportation; did you hear someone say that?

A. I heard several say something about transportation.

Q. What purpose did you have?

A. I heard it in the crowd they was in the head of the creek at Burnwell, to see about the transportation.

Q. So far as you know you were not going on an unlawful errand, were you?

A. No, sir, so far as I know. I thought I had a right to go into the woods on that occasion.

Q. Did you hear outside of these men going up to Burnwell to see about the transportation, did you hear anybody else say they were going for any unlawful purpose?

A. No, sir.

Captain Carskadon: Mr. Gillispie, did you know anything about this body of men that you met in the woods being up there?

A. No, sir.

Q. Did you expect to meet any men?

A. No, sir, I didn't expect to meet any men.

Q. Your destination, so far as you knew, was Burnwell?

A. Yes, sir.

Q. You simply ran into the men who did the firing?

A. Yes, sir.

Re-redirect examination by the Judge Advocate:

Q. What do you mean by getting out transportation, Mr. Gillispie?

A. I don't know.

Q. You don't know?

A. No, sir.

Q. When you went up to get out transportation, you had your gun, did you?

A. I had my gun with me.

Q. You had your gun along?

A. Yes, sir.

Q. And every fellow in the crowd had his gun, too?

A. Yes, sir.

Q. And you were going to get out transportation?

A. Yes, sir—well, I wouldn't say that was where they were going. I heard it mentioned in the crowd something about transportation.

Q. What is transportation?

A. They had brought in miners at Burnwell, brought them in on transportation.

Q. In other words, they are what is commonly termed "Scabs?"

A. Sir?

Q. They are what is commonly termed "Scabs?"

A. Yes, sir.

Q. You are a union man?

A. Yes, sir.

Q. And the fellows who were with you were all of them strike sympathizers?

A. I don't know whether they was or not.

Q. But anyway they were all going up to get out transportation?

A. I wouldn't say they was all going to get transportation out.

The witness is again turned over to the accused for further cross-examination by Captain Carskadon.

Q. As a matter of fact, Mr. Gillispie, it is doubtful if the men all knew what they were going for, who were in the crowd?

A. Yes, sir, it is doubtful whether they all knew it or not.

John Jones, recalled as a witness for the prosecution, testified as follows in direct examination by the Judge Advocate:

Q. You referred to the fact that when you heard the first shot fired, that it was your impression that the guards had fallen in behind you?

A. Yes, sir.

Q. Did you have reference to what is known as Baldwin guards or members of the State militia?

A. It was Baldwin guards. I was not looking for any militia. I was not looking for anybody.

Q. When you use the word "guards" in your testimony you had reference to the Baldwin guards, operating on Paint Creek?

A. Yes, sir.

Q. There has been numbers of such men operating on Paint and Cabin creeks, since the strike has been on?

A. That is so far as I can learn from newspapers. I have seen in the newspaper where there was 134 or more, or something like that. I saw that in the newspapers that was up on Paint Creek.

Q. You do not know how many guards were there of your own personal knowledge?

A. No, sir.

Q. You did not see any of them?

A. No, sir, I didn't see nary one of them.

The witness is turned over to the accused for cross-examination, but counsel
for the accused declined.

C.B. Campbell, a witness for the prosecution, was duly sworn and testified as
follows in direct examination by the Judge Advocate:

Q. Your name is C.B. Campbell?

A. Yes, sir.

Q. You are a mine guard, are you?

A. Yes, sir.

Q. Where do you live?

A. Kingston.

Q. Where were you on the 10th day of February, 1913, at the time they had
that fight above Mucklow?

A. Where, above Wacomah?

Q. Yes.

A. I was on guard there.

Q. On guard where?

A. At Wacomah.

Q. Were you on the mountain and take part in that fight?

A. Yes, sir.

Q. I will ask you to turn to that bunch of defendants over there and pick out
the men that you saw on that day. Just call them out, one at a time.

A. This man sitting right here.

Q. What is your name? (To one of the defendants)

[Defendant] A. Ernest O'Dell.

Q. You saw Ernest O'Dell?

A. Yes, sir.

Q. Now give the names of any others that you see?

A. I believe that is all I see there. That is the only one I see here.

Q. Now go ahead, Mr. Campbell, and tell this commission all that occurred
there, what you did and what you saw.

A. We were there at Mucklow that morning and there were some women and
some fellows seen these men going along the hill and they told the
superintendent up there and he wouldn't believe it and directly the
fellows at the top of the hill at Paint Creek seen the men going along the
ridge there, and all we guards went there to protect the camps and the
crowd shot us up.

Q. How many guards were up on the hill?

A. Between 18 and 22. I don't know just how many.

Q. Were you with them?

A. Yes, sir.

Q. What took place when you got up on the hill?

A. We were up on the hill and this man that was in the crowd with us hollered, Mr. Pierce hollered at them three times.

Q. Who is Mr. Pierce?

A. Civil engineer. Mr. James Pierce.

Q. Then what happened?

A. They opened fire on us.

Q. Who fired first?

A. The other side. There were several shots fired before we got to the top. There was five of us on top of the hill, and there were several fired shots before we got to the top.

Q. Anybody in your party hurt?

A. Yes, sir.

Q. How many?

A. Three.

Q. Who were hurt?

A. Vance, Bobbitt and Nesbitt.

Q. Were any of them killed?

A. Yes, sir.

Q. Who were they?

A. Vance and Bobbitt.

Q. What was Vance's name?

A. Riley.

Q. Is that a nickname?

A. I don't know. That is the only name I ever heard him go by, the name of Riley.

Q. You don't know what his other name was?

A. No, sir, I think that was his name.

Q. Was Bobbitt hurt?

A. Yes, sir.

Q. How badly?

A. He was quite badly hurt.

Q. Do you know whether he is living?

A. No, sir.

Q. He died?

A. Yes, sir.

Q. Who else was hurt, did you say?

A. T.L. Nesbitt.

Q. What is his name?

A. T.L. Nesbitt.

Q. Where were these men hurt, with reference to Mucklow? Where did the shooting take place?

A. On top of the hill, to the right of Wacomah.

Q. To the right of Wacomah, on top of the hill?

A. Yes, sir.

Q. Was that within this military district, that is, in this martial law zone, as we call it?

A. Yes, sir.

Q. About how many shots were fired upon that occasion, if you know?

A. That would be hard for me to say.

Q. Guess at it.

A. I don't believe I could.

The witness is turned over to the accused for cross-examination by M.F. Matheny.

Q. These people were at the spring, when you first detected them, were they not?

A. I don't know exactly where the spring is at. I never seen the spring myself.

Q. Did you have any court process, authorizing their arrest?

A. Sir?

Q. Did you have any court process, authorizing the arrest of anybody? When you went up there shooting at these men?

A. (No response.)

Q. Did you have any warrant to shoot at these men or to arrest them?

A. No, sir, I did not.

Q. You were not sent up there by anybody except the manager of the coal company?

A. No, sir, I was sent there by the captain of the mine guards.

Q. You were sent on top of the hill by the captain of the mine guards?

A. Yes, sir.

Q. What do you mean by that; have you a military mine guard up in that country?

A. I have a captain; Captain Levy.

Q. How many mine guards did you have operating up there at that time?

A. I don't know exactly how many there were.

Q. About how many?

A. I guess about 12 or 15, I think.

Q. Were they all armed with Winchesters and revolvers?

A. Not all of them I don't think.

Q. They go armed all the time, do they not?

A. The guards do.

Q. Travel the trains and they meet the trains at the stations, do they not?

A. They don't travel the trains that I know of.

Q. You have never seen them on the trains with Winchesters?

A. No, sir.

Q. Or their revolvers?

A. No, sir.

Q. Where did this bunch of guards operate?

A. At Mucklow.

Q. Were a part of them distributed along out by the mine, up and down the creek?

A. Not that I know of; all that I know of are at Wacomah and Mucklow.

Q. How many men have you there? The most you ever saw together?

A. Between 18 and 22, is the most I have ever seen together.

Q. Who pays them for their service?

A. The company.

Q. The coal company pays them?

A. Yes, sir.

Captain Morgan: What are your duties as a mine guard; what do you do to earn the money?

A. I am a mine guard.

Q. What kind of work do you do?

A. I keep anybody from destroying any property, to see that nobody shoots up the camp, and to keep peace.

Captain Carskadon: Are you authorized by any court to keep the peace?

The Judge Advocate objected to this question. Thereupon the accused, his counsel, the reporter and the Judge Advocate withdrew and the commission was closed, and on being opened the president announced in their presence that the objection was overruled.

A. (No response.)

Q. Are you an officer of the courts, in any way, or just an officer of the law?

A. No, sir.

Q. Are you authorized to carry guns?

A. Yes, sir.

Q. By whom?

A. By Captain Lester.

Q. Is that all?

A. Yes, sir.

Q. Did you have any knowledge that any men—any miners were going along that hill, for the purpose of shooting into you people down there at Mucklow or Wacomah?

A. They come along that hill, armed up and they was seen. They was all armed up.

Q. You had no knowledge that there was anyone going to trouble your town, did you?

A. I thought that was their intention.

Q. But you did not know that, did you?

A. There was a colored fellow that they captured there, who said that was the intention, to shoot the camps up, about dark.

Q. Who was that colored fellow?

A. I don't know his name. He was captured there.

Q. There had not been any shots fired?

A. Yes, sir.

Q. When you went up on the hill there had not been any shots fired, at you, had there?

A. (No response.)

Q. When your body of men got up on the hill, there had not been any shots fired, had there?

A. No, there had not been any shots fired until these men fired into us.

Q. So far as you know there was not going to be any shots fired?

A. Not by our side.

Q. You had no knowledge that the other side was going to fire?

A. I can't tell you.

Q. You went up there armed with Winchesters, didn't you all?

A. Yes, sir.

Q. Just tell this commission what you went up there to do, Mr. Campbell.

A. We went up there to protect this camp, to keep the fellows from coming down into the camps, to keep them from coming down into the camps and killing all the women and children. That was our intention, as to what we was going to do when we got up there.

Q. Who had charge of your party?

A. Nesbitt was leading us.

Q. What instructions were given you before you left your camp?

A. To go up there and keep the people from shooting into the camps, if we could.

Q. How?

A. On top of the hill.

Q. How were you going to keep them from shooting into the camps?

A. They told us to go up on top of the hill and sent our bunch up there, and if they fired into the camps, we would be there to protect them.

Q. To protect them, how?

A. To keep them from shooting into the camps.

Q. How were you going to do that?

A. If they shot into the camps, we didn't want them to come down into the camps.

Q. The fact is that you went up there to drive these people out of that section, did you not?

A. No, sir, we didn't.

Q. And was not your instruction when you went up there, for you to drive these people out, if you could?

A. No, sir, it was not. They sent us there if these people had been starting anything, or jumped on us, to try to keep them back, if we could.

Q. How?

A. In self defence, I suppose.

Q. That is, you went up there to meet them, so that you could shoot them in self defence, is that it?

A. No, sir, we didn't go to meet them.

Redirect examination by the Judge Advocate:

Q. Are you a miner or a regular mine guard?

A. Mine guard.

Q. You are a mine guard?

A. Yes, sir.

Q. Were you employed regularly as a mine guard on this occasion?

A. Yes, sir.

Q. Tell the commission whether or not there had been—whether or not Mucklow had been fired upon by some persons immediately before you went up on the hill.

A. Yes, sir, it was fired into a few days before we went on the hill. I don't know exactly what day it was, but Mucklow was fired into.

Q. It had been fired into more than once?

A. Not since I have been there.

Q. It was fired into a few days before you went up on the hill?

A. Yes, sir.

Q. You were carrying guns with you, I mean by guns, you were carrying Winchester rifles and revolvers?

A. Winchester rifles.

Q. I will ask you if you were carrying revolvers upon that occasion?

A. No, sir.

Q. What you mean that you were going armed, that you were carrying Winchester rifles?

A. Yes, sir.

Q. Do you know whose property this occurred on?

A. No, sir.

Q. You say Mr. Pierce called to these people?

A. Yes, sir.

Q. Who fired the first shot, you or the other fellows?

A. That other crowd fired on us. They fired several shots before we could get in place to get out of the way.

Captain Walker, member of the commission: You stated in your examination in chief, that Fred Bobbitt, I believe it was Fred Bobbitt—Mr. Bobbitt was injured in that fight; and that he is not now alive?

A. No, sir.

Q. Was that injury the cause of his death, if you know?

A. Yes, sir.

Q. He never recovered from that injury?

A. No, sir.

The witness is again turned over to the accused for further cross-examination by Captain Morgan.

Q. Where were you when Nesbitt called, with reference to the log behind which Vance was killed?

A. Where was I when he called to us?

Q. Yes.

A. I was about 50 feet from Nesbitt.

Q. Where were you with reference to this log behind which Vance was killed?

A. I was to the left behind a stump.

Q. You were behind a stump when Nesbitt called?

A. No, sir, not when he called; not when they opened fire on us.

W. O. Bobbitt, a witness for the prosecution, being first duly sworn, testified as follows in direct examination by the Judge Advocate:

Q. What relation, if any, are you to Fred Bobbitt, Mr. Bobbitt?

A. Brother.

Q. Is he now dead or alive?

A. He is dead.

Q. Where did he die?

A. He died in the McMillen Hospital in Charleston.

Q. This county and State, of course?

A. Yes, sir.

Q. When did he die and what was the cause of his death?

A. He died from the effects of a gunshot wound through the abdomen, which was inflicted on the mountains above Mucklow on the 8th day of February–9th day of February it was, I guess. (Witness examines his pockets.) I find I haven't the dates.

Q. On Monday, the 10th, to get your memory right, that is the time it is said that he was shot?

A. Yes, sir, it was on Monday and he died on Monday night.

Q. That was 1913?

A. Yes, sir.

Q. You do not know anything about the shooting yourself, do you?

A. No, sir, I couldn't hear it at all. I was in my office locked up, preparing my monthly reports and I didn't know anything about it until I was called by phone that Fred was killed.

The witness is turned over to the accused for cross-examination, but counsel for the accused declined.

Gid Ratcliffe, a witness for the prosecution, was duly sworn, and testified as follows in direct examination by the Judge Advocate:

Q. You are a mine guard at Mucklow, I believe, are you?

A. I was temporarily while the trouble was going on.

Q. What were you prior to that time?

A. Sir?

Q. What were you before you were a mine guard?

A. I was a coal digger.

Q. What are you doing now?

A. I was and am digging coal.

Q. You are now digging coal?

A. Yes, sir.

Q. Were you acting as mine guard on the 10th day of February, at the time they had that fight?

A. Yes, sir.

Q. I will ask you to just tell this commission—First, I will ask you to identify any of the defendants you know. Look over these defendants and identify all the men that you know and saw on the 10th day of February. Just stand up and identify each one that you know.

A. I can't identify none of that crowd.

Q. You don't see anyone in there that you know?

A. No, sir.

Q. Tell us now all you know that took place the day of that shooting.

A. Well, sir, I will tell you the best I can remember. I was at Mucklow when there was some men spying on top of the mountain and I was sent for by Squire Lambert. There was some several of us boys together, sent out to prevent these fellows from shooting into Wacomah. They were going that way and we went toward the top of the mountain, and a fellow by the name of Pierce was in front with us fellows, and as we topped the mountain, on one side we saw some other fellows and he hollered and asked them their business and they raised and opened fire on us.

Q. How close were you to those men?

A. Well, sir, I was in about 50 yards, I guess, of them.

Q. Some days ago you were down here and looked over these men and picked out some man that you saw there on that morning?

A. Yes, sir, I was picking them by their clothes they had on.

Q. You picked them out by the clothes they had on?

A. Yes, sir.

Q. Take a good look at these men again, look around and see if there are any that you know.

A. No, sir, I don't identify one in there; I don't identify one of their faces at all.

The witness is turned over to the accused for cross-examination, but counsel for the accused declined.

The commission then, at 6 o'clock p.m., adjourned to meet at 9 o'clock a.m. on Saturday, March 8th, 1913.

The commission met pursuant to adjournment, at 9 o'clock.

S.P. Richmond, a witness for the prosecution, was duly sworn, and testified as follows in direct examination by the Judge Advocate.

Q. Mr. Richmond, will you tell the commission your name?

A. S.P. Richmond.

Q. What is your profession?

A. Stenographer.

Q. By whom are you employed?

A. The firm of Brown, Jackson and Knight.

Q. They are corporation attorneys and represent the mine owners, in this controversy that has been going on in this district for some time, do they not?

A. I think they do.

Q. I want to get that in the record. I want to show just how bad you are. Do you know Mother Jones, one of the defendants?

A. Yes, sir, not personally acquainted with her; I have had no introduction, but I know her.

Q. I will ask if you by the direction of anybody took down any of her speeches, in the summer and fall of 1912?

A. I did; I took several of her speeches.

Q. I will ask you if you extended those speeches from your shorthand notes?

A. I have.

Q. I will ask you if you took those speeches down accurately and extended your shorthand notes accurately, to the best of your ability?

A. I did to the best of my ability, the way I understood them. I will say that in writing any public speech while there is applause, there may be a few words that you might not extend just exactly, a few words might slip you now and then during applause or something of that sort.

Q. Do you believe the transcript of those speeches is a true and accurate one to the best of your knowledge and belief?

A. It is.

Q. I will ask you to identify the several speeches you have, by giving the dates on which the speeches were delivered, and we will introduce them in evidence and read them into the record later. (The Judge Advocate hands the witness several papers.)

A. I have a copy here that I fastened altogether.

Q. Just identify them by dates and turn them over to the stenographer.

A. The first one I took was Charleston, West Va., August 1, 1912, on the levee. Second, was at Montgomery, West Va., August 4, 1912, baseball park. Third, at Charleston, West Va., August 15, 1912, upon the steps of the Capitol, and the fourth, Charleston, West Va., September 6th, 1912, at the courthouse square. The fifth, Charleston, West Va., September 21, 1912, lawn of the Y.M.C.A. I only got a part of that speech. I arrived after the speaker was pretty well along, and they are all in that cover, under that binding.

Thereupon the reporter marked each speech, to identify them, as Exhibits 1, 2, 3, 4, and 5, S.P. Richmond.

The witness is turned over to the accused for cross-examination, but counsel for the accused declined.

T.L. Lewis, a witness for the prosecution, was duly sworn, and testified as follows in direct examination by the Judge Advocate:

Q. Tell the commission your name.

A. T.L. Lewis.

Q. What is your business?

A. Connected now or associated with the *Coal Mining Review* and much of my time is taken up in correspondence.

Q. What was your former business?

A. The last actual work I did in mining was year before last. My business has been connected with the paper for nearly two years, at the present time.

Q. I will ask you if you know the defendants, Mr. Paulsen and Mr. Batley?

A. I do.

Q. And Mother Jones?

A. And Mother Jones.

Q. Of what states, if you know, are they residents?

A. Mr. Charles Batley is a resident of Missouri, Paul Paulsen resides in Wyoming, and I am not prepared to say positively where Mother Jones' residence is, that is, where she claims her home residence.

Q. What connection, if any, do the three persons have with this trouble–this industrial trouble in this State, that has been going on during the past several months?

A. I really do not know what connection they have with the United Mine Workers of America. I understand Mr. Batley is an International Organizer, and Mr. Paulsen is a member of the International Executive Board.

Q. Where, if you know, do they have their headquarters?

A. Indianapolis.

Q. Where, if you know, do they have their headquarters in West Virginia?

A. That I am not prepared to answer. I don't know.

Q. I will ask you whether or not they do not remain or stay most of the time at Charleston, West Va., or have not been for some time past?

A. I have been in Charleston on two occasions within the last two years and I met the gentlemen in Charleston on each occasion. I am not prepared to say how much of the time they spend in Charleston.

Q. Who, if you know, is in charge of the headquarters of the United Mine Workers of America, at Charleston, West Va.?

A. That I do not know.

Q. You do not know who stays in the office there?

A. Excuse me. I know the men who were in the office there, of course, the district officials, but who is in charge of the national organization I do not know.

Q. I will ask you whether or not Mr. Batley and Mr. Paulsen make their headquarters in Charleston, West Va., in the United Mine Workers of America office?

A. That I am not prepared to answer; I do not know.

The witness is turned over to the accused for cross-examination, but counsel for the accused declined.

J.H. Pierce, a witness for the prosecution, was duly sworn, and testified as follows in direct examination by the Judge Advocate:

Q. What is your name, please?

A. James H. Pierce.

Q. What is your business?

A. Superintendent of the Paint Creek Colliery Company.

Q. By whom were you employed on the 7, 8, 9, and 10th day of February, 1913?

A. Wacomah Coal and Lumber Company.

Q. Where are they located at this time, where are their headquarters at this time?

A. Mucklow.

Q. That is within this military district?

A. Yes, sir.

Q. I will ask you whether or not there was any trouble at or near Mucklow, West Va., within this district, on the 10th day of February, this year?

A. What day was that, Sunday?

Q. That was on Monday, the day the fight is said to have taken place.

A. Yes, sir, there was.

Q. Were you present when the trouble took place?

A. Yes, sir, I was there.

Q. I will ask you first to tell the commission whether or not there had been any trouble at Mucklow, prior to that date, whether or not the town had been shot into?

A. Yes, sir, the previous Friday, the town had been shot into, Friday morning.

Q. How much had it been shot up?

A. I should say between 30 and 40 shots. We found I think about 28 cartridges in one place where the shooting came from.

Q. What kind of shells, if you know?

A. Springfield.

Q. Springfield shells?

A. Yes, sir.

Q. That was on Friday?

A. Yes, sir.

Q. What if anything else happened either on Friday or Saturday; was there any other shooting into the town?

A. Not into the town; no, sir, that I know of.

Q. Just tell what took place on Monday and all that you saw up on the hill.

A. About 9:30 Monday morning we had a picket on the mountain and he phoned down that there was a gang of men coming along the ridge or going along the ridge back of Scranton mines. He also stated the number. He said there were 39 in the crowd. The guards and other people who volunteered went along up the mountain to cross over the hill there, around the tram road and back over what is known as the Cabin Creek trail, and where they saw us that is where the battle took place.

Q. Just tell us how the battle happened and what took place, who fired the first shot, and all about it.

A. I was acquainted with the country and was in the lead probably 100 feet, in advance of anyone else, and when I got to the ridge, I saw these men and I waited until the others came up, that is, some of them.

Q. When you say "the others" you mean your own people?

A. Our own people. I did not know who the men were. I had known that Mr. Cunningham and people like that were scouting the woods and for that reason I called and asked them their business and from the acts of the men—they were in consultation, some were kneeling and some were standing and they didn't hear me and I had to repeat it twice, and then somebody over to the left, not of the original crowds fired one shot, and that was the start of it. We evidently had run into three parties. Only one party was visible.

Q. The man who fired the shot to the left, was that one of your own party?

A. No, my party was all with me.

Q. Then how many shots were fired from that side and into your people, if you can tell, from the best of your knowledge?

A. That would be hard to judge. The men were equipped with automatic Marvins, each man was capable of firing seven shots without loading; some shot eleven times but I will say this, that all of our men did not get into it. It was an uphill climb and all of our men were not present.

Q. About how many men did you have?

A. On a rough guess I would say about 20.

Q. Was there any of your party hurt?

A. Yes, sir.

Q. How many and how serious?

A. Two men were killed and one man was shot through the neck, but it was not serious.

Q. Who was the man or who were the men who were killed?

A. Mr. Fred Bobbitt and Mr. Riley Vance.

Q. Who was the man wounded?

A. Nesbitt, Thomas Nesbitt.

Q. Thomas Nesbitt was wounded?

A. Yes, sir.

Q. Where were they wounded, not the location of the wound, but where did this occur, within this military district?

A. It was within this military district, and on our company property.

Q. On your company property?

A. Yes, sir.

Q. Now, you say your company property; what company was that?

A. The Paint Creek Colliery Company.

Q. Paint Creek Colliery Company?

A. Yes, sir.

Q. Did you see Vance die?

A. Yes, sir.

Q. You know the cause of his death?

A. Yes, sir.

Q. What was it?

A. A bullet wound that entered into his head.

Q. Have you seen any of the men who have been arrested, any of these defendants?

A. No, sir.

Q. In that bunch there are a number of men who have been arrested, and are being tried for these offenses; I will ask you to look them over and see if you identify any of them as being on the hill at this fight? Look them over carefully and take you time about it.

A. Is there a man in here with a black beard, tall, heavy man?

Captain Carskadon: That is for you to say.

A. No, sir, I can not positively identify any of those men.

Q. Do you know anything about the Holly Grove fight that took place on the Friday preceding this trouble?

A. No, sir, I was at Mucklow all this time.

Captain Walker: Mr. Pierce, I believe you stated that after you had gone up on the hill, you and your party, that you heard a shot fired off from the main party or over in a different direction, that was visible?

A. Yes, sir.

Q. What did your party do then, commence firing?

A. It was almost simultaneous. When I called, they grabbed their guns before, but the main body of them opened fire, the shooting coming from that direction. We did not open fire until they fired on us. The instructions are not to open fire until we are fired on.

Q. How many shots were fired before you opened fire, other than the one shot?

A. I can not say; there was so much racket.

Q. Can you give us a guess on it?

A. We didn't commence the firing. I have been criticized by everybody on the creek for calling and enquiring about their business, but I feel that I did the right thing. I did not want to get into their hands. We were simply defending ourselves.

Captain Morgan, for the defence: Mr. Pierce, you do not know then whether there was more than one shot fired before you began firing?

A. Yes, sir, there was, but I say that just one an instant before the volley.

The Judge Advocate: Then there was a volley fired before you fired? You mean the first shot, and then there was a volley; was that from your party or into your party, Mr. Pierce?

A. I mean there was one distinct shot and then a number of shots came together, and we all fired together.

Q. Then you opened fire?

A. Yes, sir.

Captain Walker: The impression that you mean to convey, after the first shot was fired, then there was a volley fired, and you all fired together?

A. The party in the middle did that. The party on the right did not open fire on us until several minutes after.

The witness is turned over to the accused for cross-examination by Captain Carskadon.

Q. After the first shot was fired, you got busy, as soon as you could, did you, Mr. Pierce?

A. Yes, sir, after the battle started. There was nothing else that we could do. We were where we simply had to protect ourselves and shoot.

Captain Morgan: Mr. Pierce, how close were you to the log at which Vance was killed?

A. A matter of about 30 feet.

Captain Walker: About how many men were up on the hill, on the other side—about how many of your men, I mean?

A. I should estimate that crowd between 30 and 40. Then there was a larger crowd coming down the hill, I couldn't estimate it.

Q. A larger crowd?

A. Yes, sir, much larger. They were seen from over in the valley. They were seen from there.

Q. Can you give us an approximate estimate of the number in that crowd?

A. They claimed there was over 150. We heard reports that there were that many.

Q. Do you think there were that many or less?

A. I don't think the men further up the creek or ridge, fired until we did. There were some trees on the ridge, on the left, but they were not visible.

Redirect examination by the Judge Advocate:

Q. You are an engineer, Mr. Pierce?

A. Yes, sir.

Q. I want you to take this map and place on it, by pencil, where your men were?

(The witness places on the map the position of his men at the time of the shooting.)

Q. I will ask you to take that map and say about how far along that ridge is Ronda, or the ridge above Ronda, from where that fighting took place and started?

A. Have you got a rule, anybody?

Q. No, we have not; you will have to estimate it with a piece of paper.

A. Ronda is just about—looks to be from two to two and one-half miles.

Q. Is Ronda between where the fight took place and the railroad, or what we would say in the general direction, south of where the fight took place? What I mean is this, I mean leaving the place where you all had your fight and following the ridge, back to the railroad, would that pass Ronda or would you have to go in the other direction to get to Ronda?

A. I am not acquainted in there. I never have been off of our own lease. I can't tell you how you would go to Ronda without going that direction.

Q. Take the map, in a general direction is Ronda south or north of where your fight took place, where the fight took place? That is, is Ronda between the main line of the Chesapeake and Ohio Railway and where the fight took place or is the fight between Ronda and the Chesapeake and Ohio Railway main line?

A. I would say Ronda—the river runs east and west, I would say Ronda was due west of Wacomah.

Q. What I am trying to get at, a man who had been at Wacomah, in this fight, and attempted to get to the Kanawha River, would he pass in the general direction of Ronda or not?

A. Very likely he would; yes, sir.

Q. He would?

A. Yes.

The witness is again turned over to the accused for further cross-examination by Captain Carskadon.

Q. Mr. Pierce, you men were all heavily armed, up on the hill, were you?

A. Yes, sir.

Q. What kinds of arms?

A. Marvin automatic rifles, and automatic Winchesters.

Q. Under what legal authority were you operating up there, Mr. Pierce?

The Judge Advocate objected to this question. The accused, his counsel, the reporter and Judge Advocate withdrew and the commission was closed, and on being opened the president of the commission announced in their presence that the objection was overruled.

A. Well, sir, I should say simply a case of self protection. Anybody that has got any manhood, when he knows people are shooting into a town, where women and children are will go up there and thereby prevent them from shooting into the women and children and injuring them.

Q. These men had not shot into them, had they?

A. No, sir, they had not, but everybody knows what would have happened, if they had not been driven away from there.

Q. Had you any evidence that they were going to shoot into the town?

A. They were there with rifles. They were evidently not going to a church meeting.

Q. They attempted to make no attack on your people?

A. They had not up to that time.

Q. What were they doing when you found them, Mr. Pierce?

A. They were in consultation about something.

Q. Sitting around a spring with their arms lying down on the ground?

A. No, sir.

Q. They were not?

A. Some of them were kneeling and some were standing up and had their rifles ready.

Q. Were they expecting an attack?

A. Evidently not, otherwise we never would have got up the hill.

Q. They were attacked?

A. No, sir, they were not.

Q. Do you think that you have a right, Mr. Pierce, to go out with a body of men and attack another set of men, who are peacably crossing your territory, even though they have been crossing your own territory?

The Judge Advocate objected to this question. . . . The objection was sustained. To which ruling of the commission, the defendants, by counsel, excepted.

Captain Morgan: Mr. Pierce, you speak of some shooting; isn't it true that there has been a great deal of shooting up that hollow?

A. Yes, sir.

Q. Isn't it true that there has been a large body of men employed by these coal companies who constantly carry guns up and down this hollow?

A. The guards employed by the coal company carry guns; yes, sir.

Q. Isn't it true that they have a number of gatling guns and machine guns up this hollow?

The Judge Advocate objected to this question . . . but the objection was not sustained.

A. Our company has owned two machine guns; what is known as a rapid fire gun.

Q. Do you know of any other machine guns up this hollow?

A. I don't know. I am not acquainted with the upper end of the creek.

Q. Mr. Pierce, what is the nature of the country where you found these men; is it improved or unimproved?

A. Unimproved.

Q. Is it not a fact that it is all wild, mountain land, heavily timbered?

A. Fairly well timbered. I don't know just what you are getting at. It is wild mountain land.

Q. The original trees on it, or practically so.

A. I don't know whether there ever has been any timber taken from there. We are timbering on that mountain, but I don't know just what is the extent of it. We are getting the mining props from back on that mountain, if this has any bearing on the case.

Q. Isn't it true, Mr. Pierce, that you have patrols of armed men through those woods every day?

A. No, sir, the soldiers are doing that.

Q. I will amend the question. Isn't it a fact that at the time of this shooting and for many days before, that you, acting in conjunction with the other guards, patrol these woods with rifles.

A. No, sir.

Q. It is not a fact?

A. No, sir.

Q. Isn't it a fact that guards did patrol these woods every day with rifles?

A. No, the only time any guards patrolled the woods was after the Friday morning's shooting. Friday and probably Saturday, but it was not our policy before. We had men working on the hills, furnished with spy glasses, that was their every protection, and the men did not patrol the hills with arms.

Q. Previous to the Friday?

A. No, sir, previous to the Friday before.

Q. Isn't it true that it was a common thing for the coal company to send armed men through those woods?

A. Not since the Baldwin men left; no, sir.

Q. Not since the Baldwin men left?

A. No, sir.

Captain Carskadon: That was originally the plan up there, was it, Mr. Pierce?

A. When the Baldwin guards were there they continually patrolled the woods; yes, sir.

Q. Mr. Pierce, isn't it true that at this time there was a very bitter feeling between the miners on the one side and the guards on the other?

A. Naturally. You mean the guards we employed?

Q. Yes.

A. By miners, you mean the strikers?

Q. By the strikers and by the guards and the union miners and the employees of the Paint Creek Colliery Company on the other side?

A. Naturally.

Q. Isn't it true that there were rumors continually being carried from the miners to you, that you were to be attacked–well, rumors coming from one side to the other, that all sorts of things were going to be done by one side or the other?

The Judge Advocate objected to this question.

Q. I will amend this question just a little. I think it is pertinent when amended a little.

Thereupon counsel for the defendants withdrew the question as propounded first.

Re-redirect examination by the Judge Advocate:

Q. You have been employed by the Paint Creek Colliery Company, how long?

A. About 13 months.

Q. Have you been on Paint Creek all of this trouble? I mean during the last year of 1912?

A. I was there all the time except the month of July, during which time I was in the hospital.

Q. Then you are familiar, have been and are now familiar with the conditions that existed?

A. I am acquainted with the conditions.

Q. I will ask you whether or not there has been employment for all the men who want work on Paint Creek during that time?

A. Yes, sir, there is employment for anybody who wants to work.

Q. I will ask you if there is not employment at other mines, for what is known as union men, and if there is not a mine in the State that do not need more men?

Counsel for the defendants objected to this question. Thereupon the Judge Advocate proceeded to qualify the witness, as follows:

Q. You are a mining engineer, I believe?

A. Yes, sir.

Q. You are familiar with the conditions in the mining country as it exists in the New River field and Kanawha River fields?

A. Yes, sir.

Q. Do you know what mines are regarded as union and non-union?

A. Yes, sir, in a general way.

Q. I will ask you from that knowledge, if you know whether or not so-called union miners who do not want to work on Paint Creek could get employment in the so-called non-union mines in the New River coal fields?

Counsel for the defendants objected to this question. Thereupon the Judge Advocate withdrew the question. The witness is again turned over to the accused for further cross-examination by Captain Carskadon.

Q. Mr. Pierce, do you feel that in protecting property, men or a body of men have authority and have the right to take life?

The Judge Advocate objected to this question, which was withdrawn.

Dave McCartney, a witness for the prosecution, who was first duly sworn, testified as follows in direct examination by the Judge Advocate:

Q. Mr. McCartney, you are employed, I believe, by the Paint Creek Colliery Company, at Mucklow?

A. Yes, sir.

Q. Were you a miner or mine guard?

A. I was a miner.

Q. Were you there on the 10th day of February at the time there was a conflict between some of the miners and mine guards in the employ of the Paint Creek Colliery Company, and certain other parties on the mountain?

A. Yes, sir.

Q. Were you in that fight?

A. I was on the hill.

Q. I will ask you to look at the defendants here and pick out any person that you can, any of the persons you saw in the fight that morning.

(Witness glances at the defendants.)

Q. Get up and take a look at them on each row.

A. This fellow back here, make him stand up.

Q. Stand up please.

(George W. McCoy stands up.)

A. I saw him there. I can not take a solemn oath that he is the one I saw there.

Q. What is your name?

A. McCoy.

Q. You are under oath and you say you are not sure whether you saw him or not?

A. No, I am not perfectly sure.

Q. What is your best belief on it?

Counsel for the defendants objected to this question. The objection was overruled, and defendants' counsel took exception.

A. Well, my best belief is that he was, but he has not the same kind of clothes. I can't go by the man's face to tell the truth, I couldn't see the man's face.

[Captain Walker, a member of the commission, and Captian Morgan, counsel for the defense, interrupted the judge advocate's examination.]

Q. Captain Walker: How close were you to him?

A. I expect in the neighborhood of 60 or 65 yards from him. This man resembles the man.

Q. Sixty or 65 yards from him?

A. Yes, sir.

Q. You are not certain that this man was there?

A. No, sir, I am not really certain.

Captain Morgan: He simply resembles the man, you say?

A. He simply resembles the same man.

Q. He might be his uncle?

A. Yes, or his brother.

Q. (The Judge Advocate) Go ahead now and tell us what took place that morning, in that fight, all that you saw of it.

A. On the morning of the fight I was called to Mucklow.

Q. Open your mouth and talk loud, we don't hear.

A. And they told us that there was a gang of fellows going around the ridge up there, and we went up there over to Wacomah–towards Wacomah and went up on the incline and went around and went on up the hill, where we met these fellows going right past them.

Q. How close were you ahead of your own party when you got up on the hill?

A. I was the third man.

Q. Tell us what took place immediately before the shooting began.

A. One of our fellows in front hollered and said "Who are you? What are you doing over there?" and then the shot was fired.

Q. Who fired that shot, your party or the other party?

A. No, the other side.

Q. Then what happened after that shot was fired?

A. Then there was shooting from both sides.

Q. Any of your party hurt?

A. Two hurt, or I should say two killed and one hurt.

Q. Who were the ones that were killed and who was hurt?

A. One by the name of Vance was killed, and Nesbitt was hurt and Bobbitt was killed.

Q. Vance and Bobbitt were killed, and Nesbitt was hurt?

A. Yes, sir.

No cross-examination by the defendants.

The commission took a recess until one o'clock p. m.

F.W. Howery testified as follows, for the prosecution, in direct examination by the Judge Advocate.

Q. You were sworn on yesterday, I believe?

A. Yes, sir.

Q. On yesterday you were asked about some telephone conversations or calls that took place between Mr. Brown, the defendant here, and a party, over your telephone, and your mind was not altogether clear as to these conversations: I will ask you if you, since you have testified, if I did not read over to you the conversation that was taken and it refreshed your memory somewhat–things you did not testify before–did you have a conversation with me at dinner time over this?

A. Yes, sir.

Q. That has refreshed your memory somewhat?

A. Yes, some.

Q. I will ask you now, if at the time that the defendant, J.W. Brown, talked to the party at Carbondale, if he did not make this statement: "That he was getting desperate and don't care who hears me and asked if they have got any men over there on the other side; that we are wanting men over here" didn't he?

A. I don't remember that.

Q. Do you remember any part of that?

A. (Witness hesitates.) No, sir, I do not think I did.

Q. At the same time, didn't you hear him say "If you have any men with red blood over there, send them over here; if ever we needed men we need them now."

A. I got part of that—"If you have men with red blood in them, we need them"—something like that. I did not catch the whole thing. It was too much of my head.

Q. Too much for your head. Didn't Mr. Brown that night call 2401 and wanted to know when the Bull Moose was going to leave?

A. I do not know what number he called. I don't think it is 2401 though, but he did ask them when the Bull Moose was going to leave.

Q. What arrangement, if any, did you hear him make about being advised when the Bull Moose was going to leave—kept posted?

A. He said he had arrangements with me to keep open—he didn't tell them it was me. He said he had arrangement with the man to keep his store open and that he wanted them to let him know concerning it every hour.

Q. Every hour. I will ask you whether or not you heard Mr. Brown ask them to send him some .44 cartridges and also some .32 special for the old man?

A. Yes, sir.

Q. Who, if you know, did he refer to, did he mean, when he said "the old man?" Who was that or did you understand?

A. That is what I couldn't tell you, who he meant. I supposed he meant himself; but then, I do not know that to be so at all. It is only my supposition for he didn't call any names—he said "for the old man."

Q. "For the old man?"

A. Yes, sir.

Q. I will ask you afterwards, if Mr. Parsons, the same night was not at the telephone down there enquiring about the Bull Moose in the store there—one of the defendants named here, G.F. Parsons: is that not true?

A. It was—Mr. Parsons?

Q. Yes; didn't he also do some telephoning?

A. Yes, sir, he had been the same afternoon.

Q. Didn't Mr. Parsons make this statement in one of those telephone conversations "Things are not looking very well right now but we will raise the devil in a little while. We can't stand everything"?

A. No, sir, I don't remember that.

Q. You don't remember that statement?

A. No, sir.

Q. Now, what, if anything, did you hear Mr. Brown say on the telephone about sending up some ammunition Sunday morning?

A. I don't think ammunition was mentioned at all. He said something about "sending that stuff up."

Q. "That stuff;" how did he say to send it?

A. He didn't say.

Q. You don't remember hearing him say how to send it; just "send up that stuff?" Didn't you hear Mr. Parsons also telephone and use this language—Parsons said "to be sure and bring that stuff up in the morning; don't risk sending it"?

A. No sir.

Q. "Be sure and bring that stuff up in the morning; don't risk sending it." Did you hear him have that telephone conversation?

A. No, sir.

Q. Anything like that?

A. I don't remember him saying "don't risk sending it, to bring it." He might have said bring it.

Q. I understand you then, you did hear Mr. Brown and Mr. Parsons both telephoning down to bring or send some stuff up?

A. Something up.

Q. Your understanding is that Mr. Brown and Mr. Parsons were the men who were the leaders or directors in that situation at Hansford?

A. Yes, sir. I was under the impression. They told me it was—they were trying to protect the town.

Q. They were the leaders aiding and doing the managing of the affairs there?

A. Yes; I mentioned to them about sending such telephones and they said they didn't care who heard it. They said we have a right to protect our town.

No cross-examination.

Thereupon came C.J. Bragg, sworn for the prosecution, who testified as follows in direct examination by the Judge Advocate:

Q. Your name is C.J. Bragg?

A. Yes, sir.

Q. What is your business?

A. I am employed as a mine watchman at Carbon.

Q. Carbon?

A. Yes, sir.

Q. Do you know Mother Jones?

A. Yes, sir.

Q. You attended a meeting of the miners' union between Colcord and Dorothy some time in January of this year.

A. Yes, sir.

Q. Upon that occasion did Mother Jones make a speech?

A. Yes, sir.

Q. What, if anything, did she say about the fellows in this trouble? Just go on now and tell us in your way what she said.

A. Well, she said that it was ridiculous, the low class as the militia came from they would come in and butcher up their people.

Q. What else did she say about the miners' fighting?

A. She said that they ought to fight; that they had a just cause.

Q. Who did she tell them to fight?

A. I don't believe she said.

Q. What statement, if any, did she ever make about fighting the United States–that if they ever came to a fight, the United States couldn't put up such an army as the United Mine Workers?

A. She said if it ever came to a fight the United States couldn't produce such an army as the United Mine Workers.

Q. What statement did she ever make as to what she would do to the Governor if she ever caught him outside of Charleston?

A. She said if she ever caught him out of the State, she would hang him to the first telephone post she could get him to.

Q. What statement about killing the Governor and what she would do if she had her way?

A. She said if she had her way she would kill the last one of them.

Q. Anything else you remember her saying?

A. No, sir, I believe not.

Thereupon came John W. Kyle (colored), sworn for the prosecution and testified in direct examination by the Judge Advocate:

Q. Your name is John Kyles–John W. Kyle?

A. Yes, sir.

Q. Where do you live?

A. Live at South Carbon.

Q. Do you know Mother Jones?

A. Yes, sir.

Q. Did you hear her make a speech on December 22, 1912?

A. Yes, sir.

Q. Saturday?

A. Yes, sir.

Q. Where was that speech made?

A. Up at Holly Grove.

Q. What, if anything, did she say to the miners about allowing transportation men to be brought in here?

A. She said they had a yellow streak up their back if they allowed transportation men to come up the hollow.

Q. What did she tell them to do?

A. I didn't hear her say anything beside that. I was only there a very few minutes.

Q. That is all?

A. Yes, sir.

No cross-examination by defendants.

Thereupon came L.D. Burns, who testified as follows in direct examination by the Judge Advocate:

Q. Your name is L.D. Burns?

A. Yes, sir.

Q. Are you a mine operator or superintendent?

A. Well, operator and manager.

Q. Whereabouts is your place?

A. At Ronda, on Dry Branch.

Q. At Dry Branch?

A. Yes, sir.

Q. I have not talked to you. You are summoned here as a witness against two of these defendants: Creigo and Craise—Harry Craise and Ernest Creigo.

A. Yes, sir.

Q. You know these two men?

A. Yes, sir.

Q. Tell us all you know of their arrest and what they were doing.

A. Well, Mr. Adkins, one of our watchmen, that was back on the ridge, brought the two fellows into our office and he also said, there is his gun.

Q. Do you know anything about it yourself?

A. Nothing further than that they brought them into our office and we found the ammunition.

Q. You saw the ammunition—do you remember who you took it off of?

A. Well, I do not just remember. One of them had—Craise had quite a bunch of Springfield cartridges and Creigo had quite a bunch of .32-20 and also had a pistol, I think—a .32 pistol.

Q. You think he did have a pistol on him?

A. Yes, sir.

Q. Did you see it taken off of him?

A. No, sir, my bookkeeper did it.

Q. Can you tell this commission whether or not there was any excitement around Dry Branch on the morning of February tenth?

A. At Dry Branch?

Q. Yes.

A. There was no excitement in the morning; no, sir. I didn't see anything or hear anything. I was at Ronda, about a mile and a half or two miles away.

Q. About two miles away from there?

A. About a mile and a half or two miles.

No cross-examination by defendants.

Thereupon came L.L. Graybeal, who testified as follows:

Q. What is your business, Mr. Graybeal?

A. Bookkeeper at Coalburg Colliery.

Q. Where do you live?

A. My home is in Greenbrier County, this State.

Q. Where were you on the tenth of February, 1913?

A. Coalburg Colliery Company, at Ronda.

Q. Do you know the defendants, Harry Craise and Ernest Creigo?

A. Yes, sir.

Q. Were you present when they were arrested on the tenth of February?

A. Yes, sir.

Q. Just tell us now what you know about their arrest and what, if anything, they had on them.

A. Mr. Adkins, one of the guards brought the two gentlemen down out of the woods in the evening of the tenth, with him, on Monday, and turned them loose down at the bottom of the hill, near the power-house. I didn't know that he had brought them down. They were strangers to me. I saw two strange men. They were looking for trouble and there were only a few men in the bottom. They were on the track and I asked them what they were doing there and what was their business and they told me they were hunting a job. I told them it was a poor time to be hunting a job and that they had better go on out of the creek. They said they were going and started and got about 100 yards and some of them said they had union badges on them and I told them to stop and went down to see if I could locate them and one of them threw his coat back–I think it was Creigo and they showed his holster under his arm. I asked him where his gun was and he said in his pocket and I went back for Cunningham and told Mr. Hampton to hold them until I got Cunningham and Cunningham came and arrested them and I took them to the office and kept them until morning.

Q. Which one did you take the gun off of?

A. I couldn't distinguish the names of any of them. They gave their names. Now as to that, I would not know.

Q. Which one did you get the gun off of?

A. The largest one of them. I didn't see them take the gun off. I only saw the holster. I was up the road when they arrested them.

Q. Do you know what time that day that shooting around took place near Wacoma and Mucklow?

A. Near five o'clock. I don't know the exact time.

Q. At five o'clock in the afternoon you arrested these fellows, had you at that time heard of the shooting on the mountain?

A. I don't think I heard the shooting.

Q. I asked if you had heard of the shooting.

A. Yes, sir; Lieutenant Taylor had just come in wounded and said that Crockett was wounded badly. Mr. Heffner came in just before that.

Q. These men were arrested after the shooting?

A. Yes, sir.

Q. Were they above or below Ronda—down the creek or higher up the creek or below Ronda, when you saw them?

A. Below the power-house—below Ronda. Adkins had brought them out of the hollow. They saw the men on the hill and it seemed as though they were scattered from the bunch of men on the hill.

Cross-examination by M.F. Matheny:

Q. You don't know that these parties were really where the shooting took place, do you?

A. No, sir; I was in the bottom, at Ronda.

Q. Isn't it a fact that there was a great deal of excitement and commotion on the creek that day?

A. Quite a bit, yes, sir.

Q. And everybody was expecting trouble?

A. Yes, sir.

Q. And these boys started on down the road after you told them to go and you would have allowed them to have gone on had you not been informed that they had on union badges, Mr. Graybeal?

A. Yes, sir. Then Adkins, after they had gone down, he told my men they had on union badges and they had gotten them over there in the woods and I didn't think it was—

Q. You didn't think union badges ought to be worn on the creek?

A. Not in that district, then, I didn't think—

Q. And the conflict on up there has grown out of this strike trouble, hasn't it?

A. Yes, sir.

Q. Does it not?

A. That is what the trouble is.

Q. So the operators and their supporters on the one hand against the union badge and the miners against the Baldwin guard badge; isn't that where the chief contention of this difficulty is?

A. Yes, sir, it seems as though the union is against the guards.

Q. And the guards against the union?

A. And that is their business up there, I guess, partly.

Q. Now, Mr. Graybeal, is this property enclosed, that is the Paint Creek mines, where this trouble occurred?

A. What?

Q. Is it enclosed land or wild woodland?

A. I don't know about the property. I couldn't tell.

Q. I mean in the Paint Creek as a general proposition; are they enclosed by a fence or is it considered woodland?

A. I went after Crockett that night, after he was wounded. I never came across a fence in about three miles. I don't know how the property is at all. That is the first time I have been in there.

Q. It is wild mountain land, isn't it?

A. Yes, sir.

Q. A big mountain running up and down, separating the waters of Paint Creek and the waters of Cabin Creek?

A. Yes, sir.

Q. And in those mountains, from the time the strike was first declared up to the time of the last declaration of martial law, there have been numerous conflicts and a lot of shots exchanged, haven't there?

A. Yes, sir.

Q. The fact of the business is there has been as high as seven or eight hundred men in the woods at one time?

A. That is the report I hear. I have not seen them.

Q. And a number of thousands of shots fired?

A. Yes, sir.

Q. And the feeling has been intense all this time, has it not?

A. Yes, sir.

Redirect examination by the Judge Advocate:

Q. You say you went into the woods after John Crockett, did you?

A. Yes, sir.

Q. What was his shape when you saw him?

A. Well, they had bound his legs up.

Q. Had he been wounded?

A. Yes, sir–been shot through his legs–his leg broken.

Q. He wasn't able to walk?

A. No, sir–carried him out on a cot.

Thereupon came R.L. Taylor, who testified as follows in direct examination by the Judge Advocate:

Q. Your name is R.L. Taylor?

A. Yes, sir.

Q. You were employed, I believe, as a mine guard on Cabin Creek on February 10th, 1913, of this year?

A. Yes, sir.

Q. Did you hear or know of some shooting that took place on the mountain between Wacoma and Mucklow along on that morning or along there on that day?

A. No, sir.

Q. You didn't?

A. Not on that day, I didn't–not until late in the evening.

Q. You didn't hear it in the morning?

A. No, sir.

Q. Were you yourself engaged in any shooting that day?

A. Yes, sir.

Q. Tell us first where it was, what time it was and all about it.

A. Well, it was, as near as I can remember, about two miles from Ronda, back between Ronda and Mucklow.

Q. You say between Ronda and Mucklow; would that be nearer the Kanawha or farther from Ronda?

A. I don't know—about the same distance from the Kanawha River to Ronda, where the shooting taken place—about the same distance.

Q. Just tell us all that took place.

A. Well, at two o'clock—I had been away from the work about ten days and I came in on Monday morning the 10th, in the morning, on the train, and I understood there was some men in the mountains by some of my men that was there and at two o'clock I took two of the men; John Crockett and a boy named Heffner and we went into the mountain. I think we left Dry Branch about two o'clock and went up Dry Branch hollow about a mile and a half and then we taken the tram-road and went in back in this direction, when we came into this point, about two miles from the railroad.

Q. That runs right up from Dry Branch?

A. Sir?

Q. Did you go to the right or left up the creek?

A. To the right, as you go up the creek. Before we got up on top of the point there, we separated and Heffner taken the south side of the ridge going up the creek and I went across through the gap in the hollow and so was climbing the other side of the hill that is on that side of the hill and I saw the boy Heffner running down from the hills below us and we hollered at him a time or two to come where we were, but he didn't stop. He said he didn't hear us and about the same time back on the point back of us there was a party come to the top of the hill and hollered at us and asked us who we was. I hollered back we were guards and I guess they didn't understand what I said. He said, "If you fellows are miners come to us, if not, we are going to kill you right in your tracks." At this time I did not see but one man. He commenced talking to somebody and after they talked they commenced coming over the top of the hill. It seemed like there were from twenty to fifty. I couldn't tell exactly how many and I hollered back—he said to come to him. I said, "I am not going to climb that hill." I said, "You meet us out on that point." It seems to be in a kind of a cove hollow and we were going to get on the point and I told them we could meet them at that point. They kept hollering and we didn't pay any attention, just walked on, Crockett and I, and he was, I reckon about three feet behind me. I had gotten in about—we had gotten in about fifty yards around the top of the hill and they kept hollering "Halt, Halt," but we didn't halt. We kept on going and I didn't think they were going to shoot and all at once they gave the command, "Ready, aim, fire," like the soldiers and at the first volley Crockett fell. I turned back to help him and he is a man weighs 210 and he raised hisself on his elbow and fell back and I thought he was shot pretty bad and I started to go to the top of the hill and when I turned they shot me and the bullet hit me I reckon two inches above the ankle and went through there and that knocked my foot out and I couldn't get along well but I got to the top of the hill and they shot at me until I got over the top of the hill. I don't know how many they shot but I know the balls rained around me pretty fast and when I got over the top of the hill several volleys were fired. I do not know who did it.

Q. What time in the day was that?

A. About five o'clock.

Q. Were you close enough to recognize any of the persons that shot at you?

A. I couldn't identify any of them. They were three hundred to three hundred and fifty yards away. Just as I went over the top of the hill I saw, I think, one or two come out on the point—some were coming out on the point I designated that we would meet them.

Q. Where was that point you designated you would meet them with reference to Ronda station or Ronda?

A. Further on—it seemed to be about south of it.

Q. Of Ronda?

A. Yes, sir.

Q. Was that point nearer to Ronda. A man coming from that point would he come out at Ronda or Dry Branch if coming back to the railroad?

A. Come out about Ronda. That is where I came out and I came a pretty direct road through the hills.

Q. I hand you a map, Mr. Taylor—a topographical map of this country showing the ridges; go over it and indicate, if you are able, with a pencil about your journey and about where you were shot, if you can. There is Dry Branch and there is Ronda (indicating on the map). Work it out if you can.

A. This branch, we followed and it seems that this ravine in here; there is a tram road runs up there and here, this is the point and we came right up in here and the shooting seemed to be right on this point in here—the shooting was done from here.

Q. Put a cross mark over the shooting place and a dot over where you were.

A. We were climbing this hill to this point right in here.

Cross-examination by M.F. Matheny:

Q. You are not able to say to the commission that a single man here on trial was in that crowd that shot at you, Mr. Taylor.

A. No, sir.

Q. And isn't it a fact that that strike on Paint Creek and Cabin Creek involves some three or four thousand men?

A. I do not know how many. I suppose a very good lot of men.

Q. And these men–these three or four thousand men, they also have quite a number of sympathizers at the nearby mines, where they are working under union contracts–is not that so?

A. Sympathizers, you mean?

Q. Yes.

A. I do not know as to that. There is quite a lot of sympathy, I suppose.

Q. You understand that to be the condition.

A. Yes, sir.

Q. And you have had charge there as a mine guard and have watched the development of this trouble, haven't you?

A. To a certain extent.

Q. Isn't it your opinion from what you have been able to gather that not only the striking miners up there have participated in some of these battles and conflicts but also a number of sympathizers from Boomer and other places have come in there?

A. I couldn't state as to that. I do not know any of them.

Q. Your information is that they have been recruited from the outside?

A. I have understood that.

Q. And that a number of people from the north side of the Kanawha River have crossed over and come into the territory–haven't you heard that?

A. I have heard that, yes, sir.

Q. And that is your belief, that they did, is it not?

A. I couldn't believe that they did. I have heard it. I do not know that they did. I couldn't state that.

Q. How many guards have been operating up in there, Mr. Taylor?

A. We had at one time one hundred and ten.

Q. They were all armed with high-power guns, were they not?

A. Yes, sir.

Q. And had some gatling and machine guns mounted?

A. Had two at one time.

Q. Built a fort?

A. No, sir.

Q. Built a concrete fort up there near Mucklow?

Objection. Question withdrawn.

Redirect examination by the Judge Advocate.

Q. Would it have been possible, considering the conditions up there and your guard system, for any number of armed men, say, as many as four or six to have gone up from Dry Branch from the outside on Monday, with their guns showing, without their having been stopped, on Monday, the day that trouble took place?

A. Well, that is not impossible for them to do it, but I had men on duty and was all about there myself and was there until two o'clock and had men on duty there and if they saw them to notify me and I do not think it possible for anybody to get up there without being seen by some of our men.

Q. If they had been seen by some of your men with rifles, would they have been permitted to go on?

A. No, sir; stopped.

Re-redirect examination by M.F. Matheny.

Q. What on duty?

A. A man on duty–patrol of men around the tipples in the daytime and in the bottom.

Q. Did you likewise have mountain patrols at times?

A. Yes, sir. I did not have any patrol out that day. I did the patrolling myself. I wanted to investigate and see if there was anybody in the mountains.

Q. And this is wild, unfenced land where the conflict took place?

A. Yes, sir.

Re-redirect examination by the Judge Advocate:

Q. Whose property was it on?

A. I do not know. I couldn't tell you.

L.T. Hensley testified as follows in direct examination by the Judge Advocate:

Q. You, I believe, helped to arrest the defendants, Ernest Creigo and Harry Craise, on the tenth day of February, 1913, did you not?

A. Yes, sir, I helped start them out of the hill with another man.

Q. Whereabouts did you help start them out of the hill? Where was that in reference to the military district, within that?

A. It is within the military district as I understand.

Q. Where was it in reference to Ronda station?

A. Back about a mile from Ronda station, on top of the ridge.

Q. Which way now, is it between the ridge–between Paint Creek or the ridge west of Cabin Creek?

A. On the ridge between Big Hollow and Paint Branch, on the top of the ridge between them.

Q. That is the ridge between Paint Creek and Cabin Creek proper–in between those two creeks?

A. Not in between the creeks; next to Ronda from the main ridge, between the two creeks.

Q. You do not understand. I don't mean the dividing line. I mean the hill on which these men were, runs between Paint and Cabin creeks?

A. Yes, sir.

Q. What time in the day on Monday did you make the arrest of these two men?

A. Well, about four; between 4:30 and 4:45.

Q. What was the circumstances of your arresting them?

A. There was some shooting in the head of Big Hollow and the men on the ridge had seen enough to phone down to send Adkins off to patrol the mountains and they saw someone in the clearing and when he started they came up in there.

Q. Did you know at that time that Taylor and Crockett were wounded?

A. No, sir.

Q. Did you go after Taylor or Crockett after they were wounded?

A. No, sir.

Q. Do you know where Crockett was wounded? Have you been there since?

A. Where they said he was, I had.

Q. Where was the shooting? You say you heard the shooting up Big Hollow; where was that with reference to where Crockett was?

A. On the hill above where Crockett was. I was on one side of Big Hollow and they were shooting off of the other side.

Q. Well, what did these two men do to make you arrest them?

A. They came up and one had a gun.

Q. Which one, if you know, had the gun?

A. The one who gave his name as Craise.

Q. Craise?

A. Yes, sir.

Q. What kind of gun did he have?

A. Well, the gun I got, .32 Winchester.

Q. What sort of arms, if any, did Creigo have?

A. I never seen his arms.

Q. You didn't see his?

A. No.

Q. What statement, if any, did they make to you in connection with that shooting?

A. They said they had got lost.

Q. Lost?

A. Yes, sir.

Q. Did you make a search of one or both at the time of their arrest?

A. Not at the time.

Q. Did you afterwards?

A. No, sir, I didn't have anything to do in it. I stayed up there after dark.

Q. What did you do with them?

A. Sent them over by a man with me.

Q. Who was with you?

A. Joe Adkins.

Q. Is he here?

A. Yes, sir.

Cross-examination by M.F. Matheny:

Q. They simply told you they were lost up there in the mountains; is that all?

A. That is all they said.

Q. They never told you anything about the shooting at all?

A. No, they never said anything about the shooting.

Q. You were one of the guards?

A. Yes, sir.

Q. How many people were operating with you?

A. One man with me.

Q. Did you have Winchesters?

A. Him?

Q. Did you have Winchesters?

A. Yes, sir.

Q. What sent you up there?

A. Well, that was the instructions, to go up there every day for a while, from the Association, I suppose.

Q. From the guard association?

A. Yes, sir.

Q. They had an association or union, did they?

A. Well, we had a leader who instructed us how to work.

Q. It was a conflict on between the mine guards and the strikers and their sympathizers, is it not?

A. I do not understand exactly what you mean.

Q. The feeling was very bitter between the two factions?

A. Might have been between some—not with me.

Q. I know, but wasn't there very bad and intense feeling existing among the miners towards the mine guards as a body; isn't that your understanding?

A. No, I didn't have any understanding about it.

Q. Well, were you in any of the former battles that took place up there?

A. No, sir.

Q. How many men patrolled the woods?

A. There was—well two or four there—anyhow there was.

Q. I mean at that time?

A. Well, I do not know, me and Adkins was altogether back on that hill.

Q. That system was kept up by all of the companies on the creek, wasn't it?

A. I don't know that.

Q. Isn't that your understanding from your connection with the other guards?

A. Well, I couldn't say.

Q. How many of these guards rode the train backwards and forwards up the Creek?

The Judge Advocate objected to this question, and it was withdrawn.

Captain Carskadon: You say you left Creigo and Craise in the mountains?

A. Yes, sir.

Q. They went down with you?

A. With the fellow with me. I stayed down there.

Q. They didn't offer any resistance to going?

A. No, sir. We told them to walk to us and they went down the hill.

Q. Went down to the station?

A. Yes, sir.

Q. Did you have any process for their arrest?

A. No, sir.

Q. Legal process?

A. I don't suppose I did.

Mr. Matheny: Don't you know you did not, sir.

A. Well, I do not know.

The Judge Advocate: You had no warrant of any sort?

A. No, sir, no warrant.

Joe Adkins testified as follows in direct examination by the Judge Advocate:

Q. You are a mine guard, I believe, Mr. Adkins?

A. Yes, sir.

Q. Employed near Ronda?

A. Yes, sir.

Q. Were you on the date of February 10, 1913?

A. Yes, sir.

Q. You were with Hensley?

A. Yes, sir.

Q. At the time Ernest Creigo and Harry V. Craise were arrested?

A. Yes, sir.

Q. What arms did either or both of those men have?

A. Craise a .32 Winchester and Creigo a .32 revolver.

Q. Did you get the revolver off of Creigo?

A. Yes, sir, after I brought him off of the hill.

Q. What other ammunition, if any, did you get off of either or both of these men?

A. Got some Springfields and Mausers, I suppose. I don't know the difference.

Q. Large calibre?

A. Yes, sir.

Q. Did one or both have them?

A. I don't think but one had.

Q. Which one had the large shells?

A. I do not remember now which one had the large shells.

Q. What statement did they make to you as to their presence in the woods, if any?

A. Said they were trying to get to the river.

Q. Trying to get to the river?

A. Yes, sir.

No cross-examination by defendants.

Emory Heffner testified as follows in direct examination:

Q. What is your name?

A. Emory Heffner.

Q. What is your business?

A. Mine business-office work.

Q. By whom were you employed on the tenth day of February, 1913?

A. I was working for the Consolidated Coal Company at that time.

Q. At what place?

A. At Ronda. I work at Dry Branch, but I was out at Ronda that day.

Q. Who were you in the mountains with?

A. Lieutenant Taylor and John Crockett.

Q. Were you with them at the time they were fired into?

A. No, sir; I was not exactly with them.

Q. Anywheres close to them?

A. Yes, sir, close to them.

Q. Tell us all you saw on that occasion.

A. Well, I was standing in the path waiting for Lieutenant Taylor and
   Crockett to come to me. We had divided on the mountain and I
   was waiting for them and I heard someone coming along the path
   and I walked back out of the path and thought I saw the boys and
   told them to hurry and I came into the path and I saw a crowd of
   men coming along, armed. I stood out in the open and when I first
   saw them I thought that it was the Ronda patrol. I know we had out
   a patrol and I thought it was the Ronda patrol and one of them
   hollered and said, "Who are you." I said I was a guard, and when
   I said that the whole crowd began scattering out and getting down
   behind stumps and things like that. It looked like they were getting ready to fire and I dropped to the ground at the same time so
   they couldn't shoot me and made my getaway around the hill about
   one hundred yards and I went on. I crawled on my hands and knees
   and got up and walked towards them again. I didn't know who they
   were. I didn't get to ask any questions and the next time I got so
   I could see the whole crowd and one man I supposed to be the leader.
   It looked like it. He had a handkerchief around his arm. He said,
   "Who are you?" I asked him who he was. He asked me again, who
   I was. I asked again who he was and he commenced talking, he said
   I want to know who you are. I said I am one of the boys. I had told
   them the other time I was a guard and it didn't seem to go well so
   I said I am one of the boys. He said, "If you are one of the boys,
   come up here." He said to the men, "Don't shoot, I want to talk to

him," and I said, "I don't know who you are." He said we are the miners from up the river. I said, "Well, if you are the miners from up the river, I have some men down the hill and I will bring them up." He said, "All right, how many have you." I said eight or ten.

I turned and whistled like I was whistling for somebody down the hill and I said, "Boys, come up here," and I kept walking along. Well, I was right out in the open and couldn't get away and when I got so the hill was high enough, I dropped on the ground so they couldn't hit me and I dropped on the ground and made my getaway down the hill and when I got down the hill about one hundred yards, the firing took place. Lieutenant Crockett was then on the hill above me and they were shooting across the top and I went on in to Ronda and told them I had met these people in the mountains and that they were shooting and I supposed they were shooting at Lieutenant Crockett, because they were in the mountains with him.

Q. You mean Lieutenant Taylor?

A. Yes, sir, and John Crockett.

Q. Who fired first, Crockett and Taylor or the men on the other hill?

A. I couldn't tell. It was so far. I was not on the hill.

Q. Did you recognize any of the men that accosted you that day?

A. I did not get a very good look at them because I was thinking about something else. I do not think I could recognize any of the men in the woods and then I was some little distance from them.

Q. Did you see the two men that were arrested at Ronda afterwards?

A. Yes, sir, I was there when they were brought in.

Q. Had you seen these men before to your knowledge?

A. Not as I know of. I couldn't recognize any of the men in the crowd at the time I talked to them. They were bunched up—all up close and lying down. I couldn't recognize any of the men at that time.

Q. Is there any other statement you want to make that you have not made about this business?

A. No, sir.

Captain Carskadon: Did any of those men fire at you?

A. No, sir.

M.F. Matheny: You spoke of Lieutenant Taylor. How did he get that title; was he a member of the militia?

A. Yes, sir.

Q. He was at that time not in the military service but in the private employment of the coal company, was he?

A. Yes, sir.

Q. You spoke about another patrol; where was that and who was in it?

A. I said I thought there was another patrol out.

Q. You said that was the custom?

A. When I first saw them I thought it was the patrol that had been put out to guard the mountains.

Q. Generally kept to guard the mines?

A. Several on the mountains for the mines, and this was pretty close to the mine.

Q. How far from Ronda?

A. Mile and a half or two miles back in the mountains from Ronda.

Q. From Ronda?

A. Yes, sir.

Q. Well, how did you get away from there; did you run?

A. When I left I ran, yes, sir.

Q. They hadn't even shot at you at that time?

A. No, sir.

Q. You didn't think it was a good place for a guard to be, did you?

A. I didn't think it was a good place for anyone to be about those men with rifles up on the cliff, with guns all pointed at me.

Q. You thought it was time to sail off?

A. Yes, sir.

Q. You didn't go back when the shooting started, did you?

A. No, sir.

Q. What did you do with your gun?

A. I kept it and took it to Ronda.

Q. Are you still guarding up there?

A. Yes, sir.

Captain Walker: About how many people did you estimate were in this party you saw on the hill?

A. At that time, between twenty-five and thirty people kept coming up from behind the hill.

Q. You say you estimate them at twenty-five to thirty?

A. Yes, sir, and I saw heads still coming up behind the rocks.

Q. What time in the afternoon?

A. Between 4:30 and 5:00 o'clock; right in that neighborhood.

M.F. Matheny: If a fellow is scared, he might be mistaken as to the number of men he saw, might he not?

(No answer by witness.)

S.P. Poindexter testified as follows:

Q. Your name is S.P. Poindexter?

A. Yes, sir.

Q. You were employed as a mine guard on the tenth of February, 1913, were you, the day Lieutenant Taylor and Crockett were shot?

A. Yes, sir.

Q. Where were you at the time Taylor and Crockett were shot?
A. What, at that time I suppose I was at Ronda.
Q. Were you in the mountains or in the town?
A. No, I was in the town.
Q. Were you present at the time they were shot?
A. I was at Ronda.
Q. Were you present with them at the time they were shot?
A. No, sir.
Q. You didn't see the shooting?
A. No, sir.
Q. Were you one of the party that went up into the woods to bring Crockett out?
A. Yes, sir.
Q. You went up too?
A. Yes, sir.
Q. Was he hurt?
A. Shot through both legs.
Q. How seriously, if you know?
A. One leg shot through here and broken, the other one through here—a flesh wound.
Q. Do you know where he is?
A. He is in the Sheltering Arms Hospital.
Q. Do you know anything about any of the trouble that led to his shooting or only know of going after him.
A. No, sir, I cannot say that I know anything about it, any more than that it was kind of expected, I suppose; got out around there and we heard shots up in the hills there and then Lieutenant Taylor came down and told us that he thought Crockett was probably killed and we went after Crockett, is all I know about it.

No cross-examination by defendant's counsel.

O.P. Morgan testified for the prosecution as follows:

Q. Your name is O.P. Morgan?
A. Yes, sir.
Q. You are employed as a mine guard, I believe?
A. Yes, sir.
Q. Whereabouts were you on the tenth of February, 1913?
A. Sharon.
Q. I believe you were with the sheriff when the arrest was made of Carl Morgan, John O'Dell, Ernest O'Dell and Joe Prince, defendants here; is that right?
A. Yes, sir.
Q. Joe Prince is an Italian?

A. Yes, sir.

Q. Tell us what time in the day they were arrested and under what circumstances.

A. Arrested about three thirty or right in around that time, sir.

Q. What time?

A. Three thirty.

Q. Of the afternoon?

A. Yes, sir, as well as I remember—between three and four o'clock.

Q. Between three and four o'clock?

A. Yes, sir.

Q. Do you recall what arms, if any, these fellows had?

A. The four men had a Springfield and Mausers, as I remember; I think one .44 rifle. I didn't pay much attention. I had one go back up the hill and get his rifle.

Q. Which one did you take back to get his rifle?

A. Italia fellow.

Q. Joe Prince?

A. Yes, sir.

Q. What statement, if any, did Joe make to you as to the rifle?

A. Joe Prince said he was looking for work. He said at first, he said he lived at Cabin Creek. I told him he didn't; that I knew everybody that lived there and I asked him if he had a rifle and he said no and I brought him down to the store and I told him I was going to beat him up if he didn't tell where his rifle was and I turned him and told him to go back and get his rifle and he went to Mrs. Clark's and got his rifle and thirty or forty rounds of ammunition—old Springfield—and I brought him back down and turned him over to Bonner Hill [Sheriff of Kanawha County].

Q. Where did those other men have their guns, Morgan, the two O'Dells?

A. A wagon came down and they put the guns in the wagon. Mr. Burns came down and told me—

Q. Don't tell that.

A. Burns came and told me, he says the men have guns and I asked one fellow what gave his name in as Jones, where his gun was and he said he gave it to a boy up there, put it in a wagon and we started back up and got the three guns out of the wagon.

Q. After you got those guns out of the wagon, did these three men admit that they were their guns?

A. Yes, sir.

Q. What statements, if any, did they make about having the guns in their possession then?

A. Didn't give any. I talked to the Italia going back up the hill and left the others there with the rest of the men. I didn't hear them make any statement. He say to me, he said I was looking for work. He said he arrived on a freight train on Paint and got lost and was going across the mountains. That is the statement he gave me and gave the company there.

Q. I will ask you if you helped to arrest four men that afternoon?

A. Yes, sir, I got the other four myself.

Q. They were Grady Everett, William Bainbridge, Bert Nutter, and Charles Lanham?

A. I did not ask them their names. I brought them down and turned them over to Hill and I went over to the train. I don't know anything about these fellows at all.

Q. You took in custody four men; who did you turn them over to?

A. Bonner Hill.

Q. The sheriff?

A. Yes, sir.

Q. Tell all about why you arrested these four men; what they were doing and whether they were armed.

A. I was taking this Italy fellow back to get his gun and I was coming out back down the hill and I seen them coming out of the woods and I was away up track from them and against I got there they came out of the woods and was going down the railroad track and I halted them and asked them where they were going and they said we are hunting for work, the same as the other fellows did and I suspicioned them, the same as the other bunch.

Q. Did you search them?

A. I brought—no, sir, I brought them all down with me—the five with me and I couldn't search them handy.

Q. You don't know whether they had any arms?

A. No, sir, I turned them over to the sheriff.

Captain Walker: They had no rifles?

A. No, sir.

The Judge Advocate: From what direction did they come in reference to Mucklow or Wacoma?

A. Came from towards the direction of Mucklow.

Q. From the hill in that direction?

A. Yes, sir.

Cross-examination by Captain Carskadon.

Q. How far is that store at Sharon from Ronda?

A. About a half a mile.

Q. About how far from where this shooting is supposed to have taken place, in which Crockett was wounded?

A. About a mile and a half or three-quarters.

Q. None of them had any arms?

A. No, sir; none of the last four I gotten.

Captain Morgan: None of them made any resistance?

A. No, sir.

Q. Did any of the first four make any resistance to going with you?

A. No, sir. Morgan tried to go over the bridge and I had to make him come back four or five times—he started to walk away when I was holding them and I had to talk to him pretty rough. He tried to walk away all the time and also the Italy—I can't think of his name—he tried to walk away.

Captain Morgan: Your instructions are to stop any suspicious parties, is it?

A. Yes, sir, that is the orders I had that day.

Captain Carskadon: You really didn't have any authority to arrest them?

A. No, sir; held them on suspicion.

Q. You never saw any of these men before?

A. No, sir.

Q. Don't know any of them?

A. No, sir.

Q. Of the eight?

A. No, sir.

Captain Morgan: None of the men made any attempt to get back in the woods?

A. No, sir, the last four didn't. They were going along about 75 or 100 yards ahead of me when I hollered to halt and I went down and asked them where they were going and they said they were hunting work. One big gentleman with a mustache on, I believe.

Q. Which one is that? (Lanham, stand up—by the Judge Advocate. He does so.)

A. That is the man. He said I am hunting for work, just the same as the other bunch said.

Q. They stopped immediately and made no effort to get away?

A. No, sir, not that I seen and didn't have any rifles with them.

Captain Carskadon: You were armed?

A. Yes, sir, I had a rifle, sir.

Captain Walker: Joe Prince, Carl Morgan, John O'Dell, and Ernest O'Dell, stand up. (They stand.) Are those the four men you spoke about seeing with the guns?

A. Yes, sir.

Q. You are certain of that?

A. Yes, sir. That is Morgan, that is Prince and these two fellows gave their names as Jones; these two gentlemen. That is the name they gave in—Jones; they said they were brothers.

Captain Morgan: You don't know whether their name is O'Dell or not?

A. No, sir. I could swear they are the fellows that I got there; I could swear to that.

Captain Walker: Let the other four, Grady Everett, William Bainbridge, Bert Nutter, and Charles Lanham stand. (They stand.) Are these the four men you got coming out of the woods?

A. They are the ones, the four, that came out of the woods.

Q. You are sure of that, are you?

A. Yes, sir.

Clara Clark testified as follows:

Q. You are Mrs. Clara Clark?

A. Yes, sir.

Q. Where were you on the tenth day of February, this year?

A. At my home.

Q. Whereabouts is that place, ma'am?

A. It is known as Paint Branch, Sharon postoffice.

Q. Sharon postoffice?

A. Yes, sir.

Q. Stand up, Joe Prince. (He does so.) Do you know that defendant?

A. Yes, sir, I know him by sight.

Q. His name is Joe Prince. He is arraigned here under the name of Joe Prince. Was he at your house on the tenth day of February, 1913?

A. Yes, sir, he stopped at my fence.

Q. What did he do when he was there?

A. He gave me a gun and about fifty cartridges.

Q. What did he give them to you for?

A. He told me he had no further use for it and asked me if I had any use for it. I told him No, I didn't know nothing about it. He said he had no further use for it; that he was going to quit running around with the men and go back to Montgomery on the river and stay where he belonged.

Q. Did he make any statement—What time of day was that?

A. It was between three and four o'clock in the evening, I think.

Q. Did he say who the men were he had been running around with?

A. No, sir, he didn't call any names.

Q. Did he say anything about what he had been doing with his gun that day?

A. No, sir.

Cross-examination by M.F. Matheny:

Q. You say he had about fifty cartridges?

A. He gave me about fifty.

Q. A box full?

A. They were not in boxes. Here is one of each kind that he gave me. He is the first gentleman that spoke to me, talked to me. He said they were twenty-two guns that they had; that they were no account–twenty-two guns and these is the cartridges they gave me.

The Judge Advocate: Did you know the other gentlemen? Could you identify the other gentlemen if you were to see them?

A. I think so. The first fellow was talking to me.

Q. Grady Everett, Bainbridge, Nutter, and Lanham, stand up. (They stand.) Look at these men.

A. No, sir, none of them.

Q. John O'Dell, Ernest O'Dell, Carl Morgan, and Joe Prince, stand up. (They stand.)

A. That gentleman right back there.

Q. What is your name?

A. Morgan.

Q. What did he tell you?

A. He came and asked me if they were working at that place, Sharon. I told him I did not know; that I was not a miner and never in the mines. He said he was lost, that he aimed to hit the Dry Branch hollow and he came in there on Paint Branch. I asked him if he knew the gentlemen coming behind him with the guns, and he said he met them on the hill; they bought those guns; that they were twenty-twos; that they were no account. That is about all he told me.

Cross-examination by M.F. Matheny:

Q. He didn't tell you that he was engaged in any of the shooting, did he?

A. No, sir.

Captain Walker: You said a while ago, Mrs. Clark, that Joe Prince gave you a gun; was that a revolver or a rifle gun?

A. A Springfield, marked on the side. An old gun. Great long.

Q. Now, the man that was following, Carl Morgan; you said they had guns. Were they like the gun given you–the condition?

A. While Morgan was talking to me he had no gun, but the three fellows behind him–one man had two guns and each of the others had a gun and when these men came to Morgan, gave him a gun and each man had a gun. Mr. Prince, you call him, gave me his gun and three of them left with guns and they left one with me.

Q. Were the guns all alike?

A. No, sir; some newer than the others; new-like guns.

Arthur J. Thompson testified as follows:

Q. You are–what is your name, Thompson?

A. Arthur J. Thompson.

Q. What is you business?

A. Acting State Historian and Archivist at this time.

Q. Where are your headquarters?

A. Third floor of the Annex Building.

Q. Do you know who publishes the *Labor Argus*?

A. Yes, sir.

Q. Who is it?

A. Mr. Boswell, I think, is the editor.

Q. Mr. Boswell. I will ask you if it is customary for the regular edition of the *Labor Argus* to be sent to the Department of the Archivist and Historian?

A. Yes, sir.

Q. Do you have in your possession any copies of that paper?

A. Yes, sir.

Q. I will ask you to identify the number of papers and the dates.

A. March sixth, February 6, February 13th, 20th, 17th; January 2nd, 9th, 16th, 23rd, 30th, December 5th, 1912, 12th, 19th, 26th, November 7th, 14th, 21st, 28th, October 3rd, 10th, 31st, September 5, 12th, 19th, 26th.

Q. That is the regular edition of the paper put out in general circulation?

A. Yes, sir.

[The Judge Advocate:] We will offer them later on. We wanted him to identify them.

No cross-examination by defense counsel.

Mr. Poindexter was recalled by the prosecution and testified as follows:

Q. Mr. Poindexter, have you got the ammunition you took off of Mr. Craise and Mr. Creigo?

A. No, sir. I turned it over to Mr. Cunningham or someone; anyhow, it was taken care of, I know. I think it was Lieutenant Taylor—he was sitting on the porch at the time. I think I turned it over to the party on the porch next to him, the last I saw of it.

Q. You can, if you are shown that ammunition you got off of those people, a similar kind?

A. I can simply say it was the same kind of cartridges, yes, sir, which I took off of these and the Dillons. A double handful. More than is there, in his pocket.

Q. Where did these come from?

A. I do not know. I did not see any of that kind.

Alex. W. Laing testified as follows:

Q. What is your business, Mr. Laing?

A. Superintendent of the Wyatt Coal Company.

Q. Where are your headquarters?

A. Sharon.

Q. Where were you on the tenth of February, 1913, that was Monday, at the time of this trouble?

A. I was at Sharon.

Q. How long have you been in the coal business?

A. Ever since I have been old enough to be connected with it.

Q. How long have you been in the coal business in this New River and Kanawha Field?

A. I came here January 23, 1907, I think.

Q. Are you the same Mr. Laing that this man Morgan, a mine guard, turned over eight persons–the eight persons who are now prisoners here, on the tenth of February?

A. Who?

Q. Morgan.

A. Yes, sir.

Q. Did you question these prisoners–these men?

A. I asked some questions, yes, sir.

Q. What names, if any, did they give you?

A. The first man gave his name when I asked him who he was as W.S. Chapman, from Houston, and he afterwards told me that Chapman was not his name and that he was Carl Morgan, from Dry Branch.

Q. Carl Morgan, from Dry Branch?

A. Yes, sir.

Q. W.S. Chapman, from Houston?

A. Yes, sir, and afterwards said he was Carl Morgan from Dry Branch.

Q. What did the others say their name was?

A. Two of the men said their name was Jones; James and John.

Q. Did they afterwards give you any other name?

A. No, sir, they did not.

Q. What about the other?

A. Well, I think the Italian gave his name as Joe Pizzanna or Pains–I do not know which.

Q. What did the other four men say was their names?

A. I don't know.

Q. Did they give you names?

A. I do not know. My wife was going to Charleston when they came down with them four and I went to meet my wife to help her to the train. Those men I would not recognize–the last four. The first four I do.

Q. John Jones and Tom Jones?

A. John Jones and James Jones.

Q. Ernest O'Dell, John O'Dell, and Joe Prince, stand up. (They stand.) Look at these gentlemen and say whether or not you recognize them.

A. That gentleman there, and this one, I recognize.

Q. What name did they give?

A. This one was Pains or Pizzanna and these two gentlemen Jones.

Q. They gave their names as Jones.

A. Yes, sir.

Q. What statements, if any, did they make about themselves, as to where they were?

A. I do not just remember that these three gentlemen made any statement as to what their business was, except that they were going to go to Cabin Creek junction.

Q. Did you have any personal knowledge of the shooting that took place that day on the mountain?

A. Nothing personal, except what we heard.

Q. I will ask you whether the papers here, this *Labor Argus*, has a pretty considerable circulation on these two creeks in this district; what is your information and knowledge as to that?

A. It has a pretty wide circulation. Quite a number of people who live close to me take the paper.

Q. I will ask you whether or not you are familiar with the districts in this; I mean, familiar with the mines in the New River and Kanawha field, in which a number of mines are unionized?

A. I am, in a general way. I do not know of any that are unionized in the New River field. I was raised in the New River field. I do not know of any of them that are located close to where I was raised—not in the New River district.

Q. Do you know of any union mines in the Kanawha field?

A. None except on the river; Eskdale, Dorothy, on Cabin Creek.

Q. I will ask you if there is any demand for union miners in the union mines?

A. I couldn't say.

Captain Walker: Carl Morgan, stand up. (He does so.) Is that the man who first gave you his name as Chapman and then afterwards as Morgan?

A. Yes, sir.

Q. You are sure of that?

A. Yes, sir.

Captain Morgan: Mr. Laing, you said this paper had a wide circulation in this district?

A. I mean the district in which I live.

Q. In the district in which you live—you referred, when you said that of the *Labor Argus*.

A. I did.

Q. Who is the editor of that paper?

A. Mr. Boswell, as I understand it, is the editor. That is my understanding. I do not know Mr. Boswell.

Rebecca Burns testified as follows:

Q. What is your name?

A. Rebecca Burns.

Q. Where were you on the tenth of February of this year.

A. Standing in my coal house.

Q. Where?

A. Standing in my coal house, getting coal to get supper.

Q. Whereabouts was that?

A. In Paint Hollow, near Sharon.

Q. Do you know Mrs. Clara Clark?

A. Yes, sir.

Q. How close do you live to her?

A. About 40 yards.

Q. Do you know when some men came up and gave her a gun; if anything you saw—

A. Yes, sir, I know the four men came along. Three had guns and one did not when they passed me, but he had just given her a gun.

Q. You saw these men come along?

A. Yes, sir.

Q. You don't know where they came from or anything about it?

A. Only out of the hollow, back of the house.

Q. What time of day?

A. Between three and four. Just about supper time—fixing for supper. I did not look at the clock.

No cross-examination by defense counsel.

Will Burns testified as follows:

Q. Where do you live?

A. Sharon, West Virginia.

Q. What are you, a miner or mine guard?

A. I am a miner.

Q. You are not the great detective yourself?

A. No, sir.

Q. Where were you on the tenth of February, 1913?

A. I worked until about one o'clock.

Q. Do you know Mr. O.P. Morgan, who was a mine guard at Sharon?

A. Yes, sir.

Q. Did you see any men coming out of the mountains that day, armed?

A. I did not see them coming out of the mountains. I saw them coming down the hill.

Q. How many were there?

A. Four.

Q. Did you know them?

A. No, sir.

Q. Did you know their names?

A. I heard their names that evening. I do not know them, personally.

Q. You are the man, I believe, that called Morgan's attention to them coming out of there?

A. Yes, sir.

Q. What was your reason for doing that?

A. The reason I called Morgan?

Q. Yes.

A. I was going down to supper and I stopped at Mr. Clover's—he had a phone—mine foreman, and I phoned. Mr. Laing answered the phone when I called the office, and I told him there was four men coming down the hollow and that three of them were armed.

Q. The four; one without anything?

A. No, sir.

Q. What kind of arms did they have?

A. Three of them; two of them these army guns—I don't know the names of them and one was a Winchester.

Q. Did these men make any attempt to dispose of the guns you saw—hide them in anyways?

A. No, sir, I did not see them.

Q. You don't know anything more than that you saw them and told Morgan?

A. Told Mr. Laing.

Q. And these were the men Morgan afterwards arrested?

A. Yes, sir.

Q. What time in the afternoon was that? What hour?

A. Between three and four.

Q. Do you know what those men had been doing and where they came from or anything about that?

A. No, sir, I don't know anything about that.

Q. Do you know anything about the shooting that took place in the mountains that day?

A. Just hearsay.

Q. You, yourself, don't know?

A. No, sir, I was working until one-thirty.

Captain Carskadon: You didn't know any of them at all?

A. No, sir.

Q. Are you an organized man?

A. I am an organized weigh boss.

The Judge Advocate: Carl Morgan, O'Dell—the two O'Dells, and Joe Prince, stand up. (They stand.) Look at these men. Do you recognize these men?

A. I have seen them before.

Q. Where?

A. At Sharon, West Virginia.

Q. Are these the four men you pointed out to Morgan?

A. Yes, sir.

Frank Smith testified as follows:

Q. What is your name?

A. Frank A. Smith, sir.

Q. What is your business?

A. I am a secret service man for W.J. Burns Detective Agency.

Q. How long have you been connected with the W.J. Burns Detective Agency?
A. I was engaged in this case the last five months, approximately; a few days less, maybe.
Q. Where were you on February 7, 8, 9, and 10, 1913?
A. February 7, 8, 9, I was down at Charleston and Cabin Creek. February 10 I returned to Charleston and had orders to go up on Paint Creek. I left on the evening train with the intention of going to Mucklow.
Q. What day was that?
A. February tenth, Monday, and I left the junction and passed up to Holly Grove. I saw nothing at Mucklow I could investigate and I stopped over at Holly Grove. Upon my arrival, as soon as the train passed, I seen a couple of men and as soon as the train passed about, approximately twenty men came from different directions and went around me and wanted to know who I am. I had a card from the United Mine Workers, Mossy Local. I showed the card and proved myself to be all right and they commenced to talk to me. The first man talked was a fellow named Steve Yeager, a Slavish fellow. I commenced talking as I know different languages. I talked to the fellow and he told me who he was and he had a Springfield rifle. Every man at the station was armed except one Anthony Knoff. He was not but afterwards he went in the store and got his gun and came out. That was the tenth of February, this month, and he told me—
Q. Don't tell about that.
A. Steve Yeager who is here present, he told me he was in the coal strike up in Pennsylvania and he knew how to handle his gun. He told me he was there almost three years and he was done waiting. He said no chance getting along as the guards can come here and they were laying there for them and he and a couple of other men—some of them I know their names and some I don't know, but I know them but I don't know their names, said that they were laying for the Bull Moose and a fellow, Henry Barry, who seemed to be the leader, came to me next and talked and he said we are going to Hansford, all the men together, when the men come up from the mountains that was the intention but all the men was not here yet, and that a couple of men came over here but that no man could pass that line without a signal; the signal they must give two whistles and three whistles answer, and they said they didn't have enough ammunition. They said Parsons did not distribute the ammunition on Sunday previous and he didn't distribute the ammunition very well; that some of the men didn't get more than thirty-five rounds and they decided to go to Hansford that relief would be needed there, they were laying for the Bull Moose but before going they wanted some supper and they decided to hold a conference and wanted to take out a couple of rails from the track, to wreck—

Q. Don't tell about that. What do you know about any of these defendants here, what they did this night; but, before that, I will ask you, where were you on Sunday, the day before.

A. Sunday, I had orders to observe the trains, who leaves, I was in Charleston.

Q. On Sunday, I will ask you if you saw the defendant, Mr. Boswell, the gentleman over there?

A. Yes, sir, I seen him.

Q. And Mr. Brown?

A. Yes, sir. Sunday morning, Mr. Boswell and Mr. Brown and three other men I know personally went from the *Labor Argus* to the K. & M. station. They had three suit cases and a couple of packages. If I am not mistaken, I think that they had newspapers around them. They left on the morning train. I couldn't follow them very closely. They knew me but I watched every train that came in on the K. & M. and I seen the same men come back about half-past seven on the K. & M. train.

Q. Sunday evening?

A. Sunday evening and I stopped one of the men I knew and started to talk with him and Mr. Brown called him for he kind of suspicioned me a little.

Q. Did you see Brown, Monday, February tenth?

A. Yes, sir, I did.

Q. What were the circumstances?

A. I seen Mr. Brown, February tenth, Monday night, after we came to Hansford. We stood around and I saw a great number of men around the station, holding conferences between them. I saw Mr. Parsons talking to one of the men. Parsons went with that man and they went into Mr. Harris' store and were in there; a couple of minutes later two boxes of dynamite; I could see very good, it was dynamite. The men carried the cases on their left shoulder and they were exposed to my view. I do not know where they deposited that dynamite. They carried it in cases and deposited it in an empty building down about the old saloon on the bank of the river. Now, after that there was orders given to put all the lights out and a couple of boys went out on the poles and turned out all of the lights separately—every light separately—turned the lights out and told me they were looking for the Bull Moose. There was quite a crowd there and they say they had the news by telegraph when the Bull Moose was coming and they were all laying for it and after I seen all what was to see and all the men with the guns and they told me what they were laying for and what they were intending to do, Mr. Brown came over.

Q. What Mr. Brown do you mean, the defendant?

A. John Brown, the gentleman sitting there next to Mother Jones. He wore a black overcoat, his head mussed up and his face red and a bad smell of liquor in his breath and his hat in his right hand, and asked me what I was doing here. I told him I held a position of inspector with Jeffreys for electric machines myself, you know, what I am to do. He said, "No, that is not all you are doing for the Jeffreys people." I said, "That is all what the Jeffreys people has out of me." The Jeffreys people didn't know what I was doing and then he told me I am in danger. He said, "Our men are slaughtered on the hill; we are not going to stand for it." He said, "We are going to stand for the right." He said, "Life is worth nothing." I said, "No, I don't know they were fighting; I only came from Mucklow and they told me to get off and they brought me to Holly Grove," and then he said, "You get out of here and go just as fast as you can down the track."

All the time we were talking, four men with Springfield rifles laying over their arms and I knew I would be shot down so I just asked Mr. Brown if he won't accompany—if he won't accompany me down the track about a hundred feet. Mr. Brown thought for quite a bit and said, "Well." Well, we went there—well, we were there and one of the men came over and said something and Brown said, "Who is running this thing, you or me." He said, "I am running this thing." He went 100 feet with me down the track and said he was going to save my life. If I lived 100 years, he said, I am adding 100 years to your life, that the best thing I can do would be to go down the track as fast as I can to Cabin Creek or somewhere and never come back. I told him I want to go and on the way down, about Crown Hill the first tipple I met about ten men, all armed and going through Crown Hill. They stopped me and they halted me and asked me what I am doing. I said I am come from Hansford. They asked me what doing. I showed my card again and a union man the first thing asked me, "Is John Brown there?" I told them yes and they said I may go and after they passed a couple of tipples I lay down behind one of the timbers and it was pretty dark and they had a flashlight and once in a while they flashed the light so I could see them making toward Hansford bunch and then I went from there down about a half a mile further and met about three or four men and they halted me again and give some kind of sign—they whistled and as a freight train passed, I couldn't hear it very well and one shot was fired at me at that time and asked me where I am going. I said, "I am going to East Bank." Well, they asked me where I come from and I told them from Hansford and John Brown told me to get out here. Well, they let me through without further question and I went on the same way and arrived at East Bank among union men and I spent that night on the river bank, etc., until next morning and I went to Cedar Grove. At Cedar Grove next morning the train was 50 minutes late and I just ran around the river bank and ferries to see anybody come and I saw a few number of men coming with rifles and belonged to Cedar Grove they said. I did not know the men.

Q. Where were you on the 27th of January?

A. January 27 I was in Cabin Creek Junction and went down to Dry Branch and some place around there—Chelyan.

Q. Did you see Mother Jones that day?

A. No, sir, not that day. I saw Mother Jones the next day, February 28th. I met Mother Jones at the station, in company with a gentleman I see, Mr. Batley, with glasses. They were there and I shook hands with Mother Jones with a few around. She was talking about a speech. She was there in Eskdale that day and made a speech and she was talking to them a little bit and told them that every time the guards beat them up they came to her crying and she said if she was a guard she would beat them up because they stand for it; that they didn't have to fight and she told them they have a yellow streak; that it was their own fault what they did. She told somebody, I don't know the name of the man, young boys, between 18 and 20 of them, they ought to get their members in Colorado and get some nerve injected into them, and she told the members in Eskdale as I was told by a miner present.

Q. Don't tell that. Just tell what Mother Jones said.

A. What is all I said.

Q. Don't tell what the miners told you she said.

Counsel for the defendants here asked the commission to hold this witness over for cross-examination after they had an opportunity to confer.

Frank A. Smith, recalled by the Judge Advocate, testified as follows:

Q. One question I omitted to ask you: You said they were laying for the Bull Moose; what was the Bull Moose; what was your understanding that the Bull Moose was?

A. The general understanding about the Bull Moose—the train was supposed to bring the troops that night.

Q. You mean the National Guard?

A. Yes, sir, the National Guard and whoever was on the train. The preparation was to meet any move to be made. The intention was to shoot up that train. You want me to point out the men I seen then?

Q. Yes.

A. That man, Harrison Ellis. That man, I don't know his name.

Captain Walker: Do you know this man's name?

A. I don't know his name. I seen him there.

Q. Is that man over there Price or Huffman?

(W.H. Huffman stands and says his name is W.H. Huffman.)

Q. You saw him where?

A. At Hansford.

Q. And this man, Harrison Ellis?

A. Yes, sir.

Q. The second man?

A. I seen Harrison Ellis, at Holly Grove and he went down to Hansford, about two hundred yards ahead of me.

Q. Who else?

A. Huffman, and I seen Mr. Parsons that night. He was in the crowd and then went back to Howery's store.

Q. Where did you see Parsons?

A. At Hansford. He didn't have any rifle. He went over there shortly before the dynamite was carted out. Parsons, I know, with another man not here and I seen Steve Yeager, a Slavish fellow, at Holly Grove.

Captain Carskadon: That is the same man?

A. Yes, sir. I saw a fellow named Parrish—right there; the first man I seen at Holly Grove.

Q. What man is that?

A. Robert Parrish, that is his name.

The Judge Advocate: Did he have a rifle?

A. Yes, sir. He was the first man I seen in Holly Grove when I got off of the train. Met him and Steve Yeager. I seen Sanford Kirk. I didn't talk to him.

Q. What did he do?

A. I seen him at Holly Grove, while we were at supper in one of the houses. He came in with another fellow with an overcoat on that is not here. He said he was worn out and tired on account he didn't have any sleep the last three nights he was out. He said if he would see one of the guards he could take his shoes off and he said he and his friends held up a freight train before he came here, behind empty cars and that he made the engineer, at the point of a gun, uncouple the train and got around and came on to Hansford. We seen the train standing on a siding. I didn't see anything behind it. Sanford was going with us to Hansford. He had a gun. He was in the party. He is the only man I see around here. Some more men I seen but they ain't here. Might be some more here that I couldn't recognize. It was dark.

Captain Walker: Did Kirk have a gun?

A. Yes, sir, he came with a gun to the house of Lawrence Perry and a couple of men went with some crowd. A couple of men ahead with some crowd going to Hansford, set of men. Two groups. Two men. Harrison Ellis was in the first group. They got about two hundred yards. Ellis in the one ahead of us.

Q. Any other of these gentlemen?

A. I seen Mr. Brown there Monday. I stated about Mr. Brown. He is the one made me leave the town of Hansford. That is the night he saved my life.

Q. All these men that you have named, all of them had guns except Mr. Parsons?

A. Yes, sir; except Parsons didn't have any gun.

Q. What connection did he have with securing the dynamite?

A. He went over with another gentleman, whose name I know, not in court, and after that, something like two minutes afterward, they seemed to supervise the removing of the dynamite from the store.

Q. Supervising the removing?

A. Yes, sir; he and another man not here.

Q. Who was that man?

A. Doug Damron or Doug Diamond. He goes by both.

M.F. Matheny: We would like to have the commission hold this gentleman for cross-examination on Monday. (Witness was excused.)

Fred Clendennin testified as follows:

Q. Your name is what?

A. Fred Clendennin.

Q. You are employed by the government in some capacity?

A. At Riverside, at Lock Three.

Q. Did you run the ferry on the morning of February 9, 1913, Sunday?

A. Yes, sir.

Q. Did you make the trip after the K. & M. train ran that Sunday morning?

A. Yes, sir.

Q. I will ask you to tell this commission whether or not on that morning any men came over bringing suitcases, and if so, how many?

A. Yes, sir, some men came over that day with suitcases.

Q. How many men and how many suitcases?

A. I don't know how many men—two or three suitcases. I didn't pay much attention to them.

Q. Was there anything about the way the men handled them that made you believe they were heavy?

A. I did not pay attention to that. I just seen the suitcases.

Q. Did you know the men that brought them over?

A. No, sir.

Q. Did you get any information at that time that those suitcases contained ammunition in them?

A. No, sir.

Q. After that?

A. Yes, sir, I heard the boys talking about them after that.

Q. But you do recollect that you had people come over on the train with the suitcases?

A. Yes, sir, men crossed the river with the suitcases.

Q. Did you know the names of these people?

A. No, sir, I did not know. No, I saw one man, Mr. Brown. I saw him before the train came in there. He didn't come on the train.

Q. Did he come with the men who had the suitcases?

A. He crossed the river at the same time.

Q. What Brown was that?

A. I don't know—Mr. Brown.

Q. Look around and see if you see that Mr. Brown.

A. Yes, sir, the gentleman over here.

Q. Mr. John Brown: he came over on the boat with the men with the suitcases?

A. Yes, sir.

No cross-examination by defense counsel. The court adjourned until Monday, March 10, 1913, at 9:00 a.m. When court resumed pursuant to adjournment, Frank A. Smith was recalled, and turned over to the accused for cross-examination by M.F. Matheny.

Q. Are you the same Smith who testified that you were a member of the Burns Detective Agency?

A. Yes, sir.

Q. How long have you been operating in this field?

A. Five months—approximately five months, maybe a little shorter, not quite five months, mighty near, though.

Q. Who employed the agency to do this special work, the coal companies or the State?

The Judge Advocate objected to this question, no ruling by the commission.

A. (No response.)

Q. I will ask you to state at this time if you are in the employment of the State?

The Judge Advocate objected to this question, his objection was sustained, and counsel for the defendants excepted.

C.M. Fenton testified as follows:

Q. Where do you live, Mr. Fenton, and what is your business?

A. I call Columbus my home but I am acting superintendent of the Columbus Iron and Steel company, over at Marting, Fayette County.

Q. Where is Marting?

A. Four miles up Smithers Creek; Smithers Creek is opposite Montgomery.

Q. About how long have you been connected with the mine, Mr. Fenton?

A. About four years, off and on.

Q. Is that union or non-union?

A. Union mine.

Q. I will ask you if during the fall and up to now there has been any demand for union men over there?

A. We have been short of men throughout 1912, up to the present time.

Counsel for the defendants objected to this question and answer and moved the commission to strike same from the record. No ruling by the commission.

Q. I will ask you this question: Does the *Labor Argus* circulate up in your mine?

A. I think it does.

Q. Have you ever had any chance to observe what the effect of the circulation of that publication has there, with reference to incite violence or otherwise?

A. I have talked with our men about some questions raised in the *Labor Argus*, and it seems to create a strained feeling between the buyer of labor and seller. I get a copy of it occasionally. It is very radical.

Counsel for the accused declined to cross-examine the witness.

Thomas Nesbitt testified as follows:

Q. You are employed as a mine guard or miner at Mucklow, or were employed there, on the 10th day of February, this year, were you?

A. Yes, sir.

Q. Which were you, mine guard or miner?

A. Miner.

Q. Were you a miner?

A. Yes, sir.

Q. I will ask you whether or not you had anything to do with or what you did in the shooting that took place on the hill above Mucklow on February 10, 1913?

A. Well, I was up there the day that they had the shooting, above Wacoma.

Q. Above Wacoma is what I mean.

A. Yes, sir.

Q. Just tell this commission how that shooting began.

A. Well, they saw the miners on the hill, somebody from Mucklow, and we went up the Wacoma mountain with the intention of heading them off, and we got up to the top of the hill we just run into them and Mr. Pierce hollered at them and they fired on us. Of course, we just had to fire on them.

Q. Were you hurt upon that occasion?

A. Yes, sir.

Q. How badly, tell the commission?

A. I was shot through the neck.

Q. Show the wound to the commission, show about where it was, indicate about where it was.

A. I was shot through there and it come out in the top of my shoulder.

Q. I will ask you if you can identify any of these prisoners as being present at the time of that shooting; for the purpose of identification, everybody on the back row stand up first. (Those on the back row stand up.) Do you identify any of those prisoners in that back row as being present at the time of that shooting?

A. No, sir.

Q. The second row, stand up.

A. No, sir, I can't.

Q. The next row stand up.

A. No, sir.

Q. The first row you can see. Do you identify any of those prisoners at all as being there?

A No, sir.

Counsel for the defendants declined to cross-examine the witness.

James Owens testified as follows:

Q. Where do you live, Mr. Owens?

A. I live in Mingo County.

Q. Where were you on Monday, on the 10th day of February, 1913?

A. Up here at Wacoma.

Q. What was your business there?

A. Loading coal up there.

Q. You were loading coal at Wacoma?

A. Yes, sir. I was not loading coal on the 10th, I was on guard duty that day.

Q. But you were employed as a coal loader?

A. Yes, sir.

Q. And not a guard?

A. No, sir, only during that trouble I was.

Q. What did you have to do with that fight, or were you in the fight that took place on the 10th day of February, 1913?

A. Yes, sir, I was up there.

Q. The rear row stand up. I will ask you to look at these men as they stand up, and see if you know any of these prisoners as being present there that day.

A. No, sir, I can't.

Q. The next row stand up.

A. No, sir, I can't.

Q. The next row get up.

A. No, sir, I can't identify any of these.

Q. You can see those sitting in the front row?

A. No, sir, I can't identify any of them to swear to them.

Q. How is that—I can't hear you?

A. I say I can't identify any of them to swear to them.

Counsel for the accused decline to cross-examine the witness.

Joseph Lytle testified as follows:

Q. What were you doing on the 10th day of February, 1913?

A. I was in Wacoma.

Q. What was your employment on that date, a guard or miner?

A. I was going to work and we were called down to Mucklow.

Q. Did you take part in the fight that occurred on the hill that morning, in which some men were hurt?

A. Yes, sir, I was up there.

Q. I will ask you to look at these men as they stand up on the several rows, and see if you identify any of these persons who were in that fight. The men in the rear row stand up.

A. No, sir.

Q. Take a look at them.

A. No, sir.

Q. The second row stand up.

A. No, sir.

Q. The next row stand up.

A. There is one man that I see resembles the one I seen, by his clothes. I can't swear positively sure that he was the man. That is the only way I could give any account of it, is that fellow with the mustache, that little fellow.

Q. What is your name? (To one of the defendants.)

A. John Siketo.

A. It is only by his clothes; I can't recognize him any other way.

Q. Now look at the front row.

A. No, sir, I can't identify any of them.

Captain Carskadon cross-examined the witness.

Q. You do not know the man's face at all that you speak of?

A. No, sir, I can't swear to any man.

Captain Walker: How close were you to the man that was firing, that you say you recognize?

A. Between 60 and 65 yards, as far as I could guess.

Q. Between 60 and 65 yards?

A. Yes, sir.

Q. Where did this shooting begin?

A. I can't tell exactly what time it started.

Q. I don't mean the time. Who shot first; did you shoot first?

A. No, sir, when we went up there we hollered at them, and hollered three times at them and they made no answer and the answer or holler was repeated, and they shot back at us.

M.F. Matheny: How many shots were fired in that conflict?

A. I can't tell you.

Q. Can you give the commission an estimate of how many men were engaged and how many shots were fired?

A. No, sir, I can't tell you how many shots were fired.

Q. During what period of time did the fight range?

A. Well, I can't tell exactly what time it was when it started, or I can't tell you exactly what time it was when it ended.

Q. Give the commission about the time that it lasted, if you can.

A. As far as I could guess it was about three quarters of an hour.

Q. And a general shooting all through the woods for three quarters of an hour?

A. Yes, sir, there was shooting right along.

Q. Pretty warm time up there?

A. Pretty warm?

Q. I mean by that the engagement was thick and fast, a hot fight about three quarters of an hour?

A. As far as I could guess it was about three quarters of an hour.

Q. Can you give the commission an estimate of how many men were engaged there on both sides?

A. No, sir.

Q. It was a mountain fight, wasn't it?

A. Yes, sir.

Q. Taking in the roughs of the mountains?

A. Yes, sir.

Q. The timber and rocks?

A. Yes, sir.

Q. Knobs and hollows?

A. Yes, sir.

Q. How far was that from the town? I mean from the creeks on either side, up to the top of this mountain where the shooting took place?

A. I can't exactly tell the distance. I can't answer that. I can't exactly tell the distance. I guess it must be pretty close to half a mile from the town, from Wacoma.

Q. Back on top of the main ridge, wasn't it?

A. Yes, sir.

Q. Were you in the battle up there?

A. Yes, sir, that was the only one I was in there, on that day.

Captain Carskadon: Did you get to the top of the hill, where the shooting actually took place?

A. Yes, sir.

Captain Morgan: Did you take any part in it?

A. Yes, sir.

Q. How many shots were fired; how many shots did you fire?

A. I can't recognize how many shots I fired. To the best of my knowledge I can't tell you.

Q. What were you shooting at?

A. What was I shooting at?

Q. Yes, what were you shooting at?

A. We were shooting over where they were. Of course we were trying to defend ourselves. We didn't know whether we shot anybody or couldn't tell whether we shot anybody or not.

M.F. Matheny: You shot at something?

A. We shot over there, of course, when they shot at us, shot the second round at us, before ever we opened up.

Captain Morgan: You aimed to hit somebody?

A. Oh, I don't know. Of course, I tried to save my own life if I could.

Q. That is not answering the question; didn't you aim to hit somebody?

A. Well, of course, I aimed to hit them as well as they did to hit me.

Captain Carskadon: What kind of a rifle did you have?

A. Marvin .30-.30.

James Bryan testified as follows:

Q. Your name is James Bryan, is it?

A. Yes, sir.

Q. What is your business?

A. What is my business?

Q. Yes.

A. Well, sir, I have been down here—

Q. I am not asking you that; what did you do on the 10th day of February, 1913?

A. Well, sir, I come down to Mucklow—

Q. I am not asking you that; were you a mine guard or miner?

A. Miner.

Q. You were a miner?

A. Yes, sir.

Q. You were in the fight that took place on the morning of February 10, 1913, between Mucklow and Wacoma, on that same day, were you?

A. Yes, sir.

Q. I will ask you to look at these men, as they stand up, and see if you can identify any of them you saw who were in that fight there. The back row stand up.

A. No, sir.

Q. The next row stand up.

A. No, sir.

Q. The next row stand up.

A. No, sir.

Q. Do you recognize anyone in the third row?

A. That one right there, looking right at me.

Q. What one is that?

A. That one with the blue overalls on.

Q. What is your name?

One of the defendants: Sanford Kirk.

Q. Look at the front bunch there.

A. No, sir.

Q. Do you see anybody else there that you recognize?

A. No, sir.

Q. How close were you to this man Sanford Kirk that you think you recognize?

A. It seemed to be about one hundred yards or about one hundred feet.

Q. What was he doing when you saw him?

A. Well, he was standing behind a tree.

Q. Did he have a gun?

A. Yes, sir.

Q. Was he shooting?

A. Yes, sir, he was shooting.

Q. Who was he shooting at, or was he shooting in the same crowd with you?

A. No, sir, at us.

Q. Now tell us about how that shooting began up there that morning.

A. We come down to Mucklow. We were down around there and Squire Lambert he spied a crowd of men going across the mountain. We got up there and run into them and one of our men hollered over and asked their business, hollered over two or three times and they turned around and shot at us.

Q. Then the firing became general?

A. Yes, sir.

Q. How long after the first shooting was it until you saw this man Kirk?

A. I suppose about ten or fifteen minutes.

Q. About what time of the day was that?

A. About twelve o'clock, I think it was.

Q. About noon?

A. Yes, sir.

Captain Carskadon cross-examined the witness.

Q. Did you know this man that you claim to identify, before you came in here this morning?

A. No, sir.

Q. Had you ever seen him before to your knowledge?

A. No, sir.

Q. You now identify him by the clothes he wears, do you?

A. Yes, sir.

Q. You don't identify his face?

A. No, sir.

Q. Then the only identification or the only similarity you see in this man to the man that you saw behind the tree on the morning is the fact that he has blue overalls on, is it?

A. Yes, sir.

Q. And I believe you stated he was behind a tree, when you saw him, something like 100 yards from you?

A. Yes, sir.

Captain Boughner: How many men did you see altogether on that day?

A. I can't tell you.

Q. About how many?

A. There seemed to be about 50 or 60 in that one bunch.

Captain Carskadon: You did not have time to look very closely, very carefully, at a man's face up there, did you?

A. No, sir.

Lieutenant H. H. Rice, 2nd Infantry, testified as follows:

Q. Mr. Rice, you are a lieutenant in the Guard?

A. Yes, sir.

Q. You came up, I believe, with the train under command of Major Davis, on the night of the 10th of February, 1913?

A. I did.

Q. Where did you detrain, at what point?

A. At a point between East Bank and Crown Hill, and we got off the train. Our company, Co. H, 2nd Infantry, of Huntington, and also Co. I.

Q. What did you do after detraining?

A. We marched along in front of the train. We understood there might be some explosives on the track and there might be some attempt to wreck our train, so we marched along to Pratt, Co. I going to Pratt and Co. H, that is my company, going to Hansford.

Q. At Hansford you arrested, I believe, Mr. G.W. McCoy, one of the defendants here?

A. Yes, sir.

Q. Tell us now the circumstances under which he was arrested; what was he doing and all about it.

A. We went down to the ferry at Hansford–(A short pause.)

Q. Go ahead.

A. We went down to the ferry at Hansford, Captain McMillen was in command of my company and I was the First Lieutenant. I went along together with a part of the company to the ferry, and when we got there we first–we had orders to capture every man–to arrest every man who was out, because we arrived at Hansford about midnight, and we had reason to believe and did believe that a lot of the people who were in the battle that day might be trying to get across the ferry, to escape out of the military zone. When we got down there we saw two men down on the river bank, near the water's edge, apparently trying to get across the river. We ordered them to halt and advanced them and they gave their names as Mr. Brown and Mr. Parsons.

Q. Were they armed or unarmed?

A. They were unarmed, though one of the men had a bottle of whisky.

Q. Go ahead. Where did you get McCoy?

A. Captain McMillen took two men and went on and they left me with a detachment to hold the ferry and I went up on the porch of a building nearby, about thirty (30) feet away and threw my flashlight along the floor and saw one man crouched down on the floor, with a bag of ammunition, under his arm, leaning on his elbow and apparently hiding. He had a homemade bag of ammunition of the Mauser type or the old Springfield type. I arrested him and called for Captain McMillen, who had just departed, and sent this man up to him. The man was G.W. McCoy, or gave his name as Mr. McCoy.

Q. After you had arrested Brown and Parsons, which you say you arrested at the ferry, and McCoy on the porch, did anybody else arrest any men that night or help to arrest anyone?

A. We helped to arrest before that time Mr. Toney, before we got to the ferry.

Q. He is not in here; did you arrest anyone else?

A. Yes, after that; soon after this, this was along between 12 and one o'clock in the morning, someone came across the river in the ferry boat or in a skiff and landed, and started up the bank. I halted him and walked up to him, threw my flashlight in his face, and asked him who he was. He had a gun in his hand and he threw it across the road, and that was Pete Britt, or gave his name as such.

Q. He is not here.

A. We sent him along also as one of the prisoners. A little later on in the morning, about four o'clock, we arrested another man; I understand he is not here, Mr. Woody. He had just come across the ferry, getting near morning then, near daylight.

Q. The men that you have just spoken of, meaning Brown and Parsons and McCoy, are the only ones who are being tried here, that you know of?

Captain Walker: Have you the ammunition that you took off Mr. McCoy? What kind of ammunition was it?

A. Ammunition of the Mauser type or old Springfield type, large, high-power cartridges. It was in a homemade bag.

Q. (The Judge Advocate hands him a bag.) Is that the bag?

A. This appears to be the bag.

Q. Look at the ammunition in there and see if it is the same kind.

A. The ammunition was of this kind, resembled that ammunition.

The Judge Advocate exhibited the bag of ammunition to the commission.

Counsel for the defendants declined to cross-examine the witness.

George Stanley Tolbert testified as follows:

Q. What is your name?

A. George S. Tolbert.

Q. You are a member of the National Guard and have been acting as orderly in the Provost Marshal Headquarters, since we have been here this time?

A. Yes, sir.

Q. I will ask you if you took the defendant, Mr. Brown, back from these headquarters to the guard house, after he had been over here in an interview with Captain Bond, and this little detective Frank Smith, the other day?

A. Yes, sir.

Q. What statement, if any, did Mr. Brown make to you about his having done something for Frank Smith?

A. He says, "I saved that damned little Jew's life the other night."

Q. Did he make any further statement about it? Did he say anything more besides that?

A. He says, "He cried like a baby," I believe. That is all he said.

Q. Did you then say anything to Brown?

A. No, sir. I says unhunh, is all I answered him.

Counsel for the defendants declined to cross-examine the witness.

Captain H.C. McMillen, 2nd Infantry, testified as follows:

Q. You are a captain in the Guard?

A. Yes, sir.

Q. And in command of Co. H on the night of February 10, 1913?

A. Yes, sir.

Q. You detrained, I believe, at Hansford?

A. Yes, sir; we detrained below Hansford.

Q. Then you marched that morning into Hansford?

A. Yes, sir.

Q. Now, tell this commission the men you arrested from the time you detrained until you got up here and what they were doing? If you haven't a list, I have one here.

A. I have a list here.

Q. Go ahead, Captain McMillen.

A. My men captured on that trip, there was one Oral Toney, J.W. Brown, G.F. Parsons, J.D. Zeller, Leonard Clark, W.H. Adkins, Pete Britt, George W. McCoy, W.E. Smith, W.M. Vickers, Jasper Sowards, and W.H. Huffman, Oscar Petry, Frazier Jarrett, and Fred Woody, I believe.

Q. How many of them, if you know, were armed?

A. Why, one J.D. Zeller, Leonard Clark, W.H. Huffman, Pete Britt, and G.W. McCoy, he had a lot of ammunition, and Jasper Sowards. It is E. Jasper Sowards, I have it on my list.

Q. What, if anything, were these men doing when they were arrested, if you know?

A. Why, I had a bunch of men stationed at the ferry to intercept anyone who should attempt to cross and it seemed that J.W. Brown and G.F. Parsons, when they were captured, were trying to get across the river. I left Lt. Rice with some men at the ferry and started back towards the depot with Brown and Parsons, and we had not gone but a few steps before we arrested one, J.D. Zeller, and Leonard Clark, and W.H. Adkins, with rifles.

Q. Tell if anyone halted you that night or your party as you came up.

A. No, sir, no one halted us that I know of.

Q. Did you see anybody that you believed was acting as outposts or pickets or anything of the sort?

A. No, sir, I did not.

Q. Now, do you see anybody else in this bunch that you know, or have any other statement that you want to make?

A. As we were going to the depot with these men, it was raining very hard that night, we were going to use the depot as a shelter or shed, a part of it, Sgt. Cochran turned over to us W.H. Huffman and Oscar Petry, who he had arrested under his orders. They were charged with loitering. We had orders to take in every man that we found out and he had these men in charge and turned them over and they stated that they were coming from Holly Grove to Crown City–to Crown Hill, was the name of the place, Crown Hill.

Captain Walker: Can you give us the name or a description of the guns that you took off of these parties, Captain?

The Judge Advocate: For the benefit of the commission I will state that Captain Bond informs me that all of these parties who have testified before him have admitted and identified their guns, and he can go on and give a lot of these details, if you want it.

The witness is turned over to the accused for cross-examination.

Q. Captain, you did not know any of these parties before that night?

A. No, sir.

Q. You only know them as being the parties by the name they gave you?

A. I never had met any of the parties before.

Q. Did you see anyone attempting to assist anyone else in escaping, Captain, or would you so construe it?

A. No, I don't believe I did.

Q. Did any of the parties whom you arrested, Captain, attempt to escape or commit any acts of violence in any way?

A. No, not that I know of.

Captain V.W. Midkiff, 2nd Infantry, testified as follows:

Q. Captain Midkiff, you were with Co. I on the night of February 10, 1913?

A. Yes, sir.

Q. I believe you arrested W. H. Adkins and William Price, two of these defendants here in Hansford and Pratt?

A. The two men I arrested, Colonel, give their names as William Price, and it seems to me that it was Boyd Holley.

Q. William Price and Boyd Holley?

A. Yes, sir.

Q. What were they doing at the time you saw them?

A. Well, they seemed to be doing sort of an armed outpost duty, around the Hansford depot.

Q. Tell the commission exactly what they were doing when you arrested them.

A. They were just standing looking up and down the track and watching around. One was armed with a Winchester repeating rifle and one a Springfield rifle, an old style army rifle.

Q. What hour of the night was it?

A. I believe it was about one o'clock, Colonel, I am not certain.

Q. Their guns were loaded and they had ammunition in their pockets?

A. Yes, sir.

Q. Did they make any statement to you, what they were doing?

A. Yes, sir. I asked them what they were doing there and they said they were guarding the town.

Q. Did you arrest any other men that morning?

A. We arrested I believe a man who was supposed to be the depot agent there. He walked out on the platform all dressed, about that time.

The Judge Advocate: He is not on this list.

Captain Morgan cross-examined the witness.

Q. Captain Midkiff, did those people attempt to escape when you arrested them?

A. They did not have much time, Captain. They were on the side next to the railroad originally, and of course when they saw me–

Q. The question is, did they attempt to escape?

A. They ran around the depot on to the light side.

Q. Into the light?

A. Yes, sir. I had already sent a sergeant and detail around on that side of the depot and I ran up there where they were and engaged them in conversation and talked to them until my sergeant came up behind them.

Q. Did they call out loud or do anything else by which they could give a signal to anyone else to escape?

A. No, sir.

Q. They did not attempt to give a signal to anyone else to escape?

A. Not that I saw.

Q. Did you have any resistance from them?

A. No, sir.

Q. Could they not have shot, if they had wanted to?

A. There is not any question about that; a man armed with a gun could shoot. Whether they could have shot me or not that is a different question.

Q. They could have shot at you?

A. They could have shot at me; yes, sir.

Q. How many men were with you when you came up where they were?

A. I was by myself. I ran around and left the point of my advance guard, when I saw them dodge around the end of the depot. I came up on them alone.

Q. You were alone?

A. Yes, sir.

Q. Anyone close to you?

A. Well, the rest of my advance guard, the point was probably 30 or 40 yards down the track behind when I got to these men.

Q. They could have offered resistance to you if they had desired?

A. I suppose they could; yes, sir.

Captain Carskadon: Captain, did these parties that you arrested there tell you what was the nature of the trouble or what was their anxiety, what they feared?

A. They said they were guarding the town. They said they were afraid the town would be shot up by someone. As near as I remember they said they were afraid the Bull Moose would come along and shoot them up.

Q. Did they say anything to you about fearing a handcar with a machine gun on it was coming down from Mucklow to make an attack on them?

A. They did not; no.

Captain Boughner: Did you have a gun in your hand when you made this arrest?

A. No, sir. The fact of the matter is they had their left side to me and their rifles hid by holding them straight up and down their right side and under their right arm, and I did not know that they were armed when I first got to them. I pulled the gun out into my hand as soon as I saw they had rifles.

Captain Carskadon: Captain, didn't it seem to be the general impression among the men around there, with whom you came in contact, when you made these arrests, that they were anticipating an attack or some trouble?

The Judge Advocate objected to the question and it was withdrawn.

A. The answer would not hurt anyone, because those three men were the only three men I came in contact with that night.

Q. These three men told you that the Bull Moose was expected to come and shoot up the town, did they not?

A. The two that I arrested with rifles told me that they were afraid that the Bull Moose would come along there and shoot up the town.

Redirect examination by the Judge Advocate:

Q. Captain Midkiff, have you been on duty in this strike zone long; during the whole period that martial law has been in effect, have you been on duty?

A. I was in the first period. We came into this district, my company did, on the 29th day of July, 1912, and left the Cabin Creek military district on the 2nd day of October, 1912, and we came into this district again on either the 15th or 16th day of November, 1912, and left the district on the 29th day of November, 1912. And then we came back this last time on the 10th day of February, 1913.

Q. During that time have you covered any considerable part of this district personally, have you been about every day, Captain?

A. Yes, sir. I have led patrols in the mountains between Burnwell and Eskdale, on Cabin Creek, and I have also led patrols up and down this creek, above Handley and over and across the mountains into Paint Creek, near Wacoma, and also up this mountain below Paint Creek.

Q. In the discharge of your duties have you come in contact with many striking miners, or union miners, in personal contact with them, and talk to them?

A. Yes, sir, a good many of them.

Q. I will ask if you know whether or not the *Labor Argus* published by Mr. Boswell is not circulated freely among them?

A. Yes, sir, it is.

Q. I will ask you to tell the commission whether the *Labor Argus* during the period that you have been on duty here has or has it not inflamed their minds intensely rather than helped this situation?

Counsel for the defendants objected to this question, the objection was overruled, and counsel excepted to the ruling.

A. (No response.)

Q. Answer the question, Captain, please.

A. Well, in my judgment, it did.

Q. You may tell the commission whether or not you yourself have read any of the accounts in the *Labor Argus*, as to the condition here and what was going on during the period of martial law–whether or not you have read it.

A. Well, I haven't read the paper regularly; now and then I would get hold of a copy of it and read it.

Q. Have the statements that you read in the paper been in keeping with facts as they existed here?

A. No, sir, they have not.

Q. What has the character of them been, inflammatory or otherwise?

A. Inflammatory; yes, sir.

Q. Do you know the defendant, Mother Jones?

A. Yes, sir, I have met her.

Q. Did you ever come in contact with her, or have an opportunity to observe her conduct with reference to these striking miners in this section?

A. Only once, sir, I heard her make one speech.

Q. When was that?

A. I heard her speak at Hansford on a Sunday–I believe it was the second Sunday before Labor Day, 1912.

Q. Was there anything in her speech that day that tended to inflame the passions of these strikers and cause violence or otherwise?

A. No, her speech that day was very reasonable; a very reasonable speech. My instructions were that if she did make an inflammatory speech and aimed to create trouble on that occasion, to stop the speech. She made a very reasonable talk to the miners. She advised them to hold out the strike all right but she also advised them in my hearing that day not to waste their money on firearms; they didn't need them, the soldiers were here and would protect them, so I didn't interfere with her speech. I didn't find anything wrong with her speech at all that day.

M.F. Matheny cross-examined the witness.

Q. Captain, isn't it a fact, that the striking miners have always respected the uniform and have been courteous to the officers and soldiers when they were given an opportunity and when they came in contact with them?

A. Well, personally I never had any trouble whatever with any of the striking miners.

Q. And don't you know it to be a fact, that a good many of them are laboring under false impressions, that the militia was coming here to shoot them up, and to shoot up their homes, and when they found out that that was not the case, weren't they friendly, and wasn't that the attitude maintained throughout all of this trouble?

A. The men themselves have never given us any trouble. Now so far as their impression that we were coming up here to shoot them up, I never heard anything like that before.

Q. And the soldiers were able to take up thousands of guns, without hurting anybody and without being hurt, or fired upon, isn't that correct?

A. I believe so, sir.

Q. Soldiers have been all through the mountains here, up and down the railroads and public highways, and in the camps, and never have been fired upon?

A. Some of our outposts at Holly Mine were fired on at night–who fired on them I don't know. I couldn't swear because I didn't see anyone.

Q. When they were fired on, then charge and countercharges were made by the miners on the one hand, and by the guards on the other, that the other side did it? Isn't that so?

A. I believe so.

Q. Isn't it a fact that this antipathy and bad will which has reached white heat at times has grown out of the conflict between the striking miners and what is known as the Baldwin guards, or coal guards, more than any other condition?

A. I don't believe I got that.

Q. Isn't it a fact that this antipathy and bad will which has reached white heat at times has grown out of the conflict between the striking miners and what is known as the Baldwin guards or coal guards, more than any other condition?

A. Well, that seemed to have been the case.

Q. The general feeling of hatred between the two contending parties, isn't that so?

A. Yes, sir.

Q. The miners claiming on the one side that their camps have been fired into and they have been arrested without cause and beaten up by a lot of these guards, and on the other hand, the guards claiming that the miners are wanting to destroy property; isn't that the condition?

A. There don't seem to be between the two factions, there don't seem to be anyone that is willing to get the other side any justice at all. It seems to be a bitter feeling, one side thinks the other side is entirely in the wrong. That is my impression—that is the impression I have of the case.

Q. There are some three or four thousand men engaged in this industrial strike or conflict, isn't that so, in addition to their sympathizers?

A. I cannot say as to the number of men.

Q. There is a considerable number?

A. Yes, sir.

Q. Well, you say, Captain, that you have been throughout the field covered by the martial law proclamation—

A. I beg your pardon, I don't believe I made any such statement as that.

Q. I thought you did. I don't want to misquote you.

A. I believe I described the territory that I had covered.

Q. In other words, you have been up and down Paint and Cabin creeks.

A. Yes, sir; Burnwell is as far up Paint Creek as I have been.

Q. This strike is confined to the two creeks, and from your observation and what you know personally and what has come to you through your connection with the military service of this State, knowing these striking miners as you do, don't you feel that you can wear the uniform and go to any of these creeks and make an arrest without resistance, or fear of bodily harm to yourself?

A. You mean in every instance, at any place?

Q. I mean as a general proposition, don't you feel that you could do it now?

A. I don't know; that would be in the nature of a boast, wouldn't it?

Q. No, I don't want it to be; I mean that you could, any other soldier could, with the uniform, that you can go into these camps and execute process without resistance, from what you know of these men with whom you have been dealing?

A. Well, I would hardly make a statement to that effect. I judge from my contact with them that there are good men and bad men among them. So far as going to serve process is concerned, if a soldier is ordered to do that, he would go and attempt to do it, whether he did it without trouble or not would remain to be seen.

Q. You have either in person, or through and by the military service under your control, executed a great deal of process, haven't you, in the military zone?

A. Why I have not made a great number of arrests myself. While I have made quite a few arrests, I usually had a detail with me.

Q. You never have met with any resistance, have you?

A. No, sir.

Q. Aside from the fanatic or hothead, and they are to be found among all classes of men, the striking miner as a rule can be handled by a man wearing the uniform, without resistance?

A. I think so; yes, sir.

Captain Carskadon: Isn't the prevailing habit these days among newspapers, Captain, to write exciting matter in them and to greatly exaggerate conditions as they find them, and sometimes to misrepresent them?

The Judge Advocate objected to this question, and the objection was sustained. Counsel for the defendants took exception to the ruling.

Redirect examination by the Judge Advocate:

Q. Captain Midkiff, you spoke of the outpost being fired on, up on Cabin Creek I believe it was.

A. Holly Mine, I believe they call it.

Q. That was at a time, after all the mine guards had been deported from this military district, was it not?

A. Yes, sir.

Q. I will ask you if it is not true that a great many insults were offered to the soldiers prior to the time martial law was declared and in the interim, prior to the time martial law was declared, if it is not your understanding that soldiers were not any more respected than anyone else?

A. Yes, sir.

Q. I will ask you to tell the commission whether or not it is not true, whether a soldier or anybody else, except during martial law, attempting to execute process had trouble; if that is not your information?

A. That is, he would have a fight?

Q. Not necessarily a fight; if they had enough force there would be no resistance, if not there would be insults?

A. There would be quite a chewing match, by calling everybody hard names.

Q. Don't you know that a good many soldiers of this guard have been called hard names, by men who are said to be striking miners and their sympathizers?

A. I believe, Colonel, the largest part of that was done by the women and children.

Q. But those women and children were the wives and children of the striking miners?

A. Yes, sir.

Q. And in sympathy with them?

A. Yes, sir.

Q. So it would not be entirely a "bed of roses" for the men to execute process alone, would it?

A. No, sir, I should say not.

Captain Morgan: You say you have done duty about five months since last July.

A. I gave the dates I have been here on duty.

Q. You were on duty in this zone when there was no martial law proclamation prevailing, were you not, Captain?

A. We came into this zone on the night of July 29th last and I believe the first proclamation of martial law went into effect on the second or third day of September, 1912.

Q. Did you have insults offered to you, or did you know of any insults being offered to any member of the National Guard during the time that martial law was not in effect; during the time before martial law went into effect?

A. That is before the first martial law?

Q. Yes, sir, before the first martial law went into effect.

A. About the only case I know of is the day the people on the train were hollering at Major Pratt and calling him names and he went on the train and arrested a man and the man tried to fight him with his fist.

The Judge Advocate: Then in the second interim, between the time martial law was raised and the time that the second proclamation of martial law was issued, what is your information as to the men who were left here with the sheriff of this county, not uniformed, as to whether or not they were insulted by the striking miners or their sympathizers? I should say in the interim that martial law was raised; between the first time martial law was raised and the second declaration of martial law?

A. I was not insulted myself, but I heard of a great many soldiers being insulted.

Q. When you came in here the second time, I will ask if that Sunday morning, I believe it was Sunday morning or Saturday night you went up Cabin Creek, that Sunday, didn't you?

A. Yes, sir.

Q. I will ask you then if the attitude of the striking miners toward the soldiers was friendly or otherwise?

A. They seemed to be bitter at that time.

Q. At that time could a man, with just his uniform have gone out and served process, unless he would have been an unusual man?

A. I believe, Colonel, I would want a few armed men along with me.

Captain Boughner: Have you ever seen anybody or gone yourself to make arrests, without being armed?

A. No, sir.

Captain Morgan: Isn't it true that on the creek–on Cabin Creek–certain members of the National Guard had been doing duty prior to the time you came in, when you said you were insulted–had been on duty as guards, and in the employ of the coal companies?

The Judge Advocate objected to this question, his objection was sustained, and defense counsel took exception to the ruling.

The Judge Advocate: Did I ask you whether or not the guns were loaded that William Price and Boyd Holley had?

A. I don't remember but I believe you did ask the question.

Q. Were they loaded?

A. Yes, sir, they were loaded.

Corporal Otis Jobe, Co. H, 2nd Infantry, testified as follows:

Q. You are Corporal Otis Jobe of Co. H?

A. Yes, sir.

Q. I will ask if you came up on the night of the 10th of February, with Co. H?

A. Yes, sir.

Q. I will ask you if acting under the direction of your officers, you made a search of the house of the defendant, G.F. Parsons, down here at Hansford?

A. He never made any orders to make any search, or we didn't have to make any search, it was laying out where you could see it.

Q. What was laying out and where did you see it?

A. A rifle.

Q. What else?

A. Ammunition.

Q. What kind of a rifle was it, and how much ammunition?

A. Mauser, and I don't remember how much ammunition there was.

Q. Whereabouts was that ammunition about his house?

A. It was in the kitchen.

Q. In Parsons' kitchen?

A. Yes, sir, it wasn't concealed.

Q. Did you make any other arrest that night, when you were coming up, Corporal?

A. I helped to make several.

Q. Do you recall now who they were?

A. Why, Parsons and Brown were two of them and I made a third going back. I don't just remember the name.

Captain Walker: Where were you when you found this rifle?

A. In his house, Parsons' house.

Q. In the house?

A. Yes, sir.

Q. What part of the house?

A. It was between the front room and dining room, there is a little kind of an offset in there, I guess that is what you call it.

Captain Boughner: Was it loaded?

A. I never examined it.

The Judge Advocate: Was it in a room or was it laying on the outside of the room?

A. Outside of the room.

Q. In other words, a man could get the gun without going into the house?

A. No, sir, it was in this little alcove, setting in there as you go in.

Captain Walker: A little hall-like place?

A. Yes, sir.

The Judge Advocate: How far is the Parsons' house from the ferry, where he was arrested?

A. I don't know.

Q. The best of your recollection, one square or half a square?

A. I suppose the best I can remember, one square.

Captain Carskadon cross-examined the witness:

Q. Did Mr. Parsons or Mr. Brown either one have any arms on them of any description when you arrested them?

A. No, they had a quart of whisky.

Q. And that was all?

A. Yes, sir.

Captain Morgan: Corporal, did it appear that any attempt had been made to conceal this gun?

A. No.

Sergeant Delbert Fisher, Co. H, 2nd Infantry, testified as follows:

Q. Sergeant, you helped to arrest Bunk Adkins, W.H. Adkins, alias Bunk Adkins, and J.D. Zeller?

A. I don't know their names; we arrested two in the first start and then coming back we arrested three more, three more on our way back to the station.

Q. Tell us what the first two did? Where arrested?

A. We were down at the river bank, one big fellow had a quart of whisky.

Q. Is that the big fellow there (Defendant Brown) with his hand up to his face?

A. That one right there.

Q. Then where did you get the other three?

A. We got the other three standing at the fence as we started back toward the depot.

Q. Were the three standing by the fence armed?

A. Yes, sir.

Q. Do you know what they were armed with?

A. No, sir, I didn't pay any attention to that.

Q. Were they armed with squirt guns, rifles, or what?

A. No, sir, rifles.

Q. Big rifles or just sporting rifles?

A. I don't remember.

Q. You don't remember what kind of rifles?

A. It was no shotgun, I know that.

Q. Was it large or small caliber rifle, if you recall?

A. That I cannot say.

Captain Morgan cross-examined the witness:

Q. Sergeant, was there any attempt on the part of any of these people to get away from there?

A. Well, the first two didn't want to come up to us when we halted them and then advanced them. We had to tell them three or four times to advance up before they would come.

Q. What time in the night was that?

A. I suppose it was twelve o'clock.

Q. Was it dark or light?

A. It wasn't light.

Q. Very dark?

A. Yes, sir, pretty dark; it was raining.

Q. Could you see the men that you halted?

A. The two?

Q. Yes, when you halted them.

A. You couldn't see to tell whether they were men or not, but I heard them walking, coming up towards us, and then we halted them and they didn't want to come up.

Q. Was it light enough to see that you were a member of the National Guard, by your uniform?

A. I don't know whether they could see it or not.

Q. Do you think it was light enough?

A. I can't say.

Q. The fact is it was too dark to see whether you were members of the National Guard or not?

A. Yes, sir, it was.

Q. There was no way for them to know, when you told them to come up there, that you were members of the National Guard?

A. No, I don't suppose there was. I don't suppose they knew who we were.

Q. You don't suppose they knew who you were?

A. I don't suppose they knew who we were.

Q. Under cover of the darkness it was possible for any of them to escape, if they had wanted to escape?

A. Oh, they could have escaped all right, because it was too dark–

Q. Too dark to see them, as they left?

A. Yes, sir.

The Judge Advocate: Sergeant, when you halted these men did they say anything, the two men at the ferry, when you halted them, did they answer you?

A. When we advanced them two or three times, then they said something; I don't remember what it was.

Q. The first time you halted them how close were you to them?

A. I guess about ten or fifteen feet.

Q. They could not have gotten away from you without you firing on them?

A. We could have fired on them, but I don't know whether we would have hit them or not.

Q. If they had called and asked if you were members of the National Guard you would have replied?

A. Yes, sir.

Q. You were in speaking distance?

A. Yes, sir.

Captain Walker: What was the name of the three men that you arrested when you came back; it has been testified to two or three times but I don't know?

A. I don't know, sir.

Sergeant Charles A. Brockmeyer, Co. H, 2nd Infantry, testified as follows:

Q. Sergeant Brockmeyer, you were with Captain McMillen's company on the night of February 10, 1913?

A. Yes, sir.

Q. Were you with him at the time Mr. Parsons and Mr. Brown were arrested at the river ferry at Hansford?

A. I was there at the time two men were arrested. I couldn't identify the men. I know there were two men.

Q. You only know them by the names given afterwards?

A. Yes, sir.

Q. Just give the circumstances under which those two men were arrested.

A. They were coming up from the ferry, we halted them and arrested them.

Q. How close were you to them when you first halted them, Sergeant?

A. I would judge about 15 or 20 feet.

Q. Were you close enough to them for them to recognize that you were members of the Guard, by your uniform, or was it too dark for that?

A. It was a dark night. It was raining and I hardly think that they would recognize us.

Q. The first two men that you arrested, did you search?

A. Yes, sir.

Q. Did you take anything off of them in the way of ammunition or arms?

A. No, sir, no arms.

Q. Did you get any ammunition?

A. No, sir.

Q. The second three that you arrested, what did they do?

A. The rest of them did that. I was left at the ferry with the detail.

Q. So you don't know about that?

A. No, sir.

Counsel for the defense declined to cross-examine the witness.

Major T. B. Davis, 2nd Infantry, testified as follows:

Q. Major Davis, you have been connected with the military establishment during the period of martial law, which is the third time you have been on duty in this district, have you not?

A. I have since July 29, 1912.

Q. Most of the time you have been, I believe, Provost Marshal, during the first two tours of martial law?

A. The first two tours, I have, yes, sir.

Q. And the third tour you have been Chief of Staff, and in the field?

A. Some, not as much as I was formerly, though.

Q. At home I believe you are a member of the machinists' union?

A. Yes, sir.

Q. And during your first tour of duty when you were Provost Marshal, you came in contact with a great many of the striking miners and talked with them?

A. Yes, sir.

Q. I will ask you to tell the commission whether or not during that time you have had any chance to observe whether the *Labor Argus* had any considerable circulation among them?

A. Did you say any considerable circulation?

Q. Yes, sir.

A. I don't know to what extent, Colonel; it had some circulation, because I frequently see it at different places.

Q. I will ask you if you didn't frequently see persons in Eskdale, where the strikers' camps were, and other places where they were congregated, reading the *Labor Argus* and cheering when anything was read out of the paper?

A. I saw it at Eskdale.

Q. I will ask you if you yourself read the articles or any of the articles that appeared in the *Labor Argus* , during any of this period?

A. Yes, sir.

Q. I will ask you to tell this commission whether or not the statements contained therein, as a general rule were true or whether or not they were calculated to inflame and arouse the passions of these strikers?

A. A good many of them; those that I knew of personally. There were several I knew not to be true. They had one particular reference to me that was absolutely false.

Q. I will ask you whether or not the temper and tone of that paper had a tendency to excite the strikers to violence or not?

A. In my opinion, yes.

Q. I will ask you if during your period of service as Provost Marshal and even before, whether or not you had any opportunity to observe the conduct of the defendant, Mother Jones, Major?

A. I did.

Q. I will ask you to tell the commission whether or not her conduct as it came under your observation was such as influenced the passions of these men, or otherwise?

A. Well, I don't know whether it did or not, Colonel, but my opinion is that it was intended to.

Q. I will ask you further to say from what you heard and saw was it in your opinion calculated to do what it was intended to do; was it likely to produce that sort of a result?

A. Yes.

Captain Morgan cross-examined the witness.

Q. Major, what particular acts did Mother Jones commit that caused you to believe that she intended to inflame the passion of those striking miners?

A. It was before martial law was ever declared, in August. I had information that she was going on the creek—coming on the creek to make a speech at Kayford. I met her at Eskdale. She was on the train that day and I told her that I would be with her the whole day and for her not to make any inflammatory speeches, that she knew what her orders were and she said she would not. I spent the entire day with her, or most of it, anyway until the train came out. She made her speech at a point probably one mile above Kayford, after considerable difficulty she had getting up there on account of the mine guards. She did not direct these miners here to resort to any violence. The question asked was her intention calculated to do that. She made parallel cases of other states, such as we had mine guards in Alabama and the miners went in and done this and crushed them, and so forth, and that was the line of it.

Q. Major Davis, you say that the mine guards stopped you on the way to Kayford?

A. No, they didn't stop us. I say she had considerable difficulty. They made her wade the creek and made it unpleasant for her all the way up.

Q. They made her wade the creek?

A. Yes, sir, the county road was in the creek; there was just a little water, probably about three inches, the county road was in the bed of the creek, at places, and I was permitted to go up the railroad, but she was not.

Q. She was not permitted to walk along the railroad track?

A. No, sir, she kept to the county road.

Q. Was any of this land, over which the mine guards refused to permit her to pass, enclosed?

A. Enclosed?

Q. Yes, by fence.

A. No, sir.

Q. Was any of it, Major Davis, cultivated or improved?

A. No, sir.

Q. Could Mother Jones have damaged any of this land by walking over it?

A. I think not.

Q. In what way, Major, did the mine guards refuse to permit her to pass over this ground?

A. Now I will have to go back again. I did not hear their conversation. I was somewhat in the rear of Mother Jones, and she would come to a point where she would want to get out of the water and I was a little distance away, not within hearing distance, I saw a halt like of her party and I asked her what was the matter later on and she told me that they wouldn't let her get off the county road, which took through the creek.

Q. You say they refused to let her go on the railroad?

A. I didn't hear the conversation but I would judge that is what they were doing.

Redirect examination by the Judge Advocate.

Q. You speak of her party; who was in her party, Major? Any considerable number of persons?

A. There was not a great number of them. Lawrence Dwyer, I remember him particularly. I remember seeing him on this occasion.

Q. They were striking miners; they were men who were on a strike?

A. Why, at the time Lawrence was; that is the one I remember. He was.

Q. About how many were with her, as many as a dozen?

A. No. There were only about two or three with her to start with; after they got to Kayford they commenced gathering in. Probably there were, after they reached the point where she was going to speak, about 150. They were gathering as she went along. They were gathering along.

Captain Carskadon conducted further cross-examination.

Q. Major, the statements that you speak of in the *Labor Argus* as being untrue, they were some statements made with reference to the militia, were they not?

A. Yes, sir, but they applied to me personally, which caused the machinists' union at our place to take action against me, and which they investigated for six or eight weeks; they found it was not true and threw it out.

The commission adjourned at 12 o'clock to meet again at one p. m.

Stipulation:

It is agreed by and between George S. Wallace, Lieutenant-Colonel, Acting Judge Advocate, and Captain Charles R. Morgan and Captain E.B. Carskadon and M.F. Matheny, Esq., representing all of the prisoners except C.H. Boswell, John W. Brown, Charles Batley, Paul Paulsen, Mary Jones, and G.F. Parsons, the commission concurring; that for the purpose of this trial, the following statement of facts is agreed to, viz.:

First. That a strike was called on Cabin Creek and Paint Creek, in Kanawha County, West Virginia, in the month of April, 1912; that during the progress of the strike the coal companies employed a large number of men, commonly called "Baldwin guards," who were armed with rifles of various kinds, including a number of machine guns; that while the strike was in progress the mine operators, by their guards, evicted a number of miners from the houses occupied by them, claiming the right to do so under their contracts and that in some of these cases the evictions were forceable; that many reports, calculated to bring on conflicts were circulated from time to time; excitement ran high and charges and counter charges of acts of violence were made by the mine guards and the strikers against each other.

Second. That the striking miners armed themselves with high-power rifles of various kind and description, but mainly Swiss and Italian Mausers; that they established camps at various points within the zone and acts of violence as a result of the conflict between the striking miners on the one side and the mine guards on the other were numerous; that these camps of the union miners have been established on private property at various places and principally at Eskdale and Holly Grove and that the union miners living in these camps have drawn from the United Mine Workers of America certain stipulated amounts, either in "grub" or money each week; that the mine-owners have claimed that the striking miners in these camps have from time to time shot into the coal plants and the miners living in these camps have contended that the guards had fired into their camps; that a number of persons have been killed and several battles have been fought.

Third. That on the first day of September, 1912, martial law was declared; troops sent into the district now covered by proclamation of martial law of February 10th, 1913, and all the arms of every kind and description that could be gotten hold of were taken in charge by the military authorities, including machine guns and rifles of the mine guards and the Swiss and Italian Mausers in the hands of the strikers and that on the third day of September, 1912, every mine guard employed in the district was deported therefrom.

Fourth. That the martial law proclamation was withdrawn about the middle of October, 1912; that the strike continued and there were other cases of disorder and violence; that martial law was again declared on November 15, 1912, and continued until the middle of December, 1912, at which time the troops were withdrawn, and between December 15, 1912, and February 10, 1913, disorders of various kinds occurred in what is called the martial law zone; that the feeling between the non-union employees of the coal companies and mine guards employed by them, on the one side, and the union miners and their sympathizers, on the other, was intense and that there were many disquieting rumors afloat at all times and that there were many acts of violence, including shootings; that the coal companies had employed armed guards and in some instances had machine guns on their property and the striking miners on the other hand had re-armed themselves with high-power rifles and that there were several shootings and conflicts that led up to the declaration of martial law of February 10, 1913, and prior to the shooting which is now being tried by this military commission.

The commission convened at 1 p.m. pursuant to recess taken for dinner.

Captain John C. Bond testified as follows:

Q. Captain Bond, you are Provost Marshal in this district?

A. Yes, sir.

Q. And as such have charge of the prisoners who are now on trial?

A. I do.

Q. I will ask you to tell this commission whether or not any of these prisoners have made any admissions to you as to the kind of guns they had in their possession at the time they were arrested and the ammunition that they had and whether or not you have kept a record of those admissions?

A. They did make such admissions and I have kept a record of it.

Q. I will ask you now to give the commission the record of the kind of arms that any of these prisoners admitted that they had and the kind of ammunition and the names of those prisoners.

Captain Morgan objected on the ground that it should be shown that the admissions were made voluntarily before they can be admitted in evidence. Colonel Jolliffe sustained the objection.

The Judge Advocate: Was there any coercion or inducements offered—Any inducements offered to or coercion upon these prisoners in the statements they made to you?

A. There was not.

Q. Go ahead now and make those statements they made to you.

A. These guns or guns and ammunition which had been captured were turned over to me with a list of the prisoners. The list was not definite as to exactly which prisoners had rifles. I placed the rifles on this table with the ammunition and sent for the prisoners, one at a time, that were supposed to have rifles and asked them to come and pick out their particular rifle and after they had done so the number of the rifle was taken.

Q. Begin and read your list to us just as it worked out.

A. E.J. Sowards had a rifle, commonly known as an Italian Mauser, No. 5059.

Q. Any ammunition?

A. According to his own statement, about thirty-five cartridges in two different bags. The ammunition was of this character. (Shows shell.)

Captain Walker: You are just identifying the guns of some of the defendants here?

A. Yes, sir—E.J. Sowards—one of the defendants.

M.F. Matheny: Does not your list show—

A. It gives a description of the gun and number, except this: there are three or four types of guns here.

The Judge Advocate: Read your list right off.

A.  W.H. Adkins, commonly known as Bunk Adkins, had a Springfield rifle, No. 246,900, shooting such ammunition as that. (Showing shell.) Boyd Holley, alias Adkins, had a Springfield rifle.

Q.  Any ammunition?

A.  To return to Bunk Adkins; he claimed that he had had but one shell, which was in the gun. Boyd Holley stated he had about forty-five shells for it. J.D. Zeller had a Springfield rifle and claimed to have but one shell for it. Leonard Clark, a Swiss—what is commonly known as a Swiss Mauser; different type of gun, shooting this kind of ammunition (Shows shell.), and thirteen shells in the gun and about twenty in his pocket. G.W. McCoy had a bag of ammunition, stating that he had about twenty or thirty Springfield shells in it. Frazier Jarrett had a Springfield rifle and about fifteen cartridges.

William Price, a Winchester rifle, calibre .32-.20 and about thirty-five or forty shells.

Captain Walker: He had a Winchester?

A.  A .32-.20 Winchester. Carl Morgan, one of the Italian Mausers, shooting that kind of ammunition (showing shell)—as I placed out before, and about twenty-four shells, he stated.

Ernest O'Dell, a Springfield rifle and three boxes of shells.

John O'Dell, a Winchester rifle, .38-.40 in calibre. He stated he had some ammunition—didn't know exactly how many.

Joe Prince, a Springfield rifle and twelve cartridges.

Ernest Creigo, a .32 Special, Smith and Wesson revolver. Now in this Springfield ammunition that was turned over—no way of telling who it came off of particularly, there were various kinds of dum-dum bullets gathered from out of it. The ammunition for the Creigo revolver, in nearly every instance, there were four little holes punched in the bullet, right around near the shell.

Q.  What is the effect of that, if you know?

A.  As I understand it, if that bullet strikes anything, it would fly into several pieces.

Q.  Any other statement you wish to make in regard to these guns and ammunition?

A.  Not that I know of.

Q.  Do you know Mr. Boswell, the defendant, the editor of the *Labor Argus* ?

A.  I do.

Q.  And Mr. Brown, the other defendant?

A.  Yes, sir.

Q.  Mr. Parsons and Mr. Batley?

A.  Yes, sir.

Q.  Do you know where they live or have their headquarters?

A.  Mr. Boswell lives in Charleston and has his office there and I understand Mr. Brown lives in Charleston. The others, I do not know.

Q. Do you know where Mr. Paulsen or Batley have their headquarters?

A. I do not.

Q. How far is it from Charleston here, by rail?

A. By rail, twenty-two miles.

M.F. Matheny cross-examined the witness:

Q. Captain Bond, you do not mean that any of these guns were taken off of any of the prisoners on the mountain, where the battle took place; they are simply guns that were gotten somewhere the day following the battle?

A. These guns were turned over in cases in which testimony has already been given. I do not know as to their being taken off of these men. A part of these prisoners were arrested, according to the records turned in, on Cabin Creek, and a part of them in Hansford.

Q. You do not know but what some of these guns were taken up in their homes and places around and about and not on the prisoners at the time they were arrested?

A. I do not know how they got them except as to what some of them stated.

Q. It is your understanding some of them really had guns at the time they were arrested, while others had no arms?

A. Well, all of those concerning whom I have testified picked out the gun as the gun they had in their possession when arrested. There is one thing further, in connection with this ammunition: the ammunition used in what is commonly known as the Italian Mauser is commonly spoken of as a poisoned bullet.

The Judge Advocate: I didn't get that last.

A. The Italian Mauser ammunition is supposed to be—to have a poisoned bullet.

Captain Morgan: Do you know that to be so?

A. I do not know. I never was shot with one.

M.F. Matheny: If that hit a fellow behind the ear, it would not matter whether it was poisoned or not?

A. Not a great deal. If struck in the hand it would.

M.F. Matheny: The prisoners represented by Mr. Matheny here move that the *Labor Argus*—that the copies of the *Labor Argus* heretofore introduced before the commission be treated as introduced for all purposes connected with this investigation.

Captain Carskadon further cross-examined Captain H.C. McMillen, who was recalled by the counsel for the defendants:

Q. Captain, I believe you were a witness here this forenoon?

A. Yes, sir.

Q. I believe that you stated that you were instrumental in the arrest of Mr. Parsons, one of the defendants?

A. Yes, sir.

Q. And that you had certain conversations with him?

A. I never had any conversations. I had no conversation.

Q. Did you not have a conversation with him over about the depot, Captain?

A. Only in the ordinary course of the duties we had to perform; like that.

Q. To refresh your memory, was there not something said to you about going down to his house there in Hansford?

A. In regard to the bad weather—a rainy night. He made a suggestion that we come down there out of the rain—bad weather, until we got to Pratt.

Q. He invited you and your men to go down to his place?

A. Yes, sir, he made that offer.

Q. Did you accept that proposition?

The Judge Advocate objected to the question, his objection was sustained, and the defense counsel took exception to the ruling.

At this point a recess was taken until 2:30 p.m., in order to give the Judge Advocate an opportunity to determine what portions of the *Labor Argus* he would offer in evidence before the commission.

At 2:30 p.m. the commission reconvened with all the members of the court present, the Judge Advocate, all counsel for the defendants except M.F. Matheny, Esq., who had left the matters in the hands of his associate counsel, and the reporter, also defendants Mary Jones, Mr. Boswell, Mr. Brown, and Mr. Parsons.

The Judge Advocate here offered and read in evidence the following excerpts or extracts from the *Labor Argus*, the copies tendered on yesterday, viz.:

Martial law has been declared on the upper end of Paint Creek in Fayette County, but not until after the Baldwin thugs had been given ample time to throw the miners out of their homes. The miners asked for martial law in this district last week, but Sen. Elkins' governor held it up until the operators and Baldwin thugs could accomplish their hellish work of illegally ejecting miners from their homes. If the reports be true the miners were ejected in the night and driven like cattle to the mountains. Men, women, and children were driven from shelter and their household goods were thrown out to be destroyed by the weather. While these wrongs were being perpetrated on a defenseless people the state's chief executive was sitting back at the capitol babbling about the "invisible law" and the "infernal lobbyist," who were the causes of the present trouble. After the miners had been ejected and driven from their homes, martial law was unnecessary. Governor Glasscock represents the interest of the "Coal Barons" so what else could the miners expect. You fellows who vote the Democratic and Republican tickets are now getting returns from the election. Stay with it, boys, if your brain is too dull to comprehend and understand you have yet got feeling in your heads and the Baldwins will club the class struggle into you if you can't get it any other way.

Mother Jones must be doing some good work for the miners judging from the way Big Business and the Coal Barons hate her. Go to it, Mother.

When you get these fellows against you it is a good sign you are doing good work.—*Labor Argus*, 12 September 1912.

A few days ago a soldier shot and killed a miner at Oakley. Since then everything that made a light has been killed, even the lightning bugs. Now since everything that made a light has been put out of business the state militia is now shooting at everything that moves. The last victim of the soldiers' fear was Bill Campbell's cow at Quarrier. The poor old bovine was not familiar with the martial law and was ignorant of the fact that when once she had laid down it was death to get up again, so when the poor old mooly raised from her bed in the weeds last Sunday night one of Gov. Glasscock's brave soldier boys was near enough to pump her side so full of steel jacket Springfield bullets that she got excited and forgot to live. Since then Bill Campbell has been doing without cream in his coffee. It is all right for the militia to kill men and lightning bugs, for they are not property, but when it comes to killing a cow it is something else, as someone will have to pay for that cow. The taxpayers are paying the soldiers' expenses and will also have to pay for the damage they do. The people pay for the beef and some one else eats the meat.

The capitalists have been making the laws to suit themselves, construing the laws to suit themselves, and executing the laws to suit themselves, and they seem to prosper since they have had everything their own way. If the working class ever learns enough to stop being a voting machine for the other fellow and go into the law-making business for themselves, construe and execute a few of these laws in the interest of their class, then the workers would prosper. Just as long as you let the other fellow ride you and then give him the whip to make you go with, just that long will you be a wage slave. Get up off your knees and fight.

If a soldier shoots and kills a workingman, a reasonable tale is concocted and the professional murderer is acquitted by his comrades, but if a citizen even makes a motion at one of the militia officers he is sentenced to two years in the penitentiary. Such is the brand of justice dealt out under martial law. And you slaves voted for it. *Labor Argus*, 19 September 1912.

Bill Baldwin's right bower Feltz wrote an article to last Thursday's *Mail* saying the Baldwin-Feltz Detective Agency would give $500 if anyone could prove an instance where one of their men had mistreated or abused a woman, or something to that effect. We are inclined to think that Baldwin's chief in West Virginia was just bluffing or doing a little cheap newspaper advertisement as no one has seen the color of that $500 he was wanting to put up. We think it is abusing and mistreating a woman when her household goods are thrown out and she and her children are driven from shelter. Do the Baldwin guards deny making women wade the creek at Holly Grove? Do they deny striking and choking women at Paint Creek Junction? Can Mr. Feltz deny that one of his men, Don Slater, brutally beat a Pole and his wife at Kayford last March? The last named case was proven to the satisfaction of twelve jurors, who found Slater guilty and he is now out on bond under a suspended sentence. Mr. Feltz will come nearer giving up $500 to keep the crimes against his thugs from being proven than he would to have them proven. Those detectives always take the public as an easy mark and this was just one of those jokes that Mr. Detective is in the habit of playing on Old Man People.

~    ~    ~

When Governor Glasscock went up to Dry Branch on Cabin Creek to investigate the killing of the Baldwin guard Hines, he made particular inquiries about how many guards were killed or wounded, but failed to ask about the miners. He was not interested in the wage slaves. It makes no difference to him if half the miners on the creek had been killed, but the mine guards represented the Governor's class; they were hired fighters and the Governor was interested in their welfare.

~    ~    ~

It has always been said that it was a hard job to keep a woman's mouth shut. Governor Glasscock is evidently of that opinion as he sent sixteen soldiers with guns and ammunition to keep an old woman over eighty years of age from making a speech and then failed. We would advise the Governor to send the whole regiment along the next time he wants to stop Mother Jones from speaking.

~    ~    ~

## CIVIL WAR ON CABIN CREEK. MINERS DETERMINED THE GUARDS MUST GO.

In the face of Governor Glasscock's "Peace Proclamation," civil war again broke out in Cabin Creek district when T.J. Hines, chief of the Baldwin guards, while drunk, arrested and attempted to kill a railroad man at Dry Branch last Friday night. From what we can learn of the affair, Hines had been drinking the most of the day and was in an ugly humor, and picked a quarrel with young Hodges and place him under arrest. Several other of the Baldwin thugs went to the assistance of their chief and the Hodge boy was taken behind the company store, out of sight of most of the men. Hines then struck Hodge with his rifle, knocking him down and began to shoot at him while he was prostrated from the blow. By this time the miners had secured their guns and gone to the rescue of Hodge and a general battle ensued between about thirteen miners on one side and thirteen Baldwin thugs on the other, and it is reported that Hines with several other of his men were killed in the fight. Hines died in the hospital from the effect of his wounds. Several of the mine guards were wounded as well as both of the Hodge boys. The mine guards were reinforced the next morning and another battle took place. The miners had taken position in the hills and drove the thugs back on the train. The miners along the entire river at once began to rally to the support of their Cabin Creek comrades and at one time it seemed that a civil war was inevitable. Under the protection of the state militia the Baldwin thugs had built forts and mounted seven or eight rapid-firing machine guns. It is reported that hundreds of miners had gathered in the mountains Sunday night and Monday and were still coming when martial law was declared. No doubt if the Governor had delayed action for another twenty-four hours the miners would have exterminated the guards in this section. If Governor Glasscock had done his duty two months ago all of this bloodshed and strife could have been averted, but he lacked the moral courage to act. This "before taking" patent advertisement that Senator Elkins hurled into the executive office of West Virginia squatted like a limber backed toad over a seething cauldron of revolt. Dominated and controlled by the corporate interests and the Baldwin strike-breakers he never realized the seriousness of the situation.

The West Virginia miners are determined to drive the Baldwin thugs from the state or die in the attempt. The strike continues to spread. The works on the upper end of Paint Creek were organized last week. This brings all of the mines in Kanawha County and those in the lower end of Fayette into the union. Between 1100 and 1200 men are out on strike over on Coal River, in Raleigh and Boone counties. We learn that since martial law has been proclaimed in Kanawha County and the guards disarmed they are mobilizing in Fayette County in and around Thurmond, where they are patrolling the railroads, watching the trains, and brutally assaulting all suspected of being connected with the mine workers. Nothing will drive the miners to open revolt quicker than the brutality of these hired thugs. If Governor Glasscock does not want a repetition of the Kanawha County bloodshed and violence he had better keep Mr. Baldwin and his thugs moving until they are beyond the state borders. If the executive of the state fails to do his duty and use his official power to move the Baldwin thugs out of the state the miners will move them by force. The Baldwin thugs must go.—*Labor Argus*, 8 September 1912

Captain Morgan: I would say in connection with this—this brings into the controversy a great many facts and I do not know but what it is my duty to object to the submission of a great deal of this for the reason that some of this and probably all of it, so far as I know, is true. If it is true, it would be my duty, as Mr. Boswell's representative, to bring in evidence showing that this is true. The statement—if it is going to be let go at this and no attempt be made to disprove the truth of the matter, why, possibly I should not object so much; but, there is an element of truth, at least, in a good deal of this that is being introduced and it seems to me that it is making a good deal of trouble, at least, and going to make this record pretty big, if we should attempt to come in here and show that those things are true that is set forth; and, for that reason I enter a formal objection and ask the court to rule upon it.

The Judge Advocate: If it takes until next year, you must not deviate from getting at the facts. The purpose in introducing these papers is to show the facts greatly exaggerated and highly colored and that they tend to do just what we say they do: inflame the minds of the miners and was calculated to bring on this conflict which finally consummated in the battle at Mucklow, and which we think the evidence has shown that he himself actively counseled and advised on Sunday evening.

Captain Morgan: You admit, as a general proposition, there are many facts stated in this and if it is your idea to show that the facts were discolored—

The Judge Advocate: I will not make that admission. Most of us know a good deal about the facts and know that in a majority of the instances they are highly discolored and put in there, as they show, to inflame the mind of the miners and bring on this trouble, and that that man is doing this for the purpose of making this trouble all the time.

The commission overruled the objection and Captain Morgan asked that an exception be noted.

From the *Labor Argus* 10 October 1912:

~ ~ ~

### SOLDIERS USED AS STRIKE BREAKERS ON CABIN CREEK–MEN, WOMEN, AND CHILDREN, THE OLD AND THE SICK BEING THROWN INTO THE HIGHWAY BY THE COAL BARONS UNDER THE PROTECTION OF THE MILITIA

~ ~ ~

### MARTIAL LAW GOING TOO FAR

Gen. Elliott, as chief of the Bull Moosers of the state and commander of the troops in the martial law zone remarked to some miners that it was better for him not to be caught talking with the miners as some one would accuse him of being partial. Such criticisms could only come from the guards and operators, yet Gen. Elliott is often seen in company with Chas.

Cabell, the Czar of Cabin Creek and other operators. He does not seem to fear the criticism of the miners and public. Not only this, but he has usurped his power and in company with Czar Cabell has gone around giving the miners orders to move out or go back to work which but shows that Gen. Elliott, as a Bull Moose and a military officer is in league with the coal barons and is using his office and influence against the strikers. This man who has always claimed to be fair and impartial has proven to be just as much a puppet and tool to the interest as the spineless Governor who appointed him. Both Governor Glasscock and Gen. Elliott promised the miners that under martial law they would not allow any transportation to be brought in or the miners to be ejected from their homes. Both of these promises have been broken. When men in their official capacity representing the law do not respect their own word and promise, how can they expect the miners to respect the law they represent? These miners are fighting for their constitutional rights that have been guaranteed to them by the state and nation, the right of free speech, peaceful assemblage, and the right to organize. These are the American citizens' birthrights and they are rights too sacred for an Esau in the form of a Bull Moose or a petty military officer to deprive them of with impunity. Under the existing conditions martial law was not intended to deprive the citizen of every civil right and to establish a military despotism, but rather to keep peace and protect the lives and property when the civil authorities were no longer able to handle the situation.

All through the pages of history we find where men of a small mental calibre have been given power they become tyrants and the West Virginia military authorities have proved no exception to the rule. When Gen. Elliott ordered the miners to either give up their homes or go back to work, he usurped a power that his office does not entitle him to. The general is quoted as saying: "God walks on sea and land, but greed rules the hills of West Virginia." It seems from the occurrences of the last few weeks that Gen. Elliott has become the victim of this same greed that numbs the hand and blinds the eye of justice. Dare he to use his soldiers to deprive the miners, their wives, and babies of a shelter? Has he no heart that he is willing to use the militia to throw the old and the young, the sick and the women out to face the elements at this season of the year? The animals will protect their female and their young and the miners will protect their wives and babies. Under martial law Gen. Elliott is giving the miners a sample of the Roosevelt Bull Moose administration, but we will advise the general to go easy as the miners are in no humor now to stand any more tyranny or oppression, either from the civil authorities, Bull Moosers, or the militia, and they number their friends and sympathizers by the thousands. If the militia officials pursue their plans to eject the miners with the soldiers a condition will arise that even the state militia will not be able to handle.

∾    ∾    ∾

From the *Labor Argus*, 3 October 1912:

All that the miners ask now is that the Governor and his military authorities keep their hands off. Should Gen. Elliott attempt to carry out his plan to eject the miners from their home with the militia we are afraid he will start something that all the state guards will be unable to stop and on his and Gov. Glasscock's shoulders will rest the responsibility for what may happen. The people are fast losing confidence in the state and military officials and another breach of faith on their part would precipitate an upheaval that would involve the entire state. The miners are determined to win this strike at any cost and are going to win or die in the attempt.

∾    ∾    ∾

From the same issue, 3 October 1912, the certificate of publication:

Statement of the ownership, management, circulation etc. of the *Labor Argus,* published weekly, at Charleston, W. Va., required by the Act of August 24, 1912.
    Name of Editor: C.H. Boswell, of Charleston, W. Va.
    Managing Editor: C.H. Boswell, Charleston, W. Va.
    Business Manager: C.S. Boswell, Charleston, W. Va.
    Publisher: The Social Labor Publishing Co., Charleston, W. Va.
    Known bondholders, mortgages, and other security holders, holding 1 per cent, or more, of the total amount of bonds, mortgages or other securities: None.
    Average number of copies of each issue of this publication sold or distributed, through the mails or otherwise, to paid subscribers during the six months preceding the date of this statement: This information is required from daily newspapers only.

                                                     C.H. Boswell.

Sworn to and subscribed before me this first day of October, 1912. S.L. Webb, Notary Public. My commission expires Jan. 12, 1920.

∾    ∾    ∾

From the same issue, 3 October 1912:

The soldier boys in the West Virginia militia have our sympathy as we know that doing strike duty is against their better nature and is anything but a pleasant task. The Baldwin guards were paid all the way from $5 to $10 a day for performing practically the same duties that the militia are forced to perform and the militiamen only draw from $15 to $35 per month and must live in uncomfortable tents while the Baldwin guards lived on the fat of the land, dressed like gentlemen even if they did not act that way and were quartered in the best and most comfortable hotels in that section. The difference is the coal barons were paying the Baldwins and had to furnish them ample pay and comfortable quarters or they would leave, but the taxpayers of the great state of West Virginia are paying the soldier boys and they cannot leave their post no matter how bad they may want to. We have always been taught to look upon our soldiers as brave, fearless men whose duty it was to protect the people of this country from any enemy who might infringe on the rights and liberties of the American citizenship and no doubt these boys who compose the West Virginia militia joined it with that idea in their minds, never thinking that as workingmen and the sons of the working class they would be called upon to turn their guns on their brother workers who were striking for their rights. They little thought that they would be called upon to protect the coal barons, the strikebreakers, and the scabs. Little did they think that they would be used as a means to oppress their already crushed and bleeding fellow workers, but these are the duties of the soldier under the present system of capitalistic government. Soldiers, fellow workers in uniform, have you the heart to shoot down your fellow workers? Do the careworn faces of the anxious mothers and the frightened stare of the ragged, half-starved child not appeal to you? Do you realize that your state officials and military officers have placed you in a position where you stand between these people and all that makes life worth while to them? You are protecting the enemies of the commonwealth and oppressing the people. The spirit of a brave man would revolt at such a task. Can you call yourselves men and stand between your fellow worker and freedom, the careworn mother and her hopes, the hungry child and its bread? Are you going to be a traitor to your class for a few paltry dollars of the master's illgotten gains? By every tie that binds man to man, your sympathies, your interest, and your birth bind you to the striking miners. Your duties as soldiers, citizens, and workingmen call upon you to protect the striking miners in the exercise of the rights and liberties guaranteed them by the state and national constitutions and a man who raises a hand to deprive these people of their blood-bought rights is a traitor to his country, a traitor to his class, and a disgrace to the mother who gave him birth. Strikebreaking is no job for a soldier. It is their duty to defend our country from the outside enemies and not to protect the enemies within.

∾   ∾   ∾

From the same issue, 3 October 1912

Gen. Elliott and Czar Cabell are going around telling the miners to vacate their houses by a certain date. This is a matter for the civil authorities to settle, and one with which Gen. Elliott has nothing to do under martial law. Our advice to the miners is to hold your houses and force the soldiers to throw you out. The Bull Moose may be the czar of Cabin Creek but there are powers yet above the military law and that is the power of the sovereign citizen. The citizenship of West Virginia is more sacred than the martial law or the 2 x 4 plutocratic stool pigeons who are enforcing it. Your home is your domain over which you are king, you have a right to protect the sacredness of your hearth from any intruder whether he be a Baldwin thug, a prostituted official, a coal baron, or the state militia, and the man who fails to exercise these rights is a coward and does not deserve the respect of his fellow citizens.

∾   ∾   ∾

From the *Labor Argus*, 21 November 1912:

The railroad men have added a star to their crown by refusing to pull the transportation men up Cabin Creek and the officials of the road have given them to understand that they will not be required to do that kind of work. We would now like to see the railroaders add a whole row of stars to their crown by refusing to haul scab coal, or pull the Bull Moose train. The Bull Moose chief and his aggregation of strikebreakers are doing more against the strikers than all the transportation men they could bring in. If Governor Glasscock's tin horns want to move let them hike it, a little walk will be good for the uniformed loafers. A man who will take up arms against his fellow workers for $1.25 a day is an enemy to his class and not deserving of any consideration from the workers.

∾   ∾   ∾

From the *Labor Argus*, 14 November 1912:

Every indication points to the fact that some of the militia officers and the Baldwin guards have gone into a partnership for the purpose of breaking the miners' strike on Paint and Cabin creeks. Just how many of the militia officers are implicated we are unable to say or just how far up it reaches, but one thing is evident from the actions of the military officers and the Baldwin guards, that a thorough understanding exists between these two organizations. On both Paint Creek and Cabin Creek we find squads of ex-members of the militia under the charge of a lieutenant or captain under the alias of watchmen doing practically the same duties of the Baldwin guards. We are informed that these men are paid by the coal operators and are under orders from Major Pratt and that Major Pratt receives his orders from that chief of the Bull Moosers, General Elliott.

When Paint and Cabin creeks got too hot for the Baldwin men and martial law was declared the operators at once got busy with the officials of the militia and under the protection of the martial law the present strikebreaking agency was organized. Just as soon as the organization was perfected martial law was declared off, and disguised as watchmen the tin horn soldiers have assumed the duties of the Baldwin thugs, patrolling the Creek and meeting and guarding transportation into the strike zone. The old Baldwin men have been sent out all over the country to secure scabs and strikebreakers. They bring them as far as Paint and Cabin Creek junctions and then turn them over to their partners, the renegades from the National Guard. All of this but goes to show that the Baldwin strikebreaking agency and the Elliott-Pratt strikebreaking agency are working together, hand in hand, and that both are under pay and subject to the instructions of the coal barons.

The "peace proclamation" failed to break the strike. The martial law failed to break it and the Baldwin thugs have failed to break it and this new organization of military thugs will fail. On Cabin Creek alone the coal operators are maintaining an army of over one hundred gunmen besides the labor agents and Baldwin men they have out hunting strikebreakers. They are paying these men from $3 to $5 a day and expenses; placing a conservative estimate on the expense of maintaining this army, it would amount to at least $650 a day or $18,500 a month. In addition to this every transportation they bring in is costing the operators all the way from $10 to $30 a head and a majority of these transportations leave without doing a day's work, and those that do stay are not practical miners and are a dead expense on the operators. But few operators on these two creeks can afford to stand this drain on their finances much longer. If the strike lasts another month the small companies will be absorbed by the big ones. The miners have this strike won in spite of the Elliott-Baldwin-Pratt agency. There is every sign of weakening on the part of a good many operators and they are only being held in line by the influence of Czar Cabell and M.T. Davis, but these two self-annointed potentates will yet have to bow their heads in defeat or go out of business. Nothing can defeat the aims of men who display such solidarity and determination as displayed by the striking miners of Kanawha County. It is a pleasure to fight for and with such men. The fight has been a hard one, but the victory will be that much sweeter, and victory shall be ours.

～　～　～

From the same issue, 14 November 1912:

When Britton and Scott go into their offices as justices of the peace of Cabin Creek district, there won't be any more "drum-head trials," with Baldwin thugs as constables, witnesses, and prosecutors.

～　～　～

From the *Labor Argus*, 26 December 1912:

We notice that the Governor has made it known that the miners' old shotguns, target rifles, and other small firearms would be returned to them December 16, but the Springfields, Mausers, and Krags would be kept in charge of the officials until after the strike, but we notice that the Governor said nothing about the Winchesters and machine guns taken from the operators and guards. No doubt but that they will be returned, if they have not already been turned over to their owners. It makes a lot of difference whose gun it is. The guards and scabs are fully armed with high power Winchesters now, but our state's chief executive seems to prefer to keep the miners disarmed and at the mercy of those outlaws and thugs. But the miners can stand it, as Little Willie is going, going, going! and he will soon be gone, and when he is gone he will be one of the deadest politicians that ever left the executive chair. He won't even have prestige enough to play his old game of ward politics in his home town.

≈   ≈   ≈

From the *Labor Argus*, 19 December 1912: The cartoon on the front page is offered in evidence.

≈   ≈   ≈

From the *Labor Argus*, 12 December 1912:

Governor Glasscock's brand of military despotism under the guise of martial law has exceeded all bounds and overrun the boundaries covered by the proclamation. It has usurped the civil authorities and extended its depredation on the rights and liberties of the people of Charleston. We had an example last Sunday morning of what can be done by the tools and hirelings of the coal baron, when a squad of soldiers and railroad detectives, better known as Baldwin thugs, came to Charleston in the dead hours of the night and at the muzzle of guns took men from their beds and made them prisoners without warrants and rushed them up to Pratt on the military train where they were thrown into the bullpen without knowing what they were charged with. Charleston and this section of Kanawha County is under civil law, here we have our municipal and county courts, these men were citizens of West Virginia and were out of the martial law zone, they had a right to a civil trial, but they were workingmen and a workingman's rights are never respected by the tools of the master class. When these men were arrested they demanded a warrant but were told by the militia captain in command that no warrant was needed; then they asked what the charges against them were and were told they would find that out when they faced the court martial at Pratt. When such crimes as this can be perpetrated on citizens of this commonwealth by an illegal military despotism, it is striking at the very foundation of the nation. Our forefathers rebelled rather than pay an extortionate tariff on tea and their descendants at this late age are expected to humbly submit to such military tyranny as this. The American eagle, that noble bird of prey, the emblem of freedom and liberty, no longer has a place on our coat of arms, for liberty and freedom have been assassinated by the vulture of greed that now flaps its hideous wings in the face of an outraged people and, perched upon the masters' machines of war and protected by their hired soldiers, it gloats over the torn and tattered remains of its bleeding victim. Justice is dead, freedom is a thing of the past, and liberty is but a dream of the future.

Where are our rights and liberties and what are they worth to us when we are subject to the will and the whims of a weak-kneed tyrant? We boast of that sacred old document and brag about our "constitutional rights and guarantees," but what do they amount to when one man can set them aside and leave us at the tender mercies of a court martial? What is the use to make laws if the governor can set them aside? The strike and the martial law have been educational. The people have learned in the last few months that they were slaves without any rights, they have learned that those who control the power of the government own the people, they have learned that where might rules justice is blind, liberty is unknown and the boasted freedom of the people is but a mockery. Must we wait until all of our rights have been abridged and all that is human has been crushed out until nothing but the brute is left before we will have the courage to get up off our knees and demand what is our own? How long, Oh People, will you beg for crumbs and accept blows?

~ ~ ~

From the same issue, 12 December 1912:

Governor Glasscock can call off his "tin horns" for a day to display them in Charleston; why couldn't he keep them here? If the presence of the soldiers was not needed in the martial law zone to preserve the peace last Tuesday it is not needed now. If they can leave for a day they are not needed at all, but they are not there to keep the peace, they are doing strikebreaking duty and the taxpayer of West Virginia is paying the bill. That is what they voted for, now they are getting results. When the Poca Elk district farmers' tax tickets come out with the assessment for military purposes they will remember how they voted.

~ ~ ~

From the *Labor Argus*, 5 December 1912:

We have read with horror of the Siberian prisons, the convict camps of the south and the slave pens of Mexico, but none of these surpass in inhumanity the military bullpen at Pratt or the darkened rooms in which the women prisoners are held under guard. Now for over a week Miss Maggie Ombler and Mrs. Lee Harold have been held prisoners in an upstairs room of B. S. Carney's house at Pratt under military guard, with blinds pulled down and windows closed these women are held prisoners of war, not even allowed to see the light of day in a close and unventilated room. One of them was under a doctor's care when arrested and tried before this mock tribunal of injustice, the court martial. When Miss Ombler asked that her witnesses be summoned she was told that she did not need any witnesses before that court, so she was tried and convicted of some imaginary crime known only to the minds of the military court.

Besides the inhumanities heaped upon those women, we are informed that a small boy who was sentenced to the reform school last week was being held a prisoner and starved because he refused to carry out the slop jars from the women prisoners' room. There are numerous other cases where the accused were not allowed to put on witnesses in their defense and were railroaded to the penitentiary, innocent of any offence. It is bad enough to see our fellow men deprived of their liberty and persecuted, but when tools of a usurped power subject women and children to these outrages it taxes human endurance to the limit. Can the sovereign citizen who believes in equity, liberty, and justice condone or defend such an outrage on society? Is manhood dead? Has the red blood of America turned yellow? Has old General Public a rubber back that he should cringe and crawl before a military despotism? It seems that the American citizens have lost that strain of blood that actuated our forefathers in '76. This is a matter that affects society as a whole. What has been done to Miss Ombler and Mrs. Harold can be done to your sister or mother, your wife or daughter. The people should rise in a body and protest against such an outrage on humanity and teach the spineless officials that they are the servants and not the masters of the people.

~ ~ ~

From the *Labor Argus*, 30 January 1913:

When Bonner Hill was a candidate for Sheriff of Kanawha County we knew he would prove but another tool of the coal barons by the fact that his campaign was financed and supported by the coal operators, and while we fully expected him to use his official power in the interest of his masters we did not expect him to stoop so low as to personally gather up scabs and strikebreakers to go to Paint Creek and Cabin Creek to take the places of the striking miners who are fighting for their rights in the face of every opposition. We were informed by two union miners that while on Kanawha Street Tuesday evening they saw Bonner Hill talking to a squad of colored men and some Italians. They went up to the squad and heard Bonner Hill trying to get these men to go up Paint Creek to take the places of the strikers. One of these men was a colored man from Hougheston and while in the crowd was approached by a man who was representing himself as a deputy sheriff who tried to get him to go up Paint Creek. When Mr. G. W. Reed of Ohley spoke to Sheriff Hill and asked him what he meant by trying to get me to go up Paint and Cabin creeks when he knew a strike was on and the conditions in that section, Hill gave him no answer but told the men he was talking with to come over to the Alderson-Stephenson building where he could finish his talk and make the necessary arrangements. This is the information just as it came to us, and we have the names and addresses of our informants who will vouch for the truth of the statement. When the sheriff of our county prostitutes his high office and descends to the level of a common scab hunter and herder, it is time the people of the county file their protest so forcibly that the sheriffs of the future would profit by the experience of their predecessor. Bonner Hill knows the conditions that exist in the strike zone. He knows that women and children are living in tents and facing the fury of the winter winds with only these thin canvass walls for protection and in the face of this knowledge he is willing to prostitute his office and try to send men up these creeks to take the bread out of those children's mouths and clothes off their backs. He would send strikebreakers to take their fathers' places and use the power of his office to defeat the striking miners in their fight for the rights and liberties guaranteed to them by the laws of the state that he has sworn to protect and defend. But Hill and his Baldwin deputies will not be able to break this strike. The deputized thugs and hired gunmen only drive the miners to desperation, and when they see their elected officials prostitute the law in the interest of the greedy coal barons they will lose faith in the law and depend on their own manhood for protection. Do your worst, Sheriff Hill, there is only a few more weeks of winter and it is not long until GREEN LEAVES will be out again.

≈  ≈  ≈

From the same issue, 30 January 1913:

We notice the *Mail* is advertising a book entitled "Civil War in West Virginia." The very fact that a paper like the *Mail* mentions this book proves beyond a doubt that it was written in the interest of the coal barons. But let that be as it may, we will warn the powers that be that unless a stop is put to the brutalities of the hired thugs there will be more civil war in West Virginia. There is a limit to human endurance and the miners are tired of being bullied and brutalized by the hirelings of the coal barons. Under the protection of the martial law the operators filled the strike zone with hired gunmen who patrol the creeks, ride the trains, and insult, abuse and browbeat the strikers just for pastime. Daily they are growing more bold and brutal in their depredations on the rights of the citizens and have even gone so far as to murder one of the strikers in cold blood. The corporation hirelings are again resorting to their old tactics of brutally assaulting the union men and strikers whenever an opportunity presents itself. It was these methods that brought about the outbreak last summer, and if a stop is not put to them, history will repeat itself this summer. Human nature will stand just so much persecution; goaded beyond that point, they become desperate and lose respect for the law and the fear of death. Courts and prisons will no longer awe them. Self-preservation, that first law of nature, is their only thought and they will fight with a desperation that knows no defeat. If the county authorities will do their duty fairly and impartially there would be no cause for or fear of trouble, but as long as armed thugs patrol the strike zone and the coal barons build and equip forts and prepare for war under the protection of the authorities there will always remain that danger of an outbreak. The county and state authorities know that peonage is being practiced on both Paint and Cabin creeks in violation of the law. They know that men are being herded by armed guards protected by machine guns mounted in forts, yet they do nothing to put a stop to this inhuman and barbarous practice, but they do send their deputy sheriffs up to guard the union camps to see that the strikers do not violate any of the sacred laws protecting property rights. If Sheriff Hill wants to do something worth-while, let him drive the hired gunmen out of the county and break up the system of peonage practiced in the slave pens of the coal barons and there will be no more "civil war in West Virginia."

~ ~ ~

From the *Labor Argus,* 23 January 1913:

The shooting of John Miller at Eskdale on Cabin Creek by one of the Glasscock-Baldwin tinhorn thugs was not only a cold-blooded murder of an innocent man but, from what we learn of the affair, was premeditated. For some time previous to the shooting the guards now called "watchmen" had been trying to start trouble at Eskdale. In the guise of deputy sheriffs and C. & O. special agents they have been riding the trains in and out the creek and of late have been getting off the cars at Eskdale and marching up and down the platform with their rifles while the train was stopping, besides using abusive and insulting language to the strikers and snapping their revolvers in their faces, with the intent to start a riot.

Failing to draw the strikers out with these infamous tactics, Maj. Payne and his right bower Michael hatched up the plot on the train going up on the evening of the 15th to murder someone in Eskdale that night and Michael was picked to do the deed. A pint of whiskey was given him to brace up his nerve, so by the time the train reached Eskdale he was just in the right condition to commit the dastardly crime. After parading the platform of the depot with Maj. Payne and waiting until the train was just ready to pull out, Michael stepped back on the train, drew his revolver, and shot and killed an innocent bystander who was leaning against the light post with his hands in his pockets. This was nothing less than a cold-blooded, inhuman, brutal murder. The stories told by the guards to the effect that Michael was struck with a rock are absolutely false, as was proved by several eyewitnesses of the whole affair. There were no rocks thrown and the lurid newspaper accounts are as false and as biassed as all the rest of their articles and accounts of this affair. The daily press, in order to serve the coal barons and condone the deed of their brutal hireling, prostituted themselves and stooped to the utterance of bare-faced lies, by saying Miller was shot and killed by a passenger on the train, while they know the thug did the shooting and at that time was under arrest for the crime. As soon as Michael shot and killed Miller he went inside of the train and gave his gun to another thug, who made away with it.

Mayor Walter Williams of Eskdale at once boarded the train and arrested Payne and Michael and took them off and brought them to Charleston that night. When he was bringing the prisoners by the Ruffner Hotel he was met by Gen. Elliott and some others of the tinhorn strikebreakers and Baldwins who took the prisoners away from Williams by claiming that martial law was still on and that the prisoners would have to be tried by the military authorities. It was later proven that these statements were also untrue and the prisoner was tried by the civil authorities. Now, we would like to know why Gen. Elliott and his thugs and strikebreakers are not guilty of interfering with an officer in the discharge of his duty. Frank Nantz was sentenced to five years in the penitentiary for this offense; now give old Gen. Elliott a dose of his own medicine. The miners were sentenced to the penitentiary on misdemeanor charges but Michael the murderer was not even sent to jail but was let out on a $5,000 bond, his guns returned to him and now he goes forth a licensed murderer. We have been informed that prior to the declaration of martial law that this man Michael was an insurance agent in Morgantown and came to this section with the Morgantown company and when his accounts were checked up by the insurance company they were found short and rather than go back to Morgantown and face his deficiency, Michael left his company and hired as a mine guard, watchman, or thug and was heard to remark that he was out for some easy money. The facts in this case stand out too bold to be disputed. Maj. Payne and Michael concocted and planned the murder. Michael was given a pint of whiskey over half of which he had drunk. On arriving at Eskdale Michael drew his gun and shot and killed Miller in cold blood. The rock throwing story as told by the thugs and published in the press was nothing more than a fabrication of lies manufactured for the sole purpose of justifying the murderer in his cold-blooded deed. All of which is a part of the strikebreaking scheme on the part of the public officials in league with the coal barons and the corporate interest.

We have no doubt but that Michael was paid to commit this murder and that the daily press was paid to publish the untrue accounts attributing the cause of the trouble to the striking miners. The very fact that Michael was not turned over to the county officials and lodged in jail as would have been done with any other murderer bears us out in making this statement. The miners who were only charged with misdemeanors were railroaded to the penitentiary and were not allowed bond, but a mine guard can murder a miner without spending a day in jail. This crime was committed against the working class, the capitalist press defended the criminal, and the capitalist politicians condoned the crime, and the working class furnished the bleeding corpse of the victim. If this is not enough to teach the working class something about the class struggle they are indeed dumb cattle fit only for slaves. If there is a law to deprive the workingman of his liberty and railroad him to the penitentiary on the smallest pretext and no law to protect the lives of the workers or to punish those who maim and murder them, then we may say to hell with the law and will advise the working class to take the law in their own hands and redress their own wrongs. The capitalists have furnished the criminal and the workers the victims long enough.

∾  ∾  ∾

From the *Labor Argus*, 23 January 1913:

Insult has been added to injury by the recommitment of Dan Chain to the penitentiary by that pitiful excuse of an executive, the Governor of West Virginia, in the face of a decision rendered by one of the ablest judges of the state to the effect that the entire martial law proceedings were illegal and nothing more than a brazen usurpation of power. It seems that the only motive of this last outrage of the governor's was to show his contempt for the people whose constitutional rights he has trampled in the dirt. By this act in the face of court proceedings he simply spits in the face of the people and treats with contempt their sacred rights and constitutional guarantees. Are West Virginians such dumb and docile cattle that they will allow a mental weakling drunk with power to hurl this defy into their teeth? Has our citizenship sunk so low? Has the manhood of this great state degenerated that they will take such a gross insult from their own servant? Why does the governor vent his pent-up wrath on this man? Is it because he is a Negro? We will remind him here that he owes his present position to the Negro vote and must say he has a poor way of showing his appreciation. If the governor thinks by persecuting Dan Chain he can effect a compromise on the pending suits against himself and that despotic abortion of his own creation, the military commission, he is sadly mistaken. Dan Chain, though a black man, is made of such material that he had rather die than sacrifice a principle or have his friends sacrifice a principle to save him. The suits will go on and will be fought out before the highest court of the nation and if they uphold the vicious decision of the state court, then the miners in the name of justice and humanity will lay their case before the court of last resort and let the people be the judge. And to the tools of plutocracy who are wielding the power of this government we say beware how you persecute a long-suffering people, lest patience ceases to be a virtue and they rise in their just and righteous indignation and demand a day of reckoning.

∾  ∾  ∾

From the same issue, 23 January 1913:

> The thugs and hirelings of the coal barons are again resorting to their brutal and murderous assaults on the miners. If a stop is not put to their tactics the miners will be forced to defend themselves as best they can. Under the martial law Major Wallace declared before the Supreme Court that the will of the governor was law. If the servant of the people can make his will law, it seems that the people who elect and pay him can declare their will law. If some steps are not taken to stop the depredations of the guards and gunmen, the miners will have to follow the example set by the state's executive and take the law in their own hands, and when they do their will will be, that the guards, gunmen, watchmen, and thugs must leave the state. For the guards, alias watchmen, alias thugs, must go, as it does not help the smell of the hole any to pull a pole cat out and put a skunk in.

From the *Labor Argus*, 16 January 1913:

> Our very benevolent governor has seen fit to exercise the "loveable" side of his nature by pardoning fifteen miners out of the penitentiary after illegally depriving them of their liberty though they were guilty of no crime against the law, and while he was in this "loveable" mode he also pardoned five Baldwin thugs who were guilty. Now no doubt the prostituted press and the subsidized sheets of the coal baron will waste several columns of their worthless editorial space eulogizing "Little Willie" for his act of made-to-order charity. He made the victims and then graciously extended them charity; he threw them into prison without cause for the empty pleasure of pardoning them out. Doubtless he thinks now these victims of his whim should prostrate themselves before him and thank him for his benevolence. We know why the governor sent these men to prison, it was just a part of his strikebreaking scheme.
>
> Now let us see why he pardoned them out and whether or not it was charity, benevolence, or fear that actuated his motives. It was not through any kindness of heart or a "loveable" spot in his warped and twisted nature that caused the governor to pardon these men but it was fear that filled his heart and his anxiety to further serve the coal barons that prompted his actions. The Supreme Court of the state had proven itself to be the venal tools of the corporate interests by rendering a vicious decision justifying the actions of Governor Glasscock and the court martial commission established under a military despotism that was antagonistic to the fundamental principles of a republican form of government. A precedent was established that will prove in the future a powerful weapon in the hands of the master class and a menace to the labor movement of the state. The attorneys for the miners had prepared to take the case before the supreme court of the nation, and Governor Glasscock and his friends know that they dare not uphold the decision of the state court, they know

that their precedent would be wiped from the records and that the governor and his military commission would be brought before the bar of justice to answer to an outraged people for their crime committed under a military despotism. There was but one way the governor could stop this case from going before the Supreme Court of the United States and that was by pardoning the petitioners. It was not sympathy, nor love, nor kindness of heart that caused him to pardon the miners but fear on the one hand and intrigue on the other. He did not want to be hauled before the court himself and he wanted that vicious precedent to remain on the records. In it all can be seen the cunning hand of the shrewd legal manipulator and Gov. Glasscock was but a tool of these legal gents who were pulling the wires for the coal operators. If these men were the criminals that they were charged with being, what right has Governor Glasscock to turn them loose on the public? But they were not criminals and the governor knew it. He also knew that when he illegally deprived these men of their civil rights and liberty that he and his commission committed a criminal act and became criminals and it was to escape the consequences of this criminal act and his just deserts that the governor pardoned all of the victims of his military court. It is time that "Little Willie" find out that the American people will not stand for military tyranny and despotism at this late age.

~    ~    ~

From the *Labor Argus*, 9 January 1913, the cartoon is offered in evidence, and from the issue of 13 February 1913 the cartoon on the first page is offered.

~    ~    ~

From the same issue, 13 February 1913:

### CIVIL WAR AGAIN IN WEST VIRGINIA
### SCORES OF MINE GUARDS KILLED
### IN BLOODY BATTLES WITH MINERS

The brutal and cold-blooded attempt of Sheriff Hill and his hirelings and thugs to murder the sleeping miners in their tents at Holly Grove last Friday night precipitated a condition that culminated in a civil war in which scores of men lost their lives. Since Friday evening a reign of terror has existed on Paint and Cabin creeks. No pen can paint the horrors of the situation. Never before in the history of the nation has a public official so prostituted himself to the interest or resorted to such cold-blooded and brutal tactics as the high sheriff of Kanawha County attempted last Friday night. The miners who had been evicted from their homes on Paint Creek last summer pitched their tents at Holly Grove where they have lived ever since, with nothing but these thin canvass walls to protect them from the rain and snow and winter wind. This tented village was detrimental to the coal barons' interest, as the strikers who made them their homes were active in keeping the transportation of strikebreakers from going up the creek and assisting them in making their escape from these slave pens. This did not suit the coal barons, so they decided to wipe out the camp at Holly Grove, even though they would have to kill every man, woman, and child in the camp. It was for this purpose that Bonner Hill, in company with some of the coal barons and their cut-throat thugs, made this dastardly and cowardly attack on the camp. There was no trouble on Paint Creek and everything was quiet until Hill and his murderous hirelings slipped up the creek in the night with lights all out on the train, and when just opposite Holly Grove at a given signal this band of bloodthirsty brutes, without provocation, opened up a murderous fire on the tents of the sleeping miners with a machine gun and high power rifles, killing Sesco Estep as he was putting his children into a dugout to protect them from the hail of bullets. Several other people were wounded, among them a Mrs. Hall, who was shot through both legs while asleep and will probably lose a foot as a result. The miners, taken by surprise, returned the fire as best they could.

We learned from a reliable source that Bonner Hill gave the order to the machine gun operator to open fire on the tents. There are a score or more witnesses who will testify that the first shots came from the train and that the train was running with all lights out. Not satisfied with this attempt to murder the miners and their families the thugs came back to Holly Grove early Saturday morning and took a position in the hills and again opened fire on the camp with a machine gun and rifles. But only the miners were the sufferers. So Governor Glasscock did not see fit to call out the militia to protect them. At last, driven to desperation by the sight of the mangled corpse of their comrade, the suffering of their wounded women, and the frantic fear of their wives and children, the miners at last took up arms to protect themselves, and the man who would not fight under these circumstances is indeed a craven coward, not deserving the name man. Is it any wonder the miners resorted to arms to rid themselves of the brutal guards and hirelings of the coal barons after being the object of a murderous attack by the authorities of the county and not furnished protection by the state? These are the causes that led up to the bloody battle that raged throughout the strike zone all day Monday and Monday night and resulted in the killing and wounding of scores of the mine guards and thugs. Driven to revolt by the inhumanities of the county officials and thugs the miners waged a relentless war of extermination on their persecutors, with the result that scores of the mine guards are known to be killed and wounded in the fight Monday while the miners never lost a man.

All day Tuesday the dead and wounded were being brought out of the creek. As a greater part of the fighting was done in the hills it will be impossible to know just how many men were really killed, and it is more than likely it will never be known as the authorities are only too anxious to hide from the world the horrors of these damnable slave pens. It is a deplorable state of affairs when the sovereign citizens are forced to resort to arms to protect their lives and the lives of their families in a state that claims to be civilized.

As long as it was only the miners being shot and murdered—as long as it was only the miners' homes destroyed and lives endangered, Governor Glasscock refused to send his tinhorns up to protect them, but just as soon as the miners were driven to revolt and the guards and thugs were getting the worst of the battle, the governor again declared martial law and rushed his militia into the strike zone to protect the coal barons and their hirelings. The guards acting under instructions from the coal barons have gradually grown more brutal and unbearable. They thought because the miners were quiet that their spirits were broken and that they would crush them with their brutalities, but their calculations were bad, they had underestimated the miners. Instead of weakening from their long struggle and suffering, they have grown stronger and more determined. The miners are not asking for any special favors. They are only asking for their constitutional and legal rights and they are going to have those or die fighting for them. It can only be settled in one way and that is by giving those men fair treatment. Justice is all the miners are asking for and this fighting and bloodshed will never stop until they get it. The "watchmen" thugs, Baldwins, and hirelings of the coal barons must go, and if the authorities refuse to do their duty, then but one recourse is left open to the miners.

≈  ≈  ≈

From the same issue, 13 February 1913:

For the third time in the last few months a military despotism has been established in West Virginia depriving her citizens of their civil rights and making a mockery of the constitution. This brazen usurpation of power on the part of Gov. Glasscock is a disgrace to the state, a blot on civilization, and an insult to a free people. The governor's military despotism under the guise of martial law amounts to no more than political persecution, and the prisoners railroaded to the penitentiary by that illegal and tyrannical court, the military commission, are nothing more than political prisoners in exile from their homes for no other cause than their activities in the interest of the working class. No doubt but that the governor and his advisors, the coal barons, think by arresting these active workers and railroading them to the penitentiary in violation of the law and constitution of state and nation that they can keep the wage slaves in humble submission, but for every man thrown in jail and denied his civil rights a thousand will awake to their condition. Let the prostituted officials, the subsidized press, and the military despotism do their worst, as they are only hastening the REVO-LUTION. Such actions as these will arouse the working class quicker than all the Socialist speakers and papers could possibly do. It is only after the tools of the ruling class have outraged justice and assassinated liberty that the working class realizes their prostitution.

≈    ≈    ≈

From the same issue, 13 February 1913:

The southern slave barons hung John Brown and brought about the Civil War. It would be wise for the coal barons of West Virginia to profit by their experience or they might start a revolution that will be equally as disastrous to their interest. John Browns are bad medicine for both aristocracy and plutocracy.

≈    ≈    ≈

From the *Labor Argus*, 27 February 1913:

The infamous Pennsylvania Cossacks have been gone some better by the Baldwin hellions of the Kanawha coal operators. Men born and reared amid the hills of West Virginia have been hounded from their homes, their wives and children insulted, beaten, and even murdered by these off-scourings gathered from the lowest depths of capitalistic society and commissioned as "police" and "deputies" by the prostituted puppets of an "Invisible Government." But the very fact that the coal barons are compelled to use these human hyenas is a good sign, for it signifies that the robbers themselves have given up all hope of justifying their system of exploitation and robbery by hypocritical "laws," and must depend entirely upon the physical force of gunmen, detectives, and militia for their continued hold upon the people whom they have plundered.

≈    ≈    ≈

From the *Labor Argus*, 20 February 1913:

THE YELLOWLEGS

Of all the contemptible things ever gathered together under the blue canopy these little under-weight, under-sized, peaked-headed counter jumpers who compose the National Guard deserve the medal.

Recruited from the slums of our cities, degenerates in both mind and body, they represent the very dregs of the survivals under capitalism. They are not deserving of real hatred, but their actions can stir up more unutterable contempt in the average healthy human animal than anything else of which we can think just now.

To illustrate: On last Sunday a detail of ten brought one of their compatriots, who had fallen under the displeasure of some of his superiors, to the county jail. Citizens along their line of march down Kanawha Street hissed and jeered them until they tried to shrink out of sight, in their yellow livery, and to place the cap-sheaf on their humiliation two bartered prostitutes who were passing in a buggy spat upon them and shrilled "scab-herders!"

At Paint Creek, Monday, a passenger on one of the C. & O. trains was moved to laughter at the ludicrous sight of two of these little manikins pacing back and forth across the bridge trying to lug weapons far too heavy for their strength. One of the yellowlegs observed the laugh and deserting his post hurried to an "officer," told him that he would "have to make that guy quit laughin' at us." He with the commission, lifting the heavy frog-sticker which was chained to his belt, to prevent it dragging on the ground, climbed up into the coach and shaking a delicate pink finger in the direction of the offender screeched: "Look ahere, you quit laughin' at MY MEN, or I'll have you yanked out of here."

And these are what capitalism expects to intimidate the workers with.

∾    ∾    ∾

From the *Labor Argus*, 20 February 1913:

## GOVERNMENT BY BLOCKHEADS

No fundamental wrong can be righted by repression. Time has limned this immortal truth upon the canvass of history. Organized force may for a time stifle the bitter cry for bread, but that imperative craving for life will again find voice. Rome felt secure after lining her highways with her massacred victims, but the echo of her crime was heard in the thundering mobs at her gates. England, France, Germany, Russia—all the countries of Europe—have sent a long procession of proletarian agitators to the scaffold and the dungeon, but still the cry for bread rings through the land. France was taught a lesson, in a whirlwind of blood, that justice never perches on the point of the bayonet. This nation writhed in the agonies of fratricidal strife because it had not learned this lesson. Though preacher and priest profaned the word of Holy Writ and desecrated the House of God to sanctify the curse of slavery, they had to yield to the decree of justice. Though Chief Justice Taney lent the weight of the nation's highest court to triple-rivet the chains upon the black man's limbs, justice struck them off with the red sword of war.

Can our "statesmen" not learn this lesson? Are they deaf to the world-wide cry for bread? Are they oblivious to the tears of women and the wail of unfed children? Don't our masters know that every bite they eat and every stitch they wear comes from the robbery and suffering of the workers? And what do they give the workers in return? Sneers and contempt, insults and bayonets, bullets and bullpens! When the workers ask for bread they get bullets. These blind blockheads of government know no argument but force—no weapons but thugs and militia. Try justice? Oh, no, that is the last thing in the world. The rulers shun justice as though she is a leper. And well they may, for her sword is meant for them. These governmental parasites will do anything but get off the backs of the workers. There they sit like a lot of leeches sucking the life-blood of the men, women, and children who toil.

No, neither the militia, the governor, nor the courts possess the wizard's power to convert robbery into justice. The governor may proclaim martial law, the militia may fill the penitentiaries with its victims, and the courts may lend legal sanction to the wrong, but wrong it will remain. You may drive the slaves back to the mines today, but tomorrow you will hear their voice again. All they ask is justice—the right to form mutual societies for self-preservation. The operators have this right, why not give it to the miners? The miner sells the most sacred of all commodities—human labor power, human life. Why not let him protect it? He has babies to feed and a fireside to maintain. You masters are living at his expense, and why not give him a modicum of justice?

No gentlemen, force will not solve this problem. Your brutality might have done it in a darker age. It will not do in this late day of the world's history. Industrial feudalism must go. You gentlemen are the classic product of a privately owned earth. To you the spirit of democracy is unknown. Your nefarious schemes of exploitation have left you no time to look about you. You still curse the nation by your intellectual medievalism. It will be a happy day for the people when they rid you of your power.

∾   ∾   ∾

From the same issue, 20 February 1913:

### AN APPEAL TO LIBERTY FROM THE MILITARY BULLPEN AT PRATT

Soul of humanity, thou Liberty, awake! arouse! Once that name was heard throughout the land. Tyrants trembled. And when thy voice as the mighty peal of thunders rent wide the open air—when like a meteor through time's eternal billows thou didst descend—when like fire from heaven thou didst enfold the land—earth rejoiced and felt a new creative sense with its soul.

Thrill to the sight and vibrate to the sound that murmurs through the heavens, breathing the essence of Justice and Love.

Then when thy congenial spirit rejoiced, and crowns and thrones and scepters lay mildewing at thy feet, Oh, Liberty, lulled by the music of thine own inspired song, didst bow thy head and sleep!

And whilst thou hast slept, serene and confiding, ocean cradled in thy vast domain, bold tyrants, mischief breeding, wove their hellish fetters 'round thee, and now thy feet in chains are bound again.

No longer now we hear thy voice acclaiming, as in the days of old when thou summoned our sires to deeds of high resolve; but mute you stand, deaf, dumb, and blind, all seeing, while tyrants devastate and desolate the land.

Here on the banks of the Great Kanawha, here where our fathers bled and died, behold thy children crushed and bleeding, behold their tears and hear their cries!

And must thy children now resign thee, once having felt thy generous breath, and should we at thy feet lie bleeding, resigned to anarchy and base, ignoble death?

Soul of humanity, thou Liberty, Awake! Arise!

Those chains are not unbreakable that 'round thy soul and mind are twined.

Unsheath thy sword! Raise high thy torch of truth and light, and strike! And when thou dost strike, strike hard!

~ ~ ~

From the *Labor Argus*, 6 February 1913:

The people of West Virginia are complaining of the many wrongs they have to endure, but when it is all summed up we can but arrive at the one conclusion, the people alone are responsible for these conditions. If the public officials prostitute themselves to the "interests," it is because the people let them. If the courts become corrupt and sell their decisions to the corporate interests in defiance of justice, it is because the people let them. Our sheriffs deputize the Baldwin thugs because we let them. The Baldwin thugs assault, brutalize and murder the workers, because we let them. The coal barons bring in their scabs, build and equip forts for their protection because the miners let them. Peonage is practiced, manhood defiled, womanhood outraged, and childhood offered as a sacrifice to the vultures of greed because the people allow it. Every wrong suffered by the people is due to their ignorance and cowardice.

The people are many and the exploiters are few, the power is ours had we but the intelligence and courage to use it. Just so long as we humbly submit to our wrongs, just so long must we bear our burdens. Just so long as the thousands of miners will submit to the tyranny of a few coal barons and their hirelings, just that long will slavery and peonage be practiced. They do to us just what we let them do. It is only with the consent of the people that their public servants become their masters. Our representatives can sell us only with our consent. The power to traffic in our lives is delegated to them by the people; they would not betray us unless we let them. Governor Glasscock overrode the constitution of the state and nation and established a military despotism, outraged justice and assassinated liberty just because the people of this state let him do it. When a few hundred guards and tin horns can terrorize 5,000 people it is only because the 5,000 are moral, mental, and physical cowards and let them. All the wrongs the people suffer are due to their ignorance of their own strength and their cowardice. The working class composes 85 per cent. of the population of this country, yet they allow the other 15 per cent. to rob, degrade, and enslave their class. Just so long as the working class allow themselves to be betrayed by the political prostitutes, robbed by the merciless masters, and brutalized by their thugs and hirelings, just that long will they have to endure these infamies. They do these things because we let them, but when intelligence takes the place of ignorance and courage supplants cowardice, then and not until then will a stop be put to the wrongs we are suffering. The martial law deprived the miners of their constitutional rights because they surrendered them. The Baldwin brutes and the tin horn thugs brutalize, club, and shoot the miners because they submit to that kind of treatment. This is a class war; for every wrong suffered by the workers the master class should be made to pay. "An eye for an eye, a tooth for a tooth and a life for a life." When the miners learn to exert their manhood and retaliate on the masters and their hirelings every wrong they suffer at their hands they will put a stop to these outrages. They ride and bleed you because you get down on your knees and let them. Now get up and make them stop.

~ ~ ~

From the *Labor Argus*, 6 March 1913:

Garroted by the governor, ravished and despoiled by the coal interests, poor, old, blind Justice received in her prostrate body the stiletto of death from the hands of the bunch of traitors whom she had fondly believed were her holiest and highest defenders—the judges of the Supreme Court of West Virginia. While her last dying murmur of "Et tu, Brute" was being wafted by kindly winds to other climes her white warm corpse was being trampled into the mire of greed by the iron-clad heels of a military despotism and her sweet sister, "Liberty," was fleeing over the hills and dales arousing in the breasts of a one-time race of freemen the emotions that moved their sires to action. When the highest court of law in West Virginia on last Friday said, in effect, that the writ of habeas corpus was a useless instrument, that the provisions of the Constitution of the United States were never intended for the protection of the toilers of the land, that the written laws of the state could be swept ruthlessly aside by the "invisible" hand that guides their prostituted actions, and the tyranny of a military despotism would be built upon the ruins of Freedom's chapel—it sounded the doom of Justice and Liberty, or it lighted the signal fires of an oncoming revolution. The decision which sent a gray-haired woman of four-score years back to the hell of a despot's prison stinks to high heaven, for it was supplied from an incision in the bowels of the putrid coal interests and the odor will cling to the bench for eons to come. Henceforth Labor will simply be wasting time in appealing to courts of law. With this decision we will probably learn that to play against the house is to lose, and to attempt to defeat the objects of the masters of greed by hauling them before the sanctimonious silk-robed parasites whom they own, body, soul and breeches, is certainly playing the game as the game-keeper wants you to play it. The courts in future will incite no feeling of awe, esteem or respect from the masses who have no part or parcel in them. They are simply the objects of withering contempt of all who love liberty and worship at the shrine of Justice. Oyez, Oyez, God save West Virginia—from her courts.

≈   ≈   ≈

From the same issue, 6 March 1913:

The state-paid mine guards are again gathering up the arms of the miners in the strike zone—confiscating the private property of others and making a laughing stock of that supposedly iron-clad constitutional guarantee that the rights of free citizens to bear arms should not be infringed. This is the course pursued by the yellows last fall, except at that time they took some of the armament of the Baldwin thugs, and the machine guns of the coal operators. The miners' arms have never been returned, but the machine guns reappeared upon the battlements of the barons and the murderers who man them carry the same side arms that the Khaki Kids temporarily deprived them of. It was simply a brazen attempt to disarm the miners and leave them at the mercy of the skunks who do the operators' dirty work.

That attempt failed as will the present one. The miners have guns, which is their right, and they know how to use them in self-defense—which accounts for their survival among the pack of murderous curs that have been turned loose on them. The miners have been driven from soil claimed by the coal barons; they have established homes on neutral lands; they have repelled murderous attacks upon these humble homes, by force. Had they done less they would deserve the contempt of any being through whom the bright red blood of manhood flows. They are not such fools as to weakly hand over their last weapon of self-preservation, knowing that they would then be compelled to cope bare-handed with the hyenas that would be loosed to ravish and rend them.

≈   ≈   ≈

From the same issue, 6 March 1913:

GOOD-BYE GLASSCOCK

For four years West Virginia has been afflicted with you and now we fear neither hell nor hereafter. Forced upon us, the bastard child of a political rape, you have lived up to the natural reputation of your political parentage and we have paid for your degeneration with blood and tears. You are hated by the masses whose deadly and stealthy enemy you have been, and the gluttonous powers which have used you as their pliant tool have only a wreath of contempt to lay upon your political grave. You came into the governorship at a time when a MAN was needed; when liberty, which had begun to feel the chains of greed tightening upon her limbs, began to stir restlessly, and look longingly for a champion. Had you been a MAN, your name would have gone echoing down the line of years to come, with Lincoln's. However, you were not a man; you were simply the cloak, the mental and physical weakling who wore the empty title of power and decorated the anteroom while the real governor–the real government–the silent invisible vampires sucked the last drop of blood from the prostrate corpse of Liberty and Justice and buried them under the starved and ravished sons and daughters of the Little Mountain State. We hope now that you will retire permanently to the home for incurables which has been your place of refuge during these four years whenever an outraged citizenship sought your presence, and that your execrated name will never again be heard among a people who will be industriously trying to efface the blot and dilute the odor your damnable contamination has left with the alleged free and sovereign state you have disgraced.

≈   ≈   ≈

From the same issue, 6 March 1913:

Among the last official acts of Weary Willie was the recalling of his private court in the martial law district and the appointment of a new commission of empty-headed, yellow-legged scab-herders to pass sentence upon the already convicted mountaineers whom the coal operators have herded into bullpens, and guard with their state-paid, uniformed guards. And the local prostitutes of publicity herald this forth as an act of justice! To mention the word "justice" in the same column with the name "Glasscock" is a crime, and the mere suggestion of a man appointing a court to try citizens of West Virginia without a jury or any other of their constitutional guarantees is a damnable, outrageous insult that our hardy forefathers would have wiped out with the blood of its author. George III was the last tyrant who tried to force upon Americans the brutal rule of the soldier and his red-coated Hessians were driven into the Atlantic. Let the coal barons' yellow-coats listen to the still re-echoing thunders from Bunker Hill and Yorktown–and take warning.

≈   ≈   ≈

From the same issue, 6 March 1913:

The men and women in the bullpens on Paint Creek are charged, among other things, with the murder of Fred Bobbitt. This guard was killed while advancing upon and firing into the homes of the miners and their families. Sesco Estep, a miner, was killed about the same time. He was fleeing from a murderous hail of bullets from an armoured train, and he carried in his arms his little child. No one has been thrown into the bullpen charged with this cowardly murder; the mighty machinery of government has not been set in motion to avenge his death, and although the human hyenas guilty of this midnight murder are well known, they walk the streets of the state's capital free. When Bobbitt met his well deserved end at the hands of men exercising the natural law of self-preservation, the incident was used as an excuse to rush 1,500 professional murderers into Paint Creek and imprison every man who has dared to ask for justice. Not satisfied with these victims, men and women who had dared raise their voice in sympathy and commendation for the struggling peons of the slave camps were dragged from afar and robbed of their rights and liberties.

～　～　～

From the same issue, 6 March 1913:

One of the charges against Mother Jones is that she feloniously swiped from the Paint Creek Collieries Company a machine gun. There are several other charges, such as arson, murder, etc., but this is the one that stands out as a capital crime. The very idea of robbing that harmless corporation of its last argument for existence! Bring on the firing squad.

～　～　～

Thereupon the prosecution by the Judge Advocate offered and read in evidence speeches made by Mother Mary Jones.

Captain Morgan, for the defendants, objected to the introduction of the above-mentioned speeches, which objection the commission overruled and to which action and ruling of the commission the defendants by their counsel then and there excepted. Thereupon the said speeches were read into the record.

The commission adjourned until nine o'clock, March 11, 1913.

The commission met pursuant to adjournment. The Judge Advocate offered in evidence the Supplement to the *Labor Argus,* Friday, February 14, 1913, as follows:

### SUPPLEMENT TO THE LABOR ARGUS

After this issue was printed its editor, C.H. Boswell, "Mother" Jones, John W. Brown, Chas. Batley, Paul J. Paulson, and numerous other representatives of labor were arrested in the City of Charleston by the Baldwin thugs and taken to Pratt to be tried by court martial. It is reported that some of those arrested are to be tried and shot. Watch daily press. This paper will be out on time as long as one of Labor's champions is unjailed.

Counsel for the defendants objected to the introduction of this supplement and moved to strike it from the record. The objection was overruled, and counsel for the defendants took exception to the ruling.

T.H. Huddy testified as follows:

Q. Please give your name.

A. T.H. Huddy.

Q. What is your business?

A. Superintendent of the Boomer Coal and Coke Company.

Q. How long have you been there?

A. Two years and 9 months.

Q. Do you know the defendant, Mother Jones?

A. I have met Mother Jones once or twice, I believe.

Q. I will ask you if you heard her make any speeches since this trouble has been going on in this Paint and Cabin Creek district?

A. I only heard one speech and that was in the early part of the season, along in the summer.

Q. About what month was that?

A. I am not positive and cannot say.

Q. Was it before or after troops were sent in here or can you say?

A. It was some months before the troops were sent in this last time.

Q. I mean in the summer; the troops came here on the 25th of July.

A. If my memory serves me right a number of troops had been here or were at the time, the first time they were sent up.

Q. What connection, if any, does Mother Jones have with the miners?

A. I don't know.

Q. What was the nature of her speech on this particular occasion? Where was that speech made?

A. Boomer.

Q. How far is Boomer from here?

A. I presume it is 8, 9, or 10 miles.

Q. Ten miles from here?

A. Yes, sir.

Q. To the east of this military zone?

A. Yes, sir.

Captain Morgan: Outside of the military zone?

A. Yes, sir.

Captain Morgan: I will put in a formal objection to this testimony.

The commission overruled the objection, counsel for the defendants took exception, and the Judge Advocate resumed his questioning.

Q. Will you now tell the commission the nature of that speech, whether it was inflammatory or otherwise?

A. At that time I can't recall of much being said that was of an inflammatory nature, at that time.

Q. Have you since that heard her make any speeches?

A. Since that time I have not heard any of her speeches, only heard of them.

Q. Don't tell what you have heard. Have you since that time, or since this conflict has been going on, had any knowledge of Mother Jones, by speeches or otherwise, going to Boomer or in that neighborhood and stirring the men up to get them to take part in this trouble?

A. In the early part of February–

Q. Of what year?

A. Of this year, Mother Jones and some others were there and held a meeting one night and made speeches; I was not present, however.

Q. What was the result of the meeting, if you know, or saw. What effect, if any, did the meeting have on anybody, Mr. Huddy?

A. At that time the men were somewhat inflamed. My reason for saying that was while the speaking was going on, we had a fire in one of our small buildings and some of the men came down from the speech, while the building was burning and they said, "Let it burn; it belongs to the company and the man renting it was a boss," and they said, "He was a company suck and one of the company's tools and to just let it burn up." The next day one of the men who made this statement I had him in my office and asked him why he said that, and he said that he had been drunk or drinking slightly and also had just come down from the speaking and the speeches were exciting and offered that as an excuse for his statements.

Counsel for the defendants objected to this answer, the commission overruled the objection, and exception was taken to the ruling.

Q. Do you recall last fall when an effort was made to get the miners at Boomer to give up their arms, to give up the guns they had?

A. I do not know of any call being made for them to give up any guns.

Q. I don't mean any call but when an effort was made by the citizens to get them to give up their guns?

A. Yes, sir.

Q. Who, if you know, prevented that purpose from being carried out and the men from giving up their weapons?

A. I don't know of anyone preventing it.

Q. Do you know whether or not Mary Jones–Mother Jones there, advised against it?

A. I will have to think. I think I will have to say that probably I had more to say about it than Mother Jones.

Q. What did you say about that?

A.  I remember now of Mother Jones saying something about guns, but just
what she said, I can't recall, but it appeared to me that Montgomery,
some of the saloon keepers of Montgomery were insisting on trying
to get martial law extended to Montgomery, that is the way I got it.
They came to Boomer and called a meeting for one Sunday, but they
didn't hold their meeting, that is the Montgomery meeting, but
Mother Jones did and then there was a meeting called two or three
days later by the Montgomery people. They again didn't show up and
the object of this meeting was to have the men give up their guns
voluntarily to the people of Montgomery. There was nobody showed
up, however. I went over to the meeting with a number of our men,
among them quite a number of our men, and we waited; and after
waiting a considerable length of time I was called on to say something.
I asked why the meeting was called and someone stated, and I then
said that we, that is the company, had several guns, didn't deny it, but
that no one had asked for our guns; that the governor had not
requested us or even the military court or anyone in authority, and
until such time we were going to hold our guns, and I told the men
in the meeting that until asked by the governor or someone in
authority, to give up their guns, I would advise them to hold them as
I thought we were going to do, and that was all that was done in that
meeting. I did say, however, while on that, if the governor or anybody
in authority did ask for our guns, then we would give them up.

Counsel for the defendants declined to cross-examine the witness.

J.H. Clagett testified as follows:

Q.  Where do you live?

A.  Boomer.

Q.  What is your business?

A.  Coal inspector.

Q.  Do you know Mother Jones, the defendant?

A.  Yes, sir, when I see her.

Q.  How long have you been at Boomer?

A.  It will be three years in May.

Q.  Did you hear Mother Jones make any speeches at Boomer along in the
summer and fall of this year—of last summer and fall, and during this
year?

A.  I heard her make one this year; yes, sir.

Q.  When did she make the speech this year, what time, about when was it?

A.  It was some time last month.

Q.  Tell this commission whether or not that speech was inflammatory or
otherwise.

A.  Well, there was some things about it were, I suppose.

Q.  Just tell what she said and let the commission be the judge of that.

A. She made the remark, she told the men if they had any guns to keep them, and when she was ready, she would send for them.

Q. Anything else?

A. And she said if there is any one of the men arrested down here that they send to the penitentiary, that they would tear up the state.

Q. Who did she say would do that?

A. She said we would.

Q. Did you hear her say anything else?

A. That is all I would say that was inflammatory.

Q. That was after the arrests had been made down here?

A. Yes, sir, after they arrested some men here at Paint Creek.

Q. That is, after the troops had come in this time?

A. Yes, sir.

Captain Carskadon cross-examined the witness.

Q. Where was this speech made, Mr. Clagett?

A. Made over the saloon, at Boomer.

Q. That is not within this military district, is it?

A. I don't know.

Q. As covered by martial law, at the present time?

A. I don't know.

Q. Boomer is not?

A. No, sir, Boomer is not in this district, I believe.

Q. Do you know whether or not Boomer is in this military district?

A. I don't know.

Q. It is not?

A. I don't know.

Q. You say Mother Jones advised the men to keep their guns; didn't the superintendent there at Boomer do the same thing, Mr. Clagett?

A. I can't say that; no, sir, he wasn't there.

Q. You didn't hear his statement a few minutes ago?

A. No, sir.

Q. You say that Mother Jones said if they sent anyone to the penitentiary down here, or anyone was sent to the penitentiary by this commission, that they would tear up the state; what did you construe her meaning?

A. I thought they would make trouble of some kind. I can't say just what she meant by it.

Q. She probably meant that it would be a struggle for the organization throughout the state or something of that sort, didn't she, Mr. Clagett, rather than physical trouble?

A. She said she make trouble of some kind.

Captain Morgan: You have no idea what kind of trouble?

A. She said, "We would tear up the state."

Q. You didn't take it by that, she meant to take up arms?

A. There was nothing more than just at that time she mentioned holding their guns. There was nothing said about taking up arms, but it was just about that time she mentioned holding their guns.

Q. You never heard her say anything at any other time, did you, Mr. Clagett, along that line?

A. Not along that line; no, sir.

Thereupon the Judge Advocate introduced in evidence and read to the commission a speech delivered by the defendant, Mary Jones, at Charleston, West Virginia, on August 15, 1912, at 2 o'clock p. m. on the front steps of the Capitol.

Harrison Ellis testified as follows:

Q. Do you know the defendant Ed Gray?

A. Yes, sir.

Q. Tell this commission whether or not you saw Ed Gray armed on Sunday preceding the fight at Mucklow; if so, where and what was he doing?

A. He was in Holly Grove.

Q. Sir?

A. He was in Holly Grove.

Q. How was he armed?

A. With a gun.

Q. What kind of a gun; was it a pistol or rifle?

A. Rifle.

Q. What time in the day was that you saw him?

A. It was about ten o'clock.

Q. In the morning?

A. Yes, sir.

Q. Do you know anything about what he was going to do with it?

Counsel for the prisoners, on behalf of this prisoner and those who are jointly charged with him, hereby object and protest to the introduction of any testimony which this prisoner may give, the same being over his protest and against his will and against the will of those who are jointly charged with him and all of whom are now being tried before this commission.

The commission then, at ten o'clock a.m., took a recess.

The commission met pursuant to adjournment at one o'clock p.m. at Pratt, West Virginia, Tuesday, March 11, 1913. They then adjourned until Wednesday morning, March 12, 1913 at nine o'clock.

The commission met pursuant to adjournment and took a recess until two o'clock p.m., March 12, 1913.

At two o'clock, the commission met pursuant to adjournment and the president of the commission announced that in reference to the motion made on yesterday relative to the testimony of Harrison Ellis the commission had prepared a statement for the record:

The commission sustains the motion made by counsel for the defendants, as to the admission of the testimony of the prisoners in this case, for the reason there is a charge of conspiracy, together with the other charges, and any testimony given by the prisoners would be indirectly against themselves, and we do not think it proper to permit the prisoners to testify under the circumstances.

However, in sustaining this motion we are not establishing a rule to be governed by in the future, as under the rule of procedure of military commissions we do not claim to be bound by the rules of evidence in the civil courts.

We would further recommend to counsel both for the state and the defendants that in the argument of motions, they will confine themselves to the motion and the law governing the same and not make inflammatory or patriotic speeches. By observing this rule you will save the commission the disagreeable duty of calling your attention to it when you attempt to so argue the motion.

We would also suggest to counsel that they do not anticipate the ruling of the commission and not to make statements to the public that are misleading and cause the publication of articles in the newspapers as appeared in the *Cincinnati Post* of today.

We do not accuse counsel purposely of doing or saying anything that would reflect on the commission but the advising of witnesses not to testify might be considered by the commission as contempt thereof and certainly such advice should not be given until the necessity arises for the same.

The commission will disregard and not consider the testimony given by Harrison Ellis, which it appears was given before counsel for the defendants was aware of the fact that he was one of the prisoners.

T.H. Huddy, recalled as a witness, testified as follows:

Q. Is your name Hudnal?

A. Huddy.

Q. You were on the witness stand yesterday and asked about giving some testimony, and I am led to believe that you did not testify fully everything you knew. I have had you summoned and want to know if you testified fully in regard to this matter. You were asked on yesterday if you ever heard the defendant known as Mother Jones make any speeches at or near Boomer of an inflammatory nature. I will ask you now if you have any recollection of anything of that sort?

A. I heard Mother Jones make a speech and I recall distinctly that I said my memory did not serve me as to just what was said. I came here not prepared. I did not know why or for what purpose I was summoned. My mind was not on those things. I had not burdened my mind with it. After you raised that question I got to thinking about it, and after thinking further, of course, I would know more about it today than I would yesterday.

Q. Just tell all you know about it.

Captain Morgan: Did you refresh your memory by talking with people?

A. No, at that time I made some notes in my notebook and after going home I examined these, and, in fact, after the question came up here, I sat around and things came to me, naturally I wouldn't recall right then just what did occur; but naturally after you put the questions to me, and I knew I couldn't answer, I said my memory was not serving me right, and I looked up certain things after I went home from my own notes.

The Judge Advocate: Go ahead and tell us what you know about it.

A. Well, this speech occurred on the 29th day of September, about two o'clock on a Sunday afternoon. The meeting was primarily called, as I understand it, for a meeting of citizens throughout the valley.

Q. Where was it?

A. At Boomer, and I with some others went up to see what was to be done, and to hear what would be said. Instead of the citizens having a meeting, the meeting was held by Mother Jones exclusively, that is in the main building, that is, in the hall; there was an overflow meeting held on the outside by Mr. Batley, because all the people couldn't get in this meeting. At this speech Mother Jones started out and remarked about conditions, the mining conditions as they existed in this state, and berated the mine operators, mine superintendents, and office clerks. I remember distinctly her calling the office clerks "two by fours"–"little two by fours." The superintendents were classed as tools of these coal barons, others were cited as human bloodhound drivers, etc. I even recall of her speaking and asking why, speaking of the superintendents' houses, why the miners did not have larger houses. Also the question was brought up about the superintendents' wives, and she said "Why are your wives and your daughters their servants?" "Why don't they do their own work?" At that time, along during the speech there were some women making some noise and talking and Mother Jones asked them "why they didn't hang over the back yard fence if they wanted to gossip and talk." Also, Mother spoke about the governor, about his so-called weakness and inefficiency and about the commission. Particularly speaking of preachers, making comments on Christ and things of that nature. She further said in speaking, not to give up the guns. There was some question about them giving up their guns, and she said "Keep your guns, and I am sorry that I haven't got money with which you can buy other guns," or words to that effect. I don't say it is quite absolutely verbatim, and further in her speech she said "The coal in these hills is rightfully yours, and if these operators don't give you what you want, go after it and get it." I wouldn't say that is just the exact wording, word for word, but that is the substance of the whole thing. There was no distinction made as between superintendent or mine foreman or mine operator; they were all classed in the same category. After the meeting downstairs Mother Jones was over where I was standing and I was introduced to her by Ben Davis, and I said to her, "Mother, you classed us all in the same box, and you gave us a lot of rotten stuff," and she said good-humoredly and in a pleasant manner, she said, "Well," she said, "I occasionally have to give the boys quite a lining up and hot stuff to hold them in line, but you understand how it is" and words to that effect. That is the substance.

Q. Do you work union or non-union miners?

A. Union supposed to be worked; union scale.

Q. How long a—You have a contract, as I understand it?

A. Yes, sir, we have a contract up until April 1, 1914.

Q. I will ask you if since this trouble, meaning since the first declaration of martial law, which was declared first on the 2nd day of September, 1912, whether or not you have had trouble with men breaking that contract, and if so, who caused it?

A. Our contract has been broken during the past year repeatedly. Several times the national officials or district officials—

Q. Of what organization?

A. Of this miners' union.

Q. Of this United Mine Workers of America?

A. Yes, sir, the United Mine Workers of America.

Counsel for the defendants objected to this line of questioning, the objection was overruled, and counsel took exception to the ruling.

Q. Go ahead.

A. We have lost considerable amount of time, just what amount I am not prepared to answer. In several of our stoppages the district officials of the U.M.W. of A. have come on the ground and ordered the men to go to work and the men did not do so, disregarding the advice and instructions of their officials. At these times there would be meetings held, not exactly at our place, but in the field on that side, which would have a tendency and did have a tendency toward keeping the men away from the work and they would insist—this I have got to give you on information. I did not hear the instructions given to the men, but I am just giving you how I got it. You understand there are some things I do not know only from what the officials tell me.

Counsel for the defendants objected, were overruled and excepted.

Q. Go ahead.

A. The officials told me that they had ordered the men to go to work and that Mother Jones had told them not to work. And placed the blame on her and on some socialist orators, not mentioning the names of the orators.

Counsel for the defendants objected and asked that the answer be stricken from the record. The objection was overruled, and counsel took exception to the ruling.

Q. I will ask you this question: Did any of the men—any of your men themselves upon the occasion that they refused to work, or did not work, give as their reason therefor that they had been advised by Mother Jones?

A. Yes, sir.

Counsel for the defendants objected to the last two questions and moved that they be stricken from the record. The motion was denied, and counsel for the defendants took exception to the ruling.

Q. On how many different occasions since September, that you can recall, have your men failed to work, in accordance with their contract, as a result of these meetings?

A. Without regard to records—without referring to records, I would say more than three or four times.

Q. I will ask you to state whether or not the speeches of Mother Jones had the effect of causing these men to quit work and to come over into Paint and Cabin creeks, to carry on the warfare with coal miners and operators?

A. I would have to answer that by saying, I don't know.

Q. Do you know of anything else of the action on the part of Mother Jones that had to do with this trouble, that has taken place on this side of the river?

A. Not unless the speech I heard her make or a part of a speech I heard her make in Charleston might be so construed.

Q. When was that speech made, if you know?

A. I don't know the exact date.

Q. About when was it now?

A. Along I would imagine early this fall.

Q. Where was it, at what point in Charleston?

A. It was on the street, paralleling the river. I think it is called Kanawha, on the river bank.

Q. I think we already have that speech in the record.

Captain Carskadon cross-examined the witness.

Q. That speech of Mother Jones' made over at Boomer, that you speak of, was there anything very inflammatory about that, over there?

A. Yes, I would so consider it.

Captain Morgan: You say she called a good many store people "two by fours?" Isn't it true that there a large number of "two by fours" in those stores?

The Judge Advocate objected to this question. The commission made no ruling, but the witness did not respond.

Captain Carskadon: I believe you state that none of your men, as far as you knew, had been led into this trouble or had gotten into this trouble of the Paint and Cabin Creek people, did you not?

A. I don't remember that question being put to me, just like that.

The Judge Advocate, in redirect examination asked:

Q. I will ask you that question now; as a matter of fact, haven't some of your men, while at work at your mine, been killed on this side of the rivers, since the trouble started?

A. We had one employe killed on Paint Creek.

Q. When was this with reference to this last difficulty?

A. It was the first shooting that occurred at Mucklow or in that vicinity.

Captain Carskadon conducted further cross-examination.

Q. In what capacity was he, that employe, working?

A. He worked for us as a miner, Check No. 63, at Mine No. 63. His name was Sam Petro.

Q. Do you know the cause of his death?

A. I can truthfully say he was shot to death.

Q. Did you see him afterwards?

A. I did.

Q. I will ask you if a person representing a cause of any nature whatever has not the right to make public speeches in furtherance or defence of their cause on proper occasions?

The Judge Advocate objected to this question, the commission sustained his objection, and defendants' counsel took exception to the ruling.

Q. Are you the gentleman who was on the witness stand here a day or two ago and advised the miners on certain occasions, if you were in their place that you would keep the arms they had and not turn them over at the present time?

A. I am.

J.C. Bell testified as follows:

Q. Mr. Bell, where do you live and by whom are you employed?

A. I live at Boomer and am employed by the Boomer Coal and Coke Company.

Q. What is your business?

A. Head clerk.

Q. Do you know the defendant, Mother Jones?

A. I have seen her once.

Q. How long have you been at Boomer?

A. About six years.

Q. Have you heard Mother Jones make any speech at Boomer?

A. One.

Q. When was that?

A. Last September.

Q. What, if anything, did she say upon that occasion in reference to the situation on this side of the river, the trouble, the strike that has been going on, on this side of the river?

A. The latter part of September the citizens of Montgomery advertised a meeting, according to this notice, to discuss martial law one Sunday afternoon. Mother Jones addressed the meeting and told them not to give up their arms, and if she had the money she would give it to them to buy more. (The witness hands the Judge Advocate a handbill.)

Q. Was that the bill that was passed around?

A. Yes, sir, this is the bill that the meeting was advertised with.

Q. Did she make any other statement of a similar kind or nature?

A. Not that I recall.

Q. Did you accordingly go to the meeting, as advertised, or did Mother Jones have the meeting advertised on this handbill? Where did she speak with reference to that meeting; did she speak there?

A. Yes, sir, she spoke there; the Montgomery crowd did not come to speak at all.

The Judge Advocate offered the handbill in evidence.

Q. Have you any other knowledge or do you know of any of your men coming over from your side of the river to take part in this trouble on this side of the river?

A. I do not know; only one of my men was killed over on this side. He was killed up here about Mucklow, last summer.

Captain Carskadon cross-examined the witness.

Q. That is, before this speech?

A. Yes, sir.

Q. That you speak of?

A. Yes, sir, that was some time in June.

Q. There had not been any speech made to your knowledge before that time?

A. No, sir.

Q. By whom was he killed?

A. You can't prove by me; I wasn't even in Boomer then; I was in Charleston at that time.

S.W. Johnson testified as follows:

Q. What do you do, Mr. Johnson?

A. What do I do?

Q. Yes, where do you live and where are you employed?

A. I live at Boomer and am head clerk for the Boomer Coal Company.

Q. Do you know the defendant, Mother Jones?

A. Yes, sir.

Q. Have you been present when Mother Jones made any speeches at Boomer recently?

A. She made one up there in the latter part of September.

Q. Did you hear that speech?

A. Yes, sir.

Q. Have you heard any since?

A. No, sir.

Q. Tell us upon that occasion, what, if anything, she said of an inflammatory nature?

A. Well, she told the boys–the most particular thing she told them was to hold on to their guns.

Q. Did she say anything more than that?

A. Well, I can't recollect; no, sir, I didn't stay to hear all the speech. I was in the hall probably 15 or 20 minutes.

Q. Tell us the best you know, everything you heard her say while you were there.

A. She berated the officials in general, especially the office help. She said the "two by four clerks and bookkeepers and the mine superintendents." "All they were paid for was to do the company's bidding."

Captain Carskadon cross-examined the witness.

Q. What do you do at Boomer, Mr. Johnson?

A. Head clerk for the coal company.

Q. You work for a coal company there?

A. Yes, sir.

Q. What, if you know, was this meeting called for, Mr. Johnson, there at Boomer on Sunday?

A. No, sir, I don't know what it was called for.

Q. As a matter of fact, wasn't it called for the purpose of getting the miners to give up their guns to certain people there?

The Judge Advocate objected to the question, the commission sustained his objection, and defense counsel took exception to the ruling.

Q. You didn't hear Mother Jones make any statements that were very dangerous there that day, did you?

The Judge Advocate objected to this question, the commission sustained his objection, and defense counsel took exception to the ruling.

Q. You didn't hear all of this speech of Mother Jones?

A. No, sir, I didn't hear it all.

Q. I believe you say you heard her tell the boys to hold their guns?

A. Yes, sir.

Q. What else did you hear her say?

A. That is about all I really heard, just along that line, as I said before, I didn't hear all of her speech.

Q. What else did you hear her say along any line?

A. Her speech was practically all the same, so far as that is concerned, about all she did was to lambaste somebody.

Q. You particularly remember just those two items?

A. Yes, sir.

Q. And that is all you distinctly remember?

A. Yes, sir, that is all.

Q. You don't remember anything she said in favor of the companies–of the coal company?

A. No, sir.

Q. Or anything she said in favor of the militia?

A. No, sir.

Q. Or the state authorities?

A. No, sir.

Captain John C. Bond, recalled to the stand, testified as follows:

Q. Captain Bond, you have heretofore been on the stand as a witness and testified?

A. Yes, sir.

Q. Upon the former occasion you offered in evidence certain bullets that were taken from the pistol belonging to Ernest Creigo. I will ask you if since that time you have fired any of those cartridges and what was the result of the test made?

A. I have fired some of them and together with Lieutenant Davis we cut one of them to see what it was. Now I have here one of the original cartridges taken from the revolver; we extracted the bullet from one of these cartridges and split it in two and found a little copper tube, in the center of that bullet, containing rather a blackish fluid of some kind. In order to see what the effect of that was, we fired it into a board and found that it blew a hole out at the rear of the bullet. We made a further test and fired some of them into a pile of sand. We found the same thing happened in the rear of the bullet, and there was something blown out through each of the little holes in the cartridge where these holes are shown. (Thereupon the Judge Advocate offered in evidence the bullets and they were inspected by all members of the commission.)

Captain Morgan: You fired none of these bullets into flesh?

A. No, sir.

At 4 o'clock p.m. the commission recessed until 4:30, when it resumed session, with Adam B. Littlepage added to the counsel for the accused.

The Judge Advocate announced that the prosecution rested.

Thereupon the prisoners, by their counsel, moved the commission that the evidence introduced against them be stricken out and that they be discharged by the honorable commission and exonerated from the charges as set forth in the specifications, because of the insufficiency of the testimony taken as a whole to establish their guilt.

Thereupon each and every one of the defendants, separately and individually, by counsel, moved the commission that the evidence introduced against them and each of them be stricken out, and that they and each of them be discharged by the honorable commission and exonerated from the charges set forth in the specifications, because of the insufficiency of the testimony taken as a whole to establish their guilt.

Thereupon, counsel for the defendants offered in evidence to the commission the proclamations issued by Hon. Wm. E. Glasscock, dated the 2nd day

of September, 1912, the 15th day of November, 1912, and the 10th day
of February, 1913.

Counsel for the defendants offered in evidence to the commission the finding
or report of the special commission appointed by Governor Glasscock,
who investigated the mining conditions on Paint and Cabin Creeks in
connection with the present labor dispute now on and which called for
the bringing forth of the militia upon the proclamation of the governor.

It is agreed, by and between George S. Wallace, Lieutenant-Colonel, 2nd
Infantry, Acting Judge Advocate, and Captain C.R. Morgan and Captain
E.B. Carskadon, representing all of the defendants, and M.F. Matheny,
Esq., and Adam B. Littlepage, Esq., counsel representing all of the
defendants, except C.H. Boswell, John W. Brown, Charles Batley, Paul
Paulson, Mary Jones and G.F. Parsons, that the prisoners could establish
that at the beginning of the strike and prior thereto the citizens living in
the mining districts of Paint Creek and Cabin Creek, as a general rule,
were peaceable and law-abiding, and that the communities above mentioned were as peaceable and law-abiding as any of the other mining
communities in the state, and for the purpose of this trial the above facts
are admitted.

Lieutenant G.C. Rippetto testified as follows in direct examination by M.F.
Matheny:

Q. Lieutenant, will you please state your official rank in connection with the
military service at this place?

A. Since the fourteenth of February, I have been Second Lieutenant.

Q. As such have you had charge, care and custody of the prisoners at various
times during that period?

A. Yes, sir; under the direction of the commanding officer and the officer of
the day.

Q. What has been their conduct and demeanor since you have had them in
charge; has it been good or bad?

A. Good. Had no trouble at all with them.

Q. And you found them to be orderly and obey commands and instructions,
have you?

A. Yes, sir.

Q. You have never noticed any disposition upon the part of them to cause
any disturbance or conduct themselves in a way unbecoming a peaceable and law-abiding citizen?

A. No, sir.

Captain Boughner: You have not had charge of all of these prisoners at all
times?

A. No, sir, just at the courthouse here.

First Lieutenant H.H. Rice testified as follows:

Q. Please state your official rank in the military service at this place.

A. First Lieutenant, Second Infantry, with Company H, from Huntington.

Q. As such, have you had charge of a portion of the prisoners most of the time since their arrest?

A. Yes, sir.

Q. What has been their general demeanor and conduct?

A. I have found them to be quiet and orderly and of good demeanor in nearly every instance. In fact, I have not noticed more than once or twice in which any of the men indicated any stubbornness—once or twice, one or two of the men—on one occasion or two.

The Judge Advocate: Who were the men that gave you the trouble you talk about?

A. No particular trouble, excepting one of the colored men; that man right over there, I believe, was acting a little stubborn on one occasion when we were marching out; but, then, he seemed to overcome that and was all right. He may have been just feeling a little badly when he came out and then, on another occasion; one—I think the other colored man up there—was slightly—was impudent to one of the officers. I think it was Captain Ridley.

W.R. Gray testified as follows:

Q. Mr. Gray, where do you live?

A. I live at Cabin Creek Junction.

Q. What is your business or occupation?

A. Coal miner.

Q. Are you being detained here by the military authorities?

A. Yes, sir.

Q. Since you have been detained, state whether or not you have been approached by Frank Smith, who now represents himself as being a Burns detective?

A. How was that question? (Question is read to the witness.)

A. Yes, sir.

Q. Did he have a conversation with you?

A. Yes, sir.

Q. Was it with regard to the trial of these prisoners?

A. Yes, sir.

Q. Tell the commission what he said to you.

A. Well, the first time ever the man called me out, I had a few words with him and was taken back and it went on then for some four or five days, maybe a week; I disremember how long or what day it was, but I was out talking to my wife and Mr. Smith came in the room where we was at, sitting in the depot over there, and he came up and spoke and I spoke to him, and he says "You need not blame me with this," he said, "It is your friend Simpson." I says, "Well, I don't blame anybody with it." He said, "You ought not to have hard feelings toward me." I said, "I haven't hard feelings to anybody." I said, "It looks hard for a man to be locked up and confined when he has done nothing to be confined for." He kept coming up closer to me and talking and he got up pretty tolerable close; anyhow, he says, "Mr. Gray, if you will make some cases against some of these other boys, I will see that you are released and I will slip you a little something on the side." And I told him, "I didn't know anything against the boys to make a case against them for." That is about all that was said.

Q. Do you see the man now in the courtroom that had that conversation with you?

(Witness looks about him. Mr. Matheny: Look behind you.)

A. That is the gentleman, sitting there.

Q. Did that happen within the military zone?

A. Yes, sir, it happened right here at the depot in the waiting room.

Q. Were these prisoners here in custody at that time—these men who are being tried?

A. Yes, sir, I suppose they were. We were all in there together until I came out with my wife.

The Judge Advocate cross-examined the witness.

Q. What day was that, Mr. Gray?

A. I disremember. I couldn't say just what day.

Q. What time of day was it?

A. I couldn't say as to that.

Q. Who was in the room beside you and Mr. Smith?

A. Well, there was some four or five ladies and I do not remember whether any men were in there or not, beside some guard was standing in the door.

Q. How many guards in there?

A. Only one; standing in the door, as well as I remember.

Q. How close to you?

A. He was standing in the door and I was sitting in this corner.

Q. Who was close to you—any person in the room? Let's get at the location; you said you were on the west side of the room?

A. Give me a pencil and—

Q. Take this as the room. This room—show by this room.

A. Like there is the door there. I was sitting in the corner back here.

Q. In the corner?

A. Not exactly in the corner—here is that little office.

Q. Were you on this side or next to the door?

A. Upper side.

Q. Sitting on the bench?

A. Yes, sir.

Q. Anybody by you?

A. My wife.

Q. Who else—how close was she sitting to you?

A. Something like the distance to that trunk. (Trunk referred to appeared to be within three to four feet of the witness.)

Q. What other ladies in the room?

A. I disremember.

Q. How close were they, if you know?

A. The other ladies?

Q. Yes.

A. I do not know. I did not pay much attention.

Q. Well, were they standing or sitting down?

A. Standing up and two of them in front of me where I was sitting.

Q. Did he bawl that out loudly or tell you—

A. Pretty low. He wasn't whispering or talking loud.

Q. What was the first thing he said?

A. We were talking when he came in and when he first came in he spoke and I spoke. He said, "You need not blame me with this, you can blame your friend Simpson."

Q. What else did he say?

A. I told him "I didn't blame anyone at all for this." He said, "I don't want you to have hard feelings to me." I said, "I haven't any hard feelings to anyone at all, but it looks pretty hard for a man to be held here in prison when he ain't done nothing to be held for."

Q. What did he say?

A. He came on up pretty tolerable close to me and said, "It is like this, Gray, you go ahead and make a case against some of those other boys and I will see that you are released and" he said, "I will slip you something on the side."

Q. Are you sure this is exactly what he said?

A. Yes, sir, I am.

Q. He didn't say anything more?

A. Of course; I do not remember if he said anything more; I would not be positive.

Q. To your best recollection that is all that was said?

A. Yes, sir.

Q. Did he ask you to swear a lie against any of these people?

A. He asked me—to convict these people.

Q. Did he ask you to swear falsely?

A. He didn't come out and ask me to swear falsely, he said convict.

Q. You said he asked you to make a case against them; do you know whether he meant for you to tell what you knew or to swear a lie against them?

A. I don't know which he meant.

Q. You would not swear a lie against them?

A. No, sir, I would not—or for them.

Q. And you never had any dealings with him in the past that would make him believe that you would swear a lie, have you?

A. No, sir; no dealings with him at all.

Q. Did you know him?

A. He stayed at my house several nights when I lived at the Junction. He stayed all night with me.

Q. You are a striking miner, are you?

A. No, sir, not at this time. I am at work at Mr. Lewis' coal works.

Q. You have been during this trouble?

A. Yes, sir, I have.

Q. A sympathizer and partisan of these parties on trial?

A. What?

Q. You are in sympathy and a partisan of these men on trial.

A. Nothing more than what is right.

Q. I am not asking you that; you are in sympathy with them?

A. Yes, sir.

Q. You are also pretty indignant with Frank Smith, after representing himself to have been a miner?

A. No, sir.

Q. You have no ill-will or hard feelings?

A. I have no ill feelings.

Q. And you think he did perfectly right in coming to you in your house as a miner—and joining the miners' local?

A. He didn't come into my camp.

Q. You know he joined the local?

A. I know he had a dues card—whether he joined the local or not, I do not know.

Q. It made you pretty mad when you heard he had come here and testified?

A. No, sir.

Q. You didn't feel bad at all?

A. No sir; I didn't have any hard feelings at all.

M.F. Matheny, counsel for the prisoners, objected to a continuation of this line of cross-examination of the witness.

Q. And you are still in that frame of mind now, are you?

A. Yes, sir, I am.

Q. What is your best recollection of that date, if you remember?

A. I couldn't tell you.

Q. Now, you referred to the first conversation; where was he when he first talked with you?

A. Why, they came and called me out the next day after I was put in the prison—they called me out into the waiting room and he asked me—he told me that "Whitley Simpson was the cause of that."

Q. Where was that?

A. There in the depot.

Q. Was anybody present then?

A. One of the soldier boys. I disremember. I would not know them–

Q. Do you know the difference between an officer or just the "soldier boys" as you call them, by their uniforms?

A. No, sir.

Q. Was there an officer present?

A. I do not know.

Q. You do not remember who was present?

A. No, sir.

Q. What time in the day was the first time he came to you?

A. I couldn't tell you that.

Q. Was there anybody present at this interview except these soldier boys, the first time he was in there and talked to you?

A. I do not know whether there was anybody in the room or not. They came in and out of the room.

Q. He made no improper proposal to you at that time?

A. No, sir.

M.F. Matheny conducted redirect examination.

Q. When did he come to see you there in reference to the time you were detained and put in the custody of the officers?

A. The first time?

Q. Yes.

A. Why, he came the next day. I do not know just what time of day. I do not remember whether in the morning or in the evening he called me out.

Q. Do you know what day you were arrested?

A. Yes, sir, on Saturday.

Q. Was that last Saturday or Saturday before?

A. I was arrested on the twenty-second of last month.

Q. He came to see you the first time on the twenty-third?

A. I ain't sure it was the twenty-third. I believe it was the next day after I was arrested. I ain't sure.

Q. How long until he returned?

A. I do not know. Couldn't say.

Q. Don't you know about how many days it was before he returned?

A. No, sir, I do not know.

Q. After you had been put in there?

A. No, sir, I do not.

Q. Well, how many days back was it from this time?

A. Well, it has been a week or such a matter. Maybe longer than that.

Q. And, it must have been some time between this–since you told us the other day–and the twenty-second of last month?

A. Yes, sir.

Captain Boughner: Did you tell anybody else about this matter before you told these gentlemen?

A. Well, I disremember now whether I did or not. I ain't sure whether I did or not.

The Judge Advocate resumed his cross-examination.

Q. Who did you first tell about this proposal—who did you tell?

A. I disremember.

Q. How did you come to tell these gentlemen?

A. Just in a conversation, the talk came up and I spoke about it.

Q. You were not on trial; how did you come to be talking to these gentlemen?

A. Well, you know how a conversational man will get to talking when all together and just talking. I disremember now who I told.

Q. And you do not know when you told them?

A. No, I disremember what day I told them; whether I told them the day I went back. I know he talked to me—I don't know whether I talked to my wife or whether I didn't.

M.F. Matheny questioned Isaac McCormick, who testified as follows:

Q. Mr. McCormick, what is your age?

A. Fifty-eight.

Q. Where did you live at the time this strike began?

A. Mucklow.

Q. Where do you live now?

A. Crown Hill.

Q. Do you know when the date of this last battle is said to have occurred— taken place on the mountain back of Wacoma?

A. Why, on the tenth of February.

Q. Do you know where Cal Newman was on that day?

A. Yes, sir.

Q. Where was he?

A. He was at Crown Hill.

Q. What was he doing there?

A. Well, sir, he was night-watching there and on that morning he had a big sow. He was up at the hospital and had heard of my hogs and was going back by my house. He was after his sow that had got out. I sent my little boy and headed her off and we drove her back down and helped him put her in the pen, somewhere about nine o'clock. It might have been a little after nine o'clock.

Q. How far was that from the place on the mountain back of Wacoma where the battle is said to have taken place?

A. I don't have much idea, Mr. Matheny—a long ways though.

Q. In the main—?

A. It was something like six or seven miles I would think. As near as I could—

Q. Do you know what time in the morning it is said the battle took place?

A. No, sir, I do not.

Q. State to the commission whether or not from what you saw and observed about him that day, whether he could have been back in the mountain participating in that battle.

A. Well, I saw him, as I stated, and helped him handle his sow in the little house–a kind of a cow house he had. I saw him about nine o'clock and somewhere about two o'clock in the afternoon he and Jud Godfrey came to my house to borrow a male hog to put in the pen with his sow. I told them to help themselves but that I didn't think they were big enough for duty. They went and looked at my hogs and they concluded that it was too small, too young and too short-legged and they went away. I was getting ready to go to the hospital to see my brother-in-law there and that is the reason I know it was just about two o'clock or a little after two o'clock and after I went home from the hospital at five o'clock I seen him and Jud Godfrey and Ott Jarrett come by with one of Ott Jarrett's hogs and take it down to put it in with his sow.

The Judge Advocate conducted redirect examination.

Q. Do you know what time the men left Crown Hill that morning to go up on the mountain?

A. I do not. I didn't know any men left Crown Hill and went on the mountain.

Q. Don't you know as a matter of fact that they had a meeting at Beech Grove the night before?

A. I don't know anything about it.

Q. Didn't you observe during the day that a great many people were out of Crown Hill?

A. I did not. I stayed right at home until I came to the hospital at two o'clock to see my brother-in-law. I just moved to Crown Hill on the fifth of February from Shrewsbury.

Q. How do you fix the time you first saw Cal Newman that morning?

A. Well, by the time that I got up and was around doing my chores about the house and milking the cows and feeding the hogs.

Q. It might have been later than nine?

A. I do not think so.

Q. It might have been later than nine?

A. It might have been later than nine but not later than ten.

Q. Did you look at the clock?

A. No, sir, but I looked at my watch. I generally carry my watch with me all the time.

Q. But you can say that you saw Cal that morning somewhere between nine and ten o'clock?

A. Yes, sir.

Q. But you don't know where he was all that time?

A. No, sir.

Adam B. Littlepage: He didn't have any gun; he had a sow?

A. He had a sow and it seemed to be "horsing" and he wanted a hog to put up against her.

The court recessed until seven o'clock, p.m. When the court resumed session at seven, M.F. Matheny made the following statement:

Gentlemen of the commission, we have taken the ages of the prisoners and they show the average age is twenty-eight years and whether or not single or married and how many children they have and with the understanding that this may be introduced, we announce our case rested.

Captain Walker: That is all right.

The Judge Advocate called Lieutenant Guthrie for rebuttal testimony.

Q. You are a Second Lieutenant of the Second Infantry?

A. I am.

Q. You have been on duty here since the declaration of martial law, February 10, 1913, have you?

A. Yes, sir.

Q. How often have you been on duty as an officer guard since that time?

A. Every other day.

Q. What is the rule as to the prisoners—as to persons seeing the prisoners except in the presence of an officer?

A. Well, they are prohibited to interview with any person except some officer or guard is present.

Q. Do you know Frank A. Smith, that little man sitting there?

A. I do.

Q. Do you know a prisoner by the name of W.R. Gray; a smooth-faced fellow with rather red hair?

A. Yes, sir, I do.

Q. Were you present on one occasion when Frank Smith had a conversation with this man Gray in the waiting room over there, at which time Gray's wife was present?

A. I was.

Q. Upon that occasion did you hear Frank Smith say anything to Gray about not being sore on him but that he should be sore on somebody else?

A. Yes, sir, I did.

Q. Who did he refer to, if you recall the name of the man?

A. I do not remember the name of the man now. It seems to me like it was Simpson—some such a name.

Q. I will ask you if upon that occasion—how close were you to Frank A. Smith, the sleuth, and to witness Gray, at the time they were talking?

A. I was within two feet of Smith.

Q. Did you at that time or could you hear everything that was said upon that occasion?

A. I could.

Q. I will ask you if you at that time heard Smith, either in words or in substance, say that if Gray would make a case against the prisoners now on trial that he would get him released and give him something on the side? Did you hear him say anything like that?

A. No, sir, I did not.

M.F. Matheny cross-examined the witness.

Q. This man Gray said the guard was standing in the door; do you know where you stood during the conversation?

A. Yes, sir, I do.

Q. Where were you?

A. I was by the stove.

Q. Do you—

A. Between Smith and the stove—between Smith and the prisoner.

M.F. Matheny: Gentlemen of the commission, at this time I want to enquire by what special license or privilege this man Smith is permitted to stay in this courtroom, when his credibility as a witness is being assailed; a privilege that has been denied all other witnesses who have testified in this case; a privilege that has not been accorded to any citizen of this state, and why a Burns detective, that has come into the homes of these prisoners, according to his own statement, with the badge of betrayal in his face, he sits around in the presence of a court enquiring after the facts in this case, where the lives and liberties of forty men are involved, and looking them with impunity in the face when you are trying to get at the facts. The more I see of this, the hotter my blood becomes. I have not assailed anybody in this case; have tried to be fair and have tried to get at the fair and unvarnished facts; and, gentlemen, I want to say that the rule of this commission is that those witnesses should be excluded from the room and this man Smith has been here from the beginning and he is exercising authority and usurping privileges contrary to the rules of this commission and I do not know by what special right he is accorded these privileges and I want to say if he is as contemptible in the eyes of this commission as he is in my eyes, from what I have seen of him, that he be excluded.

The Judge Advocate: I will have to protest against counsel. Counsel represents his clients and he is accorded all the privileges and as to what Smith may be to him or anybody else, I do not see that that has any place in this record.

Colonel Jolliffe: The gentleman will confine himself to the case.

M.F. Matheny: I am talking about the case. This man Smith is a witness and if he is believed goes right to the heart of this case. Gentlemen, you should have excluded this witness. I have not asked for a single one of our witnesses and no other witness has violated the rule of this commission and I want to say, gentlemen, this man ought to be fired out of here by this commission and the Judge Advocate.

Captain Walker: Mr. Matheny, after a witness has been examined and been on the stand, the rule has not applied and does not in any other case. There has been a number and I think you had a few after they were questioned, who were accorded that privilege. A number of officers testified and after testifying have been backward and forward in the room and that is the reason he has been permitted the same privilege.

M.F. Matheny: Gentlemen, there are other cases that will be tried on practically this same testimony and this man, as I understand it, is not in the employment of the state or the military service and this commission is here for the purpose of getting at the facts and I cannot for my life see why he is permitted to be here and we object, gentlemen, and we want this objection to be entered of record.

Captain Carskadon again questioned Lieutenant Guthrie.

Q. Lieutenant, is it your custom to always be near enough to parties whom you allow to talk to your prisoners, to hear everything that is said?

A. Yes, sir.

Q. Do you invariably do that?

A. I do it with very few exceptions.

Q. There may be times, then, when you do not get all the conversation that passes between the prisoner and the party visiting him; is that true?

A. It is not true with the exception of a man and his wife.

Adam B. Littlepage, Esq., questioned Lieutenant Guthrie.

Q. Did you know that this man, Smith, was a detective when he went in and had the talk with this prisoner?

A. No, sir, I did not.

Q. Didn't you know at that time that he was acting as a detective?

A. No, sir, I did not.

Q. Did you enquire—did he ask your permission to go in and see one of these prisoners?

A. He didn't ask permission. He had permission from the Provost Marshal to be allowed such liberties as any other person would be allowed around there. I did not know he was a detective. I—in fact, I didn't know what he was.

Q. You say that he had permission from the Provost Marshal to do what?

A. Well, the first time that I saw this man, I asked the Provost Marshal, "What about him?" and he told me that he could go in when he was present; that is, if some officer was present. That happened on one occasion when the Provost Marshal came in with him. After that he acted as any other ordinary citizen and was not allowed any other privilege that is accorded any other citizen in town.

Q. Did you always listen to his conversation with the prisoners?

A. That is the only conversation he ever had.

Q. Are you prepared to tell the commission now just what he said to this prisoner and what the prisoner said to him; all of what each said?

A. It would be very easy. It was less than a dozen words. I cannot give the exact words but the sum and substance was–

Q. Let me see if I got your answer right. Your answer was "That it would be very easy; it was less than a dozen words." Have I quoted you right.?

A. You have; yes, sir.

Q. Well, now, will you repeat what was said in less than this dozen words and what the prisoner said?

A. He said he should not be sore at him, or words to that effect.

Q. Do you know how he happened to say that?

A. Smith came into the depot while this man was talking to his wife and another lady. He tipped his hat and spoke to the ladies. The other lady spoke friendly and this man's wife kind of turned up her nose and turned her head. That evidently brought on this conversation.

Q. But the conversation was addressed to her husband and not to her by Smith?

A. Addressed–I presume it was addressed to this man.

Q. And that is all you heard?

A. That is all that was said.

Q. All that was said.

A. It was.

Q. No reply made by either the husband or the wife?

A. None that I know of.

Q. None that you know of?

A. No.

Q. Now, as I understand you, you have related to the commission that he went in there and tipped his hat to this man's wife, this prisoner's wife, and said to her husband, "You need not think hard of me" or words to that effect.

A. Yes, sir.

Q. And you heard no reply that you can now recall?

A. None that I now recall.

Q. And that is the substance of what he said to him?

A. Yes, sir, it is.

Q. As you recall it?

A. Yes, sir. That is all that was said, in substance.

Q. Do you remember where they were standing?

A. Smith was standing–

Q. In the room?

A. Smith was standing on the further side of the stove. This man, his wife and the other lady and a little child, were sitting in the depot at this corner.

Q. The upper corner?

A. Yes, sir, the upper end of the depot, in this corner, and I was standing between Smith and the prisoner on the other side of the stove.

Q. He didn't step around you to talk to Smith?

A. No, sir, he did not.

Q. And Smith didn't step around you to talk to him?

A. No, sir.

Q. And you tell this commission that you did not know that man was a detective, either?

A. I did not know that he was a detective.

Q. And had no intimation of it and no information about it?

A. None whatever.

The prosecution here announced by the Judge Advocate that it rested its case. The defendants, by their counsel, did the like.

The commission announced that the motion of M.F. Matheny that Frank A. Smith be excluded from the room is overruled.

M.F. Matheny: The prisoners, by counsel, here object to the witness, F.A. Smith, remaining in the courtroom.

Captain Walker: After the case is rested by both plaintiff and defendants?

M.F. Matheny: After the case has been rested by both plaintiff and defendants, and represents that at sundry times during the trial of this case, since he has given his testimony, that he has been present in the courtroom, notwithstanding the order of the commission that witnesses should be excluded; and further representing that all other people not interested in the trial of this case, just previous to this motion, were excluded from the courtroom, and they retired upon the order of the commission.

Captain Walker: No, sir, the commission has not done that. If they think it is safe they may come right back.

The Judge Advocate: I got up and suggested that they retire for the reason that the building was stated to be unsafe and so stated at the time that I asked them to retire.

M.F. Matheny: To which action and ruling of the commissioners, the prisoners, at the time, excepted.

Argument by Captain Charles R. Morgan for the defendants:

Gentlemen, I realize that the question you have to decide upon within the next few hours is one of extreme importance. It is important, of course, as I have stated before, as to the conditions of our state and it is even more important to these men who are arraigned here before you. It is important to them and to their families–it is important to every one of them.

I won't have very much to say, but what I say, I want to say that I feel as earnestly to be true as can be.

Now, in the first place, these people are charged under a conspiracy. They are charged with having conspired to do a certain crime.

They are charged with having committed certain crimes. They are charged with having aided and abetted in securing the release or escape of those who have committed these crimes; and, I want to say to you, gentlemen, frankly, that I do not believe, that under the law, the Judge Advocate, in his most admirable—in his admirable endeavor to make a case against these people, to support the law, as he says—I do not feel that he has established a conspiracy against these men and I believe that I can show you this, gentlemen, to be true.

Analyzing the evidence from the beginning: he takes up evidence against Brown, Parsons, and Boswell. He says that Brown—he brings in evidence to show that Brown says that the situation is desperate; and gentleman, you know that it is desperate.

He goes further and puts in evidence that Brown is telephoning over the country for men to come in. He would seek to prove that this is true; and, gentlemen, it has been shown that there has been a necessity for men to defend their homes.

He goes further and attempts to show that ammunition was brought in here by certain people and the amount of shooting that has been done here on both sides would go to show that ammunition was necessary to defend the homes of these people in this district. You know it and I know it, that it is necessary, if you are going through this country, when martial law does not prevail, that you go armed. You would go armed and so would I.

Now, gentlemen, taking up the proof of what this conspiracy was. There has not been a scintilla of evidence to prove to you, that these men who went on that mountain, whoever they may be—that those men went there for any unlawful purpose. True, you say, the Judge Advocate will say that they were not going up there looking for bees. He will say that they would not have taken their rifles if they were not going for an unlawful purpose; but that was for him to prove. One of the witnesses placed on the stand for the prosecution—one of the men who had made the so-called confession—said they said something about transportation; that he did not know what it was. Another of the witnesses said they said something about a machine gun and he did not know what it was; and, if my memory serves me correctly, the other witness said he did not know what their purpose was; and the prosecution has failed, and failed dismally, to establish a case of conspiracy.

Now, gentlemen, if we take as true the faltering statement of these people, of these people who say they were with those men who went on the hill, and if we believe that those men whom they say were with them as they went up on the hill—if we believe that this was true and that they were there, we must first establish that they were there for some unlawful purpose; and then, gentlemen, if they establish that they were there for an unlawful purpose; if those men were on their way for an unlawful purpose entirely different; for instance, such as the committing of theft; if one of these men turns out of his way, his course, and shoots another man, you could not hold that these men on their way were guilty of a conspiracy to shoot that man. That is the law and the Judge Advocate will tell you it is the law. So, gentlemen, if these men went up there for the—probably a lawful purpose, because it has not been established that it was for an unlawful purpose—if they went up there for that purpose, which had nothing to do with the killing of a man; didn't go up there in a conspiracy to kill Vance and Bobbitt but that someone with them killed Vance and Bobbitt; then, if those men were not present, aiding and abetting in the killing of Vance and Bobbitt, gentlemen, you cannot find these gentlemen guilty of a conspiracy to murder these men. You cannot find them guilty of the murder of these men unless you can show there was a conspiracy to do that or unless you can show that they were present, aiding and abetting in the killing of those men; and you know that there has not been a word of evidence going to show that any man there named—any man named in this prosecution did a single act toward the furtherance of the killing of Vance and Bobbitt.

Now, gentlemen, I am not going to go very much further.

There have been very few people named in this prosecution. There was evidence introduced showing that Crockett and Taylor were shot; but there is not a word of evidence showing by whom. There has been evidence offered that certain men were arrested in certain places. For instance, there are four men here, the commission will remember, who were arrested in the broad road without a weapon upon them, walking peaceably along. The evidence is that they were arrested by men who had not a right to arrest, and, in spite of the fact that the men who arrested them without any warrant and without any reason for arresting them—in spite of this fact, these men peaceably gave themselves up, rather than have trouble. I ask the commission if that is the kind of a man that would do killing. Is that the kind of men that had just been engaged in a murder of two men?

You know that it is not. Those men did not have to explain their presence there—it is not necessary that they do that. The fact is they were acting as law-abiding citizens, doing absolutely nothing that would go to show that they were not law-abiding citizens who had never been mixed up in any trouble. The same is true of Prince, and Morgan, and the O'Dell boys. They were behaving absolutely peaceably; gave up their guns without a struggle to people who had no authority in the world to take them from them, and the same is true of the two other men, arrested on Cabin Creek, against who the state has failed to prove its case. You show that these men had guns—had pistols or that these men had revolvers. I want to say that Judge Wallace has said that the Code of West Virginia does not lie in this district. You know that he said it and I want to say that I agree with him; and, I want to say under that, that a man who was found with a revolver is not guilty of the crime of carrying a revolver, as laid down by the statute. It is for you gentlemen to judge whether a man, who is carrying a revolver through this district, the district where the Code of West Virginia is set aside, whether or not, gentlemen, that man would be found guilty of a misdemeanor as laid down by the Code of West Virginia. It does not seem to me, considering–

The Judge Advocate: Captain Morgan, the governor who appointed this commission in his order said "Any offense against the civil law as it existed prior would continue to be an offense under the martial law." By executive order, that is the law of this place.

Captain Morgan: The only point, gentlemen, the punishment fixed for this is not fixed by statute. If you decide, gentlemen, that it is dangerous to go up and down these creeks of the time without guns or with guns, and we believe you know that to be the fact, that a man would be a fool to go through this territory unless armed. Now, we have introduced in evidence the fact that there has been great trouble existing here. The prosecution has introduced evidence that there has been a great trouble existing in this territory. The evidence shows that hundreds of persons engaged on the one side or the other in the carrying of guns and that one side is about as bad as the other. The prosecution has shown these facts; that it is a very common thing for men to go armed and that there is no intention of any intentional wrong-doing when he does go armed, and, as to no other men, excepting the ones I have named and those named by one of the Negroes, as being on the hill and the only charge against him in the world is that he was carrying a gun and I think that you gentlemen will consider that. Most of these men have never been named at all Most of them–I would say that there are twenty-five of the men here who have not been named at all and the others have been named with the men who were picked up on Cabin Creek, named by implication. Is it a case against a man, because he is in two or three miles of the place where the crime was or has been committed? Is that a sufficient case against him, that he has been committing murder? It might be a circumstance, if you would show that man had been connected in a sufficient way; that he had started to do that murder; that he had been seen aiding or abetting the people; that he was escaping, but otherwise it would not be.

Now, gentlemen, as to one of my clients, the aged lady, who has sat here so patiently and listened to the testimony: I do not want very much to say, but you gentlemen know that it is being introduced in evidence that this old lady is fighting the battles of the laboring man and has been for years and years.

You know it to be a fact that eighty years of age will sometimes cause us to say and to go further in what we say, than if we were fifty. Old age–very old age, sometime causes flinging discretion just a little bit to the winds, and, I leave it to you gentlemen, if there has been a single item of evidence introduced here that this old woman, who has been here, and has been so courteous and so patient to you all–if she has done a single act in the furtherance of this conspiracy with which she is charged. The last evidence introduced was the halting, floundering evidence of a man who heard her say, back, I think, some time in January–that he heard Mother make a speech and heard her say something about guns. This was not to shoulder your guns and march to the front. That was not the burden of her song, but it was to bury their arms. That is what she said; and, you remember that the other speeches that she made were made all the way back last summer, shortly after the poor old woman had waded the creek in order to get to the place she was going to speak. My God, it is enough to make the blood of an old woman boil when she is forced to do things of that kind; when men–when mine guards in the uniform of men–who call themselves men–will stand on each side of the creek and force an old woman to march in the middle of it, in order that she may get up to say a few words to "the boys" that she–whose interest she thinks she is advancing–Where is there a single item of evidence connecting this old woman with the conspiracy, if a conspiracy has been shown, and which we say we do not think has been shown. Now, the state has failed.

The state has failed to mention the name of Mr. Paulson–they mention that Mr. Batley was seen in Hansford and have shown that Mr. Boswell came to Hansford. They said he was guilty of publishing inflammatory re-marks, contained in the *Labor Argus*. A good many of these remarks are on a par with the remark which Mother Jones is alleged to have made that there were courts who were two by four. A good many of them are trivial–of little importance and amount to very little in the end and practically all of them, you gentlemen know, have at least a considerable foundation for truth. The most dangerous thing said in any of these remarks is that "It is time to fight." "It is time to fight." Now, my friend Judge Wallace and my friend Mike Matheny have said many a time from the hustings–they have said, "Boys, it is time to fight. If we don't fight, we are not going to roll up the proper kind of a majority this fall–it is time to fight." They have said that again and again, and I am not going to say and you are not going to say that there is anything more improbable contained in the *Labor Argus*. That is the worst thing he said, "To fight." If to say "to fight" means to go out and fight with guns and to commit murder and all sorts of things–it seems to me that there are various ways of fighting than that and that is the most serious thing that happened.

Now, gentlemen, I have taken too much of your time and I will let my labors be continued by my associate counsel.

Captain Carskadon, for the defendants:

Gentlemen of the commission:

I know that this will be tiresome to you before this argument is concluded by everyone who is entitled to speak; therefore, I shall try to make my remarks as nearly to the point and as brief as possible.

I want to say, in the first place, gentlemen, that knowing the personnel of this body sitting here tonight, as I do know you and as I have known you for a number of years past, I want to say that I believe it is unnecessary entirely to say anything–any of we gentlemen on the part of the defence, to come up here and attempt to argue to you what you should do and what you should not do in this case. You have heard the evidence just the same as the prisoners have heard it and as we have heard it. You have been informed as to the nature of the cause; as the conditions which surrounded the participants, if any of them be here, before this trial came on, and I believe that you are able amply to judge what is for the right and for the best in this matter; but, as Captain Morgan has said a while ago, gentlemen, I believe that this is one of the most important bodies and one of the most important occasions upon which any body has ever sat, to pass judgment on any effect or any crime. The state, gentlemen, in the past has made marvelous and wonderful progress. Twenty-five years ago in the state of West Virginia, we had very few men who owned any capital, and the resources of this state and this immense wealth were practically unknown to its citizens. In order to develop this splendid state, gentlemen, it was necessary to invite capital from beyond our boundaries to help us. This was done and capital from distant states came to our rescue and has been nobly assisting us in the development of this splendid territory of ours and helping us to deport to the markets of the world our splendid products. Capital, gentlemen, should have its protection and its rights should be amply and properly protected and cared for; but, gentlemen, there is also another side to this question. In order to develop this state and these vast resources, it has taken more than capital. It has taken human intellect; it has taken more than machinery, it has taken the skill and the labor of these men sitting here before you tonight. They have played their part, gentlemen, in the development of this state and in making it what it is today, and they also have interests, which are vitally placed before you today–at this present time–for your consideration.

Coming down to the real facts in the case, gentlemen, of the case as it stands before you, we do not believe that the state has made a case. We do not believe that it is properly connected up with evidence of the items it charges here in order to establish a conspiracy. It is true that Mr. Brown and Mr. Boswell and Mr. Parsons were in Hansford on Sunday night and on Monday following that day, but, gentlemen, it has not been shown here to you that they did any acts which would make the crime a conspiracy. It is true that Mr. Boswell was over at Boomer on Sunday, but there has been nothing shown that he was over there for any particular purposes, more than that some of the witnesses said that he went there, I believe, to carry a message. Mr. Paulson and Mr. Batley, I believe, are not connected in any way with this proceeding and the only charge against Mother Jones is, I believe, that she made several weeks or even months ago, a number of speeches over this section of the country; and, gentlemen, let me say right here, that the last speech Mother Jones made anywhere within this section of territory and I do not know but what it is the last one she made, was made something like three weeks before this act of conspiracy with which these prisoners are here charged took place or became a fact, if such conspiracy exists; which we deny. Do you think, gentlemen, honestly and fairly, that a speech made three or four weeks before the act is perpetrated would have stayed and retained any holding force or influence on these people here, charged with this crime; that it would have any influence that length of time afterwards? We do not believe it would. The principal feature in this act of conspiracy, as I take it, gentlemen, is the fact that on Saturday night of February ninth, I believe, or the eighth, I believe it was, or the Sunday night of the ninth, I am not sure which, a meeting was held in what they call Beech Grove. I take it to be near Crown Hill. I do not know the lay of the land definitely enough to describe it. There was said to have been a number of miners congregated at this place at that time. There has been just one witness that I recall that has been on the stand who has told that there was actually such a meeting occurred–he was there himself. He says he thinks he saw one other man that he knows that was at that meeting and this is a part of that conspiracy, that meeting supposed to have been held at Beech Grove. Nothing was said there, gentlemen, about violating any statute or committing any criminal offense at this meeting, so far as I know, or so far as came before you in evidence. The only thing that was said at that meeting was that "we will meet at six o'clock tomorrow morning."

"We will meet at six o'clock tomorrow morning." That is then all the evidence, I believe given by one of the state's witnesses, who deserted the bunch, who made this statement that they "were to meet at six o'clock in the morning." A body of men possibly went on the hill above Mucklow and above Wacoma on the morning of the tenth of February, 1913. I believe it would be useless, gentlemen, to dispute that; that there has been sufficient evidence to show that. There was certain firing done at that time—a battle took place. What the object was in those men going up on that hill has not been placed before this commission and we do not know and you do not know what the object of that was. Evidently, gentlemen, it was never made. They never congregated and went up on that hill from wherever they did go for the purpose of making an attack on the town of Mucklow, because they had gotten on down a period over beyond and were attempting still to go on. The witnesses who testified to seeing these men, who were not firing or had not entered into this firing, had gone on even beyond the place where the firing took place, headed towards Burnwell. I believe two witnesses said—one of the state's witnesses, I believe one of these colored gentlemen—said they were going to Burnwell to get transportation. The other man said they were going up the hill to get a gatling gun. I believe the majority, the biggest part of that crowd, never knew where they were going. I do not believe there was concerted action enough among these men to have a definite purpose. Surely, gentlemen, there could have been no murder commit-ted when there was no intent and when they were attacked, as we take it. One or two witnesses say that one side fired the first shot. I believe the principal witness for the state, relating the occurrence, said he came up on top of the hill and the rest of his men were something like one hundred yards behind him. He stopped and calmly surveyed the situ-ation, and his testimony, gentlemen, is that after looking over that situation and waiting for his men behind him to come up, of course, he didn't want to make any attack on these men without assistance, and after looking over that situation. He had been superintending the way to Mucklow and traveling with the boys—the miners—and he was asked by the Judge Advocate: How many of these men—how many of these faces—look over the *witnesses* sitting before him; how many of these men do you know? He said: I do not identify any man. He was there, with plenty of opportunity to calmly survey these men and could have seen whether or not any of these gentlemen were present.

We do not believe, gentlemen, even though we had the time, and we had very little time in this case; we do not believe that this could be considered murder or that the charge of murder could be sustained on the evidence of the sort that has been introduced here. There was firing on both sides. God knows how many miners were killed on the other side. We do not think the evidence shows. We do know that there was a pitched battle between two factions—two hostile forces—and we do not believe the charge of murder or conspiracy should be sustained on any such evidence as that. What is the evidence against them—very few of them—very few of these men have been identified even in name and the circumstances under which they were identified are so far-fetched and these men were so far away from them and under such circumstances it would be mere conjecture for you to even say these men were part of that conspiracy, if such you care to call it. Three or four of these men were picked up away over here on the range on the road, without arms, which certainly does not sufficiently connect them with a fight that took place on this hill when none of them were even seen.

Gentlemen, in this short time, we can only take a brief view of this situation. The state worked on this case six weeks. The defense had but two days to look over the whole situation. Not time to make a sufficient or a proper defense for these men and to attempt to do so under these circumstance would be simply foolishness. We believe that after you have carefully read over this evidence, which we know you will do, and after you have taken into consideration all of the circumstances which surround this case and these gentlemen for a number of weeks and months, a matter which is only too plain and of which you are fully conversant; these conditions which existed up here between the miners and the guards; that pitched battles have occurred in different parts of the country and, I want to say, gentlemen, that the fact that there was shooting done at Mucklow on the day or two preceding the pitched battle, which occurred on the hill above Mucklow; that the same thing occurred right over here at Holly Grove on Saturday morning and there was no firing done. I want to say in conclusion, gentlemen, that I believe that after you have fairly considered these facts, that you will come to the conclusion that no conspiracy has been proven and that these parties are innocent of the crime with which they stand charged.

Adam B. Littlepage, for the defendants:

Gentlemen of the commission, on account of not having heard all of the evidence in this case, it is possible that I can contribute but little to the proper solution of it. But because of past environments in life, and experience I have had, and from what I have read—accounts I have read of the evidence in this case and information gained from my partner as to what has gone forward heretofore in the case before this commission, I feel that it would not be improper to submit for your consideration, such consideration as you will be pleased to give it, some observations which occurred to my mind, might be pertinent.

I have always stood and expect to stand for law and order in the community in which I was born and reared—this is my native county—and for a square deal as between man and man. I am fully aware that the citizens of this county and of this state have been shocked as the result of what has occurred on Cabin and Paint creeks within the recent past, and which is the subject matter of this investigation. There is no man under the sound of my voice who lives within the state who regrets it more than I do. Good men were involved—some bad ones. I have had much experience with miners—coal miners, and the rank and file are as good as you or I. There are some agitators among them, like in all other class of business. I have had a good deal of experience with guards, the guard system in this state. I cannot say that the rank and file is good, nor I cannot say that they are all bad. This occurred to me from what I have read in this case—what I have heard of it that it is more of the efforts of the miners to justify their employment, than it was the efforts of the guards to drive the miners before them—domineering, dictating to, even imposing upon them. I am not aware that the individual members of this commission has studied between the lines of the evidence in this case and ascertained which was the imposing party—coal miners or the company guards. I want to see every man's property protected. I want to see the coal company's property protected, or railroad protected, and I want to see them all prosper. I want to see the men who are developing our resources protected and encouraged and God knows I regret the clash that has taken place. I regret it as a citizen of the state.

Never have my eyes beheld such a sight as I witness in this case: forty men, poor men, toiling men, who live scantily, part of them, according to information have hardly enough to live upon.

They divided their bread with the man who has come out today before this commission and deliberately undertaken to betray them—and that is this detective. That is the sad thing to contemplate, gentlemen of this commission. Whether he be a volunteer witness, whether he be an employee of the state, whether he be in the employ of the coal company, whether he be in the employ of the coal guards—company guards, it matters not; I say to you as a citizen I believe in a fair deal for every man.

The figure that this detective has cut in this case will live only to taunt the recollection of the people engaged in this trial—lawyers, military men, laymen and laborers. I would hate to go to your house, accept your hospitality, live upon your bread, and stab you in the back when I get an opportunity to do it. Those are the sentiments of my heart. I would be cowardly not to express them in this important presence.

Was there a conspiracy in this case upon the part of the coal miner? Was there a conspiracy in this case upon the part of the coal guards? To make good themselves in the estimation of their employment and friends, and earn their livelihood by reason of their service? Was there not a fight in this case amid the hills of West Virginia, high up on top of the hills? You have learned definitely of the killing—of the death of two or three coal company guards; you have learned with indefiniteness of some fourteen or fifteen coal miners who are sleeping the long sleep that knows no awakening as the result of that clash. Wrong? Yes, it was wrong upon the part of both sides. Armed? Yes, they were armed. Coal company guards and miners. Who were the armed men? Who fired? Who did the firing?

Who commenced it, and what purpose was it for? Was it a desire to commit murder or was it a desire to defend conceived rights?

You have got nearly forty men in the hands of the commission, and you have young men, noble looking as you are composing this high and important commission. You may live to be one hundred but I trust you never will be called upon to assume the responsibility of looking into the faces of forty poor men, each one of whom has a heart, many of whom have wives and children. Anxious? Yes. Heart stricken? Yes. The dragnet of the law has gone out through the instrumentality of the law and both ends have met, and when you have made the landing, whom have you upon trial?

The coal company's guards are all gone. Not one here. Were they not engaged in the identical conspiracy to annihilate that it is alleged the miners on the other hand were engaged in? Forty men! Whom have you? Poor, distressed, humiliated coal miners. I have stated many times heretofore and my experience justified it, that there is not a set of people in these United States so much imposed upon, so much humiliated as the coal miners, and I mean every word, every utterance when I make that statement. They have some rights. God created them as he did you and me. They have their occupation, they have their little homes that they love dearly. They didn't bring on the trouble, not one bit more than the company guards did. You may never have had any experience with the guards. When you shall have had that experience and been kicked out of the public highway and off of the railroad track, and driven, and humiliated and browbeaten–if you resist, knocked down. That is all a matter of history and it may be outside of the evidence in this case, but it is a part of the history of the state and the history of the trouble that culminated in this fight that took place.

Now, as I understand the law, gentlemen, as I take it, the specifications were drawn under the "Red Men's Act," which act is considered by lawyers to be the most liberally drawn in favor of the state and under which statute convictions can be more easily made than any other criminal statute in the state.

If two or more men combine, conspire and confederate together for the purpose of inflicting bodily harm upon another person–it has been some time since I read it, but I am giving the gist of it–and by reason of said combination and conspiracy inflict punishment or death, then it pre-scribes the penalty. I want to ask you this question, from the evidence of this case, gentlemen, if you can justify yourselves in the face of your God and my God, after looking over this court at the depressed, humble poor people and say that man, this man, that man, this man–I know he was engaged in that conspiracy, as well as I know that I am living. Now you must know that from this evidence and as a result of that conspiracy he took part in that shooting, which resulted in the death of Bobbitt and the man named. Now, how do you know, gentlemen, that Bobbitt was ever shot by a coal miner? How do you know he was not shot by one of his own side? How do you know he was not shot by his own side?

I understand from this evidence that there are two national organizers arraigned here for trial; men sent out by the national organization of the United Mine Workers of America, and there is not a [shred?] of evidence against them, that is incriminating evidence, unless it be the fact that they occupy that high and responsible position.

And poor old "Mother" Jones, eighty years old! I am not as young as I used to be and I am not as impulsive as I used to be. When a young man I was very impulsive, high strung, and would get mad and if I could not find some one to scrap with, I would get mad; I would go out and butt a tree or something, in order to get satisfaction; get under the end of the house and I would lift up on it, but as we grow older and the time goes by and the impulsiveness of the earlier nature comes and goes with the time.

This is a sad occasion to me. Never have I in all of my twenty years experience as a member of the bar looked upon and witnessed such a picture as confronts me. No man has a higher conception of the important station you occupy on this commission in this state. I have done what I could as a citizen to facilitate your investigations here. I want to do what I can as a citizen to facilitate a proper adjustment upon your part of this trouble; free from passion so as to leave no sore spots.

I have not been too severe on the man that took the bread at the table of these men out of employment for so long. When living in tents, in the hills, in the valleys with God's sun shining on them—looking down upon them, I pity them and I pity their clan. They work, they toil, they dig, and go to their houses and they will divide their last crumb with you. Nothing they have is too good for the visitor. The best chair—they may have but one, but that one is given to the visitor.

Who were engaged in this conspiracy, which one under your oath? Why, I suppose if I had been coming up the highway with a shotgun, or a rifle, or cannon, or a gatling gun, I guess I would have been here too, except you are only trying coal miners. Gentlemen, Judge Advocate, have not the coal miners been goaded? Goaded! Goaded! Who wouldn't fight when he is attacked? You come to my home to drive me away from it—yes, put it down twice, Judge, you come to my home and drive me away from it, and I will fight; yes. I would be unworthy if I did not. I say to you now and I do not want to be misunderstood, I want every reasonable and proper protection and encouragement given to the development of our state. I have tried to help them and I want a square deal for the under-man. Why, he is a simple humble outcast. Been submissive! Why, you would say, of course, they have been submissive. The power of the law is over them. Mighty it is. But they come and they go without a word, not a complaint. Now is this commission, and I do not mean it at all in any personal sense, but how are you to forget and to forgive yourselves, if we mete out punishment to the poor lowly miner and let the fellows engaged on the other side of the controversy, who are engaged in it as a matter of livelihood, but as a matter of being determined and capable of humiliating the under-man.

God's eternal truth shall shine out in this state, as I expect to tell the governor of this state, should one of them be convicted. You convict a miner and you let the company guard go and you permitting him to go, you put a premium on his conduct. I might be wrong, gentlemen of the commission.

The Judge Advocate: Let me interrupt you. Have you anything in this record of this case to base such a statement as that upon?

M.F. Matheny: I am familiar with the record and I will say—

The Judge Advocate: Let Mr. Littlepage reply.

Adam B. Littlepage: Yes, sir, I have, Mr. Judge Advocate. I may be mistaken but I leave it to your sense of honor to answer, whether I am right or wrong, after I have made my statement.

The fight that took place in the woodland was engaged in on the one side by the coal company guards, Baldwin detectives, on the other side by supposed coal miners. Is that right?

The Judge Advocate: I want to answer that in this way. Does not all the evidence in this case show that the firing, and all of it, came from wherever these defendants were there, into these people and that no firing into the—

Adam B. Littlepage: Great God, they tell me that the whole top of the mountain—

The Judge Advocate: What is the evidence in this case? It is in testimony that ten or twelve men that when these men on the mountain asked them their business, the reply to that enquiry thrice repeated was a rifle shot.

Adam B. Littlepage: I did not see this fight.

The Judge Advocate: I say it is in evidence.

Adam B. Littlepage: If you say that is the fact, I was not on that hill and I don't know about it. I am glad I was not on the hill.

The Judge Advocate: I am too.

Adam B. Littlepage: No telling how fast you and I would have run if we had been there. If we could not get behind a rock or something.

The Judge Advocate: Everybody I have heard testify yet has run.

Adam B. Littlepage: Now I might have been too general in my statement, gentlemen of the commission. I take it that underlying all the evidence that falls from the lips of the witnesses you realize that a fight was engaged in by the guards upon the one side and the miners on the other. Now, what I had reference to was, to advance this idea. You gather up one side, and you convict, and you let the other side go; not one of them are here. If there is a conspiracy on the one side there must have been on the other. Not one of them are here.

Man's inhumanity to man, causes countless thousands to mourn!

I have not intentionally trespassed upon your time. I just had these ideas in my mind and wanted the commission to have the benefit of them, so you might know what my sentiments were. I can but repeat, God knows I wish it had never happened.

I know lots of these men personally, have known them for years, some of them have been reared here. I know some of the best of these men and you are dealing with these people and dealing with people that have grown up here since you and I were boys—since the Judge Advocate and myself were boys.

That is the men's average age, twenty-eight years. Young, ambitious, poor but proud. They may some of them conceive that they were imposed upon.

God knows I believe they have been. Which one of them did any shooting, tell me? Here are two colored men who came in as state's witnesses and one of them swears they could hardly tell a man from a tree. Didn't know anybody or anything.

Gentlemen, I have finished. Let me say this to you now in good faith, one humble citizen speaking to men higher in station, go slow, be certain that you are right, let the state prove its case, and if it does not, send these people home.

Lots of poor people are looking and praying tonight on the hills, in the valleys, for loved ones you have got before you. If you had been a coal miner and living in this neighborhood, you might have been in this same situation. If I had been a coal miner and lived in this neighborhood, I might have been in the same situation. Shall the strong and the powerful crush the weak? Look on these poor men, whose protectors you are, not here to convict them unless compelled to by your oath. The state won't love you any better, nor will it respect you less.

M.F. Matheny, for the defendants:

Gentlemen of the commission, in the way of the beginning of the remarks which I am now about to make, I want to call your attention to this one fact, from which there can be no retreat, and that is, behind the effect there is always a cause.

In these prisoners before you tonight, in looking over the faces of these men who have been committed to your keeping, you see the effect.

It is my purpose at this time to first discuss with you for a brief period the cause. Old things are passing away in this country and all things are becoming new. It is true that in the evolution of things the cause moves slowly, but as certainly as God rules and the eternal principles of justice prevail, they are moving, and the truth remains that no question has ever been settled until it is settled right.

Gentlemen, for a long period in this country men set themselves to the task of making money. Political parties met in their conventions and they spoke with reference to the prosperity they had under the policies that they had pursued; but this period of evolution moved onward and in the last few years men have awakened to the fact that a nation that gives itself to spoils and to money and about the things that money represents cannot long endure; hence it was in the last political campaign that all of the political parties headed by the greatest men of this country looked, and looking they saw a star, as did the Wise Men of the East who saw the star on the plains of Judea, when the angels announced that the Prince of men had come to establish the doctrine of "Peace on earth and good will to men;" and these great men not coming from any political party, but from all of the political parties, said that you may talk about the conservation of our water powers, of our timber land, of our coal, and of our national wealth, but first and above it all stands the great question of the conservation of human rights. They looked into this industrial situation of ours and they saw men becoming rich, immensely wealthy, while the great toiling masses of this country were becoming more and more impoverished, notwithstanding that we have fertile fields and fairly rich plains and wealth incalculable locked up in the bowels of these hills. Men and women beneath the shadow of this great festive board are begging for bread and a chance to make a living by the sweat of their faces. That condition is not on the western slopes where rocks are lashing the tide of the Pacific; we do not have to go to that place on the northern shore where whispering pines bow; we do not have to go to the great Keystone State to find these conditions, but they are present in the Mountain State of West Virginia, dedicated to the principle that "Mountaineers are always free."

And, gentlemen, you are not dealing with men in this conflict but you are dealing with the cause. You are dealing with the principles and some men may say that there is nothing to settle—that there is nothing to settle; it is only a few agitators who are doing it all.

But, gentlemen, there is something to settle and we will go on until these questions are settled right, regardless of the convening of this commission. There is something, gentlemen, to settle.

When men whom the state admits have always been men of good character, men who make their living by the sweat of their brow, will shoulder their muskets and march to death, almost within the shadow of the capitol of your state, back of the effect there is a cause. It is declared in the Holy Writ that he who liveth by the sword shall by the sword perish.

Let us see if these men are the only law breakers in connection with this great industrial conflict that is going on. If I owe you a dollar, you sue me in any of the civil courts of this state, to wit, a justice of the peace. After you have given me a week's notice, I have the right to appear and demand a continuance as a matter of right and it must be given and it goes over for another week, in order that I may prepare myself for trial. But not so when I occupy your house unlawfully. The statutes of this state say that you are entitled to an expedient remedy and upon three days' written notice you can compel me to stand a trial to show why I so unlawfully retain that property, and upon the first calling of the case, although I have only had three days' notice, I am not entitled to a continuance as a matter of right, and unless I show good cause for the detention of your property and have a continuance you can force me into a trial upon that short notice. There is a question of expeditious remedy as to the other parties in this industrial conflict as admitted by the record in this case.

Gentlemen, instead of resorting to the process of the law for the purpose of evicting these men, they have resorted to the process of Baldwin guards, who forcibly evict men from their homes in violation of the statute of this state. There is one of the causes that brings the effect before you here this evening.

Another contributing cause, gentlemen, is this: It is not a trespass to walk across lands of another—

The Judge Advocate: Let me interrupt you. I disagree with you on the law; the law does not punish a trespasser on unenclosed land, but it is a trespass and you can evict them.

M.F. Matheny: The statute says, gentlemen, that if any person trespasses upon the enclosed lands of another, that he is guilty and can be fined and punished for his acts and can also be made to respond in damages; but you can see the wisdom of the legislature in the enactment of that statute, that it used the word "enclosed." Of course, at that time the vast territory of this state was unenclosed and it is far seeing by the legislature and in their wisdom they said it would not do to make it a trespass against a man who went rambling over the property of other people, which were not enclosed, and hence it is not a criminal act. It is not an act, if the damages can be recovered, under the statute of this state for a man to pass over the unenclosed lands of another.

Now, these people with these facts before them went into the mountains. They had their guns up there and I want to call your attention to the fact, gentlemen, that no coal company has the right to enforce the law by its private process.

Why, gentlemen, you know that when a man clothed with authority goes out for the purpose of summoning and that he possesses authority is known the man steeped in crime is very loath to oppose that authority of that officer and you know it to be a fact that the sheriffs and constables and a marshal when they go to execute a process, they are never fired upon, except in isolated cases, where the man is so steeped in crime that in order for him to escape the law and the punishment for the former crimes that he is willing to strike down the officer, but these cases are very rare and exceptional indeed.

And, gentlemen, whenever you place on the trains of this state men who are without the semblance of authority delegated to them by the state or the constitution, but that authority is granted by the arrogants of the very force against which they are contending, then that man under the usurpation of authority in places wherever a man has the right to be, by the usurpation of that authority he drives men to crime and causes good citizens to violate a statute that theretofore they had held inviolate and sacred, and let me say to you that the time is not here, it never has been here, and it never will come when private individuals can enforce and maintain a public duty and the more private individuals arrogate to themselves the administration of the law, which has been committed to officers in uniform, the more you will have the deplorable condition that you have here before you as the subject of this investigation.

A railroad is a common carrier. By law every man is entitled to ride upon that railroad. This railroad that runs this line, the main line and these railroads that run up these creeks are no more, gentlemen, the private property of the coal company than they are the private property of the coal miners; yet this investigation shows and the evidence upon which the commission, the special commission appointed by the former governor, William E. Glasscock, reported that these guards took possession of these trains, enquired of men where they were going, forcibly ejected them, held them up and seized and searched them at the station, denied them the privileges of the public highway and access to the postoffice of this district.

Now, gentlemen, what does it all mean? It means that men will first appeal to the law and appealing to the law and obtaining no redress, where the law says that redress should be found, then the inevitable—the inevitable comes. And when I say the inevitable, I say that which caused ancient Rome to quake, foreign destinies and thrones to shatter and crumble and fall to the earth, will take the place of representative government and it will loose its power and private arrogants have repealed. Private influences through the medium of private agencies undertake to perform a public function. If for the public, it should be performed for the public's benefit, and not to perform it to suit their own sweet will and in their own sweet way.

Now, gentlemen, American citizens will not tolerate that and that condition has been brought about in this very field and you read the declaration of martial law of the governor. Read what has occurred in this case and there you will find that it is not the men–that it is not the prisoners at the bar here; they can be exterminated here tonight and, gentlemen, as certain as God rules you cannot get away from the principles that the system is wrong and until you rid the system it must assert itself again in Paint Creek valley or somewhere in the New River hills, or somewhere on the Norfolk and Western. Like smoke shooting from the smouldering volcano or stratification of the earth somewhere they will burst asunder and the smouldering fire vent beneath will give vent to itself, because the thing is wrong and must have vent somewhere.

Would you pardon me, gentlemen, if I would call your attention here to the fact that it has broken loose in the city of Chicago today, that the investigation there shows that fifty thousand young women, as good by birth perhaps as your sister and mine, are forced to prostitution and wrong because some monster with the clutch of greed denies them an adequate wage, thereby forcing them to prostitution.

The great president of the United States and the great men of all the nations of the earth are looking at this industrial problem and they agreed, without respect to whatever political party they belong to, they agreed upon this one fundamental fact, that the people who toil must have industrial justice or industrial war and revolution is the inevitable result.

Now, what does the evidence in this case show? These men are charged with conspiracy. It is claimed that inflammatory speeches were made, calculated to excite trouble. You read the President of the United States' speeches on these industrial problems; see what he says. Read the ex-President of the United States' speeches on these problems and see what he says about it. Read Eugene Debs' speeches and see what he says about it. Read the Great Commoner's speeches and see what he has to say about it. Read the great men of the earth's speeches and see what they say about it. They say that there is an invisible force, locked in the arms of greed and spoil, that is undermining representative government–the government of the people of this country and that the courts must destroy this invisible viper that strikes its fangs into the breasts of those who toil, else the viper, perforce, will take the citadel of this republic.

These men criminals? When did they become criminals? They were not criminals prior to April a year ago. You, gentlemen, when you read that report and see what prices they were forced to pay for goods, it is enough to inspire crime. When you read the conditions under which they labor, it is enough to inspire crime. When you read the actions of the Baldwin guards, it is enough to inspire crime. When you read that time and time they were knocked down and sand-bagged or bludgeoned off of public places, where they had a right to be; these men went unpunished, while they, themselves, were dragged away to prison; it is enough to inspire crime, and, gentlemen, there must be a solution of this question—it must be solved or we are going to have more anarchy and a need for more soldiers in the state of West Virginia than we have had in the past.

Now, coming down to what are the causes and effect in this case. This man wears the uniform. Judge Wallace occupies the same function in this case, with reference to the state, that we occupy with reference to the prisoners. His word is not law. Why, gentlemen? While you members wear the uniform, yet, for the time being, you are fair and impartial judges; standing with the balance of justice poised; without any prejudice for or against either side to this controversy. Presuming and assuming, and, in fact, from our experiences with you, gentlemen, and knowing you to be men of that type who can disregard everything that you might know as a private individual, coming right down to this case, now; exercising the functions of the judiciary for the time being; you are at the first point in this case, met with the proposition that the law of this state presumes every one of these prisoners to be innocent and that that presumption follows them through the entire trial and appears at every stage thereof and there should be no conviction—no conviction unless they are proven guilty by evidence clear and conclusive, establishing their guilt beyond a reasonable doubt. Now, mark: the Supreme Court has said that the governor has the right to establish a military court and that it has power to try—to try men, how? Agreeable to and in conformity to the law of the land. Then, that being so, where is your conspiracy? What did the people say when they got together? Who was it got together? What did they do when they got together and where were they when they conceived this conspiracy? Who was present? What did they agree to do? That is the thoughts, gentlemen, that come to you as judges. Those are the facts that you must solve, basing any conclusion that you may reach in this case upon the evidence that has been placed before you.

Now, the law says, that a man of previous good character is not presumed to leap at one bound from that position as a good citizen, which he occupied in his state, to a serious violator of the law; quoting the opinion and language of one of the greatest law-writers of this country. Then, you are confronted, along with the proposition that these people are presumed to be innocent, that here are men with previous good character and who are not presumed at one bound to become serious violators of the law.

Now, then, coming right on down; where did the evidence in this case come from and what does it amount to after it reaches your council chamber?

Mother Jones made some speeches they say are inflammatory. Yet, gentlemen, in arguing these social problems, the ex-President of the United States and the Great Commoner, and the present President of the United States have seen fit to denounce the despoilers of this country in the severest terms that their vocabulary was able to command and express. Of course, the Wall Street, subsidized press came out and said they were inflammatory and that they were dangerous characters. Why, Great God, gentlemen, on such a proposition of that kind; on newspaper reports, you could convict Roosevelt, Bryan, and Wilson tonight. On their discussion of social problems, on what the newspapers have said; because those who are unfriendly and who are representatives of these United States say they are dangerous characters–they are interfering with their business, that's the trouble.

Now, it has been further shown that some three thousand or four thousand rifles were taken away from these people. Not these prisoners, but the evidence is there were three or four thousand of these strikers–miners, with their sympathizers. Are you going to pick these men out of those three or four thousand and say this man made a conspiracy and say that these three or four thousand men were not participating? They were not there and you can lay your finger on that man. How can you convict these men of conspiracy? You have to put your finger on each man and couple him with the conspiracy and say that he was present, aiding and abetting; that he did some act in furtherance of that conspiracy or committed acts of confirmation. Gentlemen, the evidence is silent when it comes to that because a number of these men have not been mentioned at all.

Then, another thing, gentlemen; the courts all recognize it; the law-writers all write about it; the judges discuss it; the lawyers argue it; and the juries consider it; and that is the interest and motive of the people who are called to testify in the case. Now, here are a lot of guards that came down here–in the first place, gentlemen, you have a right to consider, in weighing their testimony, as to the character of the men you are dealing with and in what business they were engaged, and I do not believe, gentlemen, that 'way down in the innermost depths of your soul, where your true manhood exists, that you will come to the conclusion that a man who will, for hire, go out to execute the law, without any process authorizing him to do so, a man who will ride public trains and hold up people and seize and search, when he is armed with no authority except that delegated by the coal companies. If I was on a jury, gentlemen, it would not take but a very little more for me to believe that he would just testify to anything that they wanted him to. In fact, I want this to go into the record: that I have–that I never have, gentlemen, in all my experience as prosecuting attorney, either as prosecutor or defender, seen one of these hired thugs that I would believe on oath or whom I ever attempted to use in a case where life and liberty was in the balance; and don't you know that the courts of this country recognize that rule–they say that an employed, hired detective, whose testimony is unsupported, is not sufficient; and, gentlemen, in many of the states of the United States, public counsel have seen fit to impose the restriction upon police testimony; that no conviction shall be had upon their unsupported testimony, unless it is corroborated in the main as to all material facts at issue.

And, as to Smith: he came in here, posing as a workingman. He desecrated the union label; he brought into shame and disgrace the union card; he went into the house of innocent, unsuspecting people; a people who had been wrought up; a people who were not at themselves; and, instead of advising them to keep the law and counseling and aiding and abetting them, he laid a trap with the cold, stealthy tread of the tiger, seeking for its helpless prey; he coiled himself in the grass by the path, along which they trod, as the viper would cover himself for the coming of the innocent child; he ate their bread, when bread they had none to spare; and then he comes into court and uplifted his hand in the presence of Almighty God, to say that he had told the truth and yet shows at the same time, if any conscience he had, that he had violated all the higher sentiments of those finer impulses that enter into the bosom of the true, manly man, and stands in this presence the betrayer of a sacred trust; paid, gentlemen, paid, paid, paid to take liberty and life. They can condemn this gray-headed woman, whom the boys call "Mother;" it makes but little difference to her, because she has gone down the slope to that point where the sun, fast receding, strikes its golden rays high in the hilltops. But a few more days, at least, and it will be said of her "well done;" but, gentlemen of this commission, where the white hair is this evening, there will be a halo of glory, all of gold and her picture will adorn the walls of the children begotten in tents and her face will shine from the frame of humble homes long after the man who has betrayed his trust has been consigned to oblivion, unwept, unhonored and unsung. I would rather be Boswell; I would rather be Brown, I would rather be Mother Jones, Batley and these other boys over here, and be guilty of everything that is alleged against me—against them in these charges— than to go from this courtroom having betrayed the confidence of my fellowmen.

Gentlemen, wipe his testimony out. I ask you as mountaineers and for the fair name of the state, God grant it, if you would believe the testimony of a man who admits upon the stand, in the presence of his fellowmen, that he is a betrayer for money and for a price.

Now, the next thing, gentlemen: the interest of witnesses. I have discussed that; and passing from that: It is admitted that there were 120 Baldwin guards on that creek; coal guards or whatever you may call them; that they had gatling guns; that they had other guns. Now, listen, gentlemen, by what process have they got those guns? They had to sit down and order them—deliberation. Pay for them—deliberation. Wait for them to come—deliberation. Install them—deliberation. Employ men to use them—deliberation. Now, what does that mean? That means a private enforcement of the law—by force. That means an open invitation to battle. That means that we are not going to submit to it; we are going to shoot. Where was the law at this time? Where were the officers? Where were the peace warrants? Where were your criminal courts? They say the civil authorities couldn't cope with it. Then the law of this state is, that when the civil authorities cannot cope with it that the military shall occupy. They say it is expensive—that is not the question. The law ought to be enforced through and by the medium of those selected for that purpose; and, gentlemen, whenever you allow one of the coal companies to erect a gatling gun, to buy Winchesters, to employ guards, then another coal company can do the same thing and another can do the same thing; and, if the coal companies can do that, then the saloon keepers could do it; then, by analogy every merchant could do it and, following the same line of reasoning every farmer could do it and, if you go on down the line, some time in the evolution of things it would come to the point where the miners would have to do it. The system is wrong and you cannot win this industrial battle—these industrial battles—by the force of the Winchesters, on either side; and if the miners have used the Winchesters, they have done wrong; yet, you must recollect that it takes two people to fight a battle and that these miners couldn't go out here and fight a battle with themselves, where they are all on the same side, asking for the same thing. There was force on the other side, gentlemen, and let me tell you that the state of West Virginia cannot afford, in this conflict, to take one side of these contending armies and cast them in prison and in jail and deny them their rights, and disarm them and leave the other people in complete operation and complete control. Now, gentlemen, it is a serious thing to convict a man and it ought not to be done except the evidence establishes guilt beyond a reasonable doubt. You gentlemen have been sworn to pass upon these people and you ought to have the evidence convincing you beyond a reasonable doubt, that they were wrong; that they have been present—guilty, and that there has been nothing shown in justification or in mitigation.

Gentlemen, the statute of this state says that when a man is killed or wounded—a homicide has been committed, the presumption is that it is murder in the second degree; so, if I am traveling the highway and I kill a man and he is found on the highway and I admit that, then, under the law I am guilty of murder in the second degree; because the law says so—a prima facie case; but, if in mitigation of that and in justification of that I can show that I did not take the life of that man in malice but that he came out on the highway and intercepted me and demanded of me money;

and laboring under these conditions, I took his life; thereupon, the law says that I am guilty of no offense but that my act was justifiable. So it is in this case. If conditions met conditions; if force met force; if both sides were wrong; if neither side had the right to gatling guns, and it was a condition moving against a condition, cause moving against cause, wherein the personnel of men was lost sight of, then the individual is swallowed up in the cause and it becomes a fight for the existence of the cause and as to which cause was right; therefore, before you could find out in this case as to whether these men should be justly punished, you would have to enquire into the conditions in the cause–the individual members are swallowed up in the cause itself.

The governor said that it was war. The papers said that it was war. People who rode through here and heard these reports said it was war. The proclamation of war was pinned upon the trees; and there was set forth the fact that a terrible condition existed in this valley. Three or four thousand men were armed with all kinds of guns and reports would come to them that their wives and children were going to be slaughtered. It matters not whether these reports were true or not. Reports would go out to this side, that the miners were going to shoot up the town and they would get ready. That called forth a strained, intensified relationship between the battling forces and the law recognizes the condition of a man's mind; so much so that it will reduce a killing which would be murder under certain circumstances to voluntary manslaughter only, because of the fact that the man was working beyond the normal self and was not, at the time, a reasonable, rational citizen, with that cool deliberation and calculative presence of mind that he always contained, before he can be guilty of murder in that sense–in a legal sense. Now, these men were wrought up to a high pitch. You take Creigo–investigate that boy's character and I dare say, gentlemen, there is not a man who wears the uniform, nor attorney who is practising before you, whose character is as spotless or more so than the young man, Creigo. In talking with the doctor he said that he never had been over here in this trouble, yet he felt that it was his duty to come over here–felt it was his duty. Let me tell you, whenever conditions get so strained that men are willing to leave their wives and children and take their Winchesters and cross the river to go to the place where the causes are in operation, there is something moving on the mind of men and there is not responsibility that would be in acting under normal conditions. Therefore, gentlemen, in dealing with these men, you must deal with them in that sense, remembering that the law recognizes the various conditions under which men act in the commission of offenses and grade the punishment accordingly.

Now, the next thing, gentlemen, then I want to close, and that is this. The constitution says that a man has the right to be present at his trial and that he can go upon the stand if he wants to or that he can refrain from going upon the stand if he desires. That is not a question for the prosecution and our Supreme Court has gone so far as to say that if the prosecutor refers to that fact in his argument, that it is a reversible error—an error that will justify the setting aside of the verdict that may be reached, adverse to the man on trial, because it is a sacred right; it is a constitutional right; it is a right that he cannot waive; it is a right that the state can, under no circumstances, usurp; and, these men now, believing that no case has been made against them, reserve unto themselves their constitutional right to stay off of the stand; and, of course, gentlemen, you would not infer—because it would be a rash inference to infer from that—that they were guilty of crime. But, suppose it might be argued here, that those who were not guilty, if others were, they ought to go on the stand and tell.

I believe this, gentlemen, that in times of peace, when men are normal, if men go out and commit arson or robbery or any of the high crimes, and one of them betrays the trust, while I have—while I would still have more respect for the other fellows who did not betray it—there might be some excuse for him going on the stand and telling all he knew about it, when he knew they were all caught anyway; but, in an industrial conflict, where cause is meeting cause, and the personnel of the men is lost and their individuality becomes swallowed up in a movement, then I say a man would be a traitor and a betrayer of the trust and be unworthy of the confidence of his fellow men if he would go on the stand and tell; and, God being my helper, I would quit the cause of any man that would break away from his allegiance—an allegiance sealed with the blood of comrades—break down the barrier and betray the trust—give away anything that had happened; but, they have not done that in this case. These defendants have stood where they have stood from the first day to the last of the trial. They are the same good citizens they were on the first day of last April. They are the same good citizens that this record shows they have always been; and, when the law of justice eventually finds its way into the benighted hills, now murky with fog and obliterated with the clouds that have been hovering over and shadowing the homes and lives of wives and children in these mountains for the past twelve months—I say, eventually, when the torch light of justice does come to illuminate those humble homes to which they return, they will return there the same good citizens that they were when they left; and, gentlemen of the jury, gentlemen of the jury, I want to say to you—I call you jurors because there are five of you who must pass upon this case.

The great Empress of France, when her eyes were growing cold in death and after her voice was weakened and trembly and she had bid farewell to those about her, her eyes lit up again and a halo of glory crossed her brow, and she said to the King, who was standing by, "One more word." She said, "In this, the moment of my departure, I am ready to testify that I have so lived that I have never caused a tear to flow." I want you to decide this case, gentlemen, upon the evidence, and you can do it, in a way that you will not cause another tear to flow. The wives of all of these men have been sewing tears into their garments long enough. Their home, humble though it is, to them is a palace, wherein reign men, strong men; without money, but with character, admitted by the state to be as good as any character of any citizen of this state. And you, gentlemen, will not send these people away from their wives and their children and brand them as criminals and disgrace the fair name of your state by saying we remove them—we remove them who have made this state great and prosperous and helped to build up our industries. Who have brought forth the railroads and made it possible for you and I to make progress in their midst, and, at the same time leave the Baldwin guards in control with their Winchesters, gentlemen, with their Winchesters still howling and barking over the homes of the wives and children they have left behind. You may say this is sentimental; that I ought not to say these things. You may say a man ought not to get any sympathy in a case. Gentlemen, sympathy in the human breast is just as important as judgment in his head. When God Almighty created man in his own image, he gave him the five senses of seeing, hearing, tasting, feeling, and smelling, and then he gave him the emotion to love and he gave him the passion of hatred and he looked upon him and still the structure was incomplete and then, gentlemen, he put on the final touch and gave him that God-given something we call sympathy, that enables him at all times and under all circumstances to reach out across the chasm with the tender hand of mercy and of loving sympathy and say to him, "My brother, you may have been wrong, but I am going to give you another chance." There may be a time when we will all want a chance; and, there may be a time in this life, when we will all be wanting a chance before an earthly court; but, gentlemen, away down yonder, at the end of the lane, when the trump of God shall sound and when one foot is placed upon the land and the other upon the sea, and it is declared that time shall be no more, then we will ask the Unerring Judge, if he can do nothing more, to look over our faults and judge us in mercy and give us one more chance.

Gentlemen of the jury, in the name of that Judge that gives us all light, I want you to take the principles of the One who came and announced his doctrine two thousand years ago; the doctrine on earth of "peace on earth, good will to men" and apply that doctrine in this case; let that good will go out to these unfortunate people who are fighting for a cause that they believe to be right and who have, gentlemen, borne all that human frame and human understanding is capable and susceptible of bearing. I have taken a long time, gentlemen, but we have expedited this case by agreement, without criticism. It takes a long time to try forty people. I know, while we have been tedious in many things, that you have listened to me patiently, because you realized it is not a conflict of property here; it is a question of life and liberty; a question of which, if you take unjustly, you cannot restore. If you make a mistake today, it cannot be corrected. The Judge Advocate will say, "Send it to the Governor," but the governor will say, "Five men on the ground had better judgment than I have." Perhaps he would say that, but I believe if he would come here and sit in this court, with his great, warm, throbbing heart, and into the faces of these prisoners tonight, seeing this picture as I see it; that before the morning sun comes up over the eastern hills, striking its golden shafts down into these valleys that have been desecrated by Baldwin guards and consecrated by the blood of honest men within the last month—within the last twelve months, I believe he would say: "Sign a pledge that you will be the same good citizens that you used to be and go back home and embrace those from whom you have been separated for lo these many days.

Gentlemen, I want to thank you, to thank the Judge Advocate for his courtesies; I want to thank the members of this commission for the courtesies extended. I want to extend to all of the boys who wear the uniform my heartfelt thanks for every act of kindness they have shown me. I want to thank the two boys who wear the uniform and who have so ably assisted me, counselling and advising with me. I want to thank you all, and, above all, gentlemen, I feel glad of this one thing, that when I sit down, my action here can be made a matter of history; where everything we have said and done can be spread on the parchments of this state, that all may see, and God knows I have not said anything that I would be ashamed for the citizens of this state to see in the newspapers or published, and, with good will towards all, and malice toward none, I put the destiny of these prisoners into the hands of the commission, who I believe are honest and thoroughly capable to decide this case according to the law and the evidence, doing full justice to all.

Argument of the Judge Advocate, George S. Wallace:

Mr. President and gentlemen of the commission: It is not my purpose to make you a speech. You have heard two very eloquent speeches. I can say at the conclusion of the present trial that these prisoners have had everything that they could possibly have had in any court in this country. This commission has been very fair, indeed. They have given to the prisoners every single benefit that the law throws around them. We have sat as a military commission; that the laws of this state, for the time being are suspended and you are sitting here under the laws of war to come at the very truth of this matter and to investigate and find out whether or not these prisoners are guilty of the offense with which they are charged. Every time that counsel for the defendants have invoked the aid of the strict common law rule in the conduct of the case, this court has sustained them, and I have no complaint.

I now desire to say to this commission that in all confidence I believe a case has been made on the part of the state and it will be my purpose to analyze the evidence and discuss it with this commission.

Before getting down to that I want to call attention to what I believe to be some of the fallacies of the argument of the distinguished gentleman who has just sat down. He is dealing in generalities but has not taken up the case. He has taken up causes and their effect. He has talked about the industrial war. We are aware of the fact that industrial war has been going on in this country and we are sorry for those who suffer by reason of that conflict. But, gentlemen, we are not here today to measure or to decide this case by what Mr. Matheny thinks about it. We are not here to weep with these gentlemen like my distinguished friend, Adam Littlepage; because he sees it from their viewpoint. We are not here to measure it in that way but we are here to hold the scales of justice squarely to our eyes and weigh the facts and the evidence as it comes and let the scales fall against these prisoners or for them. We are not here to hear the Baldwin guards railed against. We have heard too much of it. All we hear is that the Baldwin guards did it; but, I want to ask, did the Baldwin guards buy high-power rifles that these gentlemen were shown to have? Did the Baldwin guards buy the pistol for Creigo, that not only shot solid bullets that will cause death but carried a bullet that explodes and some substance in it of which we know not. Not only shoots his victim down to kill him but to do that which is forbidden by the laws and rules of civilized warfare. When the court of the nations met at the Hague and formulated laws governing armed conflicts between men when they submit their causes to the arbitrament of the sword, they said at that time, we will no longer use explosive bullets, yet some of these gentlemen you have here you have heard such an eloquent plea for have violated that. Not only violated the law of your state but have gone to work and violated the laws of the nations of the earth—actions they have frowned on.

My friend wants to know why some of the Baldwin guards are not on trial here. You didn't hear the evidence as stated by every witness on the stand which was that every shot—that the first shot that was fired came from these prisoners or some of them, and that after the men asked them what they were doing there, their reply was a gunshot.

My friend has undertaken to say to you that these men had no right to be up there and hail them. I say to you the law is that is is trespass to go upon the lands of a person, whether enclosed or unenclosed. The statute inflicts a penalty upon a man if that man goes upon enclosed lands and destroys the garden or orchard higher than the penalty of passing through unenclosed lands. These men were in an armed body, coming from where? They had not been evicted from any houses on that land. They did not belong there but came from across the river, from Elk Ridge, Crown Hill, some six, eight, or ten miles; armed with high-power rifles, going where? On a peaceable mission? The man who called to them thrice was not a thug, Mr. Pierce. A man of as high a character as any gentleman sitting on this court. A man who impressed me as having as much character as any gentleman who has been in this case or in this room. He called upon these people to answer him and their answer was a gunshot. In this case once or twice, matters have come out and there has been something said about Baldwin guards shooting. We hear rumors here and rumors there and this commission is ready and willing to try the Baldwin guards as readily as it will anybody else, but I want to say that we cannot try but one at a time. What the Baldwin guards may have done last spring does not justify this now.

My friend tells you—undertook to tell you that men have been evicted. That may have been true, but I do not see that has anything to do with the trial of this case. These men were not evicted. These men came from Carbondale and Oakley and from across the river. They have not been evicted. That does not justify them or help them any. They talk about character. We have not assaulted anybody's character, but we admitted that the mining communities on Paint Creek and Cabin Creek were just as good as any other community in the state. How about these gentlemen who do not live there? Does that help them?

Now, then, coming down to the interest of the witnesses. The whole object of their talk has been this man, Smith. They have gone to work and Mr. Matheny tells you that he would do almost anything than do what that man did. Gentlemen, I want to ask you now and want to know—a man who testifies before this commission about men that have been gathering together with arms, to murder, to commit arson and things of that sort: is it such a crime when a man comes and testifies before you, that he is unworthy of belief himself because he has gone to work and broken a pledge, if you please? That a man must not betray a man who is about to commit a murder and come into court and just tell the truth, about men preparing to destroy a train, because he has a U.M.W. card? Does that carry an obligation of that sort? Gentlemen, if that is the kind of an organization you have got, then it ought to perish from the face of the earth. We are not here to assail the organization. We do not care anything about it. When a man gets up and talks about the sacredness of his obligation, does the fact that a man comes and tells the truth brand him as being worse than anybody in the world? They would have you believe that this man ought to take his place with a Judas because he has come here and undertaken to tell the truth. Let us see–has he not told the truth? Has he been contradicted in anything or has he been corroborated? Gentlemen, he told you that he was at Hansford the night that this man Brown talked to him and saved his life. Didn't your orderly state to you–tell you that he took Brown out and that Brown told him that he had saved that fellow's life and didn't that corroborate it? Didn't he tell you that these men were bringing ammunition from Charleston on Sunday morning? Didn't Clendennin, the ferryman come into court here and tell you that they had–

Captain Morgan, for the defendants: I beg your pardon, that is not in evidence. Mr. Clendennin didn't say there was ammunition in there. He said they had suitcases and never said what was in them.

The Judge Advocate: I think that is right. The telephone message from Howery's–he said send up that stuff; that they needed some .44's and .32 specials and telephoned them to get it up next day, on Saturday. On next day these gentlemen were seen going to the train with the dress suitcases–Sunday morning. They crossed with the dress suitcases and then he met them. Of course you couldn't see through them to see that they had ammunition inside of them. What interest did Mr. Brown have in it? He met them. Don't that corroborate that man, Smith? They undertook to break him down. You heard Guthrie's testimony.

Now, gentlemen, let's see now where we are on the question of law. I have got some charges in here. The charge is first of conspiracy, for the purpose of taking away personal property, and in pursuance of that conspiracy, the wounding of three men.

Second: Murder.

Third: Conspiracy for the purpose of inflicting bodily injury and the wounding of the three men.

Fourth: Conspiracy.

Fifth: Accessories after the fact.

(The Judge Advocate here read sections of Chapter 148 of the Code, known as the "Red Men's Act.")

Now let us see what and how conspiracy has to be proved:

"The rule that conspiracy must first be established prima facie before the acts of one confederate can be received in evidence against another cannot well be enforced where the proof depends upon a vast number of isolated circumstances. In any case where the whole evidence shows that a conspiracy actually existed, it will be considered immaterial whether the conspiracy was established before or after the acts and declarations of the members."

Spies vs. People, 122 Ill. 237

State v. Winner, 17 Kansas 298
Loggins v. State, 112 Texas Appeals 65
Amer. & Eng. Encyc. of Law, 2nd ed., p. 867.
How can conspiracy be proved?

"It is not necessary, in order that the facts of a conspiracy may be established, that it should be proved by evidence of the express agreement or compact between the alleged conspirators, or by direct evidence of any agreement or contract. A conspiracy may be proved inferentially, or by circumstantial evidence. Conspiracies, from their very nature, it has been said, are usually entered into in secret and are consequently difficult to be reached by positive testimony, which renders it peculiarly necessary and proper to permit them to be inferred from circumstances."

Now, let us see how that applies to this case here.

Who are the conspirators in this case and the men on whom more than anybody else rests the responsibility for the wounding and loss of life on this mountain? The defendants Brown, Parsons, and Boswell.

Now let us see what we have. You have got first, on Mr. Boswell, a paper that he has been publishing and circulating in this community for a number of months. In that paper, to say the least, it preaches death and destruction. The most trivial things, which every man knows without anybody telling him, have been exaggerated and highly colored. Everything in the world has been done to enflame the minds of these people against the other parties. Not satisfied with that, on the day before, on the Saturday before this conflict came up, the evidence shows that Brown and Parsons were in constant communication with the *Labor Argus* at Charleston. It shows that upon that occasion the telephone call went to the *Labor Argus* at Charleston, asking for the ammunition; the evidence shows that on Sunday morning preceding the fight that Boswell left Charleston with the men with dress suitcases. On the Sunday preceding this trouble Brown and Parsons were telephoning across to Carbondale asking for men with good, red blood to come over. At that same time we find Boswell over at Carbon in conference with this man Creigo; in conference with Nutter and in conference with others and, what were they there for? What are they doing? Getting up the ammunition; asking for red blood; asking for something else; and right here at Hansford on that day, the men are gathering. Truly an incriminating action. They phone across and bring men in from the hills.

Where is Boswell? Not on the firing line like some of the other defenders of his cause. He is telling his men to face the bullets, but he is not here himself. Didn't do as he had told them to do. Parsons and Brown, at least, had the courage of their convictions and were there on Sunday morning, tolling off the men and telling them what to do. Sunday night, the meeting at Beech Grove and in pursuance of that meeting where are the men on Monday morning? They went into the hills and then you had that conflict. What was their purpose in going there? Just look at a lot of those men there. There are men engaged in this strike that do not know what they are there for. They don't know whether they are going to get out transportation or going to get out a gatling gun. Don't know what for, but a lot of these people who are telling them, without informing the men, driving them to it. They are more guilty than the men who went on the hill. When the guards there came in contact with these men and engaged them as you know, they scattered to the west side of the hill and then fired into Crockett and Taylor, wounding them. I say that it is all part of one great conflict—a part and parcel of this one transaction. Not satisfied with that they went down here that night, getting reports from below, telephoning for reinforcements and you know what came on. To get rid of the soldiers coming on the Bull Moose soldier train, to shoot them up.

Then you find your men Parsons and Brown down at the ferry in the dead hours of the night, trying to get away. What were they going for? What were they trying to do? Again, Smith said that Parsons was drinking that night when he saved his life. The evidence of this man—not Parsons but Brown—the evidence is that when Brown was taken up that night that he had whiskey on him. He had been drinking. There is not one thing in this world so isolated; the men in there, the firing. When a man begins lying, he cannot tell one that will gibe in and this fellow told the truth—it gibed all through. I say, gentlemen, the evidence has shown that Brown, Parsons, and Boswell were the arch conspirators; they planned this matter and helped to work it out and it was worked out and as a result of that murder was committed, men who are here. Now they talk about sending them home to their families. That sounds good. They tell you that their families are back praying tonight and today over the result of your deliberations. Is there anybody here tonight praying for Bobbitt's wife and baby and asking you to bring them back? Who will now take care of that little girl child growing up in this world to face the battle of life, while Mr. Matheny tells you that there are 50,000 girls in Chicago reduced to prostitution on account of the lowness of the wage scale? Who is going to stand behind that little girl and protect her? There is no evidence here that Bobbitt left any money. His life was sweet to him; as sweet as it is to you or to me or anyone here. Crockett lies over here in the hospital, suffering as a result of a gunshot wound. There is nobody here talking for Vance, who sleeps in his silent grave as a result of this fighting.

So far as Paulsen and Batley are concerned, I say to you frankly, I do not find anything in this evidence that warrants their being held.

So far as Mother Jones is concerned, she has no doubt been—has largely contributed to this trouble; her utterances have been more or less remote. She has been in here making speeches and helping to keep it up. She may have thought she was doing right. From the viewpoint of peace and order, at least, she was wrong; but, whether or not this evidence will connect her up with this conspiracy, it is more difficult for me to say. That is a matter I leave to the commission; but, I frankly say that I do not think the evidence is very strong against her.

Now, then, coming down to the question of the guilt of these prisoners arraigned here. I have arranged them in three groups: Charles Kenney, George Lavender, A.D. Lavender, Charles Wright, Charles Gillespie, John Jones, Cleve Vickers, E.B. Vickers, Tom Miskel, Ed Gray, Ernest O'Dell and John O'Dell have been identified as having been up on top of the hill with the crowd, a part of which took part in the shooting into Vance and Bobbitt, in which they were killed and Nesbit was hurt.

Captain Morgan: I beg your pardon. The O'Dells are not mentioned.

The Judge Advocate: I took it down at the time. I will find it if the gentleman will be quiet. I checked it up tonight.

Captain Morgan: The evidence is that he resembled a man on the hill.

The Judge Advocate: That may have been the exact language he used. He was identified as being there and I will read it.

Captain Morgan: He resembled a man on the hill.

Captain Carskadon: He said he would not swear it was the man.

The Judge Advocate: C.D. Campbell was asked: Look at those gentlemen over there and pick out the men you saw on that day. Just call them out.

A. This man right here.

Q. What is your name?

A. Ernest O'Dell.

Q. You saw Ernest O'Dell.

A. Yes, sir.

Captain Carskadon: Read the rest of it.

The Judge Advocate: I will not read any more. That is what he said. He identified the man as being there.

Captain Morgan: He said he resembled the man. Read the rest of it.

The Judge Advocate: I do not desire to be interrupted any further. I did not bother you gentlemen.

I believe he was there. On cross-examination three men identified him in just the same way. Let's see about the O'Dells. Ernest O'Dell, John O'Dell, Morgan, Joe Prince, and Bert Nutter were arrested over on Cabin Creek side, and when the O'Dells were arrested they gave the wrong name. They undertook to show their name was Jones. They had rifles—were armed. What did that mean? What were they doing there? Where were they going? Where coming from? Arrested right on the west slope. They had been up in the mountains. Coming from that direction and going towards the river. When they were caught, what did they do? Just what any other guilty man would. Tried to conceal their identity by giving wrong names. Let's see a little more about that.

Now, over on the Cabin Creek side you have: Creigo, Craise, Morgan, Ernest O'Dell, John O'Dell, Joe Prince. Five of these were arrested together. The O'Dells, Morgan, Prince, and Bert Nutter, as I recall, were arrested together.

Now, isn't it a fair inference; don't you know that if Ernest O'Dell was on top of the hill the balance of them were with him? Bert Nutter was there on the other side of the river with Boswell the evening before. Now, is that just an accident? Boswell was over there—what was he doing? Brown was telephoning for men with red blood in their veins. These men were here with high-power rifles. They evidently had red blood.

Then, Charles Lanham, Grady Everett, and William Bainbridge were all arrested on that side. They all lived over here and gave no account of themselves. You have Creigo, the man who had the explosive bullets; Craise who had rifles and Morgan who gave the wrong name and O'Dell who gave the wrong name and John O'Dell, Joe Prince, Bert Nutter, Lanham, and Bainbridge over there together. The evidence shows they came from the other side of the river. What would you infer from that?

It seems to me, gentlemen, that it is all part and parcel of the same occurrence and I think the evidence will warrant you in so finding.

Now Boyd Holley, Henderson Ellis went from Holly Grove to Hansford.

Bunk Adkins, Boyd Holley, J.D. Zeller, Leonard Clark, G.W. McCoy—he was identified as being on the hill, just in the same way that O'Dell was. The man said he identified him; he believed it was him. He said it looked to him to be him to the best of his knowledge—he believed it was. He had a bag of cartridges—high-power cartridges. What did he have them for? What was he doing there?

Frazier Jarrett, William Perdue, J.E. Sowards, W.H. Huffman came from Holly Grove. Steve Yeager came from Holly Grove. Bob Parris went to Holly Grove. Sanford Kirk—you know what Kirk told Smith, the man they regard as so contemptible. He told him he had not had any sleep for three nights. He said I seen him at Holly Grove. He is the man who said he took his shoes off when he would see one of the guards. What did he take his shoes off for? What was he doing? Was he not in that crowd, in that bunch? Now, one thing more about this man Kirk. He told Dr. Wilson that he thought it was his duty to come over here. He had never been before but he came over and took a part in this. Is Doctor Wilson a Baldwin guard? The evidence in this case does not depend on Baldwin guards or so-called Baldwin guards. Fifteen or twenty men came out calmly and took part in that conflict. Two or three were identified. That seems to be a pretty good record.

Howery was not a Baldwin guard. He tells us about Parsons telephoning. He was not a Baldwin guard. Dr. Wilson is not a Baldwin guard. He tells us about Creigo. Bert Nutter was with Boswell Sunday. He tells us about the men living at Carbondale. King was not a Baldwin guard. Jones and Gillespie were not Baldwin guards. They belonged to the bunch. They did not desert the bunch but they went on the stand and told the truth about the facts. Suppose now that they had been thrown out. Campbell was not a Baldwin guard or a policeman. This man Pierce was not a Baldwin guard. It seems to me, gentlemen, that this case has been made out without any Baldwin guards.

The facts as established, then, are: that there had been great trouble in this community; a great many men hurt at different times; a great many things to stir up the minds of the people; that they became hot-headed. I may add that it has not been shown that these defendants had anything particularly to do with this up to this particular time. On Saturday night and Sunday, these men calmly prepared for this fight on Monday. On Monday they put it into effect and men lost their lives. On Monday night they were getting away as fast as possible and working towards the river.

Now, as to the question as to the kind of an offence. I say to you very frankly that my friend Matheny stated the law as to murder correctly. Murder in the first degree is a wilful, deliberate, premeditated murder, or murder by lying in wait, by poison, robbery, or arson.

This statute, however, makes it, under the Red Men's Act if a conspiracy result in murder, it is murder in the first degree.

But, as Mr. Matheny says, if a man goes out and kills another, the presumption is that it is murder in the second degree, punishable from five to eighteen years in the penitentiary. If the state shows that it was done wilfully, maliciously, deliberately, and premeditatedly, then it becomes murder in the first degree, punishable by hanging or by a life imprisonment.

If the defendants wish to reduce it to manslaughter, then they have to show by a preponderance of the evidence that the murder or homicide was committed in hot blood or in great provocation.

Now, let us take up this evidence here.

Everything—we have got an agreement—everything we know about it is in the record. It probably will or might take away the murder in the first degree, but under no process of reasoning can it reduce it to voluntary manslaughter.

It is true that every man recognizes that property rights are not as high as human rights, still property has some rights. On Friday before the fight at Mucklow, nothing had been done to these gentlemen, the visiting gentlemen as we will call them; they came from the other side of the river. They had not been up there. They came over Sunday night and Monday morning and were seen coming across the ridges, making in that direction. What was their object? The people at Mucklow knew they had been shot into on Friday. They had perfect knowledge of what had been done. These men were plainly armed—in daylight, when coming up the hill. After they were hailed the third time there was a rifle shot, then the volley, and then the men fell. Gentlemen, can that be justified? They cannot get away with it.

Let us see what the law says:

"If one conspirator, proceeding according to the act intended, commits a crime, his associates may be held responsible, though the crime committed be not the particular result intended, if it be a natural result or probable consequence of the course of action agreed upon."

Now, what is that course of action agreed upon? The course of action agreed upon was that these people went up into the mountains for some purpose. It was not a lawful purpose in any way you look at it. If they were going to get a gatling gun at Burnwell, that was not lawful. If they were going to get out the transportation, it was not lawful. It don't make any difference from our side of the controversy. That is the law as it is written. Let it be peaceable or otherwise. People have got to obey the law. It is not what Mr. Matheny may think about it or what I may think about it, or what we would like to have it, or as the strikers would like to have it, but what the legislature has said about it and that is the law I am reading.

Further:

"If divers persons come in one company to do any unlawful thing, as to kill, rob, or beat, or to commit a riot, or to do any other trespass, and one of them, in the doing thereof, kill a man, this shall be adjudged murder in them all that are present in that party abetting him or consenting in the act, or ready to aid him, although they did but look on."

Gentlemen, that is the law of the case.

Now, we know that war exists here. The governor's proclamations are in evidence, showing the reasons for the existence of the war. If the criminal courts and juries of this county had done their duty, you and the balance of us would not be here performing this disagreeable and unpleasant duty we are performing tonight.

If the juries of Kanawha County had sat in the jury box and listened to the evidence and passed impartially upon it, with respect to the Baldwin guards on the one hand and the miners on the other, there would have been no occasion for this condition. But they have not done so. We know that a number of crimes have gone unpunished and that report in this case says so. We have nothing to do with that. You are trying this case before you—to examine into the evidence and to pass your verdict upon that.

Captain Carskadon: They didn't swear to convict.

The Judge Advocate: Something was done here that I have never heard of before. These gentlemen were put on their voir dire. The presumption is that unless you have some specific cause, the member of the commission is not put on his voir dire. I am not asking this commission to punish any man here. I have nothing in my heart against them. I say to you that I have just as much sympathy for every man who sits there as Adam B. Littlepage, Mike Matheny, or any other persons. It is my duty to stand impartially between them, and I ask you gentlemen to do your duty, not from their viewpoint, not from my viewpoint, but right, squarely under your oaths and in accordance with the law and the evidence and put the punishment where it belongs, and then we will break up this lawlessness in this great state and clear her fair name in the respect of the world.

It has gone forth all over the world that West Virginia cannot govern herself through her courts and that the Executive has convened a military tribunal because of the weakness of her civil courts or the corruption or venality of the courts.

Stand up like men. Do your duty. I hope when we go out of here that the masses and our friends will not say, you did not have the courage of your convictions to stand up and apply the law as it is written.

I thank you gentlemen.

Thereupon the commission was adjourned until nine o'clock tomorrow morning.

The transcript proper ends at this point. The remaining six pages of the typescript contain forms for verdicts, with blanks for names and for "Guilty" or "Not Guilty" listings against the various charges and specifications. The commission submitted their verdicts and sentences under seal to Governor Henry D. Hatfield, but he never revealed them to the public.

# INDEX

ACLU (American Civil Liberties Union), vii

Adkins, Joe, 158, 165, 166, 167–68

Adkins, W.H. "Bunk," 197, 198, 207–9, 215, 303

admissibility, of prisoners' testimony, x, 30–31, 250–51

African American miners, 71–72, 233. *See also* Ellis, Harrison

American Civil Liberties Union (ACLU), vii

Anderson, J.C., Jr., 14–15

anti-trust law and suits, viii, 75, 82

*Appeal to Reason, The,* 83

arrests: of Batley, Boswell, and Paulsen, 20, 245; of Brown, 30, 196, 197, 209, 245; of Craise and Creigo, 28, 158, 164–65, 167, 177; of Everett, Lanham, Morgan, Nutter, O'Dells, and Prince, 28, 173–74, 175, 178–79, 302–3; of Huffman, Jarrett, McCoy, Petry and Sowards, 197–98; of *Labor Argus* editors after strike settlement, 59; of Mother Jones, 3, 17, 40, 245; of Parsons, 30, 196, 197, 209, 216–17

Associated Press, 34

Atkinson, George W., 65

attorneys, relations among, x–xi. *See also names of attorneys*

Avis, Samuel B., 6–7, 76, 79

Backus, B.F., 113–14

Bainbridge, William, 28, 173–74, 175, 178, 303

Baldwin, Roger, vii

Baldwin-Felts Agency guards: *Labor Argus* on, 42, 43, 217, 218–20, 223, 225–26, 227, 231–32, 234, 241, 242; Mother Jones's speeches on, 47; role in Cabin Creek and Paint Creek strike, 5, 6–7, 10, 12, 78, 79; role in Colorado strike of 1913-14, 63; transcription of testimony on, 133–40

Ballantine, Henry Winthrop, 68

Barry, Henry, 182

Batley, Charles: arrest of, 20, 245; closing arguments on, 53, 275, 301; discussion of evidence against, 53; habeas corpus proceedings for, 20, 22–24, 89 nn 51 and 53, 95 n 133, 103; plea, 100, 102; release of, 55; statement denying jurisdiction of court, 26; transcription of testimony against, 109, 143, 144, 185, 215, 216, 252

Belcher, Albert M.: and court-martial, 31, 63–64, 65, 89 n 63; in habeas corpus hearings, 20, 21, 22, 24; political affiliation of, 76

Belcher, Tip, 55, 120, 124, 126

Bell, J.C., 40, 255–56

Bethel, Col. W.A., 32–33

Bill of Rights, 68, 71, 94 n 124

Black, Henry K., 7

Blont, J.W., 108

Bobbitt (man assaulted by Ray Morse), 86 n 9

Bobbitt, Fred, killing of: closing arguments on, 53, 273, 301, 302; discussion of, 22, 26, 46; transcription of testimony on, 100, 101, 135, 139, 145, 153, 245

Bobbitt, W.O., 140

Bond, Capt. John C., 67, 214–16, 258

Boomer Coal and Coke Company, 40

Boren, C.M., 107–8

Boswell, Charles H.: arrest of, 20, 245; closing arguments on, 51, 53, 272, 275, 277, 300, 304; discussion of testimony and evidence against, 26–27, 30, 51, 53, 73; habeas corpus proceedings for, 20, 22–24, 89 nn 51 and 53, 95 n 133, 103; plea, 100, 102; release of, 58; sentence of, 55, 56, 91 n 97; statement denying jurisdiction of court, 26; transcription of testimony against: by Backus, 113; by Bond, 215; by Howery, 103; by Laing, 179; by Smith, 183; by Thompson, 177; by Wilson, 109, 111–12; written evidence against, 41–46 (see also *Labor Argus*)

Boughner, Capt. (attorney), transcription of questioning by: of Bryan, 194; of Gray, 265; of Jobe, 206; of Midkiff, 200, 205; of Rippetto, 259

Bowe, Clyde E., 55

Bragg, C.J., 155–56

Brandeis, Louis D., 95 n 131

Britt, Pete, 196, 197

Brockmeyer, Sgt. Charles A., 209

Brown, Jackson and Knight (law firm), 37–38, 142

Brown, John W.: arrest of, 30, 196, 197, 209, 245; closing arguments on, 53, 272, 277, 299, 300–301; discussion of testimony against, 26–27, 28, 29, 30, 53, 73; plea, 99, 102; release of, 56, 58; sentence of, 55, 56; socialist political activities discussed, 8, 9; statement de-

nying jurisdiction of court, 26, 89 n 58; transcription of testimony against: on arrest, 196, 197, 209; by Backus, 113; by Bond, 215; by Boren, 108; by Brockmeyer, 209; by Clendennin, 187–88; by Fisher, 207; by Howery, 103–6, 153–54, 155; by Jobe, 206, 207; by King, 115, 116–18, 119–20; by McMillen, 197; by Rice, 195, 196; by Smith, 183–84, 186; by Wilson, 109–10; by Wright, 120–21, 124–25

*Brown, Nance and Mays v.* See *Nance and Mays v. Brown*

Bryan, James, 193–95

Bull Moose (Progressive) party, 5, 8, 13–14, 79

Bull Moose Special train, 29, 182, 183, 185, 195, 200

Burdette, Frank C., 7, 79, 86 n 9

Burks, Ben, 14–15

Burns, J.W. agency. *See* J.W. Burns agency guards

Burns, L.D., 157–58

Burns, Rebecca, 179–80

Burns, Will, 180–81

Cabell, Charles A.: and Cabin Creek strike, 13, 60; household of, 86 n 6; *Labor Argus* on, 222, 224, 226; relations with miners summarized, 5–6

Cabin Creek strike. *See* Paint Creek and Cabin Creek strike

Cairnes, Thomas, 9, 37, 58, 86 n 14

Campbell, C.B., 134–40, 304

C.& O. Railroad, 12, 15

Carbaugh, H.C., 67–68

Carney, B.S., 228

Carney, Isabel, 18, 20, 34, 58, 59

Carskadon, Capt. Edward B.: closing argument by, 51, 276–79; on closing arguments by Wallace, 302, 305; court-martial role discussed, 38, 51; introduced as council, 100; transcription of cross-examinations: of Bell, 256; of Boren, 108; of Bryan, 194–95; of Campbell, 137–39; of Clagett, 249; of Davis, 212; of Gillispie, 132, 133; of Gray, 269; of Heffner, 169; of Hensley, 166–67; of Huddy, 254, 255; of Jobe, 207; of Johnson, 257–58; of John Jones, 129; of Lytle, 191, 192, 193; of McMillen, 216–17; of Midkiff, 200, 204; of Morgan, 173–74; of Pierce, 146, 147, 148–49, 150–52; of Smith, 186; of Wilson, 112; of Wright, 123, 125

Catholicism, 72

census data on Paint Creek and Cabin Creek miners, 73

Chain, Dan ("Few Clothes" Johnson), 66, 233

charges, against court-martial defendants, 100–102, 245

*Charleston Daily Mail,* 16, 36, 40

*Charleston Gazette,* 36, 90 n 72

Charleston *Labor Argus.* See *Labor Argus*

child labor laws, 4

Chilton, W.E., 93 n 111

church, Mother Jones's speeches on, 47–48

civil actions, resulting from Paint Creek and Cabin Creek strike, 66–67

Clagett, J.H., 248–50

Clark, Clara, 175–76, 180

Clark, Leonard, 197, 215, 303

Clarke, John H., 95 n 131

Clayton Antitrust Act, viii, 82

Clendennin, Fred, 187–88, 299

closing arguments, 51–55, 271–306; by Carskadon, 51, 276–79; for defendants, 51–53, 271–96; discussion of, 51–55; by Littlepage, 51, 279–84; by Matheny, 51–53, 284–96; by Morgan, 51, 271–76; for prosecution by Wallace, 53–55, 296–306; transcription of, 271–306

Colorado strike of 1913-14, 4, 63, 75, 80, 82, 83

Commission on Industrial Relations, 62

Committee on Education and Labor investigation. *See* Senate Committee on Education and Labor investigation

congressional investigation. *See* Senate Committee on Education and Labor investigation

constables, 78

*Constantin, Sterling v.,* 70

Corbin, David, ix

court-martial: admissibility of prisoners' testimony, x, 30–31, 250–51; charges, 100–102, 245; closing arguments (*see* closing arguments); conclusions of present study on, 74–84; defense testimony, 40–41, 259–67; Donahue Commission report as evidence in, 41, 97, 259, 287; *Labor Argus* as evidence in, 30, 42–46, 97, 216, 217, 220–21; *Labor Argus* on, 244–46; legal issues summarized, 84; legality challenged, 26, 31–32, 64–65, 67–71, 76, 89 n 58, 93 n 112; martial law proclamations as evidence in, 41, 258–59; motion for striking of evidence and exoneration of defendants, 258; motion to exclude Smith from courtroom, 51, 268–69, 271; motion to quash charges, 102; pleas by defendants, 26, 99–100, 102; political aspects of, 38, 76–77, 90 nn 75 and 76; procedures for, 25–26; profile of typical defendant, 73; prosecution testimony, 26–31, 39–40, 50–51, 103–258, 267–71 (*see also under names of witnesses and defendants*); publicity on, 33–35, 38, 90 nn 69 and 70, 91 n 87, 251; and racial issues, 72; sentences and verdicts, 55–56, 58, 74–75, 81, 91 n 97, 306; stipulations, 30,

41, 212–14, 259; suspension of, x, 31–33, 89 n 63; testimony on battle of Mucklow (*see under* Mucklow, battle of); verdicts and sentences, 55–56, 58, 74–75, 81, 91 n 97, 306; written evidence in (*see* written evidence). *See also* arrests; speeches (Mother Jones), as evidence in court-martial

Coxey, Jacob S., 3

Craise, Harry: arrest of, 28, 158, 164–65, 167, 177; closing arguments on, 303; discussion of testimony against, 28; transcription of testimony against, 109, 113, 157, 158, 164–68, 177

Creigo, Ernest: arrest of, 28, 158, 164–65, 167, 177; charges against, 102; closing arguments on, 293, 297, 300, 303, 304; discussion of testimony against, 28; sentence of, 55; transcription of testimony against: by Adkins, 167–68; on arrest, 158, 164–65, 167, 177; by Backus, 113; by Bond, 215, 258; by Burns, 157; by Graybeal, 158; by Hensley, 164–67; by Howery, 104; by Poindexter, 177; by Wilson, 109, 110–11

Cripple Creek strike, 4

Crockett, John, wounding of: closing arguments on, 53, 273, 301; discusson of, 28; transcription of testimony on, 101, 159, 160, 161–62, 165, 168–69, 170–71

Cunningham, Dan, 17, 40, 158

Darby, William, 121
Davis, M.T., 226
Davis, Maj. T.B., 209–12
Dayton, Alston G., 75, 80
Deal, Walter, 124, 126, 127
Debs, Eugene V., 83, 92 n 107
delegations and petitions to governor, 3, 17, 49–50, 54
Democratic party, 8–9, 76, 77, 78, 81–82

Department of Labor, 62–63, 81–82
Detroit, martial law in, 70
Diaz, Porfirio, 4
Donahue, Bishop P.J., 21, 72. *See also* Donahue Commission
Donahue Commission: contents of report, 41, 80; and ethnic issues, 72; investigations, 12, 41; report as evidence at court-martial, 41, 97, 259, 287
Douthat, R.S., 100
Dwyer, Lawrence, 56–57, 91 n 94, 212

Education and Labor subcommittee investigation. *See* Senate Committee on Education and Labor investigation
election of 1912, 8, 78
Elkins, Stephen B., 8, 42, 48
Eller, Ronald D., viii
Elliott, Gen. Charles D.: on ethnic issues, 72; *Labor Argus* on, 221–23, 224, 226, 232; opinion on court-martial and strike, 38; political affiliation of, 77; political ambitions of, 90 n 75; and publicity on court-martial, 33, 34, 38
Ellis, Harrison: closing arguments on, 303; discussion of testimony of, x, 30–31, 35, 39, 72; transcription of testimony against, 103, 185–86; transcription of testimony of, 250
Engdahl, David, 71
Estep, Sesco, 15, 40, 245
ethnic issues, 71–73
Everett, Grady: arrest of, 28, 173–74, 175, 178; discussion of testimony on, 28; transcription of testimony against, 109, 113, 173–74, 175, 178
evidence, written. *See* written evidence)
*Ex parte Milligan,* 69, 89 n 53

Fairley, William, 62
Fairman, Charles, 68–69, 70

Federal Reserve Act, viii
Federal Trade Commission, viii
Feehan, Frank, 62
Fenton, C.M., 188–89
Fisher, Sgt. Delbert, 207–9

Gillispie, Charles, 55, 126, 129–33, 302, 304
Glasscock, William E.: *Labor Argus* on, 42–43, 44, 217, 219, 222, 223, 234–35, 236, 237, 241, 243–44; and legislative session of 1913, 13–14; Mother Jones on character of, 81; Mother Jones's speeches on, 47, 48, 50, 156; and Paint Creek and Cabin Creek strikes, ix, xi, 3–8, 12, 16, 25, 41, 54, 66, 74, 77–81; pardon of Nance, Mays and others by, 22; political career summarized, 5; proclamations of martial law as evidence in court-martial, 258–59; strike-related civil cases against, 66; testimony before Senate investigation, 62, 80
Glenn, Garrard, 70–71
Goff, Nathan B., 60, 87 n 28
Graham, Jonathan T., 67
grand jury, 7–8, 78–79, 86 n 9
Gray, Ed, 55, 250, 302
Gray, W.R., 41, 51, 260–65, 267–71
Graybeal, L.L., 158–60
guards, company: National Guard members as, 8; Wertz bill on, 14. *See also* Baldwin-Felts Agency guards; J.W. Burns agency guards
Guthrie, Lt. August S., 50–51, 53, 267–71

habeas corpus proceedings, 20–24, 36, 45–46, 64, 66, 67–68, 95 n 133; *Labor Argus* on, 242–43; *In re Shanklin,* 20–21, 23, 24, 64. See also *In re Mary Jones et al.; Nance and Mays v. Brown*
Haggerty, Thomas, 58
Hamilton, James, viii

Harold, Lee, 228
Hatfield, Henry Drury: and court-martial, x, 25, 26, 31–32, 74–75, 81; and court-martial sentences, 55, 56, 58, 74, 81, 306; in election of 1912, 8; and legislative session of 1913, 14; Mother Jones on character of, 81; Mother Jones's meetings with, 57, 60; and Paint Creek and Cabin Creek strike, ix, 25, 56–59, 75, 77, 81, 91–92 n 101; professional activities summarized, 25; and Senate investigation, 62, 81, 92 n 107; strike-related civil cases against, 66; suppression of Socialist press by, 59, 66–67
Hawaii, martial law in, 70
Heffner, Emory, 28, 159, 161, 168–70
Henderson, Gordon D., 94 n 124
Hendricks, Everett, 131
Hensley, L.T., 164–67
Henson, J.O., 89 n 51
Hill, Bonner: activities of, 15, 28, 31, 64; discussion of testimony on, 28; *Labor Argus* on, 229–30, 231, 235–36; transcription of testimony on, 172, 173
Hitchman Coal and Coke Company strike, 75, 76
*Hitchman Coal and Coke Company v. Mitchell,* 75, 76, 80, 95 n 131
Holley, Boyd, 198–200, 205–6, 215, 303
Hollis, A.J., 20
Holly, Sally, 40
Holmes, Oliver W., 95 n 131
Houston, Harold W.: and court-martial, 31, 63–64, 89 n 63; in habeas corpus hearings, 20, 21, 22, 24; political affiliation of, 76; socialist political activities discussed, 8
Howery, F.W.: closing arguments on, 303; discussion of testimony of, 26, 28; transcription of testimony of, 103–7, 153–55; transcription of testimony on, 108

Huddy, T.H., 40, 246–48, 251–55
Huffman, W.H., 185, 186, 197, 198, 303
Hughes, Charles Evans, 70
*Huntington Socialist and Labor Star,* 9, 59, 66–67

Imperial Coal Company, 5
Industrial Corporation, 10, 11
injunctions, against striking unions, 76
*In re Mary Jones et al.,* 20, 22–24, 89 nn 51 and 53, 95 n 133; cited in later cases, 67; cited in scholarly debates, 64, 67, 68, 69; and Walker's participation in court martial, 103
*In re Shanklin,* 20–21, 23, 24, 64
investigative committee. *See* Senate Committee on Education and Labor investigation
Irwin strike, 80
Isseks, Morris Shepp, 70
Italian miners, 72, 73

Jackson, John J., 4, 131
Jacobs, P.T., 65
Japanese in U.S., incarceration during World War II, 70
Jarrett, Frazier, 115, 197, 215, 303
Jobe, Cpl. Otis, 206–7
Johnson, "Few Clothes" (Dan Chain), 66, 233
Johnson, S.W., 256–58
Jolliffe, Clarence F., 14, 38, 76, 214, 268
Jones, John: closing arguments on, 302, 304; discussion of testimony of, 27; transcription of testimony against, 124, 130; transcription of testimony of, 125–29, 133–34
*Jones, Mary, et al., In re. See In re Mary Jones et al.*
Jones, Mary Harris "Mother": and ACLU, vii; activities after release, 63, 83; arrest leading to court martial, 3, 17, 40, 245; and battle of Mucklow, 15–16, 17, 40; and beatings of scab laborers, 21, 88 n 46; bibliography, 85 n 2; closing arguments on, 54, 274–75, 277, 282, 289, 291, 301–2; with delegation to governor, 3, 17, 88 n 36; on difference between Glasscock and Hatfield, 81; and elections of 1912, 9; habeas corpus proceedings for (see *In re Mary Jones et al.*); Hatfield's meetings with, 57, 60; imprisonment after court-martial, 56, 58, 59; imprisonment for court martial, 18–19, 24, 57, 88 n 38; injunctions against, 76; interviews with journalists, 33–35, 90 nn 69 and 70; involvement with Socialist party, 4, 9, 83; involvement with UMWA, 3, 4, 9–10, 59, 86 nn 14 and 16; *Labor Argus* on, 9, 245; labor organizing career summarized, 3–4; mail communication during imprisonment, 18, 20, 65–66, 88 n 38; and Paint Creek and Cabin Creek strike, vii, 6, 9–13, 15–17, 21, 60, 82–83, 88 nn 36 and 46; plea in court-martial, 100, 102; release after court-martial, 59–60, 82, 83; and Senate investigation, 62; sentence of court-martial, 56; summary of court actions against, vii–viii; transcription of testimony against: by Backus, 113–14; by Bell, 255–56; by Bragg, 155–56; by Clagett, 248–50; by Davis, 210–12; by Howery, 103; by Huddy, 246–48, 251–55; by Johnson, 256–58; by Kyle, 156–57; by Lewis, 143; by Midkiff, 201; by Richmond, 142–43; by Smith, 185; by Wilson, 109; by Woods, 114. *See also* speeches (Mother Jones), as evidence in court-martial
justices of the peace, 78
J.W. Burns agency guards, 28. *See also* Smith, Frank

*Kanawha Citizen,* 31, 33–34, 36, 64, 89 n 63
Kanawha Coal Operators Associations, 5
Kanawha County census for 1910, 73
Kenney, Charles, 55, 120, 124, 126, 302
Kent State shootings, 71
Kern, John Worth, 19, 20, 60, 82, 92 n 104
*Keyser Mountain Echo,* 36
King, Harry, 115–20, 304
Kirk, Sanford, 186, 193–95, 303
Knoff, Anthony, 182
Kyle, John W., 156–57

*Labor Argus:* arrest of editors after strike settlement, 59; on Baldwin-Felts Agency guards, 42, 43, 217, 218–20, 223, 225–26, 227, 231–32, 234, 241, 242; on battle of Mucklow, 235–37; on Cabell, 222, 224, 226; certificate publication (3 Oct. 1912), 223; closing arguments on, 51, 275, 300; on court martial, 244–46; on Davis, 226; discussion of testimony on, 27, 36; on Elliott, 221–23, 224, 226, 232; as evidence in court martial, 30, 42–46, 97, 216, 217, 220–21; on Glasscock, 42–43, 44, 217, 219, 222, 223, 234–35, 236, 237, 241, 243–44; on habeas corpus proceedings, 242–43; on Hill, 229–30, 231, 235–36; on martial law, 45, 217–20, 221–35, 237–38, 241–42; on Mother Jones, 9, 245; motion for introduction into evidence transcribed, 216, 217, 220–21; portions placed in evidence transcribed, 217–19, 221–46; on prison conditions, 228–29; sympathies with miners summarized, 36; transcription of testimony on: by Boren, 108; by Davis, 210, 212;

by Fenton, 189; by Laing, 179; by Midkiff, 201; by Thompson, 177
Labor Department, 62–63, 81–82
labor law, development summarized, 81–82
Laing, Alexander W., 177–79
Lane, Winthrop D., ix
Lanham, Charles, 28, 173–74, 175, 178, 303
Lavender, A.D., 55, 124, 126, 302
Lavender, George W., 55, 120, 124, 126, 127, 302
Lee, Howard B., ix
Lewellyn, T.J., 19
Lewis, T.L., 59, 80, 143
Lilly, A.A., 31, 32, 89 n 63
Lithuanian miners, 73
Little, Tom, 15
Littlepage, Adam B.: closing argument by, 51, 279–84; and court-martial, 41, 51, 258, 267, 269–71; political affiliation and career of, 76, 77
Littlepage, Samuel D., 31–32, 33, 63
Lytle, Joseph, 190–93

mail communication, by Mother Jones during imprisonment, 18, 20, 65–66, 88 n 38
Maitland, Sir Frederick, 74
Marie, Tom, 130
martial law: ending of, 8, 13; initial declaration of, xi, 3, 7, 41, 74; *Labor Argus* on, 45, 217–20, 221–35, 237–38, 241–42; legality challenged, 22, 23–24, 67–71; Mother Jones's speeches on, 47; proclamations as evidence in court-martial, 41, 258–59; reimpositions of, 12, 16, 41; results of, 7–8, 10
Martine, James E., 61–62
*Mary Jones et al., In re.* See *In re Mary Jones et al.*
Matheny, M.F.: closing arguments by, 51–53, 284–96; court-martial role discussed, 29, 30, 51–53; introduced as council, 100; motion

to exclude Smith from courtroom, 51, 268–69, 271; motion to quash charges, 102; objections to cross-examination of Gray, 263; relations with junior attorneys, xi; transcription of cross-examinations: of Bond, 214, 216; of Campbell, 136–37; of Clark, 175–76; of Gillispie, 131; of Gray, 268–69; of Graybeal, 159–60; of Heffner, 169–70; of Hensley, 166, 167; of John Jones, 127–28; of Lytle, 191–92; of Midkiff, 202–4; of Smith, 188; of Taylor, 162–63, 164; of Wilson, 112; of Woods, 115; of Wright, 122–23; transcription of direct examinations: of Gray, 260–61, 264; of McCormick, 265–67; of Rippetto, 259

Mathews, W.G., 64–65, 93 n 111

Mays, L.A., 21–22, 89 n 48. See also *Nance and Mays v. Brown*

McCamic, Charley, 130

McCartney, Dave, 152–53

McCormick, Isaac, 265–67

McCoy, George W., 152, 195–97, 215, 303

McMillen, Capt. H.C., 30, 195, 197–98, 209, 216–17

media coverage. *See* publicity

mediation system, 82

Mexican revolution, 4

Michael (guard), 231–32

Michigan copper mine strike, 83

Midkiff, Capt. V.W., 198–206

Miller, John, 231–32

*Milligan, Ex parte*, 69, 89 n 53

Miskel, Tom, 55, 126, 127, 302

*Mitchell, Hitchman Coal and Coke Company v.*, 75, 76, 80, 95 n 131

Mitchell, John, 4

"Money Trust" hearings, viii

Montgomery, Samuel B., 37, 76

Morgan, Carl: arrest of, 28, 171–73, 174–75, 178–79, 302–3; closing arguments on, 273, 302–3; discussion of testimony on, 28; transcription of testimony against, 171–73, 174–75, 176, 178–79, 180–81, 215

Morgan, Capt. Charles R.: closing arguments by, 51, 271–76; on closing arguments by Wallace, 51, 271–76, 302; court-martial role discussed, 30, 38, 51; introduced as council, 100; on introduction of *Labor Argus* into evidence, 220–21; objection to Huddy's testimony, 246; objection to introduction of Mother Jones's speeches into evidence, 245; objection to questioning of Bond, 214; transcription of cross-examinations: of Bond, 216; of Campbell, 137, 140; of Clagett, 249–50; of Davis, 211–12; of Fisher, 207–8; of Gillispie, 132; of Huddy, 252, 254; of Jobe, 207; of Lytle, 192–93; of McCartney, 152–53; of Midkiff, 199–200, 204–5; of Morgan, 174–75; of Pierce, 147, 149–50; of Wright, 122; transcription of direct examinations: of Boren, 107; of Wilson, 112

Morgan, O.P., 171–75, 178, 180–81

*Morgantown Post-Chronicle*, 36

Morse, Ray, 86 n 9

Morton, Quinn, 5, 15, 16, 61–62

motions: to exclude Smith from courtroom, 51, 268–69, 271; for introduction of *Labor Argus* into evidence, 216, 217, 220–21; to quash charges, 102; for striking of evidence and exoneration of defendants, 258

*Moyer v. Peabody*, 24, 67, 69, 70

Mucklow, battle of: charges related to, 100–102; closing arguments on, 53, 277–79, 301, 304–5; discussion of testimony on, 27–29, 39, 53, 56, 72; history discussed, 14–17, 87 nn 32 and 33; *Labor Argus* on, 235–37; stipulation on, 212–14; transcription of testimony on: by Bryan, 193–95; by Campbell, 134–40; by Gillispie, 129–33; by Graybeal, 158–59; by Heffner, 168–70; by Hensley, 165, 166; by Howery, 104; by Huddy, 255; by John Jones, 125–29, 133–34; by Lytle, 190–93; by McCartney, 152–53; by McCormick, 265–67; by Nesbitt, 189–90; by Owens, 190; by Pierce, 144–52; by Poindexter, 170–71; by Ratcliffe, 140–41; by Smith, 181–87; by Taylor, 160–64; by Woods, 115–16; by Wright, 121–25

Nance, S.F., 21–22, 66, 89 n 48. See also *Nance and Mays v. Brown*
*Nance and Mays v. Brown*, 21–22, 24, 37, 89 n 48; cited in later cases, 23, 32, 67; cited in scholarly debates, 64, 68, 69, 70
Nantz, Frank, 232
National Commission on Civil Disorders, 71
National Guard: cost of, 25; court-martial witnesses from, 41, 50–51; as guards for court-martial prisoners, 18; Kent State shootings by, 71; members' opinions on West Virginia strike and court-martial, 38–39; and politics, 38, 90 n 76; role with Colorado strike of 1913-14, 63; role with West Virginia strike, 5, 7, 8, 12, 13, 17, 78, 79; transferred from West Virginia strike to flood relief, 59. *See also* martial law
Neely, Matthew Mansfield, 8
Nesbitt, Thomas L.: charges related to wounding of, 100–101; closing arguments on, 53, 302; discussion of wounding of, 53; transcription of testimony of, 189–90; transcription of testimony on, 135, 138, 140, 146, 153
New Deal, 82
Newman, Cal J., 41, 55, 126, 265–67

*New York Call*, 34–35, 36, 83, 90 n 69
Nutter, Bert: arrest of, 28, 173–74, 175, 178, 302–3; closing arguments on, 302–3, 304; discussion of testimony on, 28; transcription of testimony against, 109, 111, 113, 173–74, 175

O'Dell, Ernest: arrest of, 28, 171–73, 174–75, 178–79, 302–3; closing arguments on, 273, 302–3; discussion of testimony on, 28; transcription of testimony against, 134, 171–73, 174–75, 178–79, 180–81, 215
O'Dell, John: arrest of, 28, 171–73, 174–75, 178–79, 302–3; closing arguments on, 273, 302–3; discussion of testimony on, 28; transcription of testimony against, 171–73, 174–75, 178–79, 180–81, 215
Ogden, Howard N., 65
Older, Cora, 34, 38, 91
Older, Fremont, 34
Ombler, Maggie, 228
Owens, James, 190

Paint Creek and Cabin Creek strike: bibliography, viii–ix; civil actions resulting from, 66–67; Colorado strike of 1913-14 compared to, 63; consequences summarized, 61; delegations and petitions to governor on, 3, 17, 49–50, 54; events decribed, 4–13, 14–17; Glasscock and, ix, xi, 3–8, 12, 16, 25, 41, 54, 66, 74, 77–81; government changes following, 79; Hatfield and, ix, 25, 56–59, 75, 77, 81, 91–92 n 101; industrial changes following, 79–80; *Labor Argus* on, 36, 42–46; law enforcement inadequacies for dealing with, 78, 81; Mother Jones and, vii, 6, 9–13, 15–17, 21, 60, 82–83, 88 nn 36 and 46; Peace Proclamation, 6;

and politics, 8–9; public opinion and publicity on, 35–39, 83, 90 n 72; scab labor during, 10–12; settlement of, 56–59, 75, 77, 81, 91–92 n 101; stipulations on, 41, 212–13, 259. *See also* Senate Committee on Education and Labor investigation

*Parkersburg News-Dispatch,* 36

Parrish, Robert, 115, 186, 303

Parsons, George F.: arrest of, 30, 196, 197, 209, 216–17; closing arguments on, 53, 272, 277, 300–301, 304; discussion of testimony against, 26–27, 28, 29, 30, 53; plea, 100, 102; release of, 58; sentence of, 55, 56; statement denying jurisdiction of court, 26; transcription of testimony against: by Bond, 215; by Boren, 108; by Brockmeyer, 209; by Howery, 103, 105–6, 154–55; by Jobe, 206–7; by King, 115, 116, 117–18, 119–20; by McMillen, 197, 216–17; by Rice, 195, 196; by Smith, 182, 183, 186–87; by Wilson, 109

Patrick, W.H., 55, 115

Paulsen, Paul J.: arrest of, 20, 245; closing arguments on, 53, 275, 301; discussion of testimony of, 86 n 16; habeas corpus proceedings for, 20, 22–24, 89 nn 51 and 53, 95 n 133, 103; release of, 55; transcription of testimony against, 143, 144, 216

Payne, Maj., 231–32

Peabody, James H., 24

*Peabody, Moyer v.,* 24, 67, 69, 70

Perdue, William, 55, 115, 303

Perry, W. Lawrence, 55, 186

petitions and delegations to governor, 3, 17, 49–50, 54

Petro, Sam, 255

Petry, Oscar, 55, 197, 198

Pew, Marlin E., 35, 90 n 70

*Philadelphia News-Post,* 35

Pierce, James H.: closing arguments on, 53, 298, 304; discussion of testimony of, 27–28, 29; discussion of testimony on, 27, 53; transcription of testimony of, 144–52; transcription of testimony on, 135, 139, 141, 189

Pike, Jim, 55

*Pittsburgh Leader,* 20

pleas, 26, 99–100, 102

Poindexter, S.P., 170–71, 177

Polish miners, 73

politics: and court-martial, 38, 76–77, 90 nn 75 and 76; and National Guard, 38, 90 n 76; and Paint Creek and Cabin Creek strike, 8–9

Populist party, 3

Post Office Department, 65–66

Pratt, Maj. James I., *Labor Argus* on, 225, 226

President's Commission on Campus Unrest, 71

Price, William, 198–200, 205–6, 215

Prince, Joe: arrest of, 28, 171–73, 174–75, 178–79, 302–3; closing arguments on, 273, 302–3; discussion of testimony on, 28; transcription of testimony against, 171–73, 174–76, 178–79, 180–81, 215

prison conditions, 18–19, 88 n 37, 228–29

prisoners' behavior, testimony on, 259–60

prisoners' testimony, admissibility of, x, 30–31, 250–51

Progressive (Bull Moose) party, 5, 8, 13–14, 79

publicity: on court-martial, 33–35, 38, 90 nn 69 and 70, 91 n 87, 251; on strike, 35–36, 83, 90 n 72. See also *Labor Argus*

racial issues, 71–72, 233

Rankin, Robert S., 70

Ratcliffe, Gid, 140–41

Red Men's Act, 26, 53, 100–101, 281, 299, 304

Reid, William Bruce, 33–34
release of court-martial defendants, 55, 56, 58, 59–60, 82, 83
religious issues, 47–48, 72
Republican party, 8–9, 13, 14, 77, 78, 81
revolution, *Labor Argus* on, 238
Rice, Lt. H.H., 195–96, 259–60
Richmond, S.P., 141–43
Rippetto, Lt. G.C., 259
Roark, James E., 71
Robinson, Ira E., 23–24, 64, 67, 68, 77, 89 n 53
Roosevelt, Theodore, 4, 5
Russian miners, 73

scab labor, 10–12, 133
Schiller, A. Arthur, 70–71
Seachrist, John, 55
Senate, 1913 session of, 13–14, 87 n 28
Senate Committee on Education and Labor investigation: establishment of, 60, 80, 82; history summarized, viii; proceedings, 7, 61–63, 80, 81, 88 n 46, 89 n 63
Senate investigation. *See* Senate Committee on Education and Labor investigation
sentences and verdicts, 55–56, 58, 74–75, 81, 91 n 97, 306
*Shanklin, In re. See In re Shanklin*
Shaw, C.R., 11
sheriffs, inadequacies for dealing with strike, 78. *See also* Hill, Bonner
Sherman Anti-Trust Act, 75, 76
Sherwood, Capt. R.E., 59, 88 n 38
Sikes, Austin M., 100
Siketo, John, 55, 191
Slavic miners, 72, 73
Smith, Frank: attempt to suborn evidence, 41, 261–65, 267–71; closing arguments on, 52, 53, 54, 291, 298, 301; courtroom behavior of, 51, 91 n 87; discussion of testimony of, 28–29, 40, 52, 53, 54;

discussion of testimony on, 40–41, 51; motion to exclude from courtroom, 51, 268–69, 271; transcription of testimony of, 181–87, 188; transcription of testimony on, 196–97, 260–65, 267–71; Wallace's possession of report by, 37
Smith, W.E., 197
*Socialist and Labor Star. See Huntington Socialist and Labor Star*
Socialist Labor party, 3
Socialist party, 4, 8, 9, 59, 76, 78, 83, 92 n 107
Socialist Printing Company, 66
Sowards, Emory Jasper, 103, 197, 214, 303
speeches (Mother Jones), as evidence in court-martial: bibliographic information, 97; closing arguments on, 54, 275, 277, 289, 302; discussion of, 30, 37–38, 39–40, 46–50, 54, 97; transcription of introduction of speeches into evidence, 142–43, 245, 250; transcription of testimony on, 113–15, 156–57, 185, 201, 211, 246–50, 251–58
Staton, J.E., 13, 87 n 25
Stehl, John, 11
*Sterling v. Constantin,* 70
stipulations, 30, 41, 212–14, 259
Stotts, Dallas, 19, 59
strikes: Colorado strike of 1913-14, 4, 63, 75, 80, 82, 83; Cripple Creek strike, 4; Hitchman Coal and Coke Company strike, 75, 76; Irwin strike, 80. *See also* Paint Creek and Cabin Creek strike

Taylor, Lt. R.L.: closing arguments on, 273, 301; discussion of testimony on, 28, 29; transcription of testimony of, 160–64; transcription of testimony on, 101, 159, 165, 168–69, 170–71, 177
Thompson, Arthur J., 176–77
Tincher, Thomas, 9

Tolbert, George Stanley, 196–97
Toney, Oral, 196, 197
Townsend, T.C., 3
UMWA. *See* United Mine Workers of America

*United Mine Workers Journal,* 36
United Mine Workers of America (UMWA): anti-trust proceedings against, 76; challenge to martial law by, 7; and Colorado strike of 1913-14, 63, 80; and court-martial, 31–33, 37; court-martial of organizers, 20, 53, 55 (*see also* court martial); in habeas corpus proceedings, 22; and *Hitchman Coal and Coke Company v. Mitchell,* 75; injunctions against, 76; internal problems of, 80; and Irwin strike, 80; Mother Jones with, 3, 4, 9–10, 59, 86 nn 14 and 16; in Paint Creek and Cabin Creek strike, 4, 5, 6, 8, 9–10, 11, 12, 13; in Paint Creek and Cabin Creek strike settlement, 57–59, 81, 91–92 n 101; and Senate investigation, 62; transcription of testimony on, 108, 143–44, 253
United States Department of Labor, 62–63, 81–82
United States Senate. *See* Senate

Vance, W.R., 53, 100, 101, 135, 140, 145, 146, 153, 273, 301, 302
verdicts and sentences, 55–56, 58, 74–75, 81, 91 n 97, 306
Vickers, Cleve, 55, 126, 302
Vickers, E.B., 55, 103, 126, 302
Vickers, W.M., 197
Vrasic, Harry, 109

Wacomah Coal Company, 27
Walker, Capt. Samuel L. (attorney): economic/political connections of, 38; and habeas corpus proceedings, 102–3; on motion to exclude Smith from courtroom,

269, 271; transcription of questioning by: of Bond, 215; of Campbell, 139; of Clark, 176; of Fisher, 209; of Heffner, 170; of Jobe, 206, 207; of John Jones, 129; of Lytle, 191; of McCartney, 152; of McMillen, 198; of Morgan, 173; of Pierce, 146–47; of Rice, 196; of Smith, 185; Wright, 124
Wallace, George Selden (Judge Advocate): closing arguments by, 53–55, 296–306; on closing arguments by defense, 274, 283, 286, 297–99; court-martial role discussed, 27, 29–30, 32–33, 35, 37–38, 39, 53–55, 77; ethnic labels used by, 72; fee for court-martial services, 77; in habeas corpus hearings, 21, 22, 24, 37, 89 n 51; and Hollis's interview of Mother Jones, 20; *Labor Argus* on, 234; legal role summarized, ix, 7; on motion to exclude Smith from courtroom, 271; political affiliation of, 76; in scholarly debate on legality of martial law, 68; in strike-related legal matters after settlement, 66; and suspension of court-martial, 32–33; transcription of cross-examinations: of Gray, 261–64, 265; of McCormick, 266; of Rice, 260; transcription of direct examinations (*see under names of witnesses and defendants*)
War Labor Board, 82
*Wayne News,* 36
Wertz bill, 14
Western Federation of Miners, 4
*Weston Independent,* 36
West Virginia Bar Association, 64–65, 93 nn 111 and 112
*Wheeling Majority,* 36
White, John P., 4, 9, 57, 58, 59, 62, 76, 77, 81, 92 n 107
Wiener, Frederick Bernays, 94 n 124
Williams, John Alexander, viii–ix

Williams, Walter, 6, 232
Wilson, S.M. (Dr. Wilson), 104–5, 108–12, 303, 304
Wilson, William B., 19, 65–66, 81–82
Wilson, Woodrow, 8, 19, 63, 81–82
Wister, John, 11
Wood, C.C., 40, 114–15
Woody, Fred, 196, 197
World War I, 82
World War II, 70–71
Wright, Charles, 27, 120–25, 302

written evidence: Donahue Commission report, 41, 97, 259, 287; *Labor Argus,* 30, 42–46, 97, 216, 217, 220–21; martial law proclamations, 41, 258–59. See also speeches (Mother Jones), as evidence in court-martial

Yager, Steve (Steve Yeager), 182, 186, 303

Zeller, J.D., 197, 207–9, 215, 303